D0085277

PLAYS BY RENAISSANCE AND RESTORATION DRAMATISTS
General Editor: Graham Storey

ETHEREGE

VOLUMES IN THIS SERIES

PUBLISHED

The plays of Cyril Tourneur, edited by George Parfitt: *The Revenger's Tragedy*; *The Atheist's Tragedy*

The selected plays of Philip Massinger, edited by Colin Gibson: *The Duke of Milan*; *The Roman Actor*; *A New Way to Pay Old Debts*; *The City Madam*

The selected plays of Thomas Middleton, edited by David L. Frost: *A Mad World, My Masters*; *A Chaste Maid in Cheapside*; *Women Beware Women*; *The Changeling* (with William Rowley)

The plays of William Wycherley, edited by Peter Holland: *Love in a Wood*; *The Gentleman Dancing Master*; *The Country Wife*; *The Plain Dealer*

The comedies of William Congreve, edited by Anthony Henderson: *The Old Batchelor*; *The Double-Dealer*; *Love for Love*; *The Way of the World*

FORTHCOMING

The selected plays of John Marston, edited by M.D. Jackson and Michael Neil: *Antonio and Mellida*; *Antonio's Revenge*; *The Malcontent*; *The Dutch Courtezan*; *Sophonisba*

The selected plays of Ben Jonson, edited by Johanna Procter: *Sejanus*; *Epicoene*, or *The Silent Woman*; *Volpone*; *The Alchemist*; *Bartholomew Fair*

The selected plays of John Webster, edited by Jonathan Dollimore: *The White Devil*; *The Devil's Law Case*; *The Duchess of Malfi*

The selected plays of John Ford, edited by Colin Gibson: *'Tis Pity She's a Whore*; *The Broken Heart*; *Perkin Warbeck*

THE PLAYS OF
SIR GEORGE ETHEREGE

The Comical Revenge; or, Love in a Tub

She Would If She Could

The Man of Mode; or, Sir Fopling Flutter

EDITED BY
MICHAEL CORDNER
Lecturer in English, University of York

CAMBRIDGE UNIVERSITY PRESS
CAMBRIDGE
LONDON NEW YORK NEW ROCHELLE
MELBOURNE SYDNEY

Published by the Press Syndicate of the University of Cambridge
The Pitt Building, Trumpington Street, Cambridge CB2 1RP
32 East 57th Street, New York, NY 10022, USA
296 Beaconsfield Parade, Middle Park, Melbourne 3206, Australia

First published 1982

Printed in Great Britain at the University Press, Cambridge

Library of Congress catalogue card number: 82–1180

British Library Cataloguing in Publication Data

Etherege, Sir George
The plays of George Etherege. – (Plays by Renaissance and Restoration dramatists)
I. Title II. Cordner, Michael III. Etherege, Sir George. Comical revenge, or, Love in a tub
IV. Etherege, Sir George. She would if she could
V. Etherege, Sir George. Man of mode, or, Sir Fopling Flutter VI. Series
822′.4   PR 3432

ISBN 0 521 24654 7 hard covers
ISBN 0 521 28879 7 paperback

PREFACE TO THE SERIES

This series provides the best plays (in some cases, the complete plays) of the major English Renaissance and Restoration dramatists, in fully-annotated, modern-spelling texts, soundly edited by scholars in the field. The first three volumes are devoted to Renaissance dramatists; other volumes present the work of such Restoration playwrights as Etherege and Wycherley.

The introductory matter in each volume is factual and historical rather than critical: it includes, where appropriate, a brief biography of the playwright, a list of his works with dates of plays' first performances, the reasons for the volume editor's choice of plays, a short critical biography and a note on the texts used. An introductory note to each play then gives the source material, a short stage-history, and details of the individual editions of that play.

Short notes at the foot of the page are designed to gloss the text or enlarge on its literary, historical or social allusions. In some volumes editors have added more substantial explanatory notes and have commented on textual variants.

The volumes are intended for anyone interested in English drama in two of its richest periods, but they will prove especially useful to students at all levels who want to enjoy and explore the best work of these dramatists.

Graham Storey

CONTENTS

ACKNOWLEDGEMENTS

I am very grateful for suggestions and assistance to Richard and Marie Axton, Anne Barton, Sandra Billington, John Buttrey, Ronald Clayton, Claire Cross, Norman Hampson, Nick Havely, Peter Holland and Norman Stevenson. The largest debt, however, is to Niccy – for encouragement and endless patience.

Michael Cordner, York
September 1981

INTRODUCTION

Life

The most likely date for the playwright's birth seems to be the second half of 1636. His paternal grandfather, 'George Etherege, gent.' (b. 1576), was a well-to-do London vintner, who held shares in the Virginia and the Bermuda companies. As a young man, the dramatist's father, Captain George Etherege (b. 1607), went to look after the grandfather's shares of land in Paget's Tribe, Bermuda. Returning to England in 1634, Captain George married Mary Powney, a gentleman's daughter from Maidenhead (which town the grandfather had made his home, in preference to the capital, some time after February 1628). The future Sir George was the eldest son (though not the eldest offspring) of this marriage.

Also in 1636, his father purchased a place at Court 'worth about two hundred pounds per annum before the troubles' – that of purveyor to Queen Henrietta Maria. When the Civil War forced the Queen into exile in 1644, Captain George presumably accompanied her into exile. The likelihood is that he never returned to England, since he died in France in 1650. The responsibility for looking after his wife and children seems to have devolved upon his father.

There is an unsubstantiated (and probably unreliable) tradition that the dramatist was a pupil at the Lord Williams's Grammar School at Thame. However that may be, he later gave signs of having received a sound education, could quote from Horace in the original and read and write French with ease.

The grandfather took care to ensure that the fatherless children would be able to earn their own livings and, in 1654, apprenticed the eldest boy to George Gosnold, a leading Beaconsfield lawyer with a substantial practice there and in London. As an articled clerk, Etherege would have lived in his master's house and been treated as one of the family. His signature appears on Beaconsfield documents until 14 August 1658.

For the next stage of his legal education Etherege went to Clement's Inn in London, of which Gosnold, already a senior member, was to become principal in 1670. Etherege was formally admitted there on 19 February 1659. His studies would have included attending (and taking notes on) trials in the neighbouring lawcourts, receiving instruction in the law from barristers of the parent Inns of Court, and trying to master

Law-Latin and Law-French. This must also have been a time of social polishing for him, and there would have been plentiful opportunities (in the Inns and in London generally) for him to acquire genteel accomplishments.

His grandfather's death in 1658 produced a protracted lawsuit over the latter's estate, which was finally settled in George Etherege's favour in July 1659. From the autumn of that year until the winter of 1663 he disappears from sight. Even if he had not yet received cash in hand, he now had expectations sufficient to enable him to raise money by borrowing, and Frederick Bracher, the editor of Etherege's letters, has suggested that he may well have taken advantage of this to travel to France for the same reasons which would one day take his own Sir Frederick Frollick there (*The Comical Revenge*, act three, scene four, lines 39–41). (This would confirm an eighteenth-century tradition, preserved by William Oldys, that he 'travelled into France, and perhaps Flanders also, in his younger years'.)

When he reappears in London in 1663 we find him conducting a free-speaking verse correspondence with Lord Buckhurst to whom, in the following year, he was to dedicate *The Comical Revenge*. With almost magical ease (or at least so it seems in the present state of our knowledge) he was showing himself to be on terms of intimacy with a prominent young aristocrat, and over the next couple of years he became well established as a central member of the group of wits and courtiers which included John Wilmot Earl of Rochester and Sir Charles Sedley.

The success of *The Comical Revenge* raised great expectations for his second comedy, *She Would if She Could*, the first performance of which in 1668 was attended by Charles II. That year also brought him a tangible sign of Court favour with his appointment as a Gentleman of the Privy Chamber in Ordinary, and, still in 1668, he went (as a secretary to the Ambassador, Sir Daniel Harvey) on a diplomatic mission to Constantinople. He returned to England (via Paris) in the autumn of 1671.

The next years seem to have been mainly spent in a life of pleasure in London. He did not escape his share of the notoriety which the Court Wits' life-style inevitably earned for them. There was an abortive duel in Covent Garden and a tavern quarrel during which a man who attempted to part Etherege from his opponent 'was runn with a sword under the eye'. Above all, in 1676 (the year of *The Man of Mode*), Etherege was present at Epsom in the nocturnal skirmish with the watch which ended tragically in the death of Captain Downs.

At some point between 1677 and 1679 Etherege was both knighted and married; gossip connected the two events, alleging that the knighthood was bestowed on him in order to enable him to net a 'rich old widow', Mary Sheppard Arnold. The marriage does not appear to have been a success, and his wife did not accompany him to Ratisbon in 1685.

In the early 1680s a fondness for gambling is rumoured to have grown into a near addiction, and he was losing heavily. When the new king, the Catholic James II, appointed him to be Resident at the Diet of Ratisbon (now Regensburg) in 1685, he does not appear to have been reluctant to leave the country, perhaps escaping heavy gambling debts.

His time at Ratisbon, however, was not to be a happy one. The freedoms he was accustomed to allow himself sorted ill with the extreme formality of the community of diplomats with whom he now had to deal, and he did not succeed in sufficiently tempering his behaviour to meet the demands of his new situation. Indeed, his hostile and conspiratorial secretary sent home lurid accounts of the outrageous excesses perpetrated by his superior. Even if, as seems likely, the secretary's malice and distaste for Etherege caused him to exaggerate, it yet remains clear that discretion was still not one of the latter's qualities.

Late in his time at Ratisbon, Etherege realized the harm being done him by the stories which were now crossing Europe about him, and he began to take his duties more seriously, thus finding to his surprise that he was actually beginning to enjoy them. But his diplomatic career was now overtaken by events at home. He responded to the news of the 1688 Revolution with feelings of simple loyalty to James II, with whose fortunes he threw in his lot.

His last years are shrouded in mystery. He is not named in the surviving list of the Court in exile (although he seems to have been in Paris while the latter was at Saint-Germain), nor is the date of his death certainly established. Various possibilities have been recorded, though the most reliable seems to be 10 May 1692. Among the records of the Benedictine cloister in Ratisbon there is entered the claim that he was converted to Catholicism before his death.

Works

Etherege's main claim to fame today is centred on his three comedies:

The Comical Revenge; or, Love in a Tub	1664
She Would if She Could	1668
The Man of Mode; or, Sir Fopling Flutter	1676

In the Restoration and early eighteenth century, however, he was also famed for his facility in a kind of light verse much to the period's taste. His poems were frequently transcribed and widely known, and his songs were repeatedly set to music (by, among numerous other composers, Henry Purcell). The modern editor of the poems, James Thorpe, reported that he had 'found them in more than fifty contemporary manuscripts and in about a hundred and fifty printed books of the Restoration and early eighteenth century'. As a result of this enthusiasm, the songs written for the plays enjoyed a life quite independent of their original dramatic context. This was the case not only with such lyrics as Gatty's 'To little or no purpose I spent many days' from act five, scene one, of *She Would if She Could* (the subject, for example, of a very beautiful setting by John Eccles), but even with Sir Fopling's 'How charming Phillis is, how fair' from act four, scene two, of *The Man of Mode*, although that song's satirical intent (as the best Sir Fopling can manage) was inevitably quite masked when the words were reprinted in songbooks or collections. A text of the poems and songs and a detailed account of their popularity can be found in James Thorpe (ed.), *The Poems of Sir George Etherege* (Princeton University Press, 1963).

One other aspect of his output deserves noting here. A large number of his personal and business letters survive, the overwhelming majority deriving from his years in Ratisbon. They provide a great deal of material of interest for the interpretation of the plays. They have never been reprinted in their entirety, but two editions provide a substantial sampling of what is available: Sybil Rosenfeld (ed.), *The Letterbook of Sir George Etherege* (London, Oxford University Press, 1928); Frederick Bracher (ed.), *Letters of Sir George Etherege* (Berkeley, University of California Press, 1974).

The text of this edition

The first quartos of each of the plays are the only texts with real authority and accordingly form the basis of the present edition. Though not free from error, their slips are mostly trivial and easily recognized, and I have tried to accept emendations of their readings only when this appeared absolutely necessary. This means that, in preparing the text of *The Man of Mode* in particular, I have preferred on a number of occasions the first quarto version to the alterations of it included in most modern editions. All such decisions are accompanied by a note explaining the reasoning that lies behind them.

In one other way I have adopted a more conservative policy than is normal in modernized texts. I have tried to limit to a minimum the changes made in the punctuation of the quartos because of the many valuable hints about phrasing which the latter offers an actor. There have inevitably been a number of occasions on which it has seemed necessary to intervene in order to avoid the possibility of real confusion for the modern reader. But there appeared to me to be no virtue in so thoroughly reordering the punctuation that it became, in effect, merely a tool of syntactical identification. The latter course seems to me to be a positive hindrance to the actor; he has to discard much that the altered punctuation will have suggested to him before he can learn to speak the text freely and fluently.

I do not mean to imply that I regard the original punctuation as having prescriptive authority. There is no one correct way of delivering a speech, and much in theatrical interpretation has to depend upon the breathing-patterns, timbre of voice and physical rhythm of the individual actor. In any case, we have often no way of knowing in particular instances whether a detail of punctuation is attributable to Etherege or to some other person (the type-setter, for instance) who may have intervened between the original manuscript and the play's appearance in print. But a way of punctuating which implies a way of speaking is, in a dramatic text, surely preferable to one that does not.

In 'modernizing' the punctuation of seventeenth-century play-texts editors often put themselves in the odd position of rejecting usages common in the printed versions of plays written in the 1970s. Thus, for instance, in David Edgar's *Destiny* (London, Eyre Methuen, 1976) one character is given this line: 'One doesn't, like, the dentist' (p. 94). But when, in the first quarto of *The Man of Mode*, Dorimant asks Lady Woodvill, 'Do you not know, Sir *Fopling*, Madam?' (act four, scene one, lines 397–8), Carnochan and Barnard, in their editions, both choose to erase the first comma. If such editorial principles were applied to modern texts, many passages would appear in a form different from that which their authors desired. The following, for instance, would be candidates for revision:

KENDAL. They're keen to do it JT.
HARRIS. Yes Ken's lads are turning out just like their father.

(Edward Bond, *The Worlds* (London, Eyre Methuen, 1980), p. 12)

CURLY. I know, but I couldn't last an evening. It's – what – not yet eight and already I'm half the man I am . . .

(David Hare, *Knuckle* (London, Samuel French, 1974), p. 17)

KEV. Twenty-two blokes out there – and do you know something Bill boy. Not one of them knows the first bloody thing about insurance.

(Barrie Keeffe, *Gimme Shelter* (London, Eyre Methuen, 1978), p. 17)

In the Keeffe example, in addition to a comma, a question-mark would presumably be interpolated. But, although grammatically identifiable as a question, that phrase should not be spoken as if it really sought an answer, and so Keeffe's omission of the sign is helpful to the actor. A similar practice is often observable in the Etherege texts, and I have tried (wherever possible) not to disturb it.

For another example we can turn to Simon Gray's *Otherwise Engaged* (London, Eyre Methuen, 1975): 'No doubt it seems a rather squalid one, to you' (p. 36). A parallel usage can be found in *The Man of Mode*, I i 60–1: ' . . . that she may look sparkishly in the Fore Front of the Kings Box, at an old Play'. (For the tang implied in those last four words, see the note to these lines in the text of the play.) Once again, both Carnochan and Barnard erase the offending comma. Yet such hints can be invaluable to the actor, especially if he does not think of the comma as inevitably suggesting a pause, but merely as a request that what follows should be given a different emphasis from what has gone before. He could indeed achieve this with a pause, but he could equally well use, say, a rising or falling inflection or a change of tonal-colour.

Another practice modernizing editors too often erase but modern playwrights find indispensable can be illustrated from Howard Brenton's *Weapons of Happiness* (London, Eyre

Methuen, 1976): 'How did a silly little girl in South London, get hold of those names?' (p. 35). Brenton has written the speech down as he hears it. He knows that the actor will be grateful for suggestions about how he should breathe his part and, therefore, about which words should be grouped with which. Accordingly, for Brenton as for Etherege, commas coming in syntactically indecorous places are a wholly natural way of punctuating speeches. It would be idle to claim that the Etherege first quartos are systematically and deliberately punctuated with a view to making the actor's life easier; but it seems to me clear that the mode of punctuation generally favoured in them is much more adjusted to the latter's needs than that introduced by Carnochan and Barnard. The modern reader may find that some passages in the following pages cause him a moment of hesitation on first acquaintance; but I hope that this is a price worth paying for a text that can assist us in imagining more vividly how the dramatist's lines might actually sound when shaped by the human voice.

There are four other topics which need to be briefly mentioned here:

(1) There is the question of Dufoy's French accent in *The Comical Revenge*. Where a French word seems intended I have altered the spelling accordingly, but otherwise I have left Dufoy's speeches as they stand in the first quarto. The same English word often recurs with an accent differently placed or omitted when previously included; but I have resisted the temptation to standardize these. Though such inconsistencies are quite likely to have been accidental, they are not inappropriate to the vagaries of emphasis into which an inexperienced speaker of a foreign tongue is likely to be driven in the heat of the moment.

(2) At a number of points in *The Comical Revenge*, Etherege writes (seemingly unselfconsciously) occasional ten-syllable phrases in easily recognizable metrical patterns but in contexts where there seems to be no consistent intent to order the dramatic speech as verse. I have printed such passages as prose.

(3) I have to a limited extent standardized the forms in which the characters' names appear in the stage-directions. In *The Comical Revenge*, for instance, Sir Nicholas appears in a variety of guises. For the speech-headings I have adopted 'SIR NICHOLAS' as the standard form. Such changes are made silently, but any other stage-direction introduced by me is identified as such by being enclosed in square brackets. Scene

locations are given at the beginning of scenes only when these are provided in the quartos.
(4) In the notes to the play-texts the first quartos of *She Would if She Could* and *The Man of Mode* are identified as *1668* and *1676* respectively. *The Comical Revenge* appeared in two quartos within one year. When there is a difference in readings between these, they are cited as *1664a* and *1664b*; readings common to both, however, are quoted as *1664*. The subsequent quartos are identified in similar fashion, as are citations from the collected editions (from *1704* onwards).

Also in the notes to the play-texts, references to Samuel Johnson's indispensable *Dictionary* and to Morris Palmer Tilley, *A Dictionary of the Proverbs in England in the Sixteenth and Seventeenth Centuries* (Ann Arbor, University of Michigan Press, 1950) are identified by being followed by the appropriate surname.

A select bibliography

Biography

Frederick Bracher has usefully summarized, and added to, the still scanty sources for Etherege's biography in the introduction to his *Letters of Sir George Etherege* (Berkeley, University of California, 1974) and in 'Etherege at Clement's Inn', *Huntington Library Quarterly*, 43 (1979–80), 127–34. (The account of Etherege's life in the opening section of this introduction is indebted to both these essays.)

Editions

Only two previous modern editions have provided texts of all three Etherege comedies. In 1888 A. Wilson Verity edited an Etherege *Works* (London, John C. Nimmo). This is a pioneering piece of work, but Verity worked from the first collected edition of 1704 the text of which derives from the first quartos but which introduces errors of its own not found in the latter. Some of these are carried over into Verity's volume.

This mistake was carefully avoided by H.F.B. Brett-Smith in his two-volume, old-spelling *Dramatic Works* (Oxford, Basil Blackwell, 1927), a painstaking and splendidly accomplished labour of love. The quality of the text which Brett-Smith produced has put all subsequent editors in his debt, and he also contributed a number of illuminating annotations. Charlene M.

Taylor has edited *She Would if She Could* for the Regents Restoration Drama Series (London, Edward Arnold, 1972), and the play has also appeared in two modern anthologies of comedies from the period: Dennis Davison (ed.), *Restoration Comedies* (London, Oxford University Press, 1970) and A. Norman Jeffares (ed.), *Restoration Comedy* (4 vols., London, The Folio Society, 1974). The latter also includes *The Man of Mode*, which indeed appears in a large number of collections of post-1660 drama. In addition, it has received three notable single-play editions: by W.B. Carnochan for the Regents Restoration Drama Series (London, Edward Arnold, 1967), by John Conaghan for the old-spelling Fountainwell Drama Texts (Edinburgh, Oliver and Boyd, 1973) and by John Barnard for the New Mermaids (London, Ernest Benn, 1979).

I have greatly benefited from the work of previous scholars, and annotation derived from their texts is acknowledged by citing the relevant editor's surname in brackets afterwards.

Criticism

Etherege's first two plays have received much less critical attention than his last. Much valuable information, however, about the dramatic context from which *The Comical Revenge* derives can be found in Alfred Harbage, *Cavalier Drama* (New York, Modern Language Association of America, 1936), and two books which address themselves to wider themes in the period's drama and yet examine in some detail all three Etherege works are Thomas H. Fujimura, *The Restoration Comedy of Wit* (Princeton University Press, 1952) and Norman N. Holland, *The First Modern Comedies: the Significance of Etherege, Wycherley and Congreve* (Cambridge, Mass., Harvard University Press, 1959).

There is only one book-length study of Etherege of note – Dale Underwood, *Etherege and the Seventeenth-Century Comedy of Manners* (New Haven, Yale University Press, 1957). This seeks to set the plays within the context of a tradition of libertine thought and is clearly a work of substance with which all subsequent commentary on Etherege has had to reckon. But it contains some emphatic misreadings and provoked from John Hayman a review which deftly sketches an alternative point of view – 'Poise is not equivocation', *Essays in Criticism*, 10 (1960), 94–9. Hayman has also published one of the best essays on *The Man of Mode* ('Dorimant and the comedy of a man of mode', *Modern Language Quarterly*, 30 (1969), 183–

97), which makes illuminating use of contemporary, especially French, courtesy books in commenting on the play.

In a provocative essay, Jocelyn Powell argues that an 'ambiguity of response', a 'floating between laughter and indignation', is 'the essence of Etherege's comedy' ('George Etherege and the form of a comedy', in J.R. Brown and B. Harris (eds.), *Restoration Theatre*, Stratford-upon-Avon Studies no. 6 (London, Edward Arnold, 1965), pp. 43–69). Ronald Berman, focusing on the use of Waller quotations in *The Man of Mode*, claims that 'in a literal sense the play is a running commentary' on that poet's work ('The comic passions of *The Man of Mode*', *Studies in English Literature, 1500–1900*, 10 (1970), 459–68), and Leslie Martin finds in 'an exquisite parody of a stock character in heroic drama, the termagant heroine' an explanation of the particular response aimed at in the portrait of Mrs Loveit in that work ('Past and parody in *The Man of Mode*', *Studies in English Literature, 1500–1900*, 16 (1976), 363–76). In his pioneering *The Ornament of Action: Text and Performance in Restoration Comedy* (Cambridge University Press, 1979) Peter Holland has brought contemporary scenic convention to bear upon the interpretation of the plays.

A harsher (though, unfortunately, factually inaccurate) account of the comedies is provided by John Traugott ('The rake's progress from court to comedy: a study in comic form', *Studies in English Literature, 1500–1900*, 6 (1966), 381–407). A more plausible (if still debatable) account of the style of *The Man of Mode* as 'tough and realistic' can be found in Paul C. Davies, 'The state of nature and the state of war: a reconsideration of *The Man of Mode*', *University of Toronto Quarterly*, 39 (1969), 53–62. Emphasizing the use of religious language in the latter play, David Krause advances a view of Dorimant and Harriet as abandoning 'themselves to Satanic laughter' ('The defaced angel: a concept of satanic grace in Etherege's *The Man of Mode*', *Drama Survey*, 7 (1968–9), 87–103). Though his opinions are more extreme than some, Krause's desire to discern a pattern in the comedy's religious references has been shared by a number of other writers, and in *Likenesses of Truth in Elizabethan and Restoration Drama* (Oxford, Clarendon Press, 1972) Harriett Hawkins offers an analysis of this phenomenon and some thoughts of her own on the play.

In spite of a great deal of scholarly activity, however, the plays have contrived to remain elusive, and little agreement on matters of substance has been achieved between the various interpreters. This is so markedly the case, in fact, that two recent essays on *The Man of Mode* have been almost as much concerned with this history of critical disagreement as with the play itself – Robert D. Hume, 'Reading and misreading *The Man of Mode*', *Criticism*, 14 (1972), 1–11 and Brian Corman, 'Interpreting and misinterpreting *The Man of Mode*', *Papers on Language and Literature*, 13 (1977), 35–53.

THE COMICAL REVENGE

WD

INTRODUCTORY NOTE

The Comical Revenge; or, Love in a Tub includes numerous incidents and exchanges generally reminiscent of earlier comedies (especially those of the 1620s and 1630s), but no definite source for any part of it has been convincingly identified.

The play's first recorded performance was on 27 April 1664 on which date John Evelyn noted that he had been to see 'a facecious Comedy Cald Love in a Tub'. This is not likely to have been its premiere, which probably took place either earlier in April or in March 1664.

It was acted by the Duke's Company at the Lincoln's Inn Fields theatre and enjoyed a great success. According to John Downes, 'The clean and well performance of this Comedy, got the Company more Reputation and Profit than any preceding Comedy: the Company taking in a Months time at it 1000*l*.' Downes also provides a cast-list: 'Mr. *Betterton*, performing Lord *Beauford*; Mr. *Smith*, Colonel *Bruce*; Mr. *Norris*, *Lovis*; Mr. *Nokes*, Sir *Nicholas Cully*; Mr. *Underhill*, *Palmer*; Mr. *Saunford*, Wheadle; Mrs. *Betterton*, *Graciana*; Mrs. *Davies*, *Aurelia*; Mrs. *Long*, the Widow; Mr. *Harris*, Sir *Frederick Frollick*; Mr. *Price*, *Dufoy*.' He also added a celebratory couplet: '*Sir* Nich'las, *Sir* Fred'rick; *Widow and* Dufoy, / *Were not by any so well done*, Mafoy' (*Roscius Anglicanus*, London, 1708, pp. 24–5). The importance of the contribution of two other actors to the comedy's success is suggested by the irascible comments of Pepys (29 October 1666) on a performance in the Great Hall, Whitehall, attended by 'the King and Queen, Duke and Duchesse, and all the great ladies of the Court; which endeed was a fine sight – but the play, being *Love in a Tubb*, a silly play; and though done by the Duke's people, yet having neither Baterton nor his wife – and the whole thing done ill, and being ill also, I had no manner of pleasure in the play'.

In spite of such adverse comments, however, *The Comical Revenge* proved well able to hold a place in the London playhouse repertoire into the eighteenth century, although, in the later decades, its appearances were inevitably rarer. The last known performance there was on 16 December 1726.

It was first published in 1664, with a second edition later that year. Additional quartos followed in 1667, 1669, 1689, 1690 and 1697.

THE EPISTLE DEDICATORY

TO THE HONOURABLE CHARLES LORD BUCKHURST.

MY LORD,

I could not have wished myself more fortunate than I have been in the success of this poem: the writing of it was a means to make me known to your lordship; the acting of it has lost me no reputation; and the printing of it has now given me an opportunity to show how much I honour you.

I here dedicate it, as I have long since dedicated myself, to your lordship: let the humble love of the giver make you set some value upon the worthless gift: I hope it may have some esteem with others, because the author knows how to esteem you, whose knowledge moves admiration, and goodness love, in all that know you. But I design this a dedication, not a panegyric; not to proclaim your virtues to the world, but to show your lordship how firmly they have obliged me to be,

My lord,

Your most humble and faithful servant,

GEO. ETHEREGE.

Charles Lord Buckhurst: see Additional Note.

2 *success*: fate (good or ill).

2 *poem*: work.

THE PROLOGUE

Who could expect such crowding here today,
Merely on the report of a new play?
A man would think y'ave been so often bit
By us of late, you should have learned more wit,
And first have sent a forlorn hope to spy
The plot and language of our comedy,
Expecting till some desp'rate critics had
Resolved you whether it were good or bad:
But yet we hope you'll never grow so wise;
For if you should, we and our comedies
Must trip to Norwich, or for Ireland go,
And never fix, but, like a puppet-show,
Remove from town to town, from fair to fair,
Seeking fit chapmen to put off our ware.
For such our fortune is this barren age,
That faction now, not wit, supports the stage:
Wit has, like painting, had her happy flights,
And in peculiar ages reached her heights,
Though now declined; yet could some able pen
Match Fletcher's nature, or the art of Ben,
The old and graver sort would scarce allow
Those plays were good, because we writ them now.
Our author therefore begs you would forget,
Most rev'rend judges, the records of wit,
And only think upon the modern way
Of writing, whilst y'are censuring his play.
And gallants, as for you, talk loud i' th' pit,
Divert yourselves and friends with your own wit;
  Observe the ladies, and neglect the play;
  Or else 'tis feared we are undone today.

---

3 *bit*: cheated.
5 *forlorn hope*: one deputed to undertake a perilous mission (originally, it meant 'a picked body of soldiers, detached to the front to begin the attack').
7 *Expecting*: waiting.
7 *desp'rate*: ready to risk anything.
11 *trip*: make a short trip (in contrast to the longer journey to Ireland).
11 *Norwich . . . Ireland*: see Additional Note.
14 *chapmen*: customers.
14 *put off*: sell, get rid of.
18 *peculiar*: special.
20 *Fletcher's nature, or the art of Ben*: see Additional Note.
24 *records*: accented on the second syllable.
26 *censuring*: judging (not necessarily unfavourably).

DRAMATIS PERSONAE

The LORD BEVILL, father to Lovis, Graciana, and Aurelia

The LORD BEAUFORT, servant to Graciana

COLONEL BRUCE, a Cavalier, friend to Lovis, in love with Graciana

LOVIS, friend to Bruce

SIR FREDERICK FROLLICK, cousin to the Lord Beaufort

GRACIANA, a young lady, in love with the Lord Beaufort

AURELIA, her sister, in love with Col. Bruce

MRS RICH, a wealthy widow, sister to the Lord Bevill, in love with Sir Frederick

LETITIA, a girl, waiting upon Aurelia

BETTY, waiting-woman to the Widow

DUFOY, a saucy impertinent Frenchman, servant to Sir Frederick

CLARK, servant to the Lord Beaufort

SIR NICHOLAS CULLY, knighted by Oliver

WHEADLE and PALMER } gamesters

MRS GRACE, a wench kept by Wheadle

JENNY, her maid

MRS LUCY, a wench kept by Sir Frederick

A COACHMAN belonging to the Widow

A BELLMAN

FOOTMEN, LINKBOYS, DRAWERS, and other ATTENDANTS

[A CHIRURGEON]

[Four or five VILLAINS]

---

3 *servant to*: suitor to, lover of.

19 *knighted by Oliver*: see note to I ii 178.

THE COMICAL REVENGE; OR, LOVE IN A TUB

ACT I

SCENE I

An antechamber to Sir Frederick Frollick's bedchamber.

Enter DUFOY, *with a plaister on his head, walking discontentedly; and* CLARK *immediately after him.*

CLARK. Good-morrow, monsieur.

DUFOY. Good-mor', – good-mor'.

CLARK. Is Sir Frederick stirring?

DUFOY. Pox sturré himé.

CLARK. My lord has sent me –

DUFOY. Begar me vil havé de revengé; me vil no stay two day in Englandé.

CLARK. Good monsieur, what's the matter?

DUFOY. De matré! de matré is easie to be perceive; dis bedlamé, mad-cape, *diable de* matré, vas drunké de last night, and vor no reason, but dat me did advisé him go to bed, begar he did striké, breaké my headé, jernie.

---

s.d. *plaister*: plaster.

6 *Begar*: 'by God'.

9 *matré*: As Brett-Smith observes, '*matter* and *master* are both reduced to *matré* in Dufoy's pronunciation'.

10 *bedlamé*: madman, lunatic (the term being derived from the name of the Hospital of St Mary of Bethlehem in London, an asylum for the insane).

10 *mad-cape*: possibly, reckless, wildly impetuous; but the word retained elements of a stronger meaning ('madman', 'maniac'), making it almost a synonym for 'bedlam'.

10 *diable de matré*: devil of a master.

12 *go to bed*: from *1664b* onwards the early editions here emend to 'to go to bed'. This is an entirely plausible reading, as also, however, is that of *1664a*, which is therefore here retained.

13 *jernie*: a profane oath, a corruption of 'je renie Dieu' ('I renounce God').

CLARK. Have patience, he did it unadvisedly.

DUFOY. Unadvisé! didé not me advise him justé when he did ité?

CLARK. Yes; but he was in drink you say.

DUFOY. In drinké! me vishé he had ben over de head and de ear in drinké; begar in France de drink dat van man drinké do's not crack de noder man's brainé. Hark! – (SIR FREDERICK *knocks*) He is avake, and none of de peeple are to attende himé: Ian! Villian! day are all gon, run to de *diable*; (*Knocks again*) have de patience, I beseech you. (*Pointing towards his master's chamber.*)

CLARK. Acquaint Sir Frederick I am here from my lord.

DUFOY. I vil, I vil; your ver umble *serviteur.*

Exeunt.

SCENE II

Sir Frederick's bedchamber.

Enter SIR FREDERICK *in his nightgown, and after him* DUFOY.

DUFOY. God-mor, good-mor to your vorshippé; me am alvay ready to attendé your vorshippé, and your vorshippe's alvay ready to beaté and to abusé mé; you vare drunké de lasté nighté, and my head aké today morningé; (*Showing his head*) seé you heré if my brayné have no ver good *raison* to counsel you, and to mindé your bus'nessé.

SIR FREDERICK. Thou hast a notable brain; set me down a crown for a plaister; but forbear your rebukes.

DUFOY. 'Tis ver couragious ting to breaké de head of your *serviteur*, is it noté? Begar you vil never keepé de good *serviteur*, had no me love you ver vel. –

---

14 *unadvisedly*: Clark uses the word to mean 'rashly'; but Dufoy (line 15) takes it in the sense of 'lacking advice'.

22 *are to attende himé*: i.e. are present to attend on him.

22 *Ian! Villian!*: see Additional Note.

26 *serviteur*: servant.

6 *raison*: reason.

8–9 *set me down*: record me as owing you.

SIR FREDERICK. I know thou lov'st me.

DUFOY. And darefore you do beaté me, is dat de *raison*?

SIR FREDERICK. Prithee forbear; I am sorry for't.

DUFOY. Ver good satisfaction! Begar it is me dat am sorrié for't.

SIR FREDERICK. Well, well.

DUFOY. De *serviteur* of my lord your cousin be comé speak vid you.

SIR FREDERICK. Bring him in.

Exit DUFOY.

I am of opinion that drunkenness is not so damnable a sin to me as 'tis to many; sorrow and repentance are sure to be my first work the next morning: 'slid, I have known some so lucky at this recreation, that, whereas 'tis familiar to forget what we do in drink, have even lost the memory, after sleep, of being drunk: now do I feel more qualms than a young woman in breeding.

Enter DUFOY *and* CLARK. DUFOY *goes out again.*

Clark! What news from the god of love? he's always at your master's elbow, h'as jostled the devil out of service; no more! Mrs Grace! Poor girl, Mrs Graciana has flung a squib into his bosom, where the wild-fire will huzzay for a time, and then crack! it flies out at's breeches.

CLARK. Sir, he sent me before with his service; he'll wait on you himself when he's dressed.

SIR FREDERICK. In very good time; there never was a girl more humoursome, nor tedious in the dressing of her baby.

Exit CLARK.

---

24 *'slid*: a mild oath, an abbreviation of 'God's lid'.

26 *familiar*: common, usual.

28 *qualms*: faintness, sickness (usually, of the stomach).

33–4 *squib . . . wild-fire . . . huzzay*: see Additional Note.

36 *before*: ahead of him.

36 *with his service*: to pay his respects to you.

38 *In very good time*: expressing ironic acquiescence or disbelief: 'of course!', 'to be sure!'

39 *humoursome*: whimsical, capricious.

40 *baby*: doll.

Enter DUFOY, *and* FOOTBOY.

DUFOY. Hayé! heré is der ver vine varké begar, de ver vine varké! –

SIR FREDERICK. What's the business?

DUFOY. De business! de divil také mé if daré be not de whole regiment army de hackené cocheman, de linke-boy, de fydler, and de shamber-maydé, dat havé beseegé de howsé; dis is de consequance of de drink vid a poxé.

SIR FREDERICK. Well, the coachmen and linkboys must be satisfied, I suppose there's money due to 'em; the fiddlers, for broken heads and instruments, must be compounded with; I leave that to your care; but for the chambermaid, I'll deal with her myself; go, go, fetch her up.

DUFOY. De pimpé, begar I vil be de pimpé to no man in de Christendomé; do you go vech her up; de pimpé – *Exit* DUFOY.

SIR FREDERICK. (*to the* FOOTBOY) Go sirrah, direct her. (*Exit* FOOTBOY) Now have I most unmanfully fallen foul upon some woman, I'll warrant you, and wounded her reputation shrowardly: oh drink, drink! thou art a vile enemy to the civillest sort of courteous ladies. –

Enter JENNY, WHEADLE*'s wench's maid.*

Oh Jenny, next my heart nothing could be more welcome.

---

45 *hackené*: a four-wheeled coach, kept for hire.

45–6 *linke-boy*: a boy hired to carry a link, a torch made of tow and pitch, etc., to light clients through the streets.

52 *compounded with*: come to terms with.

58 *sirrah*: used with an assumption of authority and superiority on the part of the speaker. Dufoy later deeply resents Cully's use of it in their confrontation (V ii 230).

61 *shrowardly*: severely, shrewdly (*OED* lists it as a nonce-word, created by Etherege from 'shrewdly' on the model of 'frowardly').

62 *civillest*: frequently used by Etherege almost as a code-word for 'obliging sexually'; cf. *She Would*, I i 12.

64 *next my heart*: nearest to my heart, dearest (used in apposition to 'Jenny').

JENNY. Unhand me; are you a man fit to be trusted with a woman's reputation?

SIR FREDERICK. Not when I am in a reeling condition; men are now and then subject to those infirmities in drink, which women have when th'are sober. Drunkenness is no good secretary, Jenny; you must not look so angry, good faith you must not.

JENNY. Angry! we always took you for a civil gentleman.

SIR FREDERICK. So I am i'troth I think. –

JENNY. A civil gentleman will come to a lady's lodging at two a clock in the morning, and knock as if it were upon life and death; a midwife was never knocked up with more fury.

SIR FREDERICK. Well, well, girl, all's well I hope, all's well.

JENNY. You have made such an uproar amongst the neighbours, we must be forced to change our lodging.

SIR FREDERICK. And thou art come to tell me whither; – kind heart! –

JENNY. I'll see you a little better-mannered first. Because we would not let you in at that unseasonable hour, you and your rude ranting companions hooped and hollowed like madmen, and roared out in the streets, 'A whore, a whore, a whore'; you need not have knocked good people out of their beds, you might have met with them had been good enough for your purpose abroad.

SIR FREDERICK. 'Twas ill done Jenny, indeed it was.

JENNY. 'Twas a mercy Mr Wheadle was not there, my mistress's friend; had he been there sh'ad been quite undone. There's nothing got by your lewd doings; you are but scandals to a civil woman: we had so much the good will of the neighbours before, we had

---

71 *secretary*: keeper of a secret.
88 *rude*: barbarous, unmannerly.
88 *ranting*: swaggering, scolding, raving.
88 *companions*: fellows, mates (with a contemptuous inflection).
88 *hooped*: shouted derisively.
89 *hollowed*: cried (as to hounds in hunting).
93 *abroad*: i.e. on the streets.
97 *lewd*: low, vulgar.

credit for what we would; and but this morning the chandler refused to score a quart of scurvy-grass.

SIR FREDERICK. Hang reputation amongst a company of rascals; trust me not if thou art not grown most wondrous pretty. (*Offers to hug her*)

JENNY. Stand off, or I protest I'll make the people in your lodging know what a manner of man you are.

SIR FREDERICK. You and I have been intimate acquaintance; – why so coy now, Jenny?

JENNY. Pray forbear: – you'll never leave till I shriek out; – (*Noise within*) your servants listen, hark – there's somebody coming.

Enter BEAUFORT.

My mistress charged me to tell you she will never see your eyes again; she never deserved this at your hands, – poor gentlewoman: – you had a fling at me too, you did not whisper it, I thank you: 'tis a miserable condition we women bring ourselves to for your sakes. (*Weeps*)

BEAUFORT. How now cousin! what, at wars with the women?

SIR FREDERICK. I gave a small alarm to their quarters last night, my lord.

BEAUFORT. Jenny in tears! what's the occasion, poor girl?

JENNY. I'll tell you, my lord.

SIR FREDERICK. Buzz; set not her tongue a-going again; (*Clapping his hand before her mouth*) sh'as

---

101 *chandler*: retailer of provisions (a lowly kind of tradesman; therefore the sense here is '*even* the chandler . . . ').

101 *score*: allow on credit (literally, to record (debts) by means of notches on a tally).

101 *scurvy-grass*: the reference here is to a kind of ale medicated with scurvy-grass, a plant believed to assist in the cure of scurvy.

103 *rascals*: people of low birth or station.

105 *protest*: declare.

109 *leave*: stop.

120 *alarm to their quarters*: sudden or unexpected attack on enemy positions.

122 *occasion*: cause.

125 *Buzz*: an exclamation of impatience, commanding silence.

made more noise than half a dozen paper-mills: London Bridge at a low water is silence to her; in a word, rambling last night, we knocked at her mistress's lodging, they denied us entrance, whereupon a harsh word or two flew out, 'Whore' – I think, or something to that purpose.

JENNY. These were not all your heroic actions;

Enter DUFOY.

pray tell the consequence, how you marched bravely at the rear of an army of linkboys; upon the sudden, how you gave defiance, and then waged a bloody war with the constable; and having vanquished that dreadful enemy, how you committed a general massacre on the glass-windows: are not these most honourable achievements, such as will be registered to your eternal fame, by the most learn'd historians of Hicks's Hall.

SIR FREDERICK. Good sweet Jenny let's come to a treaty; do but hear what articles I'll propose.

JENNY. A woman's heart's too tender to be an enemy to peace.

They whisper.

DUFOY. Your most humble *serviteur*, my lord.

BEAUFORT. Monsieur, I perceive you are much to blame; you are an excellent governor indeed.

---

127 *paper-mills*: frequently invoked in seventeenth-century writing to describe a woman's raucous tongue.

128 *London Bridge at a low water*: 'in the seventeenth century the piers and starlings of London Bridge damned the river to such an extent that at low water there was a pronounced and noisy *fall* through the arches' (Brett-Smith).

128 *silence to her*: i.e. silence in comparison to her.

129 *rambling*: wandering the town, but with a secondary meaning of 'going out in search of sex' (for the latter, see J.D. Patterson, 'The Restoration *Ramble*', *Notes and Queries*, 226 (1981), 209–10).

136 *gave defiance*: declared hostilities.

139 *glass-windows*: a common target of Restoration street marauders; see, for example, the prologue to John Dryden's *The Wild Gallant*, *Dramatic Works*, ed. Montague Summers (London, Nonesuch Press, 1932), vol. 1, p. 67.

141–2 *Hicks's Hall*: the sessions-house of the Justices of the Peace of Middlesex.

144 *articles*: terms.

149 *governor*: tutor.

DUFOY. Begar do you tinké dat I amé de bedlamé? No tingé but de bedlamé can governé himé.

SIR FREDERICK. Jenny, here's my hand; I'll come and make amends for all – pretty rogue. –

DUFOY. Ver pret rogué, vid a poxé.

JENNY. What rude French rascal have you here?

DUFOY. Rascalé! Begar ver it nod vor de reverence of my matré I vod cut off your occupation. French rascalé! Whore English –

SIR FREDERICK. Dufoy, be gone, and leave us.

DUFOY. I vil, I vil leave you to your recreation; I vishé you ver good pastimé, and de poxé begar.

Exit DUFOY.

JENNY. I never heard a ruder fellow. – Sir Frederick, you will not fail the time.

SIR FREDERICK. No, no, Jenny.

JENNY. Your servant, my lord.

BEAUFORT. Farewell Jenny.

Exit JENNY.

SIR FREDERICK. Now did all this fury end in a mild invitation to the lady's lodging.

BEAUFORT. I have known this wench's mistress ever since I came from travel, but never was acquainted with that fellow that keeps her; prithee what is he?

SIR FREDERICK. Why his name is Wheadle; he's one whose trade is treachery, to make a friend, and then deceive him; he's of a ready wit, pleasant conversation, throughly skilled in men; in a word, he

---

150 *bedlamé*: *OED* offers no instances of 'bedlam' in the sense of 'a keeper or custodian of madmen'; so Dufoy presumably means that a man would have to be as mad as Sir Frederick to be a fit 'governor' for him.

153–4 *rogue*: (1) on Sir Frederick's lips, a playful term of endearment (2) on Dufoy's, a scornful epithet (applied abusively to servants).

156 *vor de reverence*: out of respect for.

157 *occupation*: playing on the popular use of the verb 'to occupy' to mean 'to have sex with', which led to the word being rarely used in seventeenth-century literature.

163 *fail the time*: fail to keep the appointment.

172 *Wheadle*: in the late seventeenth century 'Wheadle' (i.e. 'wheedle') carried strong associations of cheating, knavery.

175 *throughly*: perfectly, completely.

175 *skilled in men*: knowledgeable about human nature.

knows so much of virtue as makes him well accomplished for all manner of vice: he has lately insinuated himself into Sir Nicholas Cully, one whom Oliver, for the transcendent knavery and disloyalty of his father, has dishonoured with knighthood; a fellow as poor in experience as in parts, and one that has a vainglorious humour to gain a reputation amongst the gentry, by feigning good nature, and an affection to the king and his party. I made a little debauch th'other day in their company, where I foresaw this fellow's destiny, his purse must pay for keeping this wench, and all other Wheadle's extravagances. But pray, my lord, how thrive you in your more honourable adventures? Is harvest near? When is the sickle to be put i' th' corn?

BEAUFORT. I have been hitherto so prosperous,
My happiness has still outflown my faith:
Nothing remains but ceremonial charms,
Graciana's fixed i' th' circle of my arms.

SIR FREDERICK. Then y'are a happy man for a season.

BEAUFORT. For ever.

SIR FREDERICK. I mistrust your mistress's divinity; you'll find her attributes but mortal; women, like jugglers' tricks, appear miracles to the ignorant; but in themselves th'are mere cheats.

BEAUFORT. Well, well, cousin; I have engaged that you this day shall be my guest at my Lord Bevill's table; pray make me master of my promise once.

---

178 *Cully*: one easily deceived, a simpleton.

178 *Oliver*: Cromwell, Lord Protector (1653–8). Knighthoods conferred by him were inevitably a subject of mockery after Charles II's return in 1660.

180 *fellow*: a word used for someone of very lowly station or origin.

182 *humour*: whim, desire.

183 *the king*: Charles II, in exile on the Continent at the time of the play's action.

186 *all other*: all the rest of.

191 *faith*: ability to believe in it.

192 *ceremonial charms*: marriage rites – 'charms' (in its meaning of 'a magician's incantation', here applied to the priest's words) leads to the next line's reference to 'circle': the magician invoking dangerous spirits inscribed a circle they could not invade.

198 *jugglers*: performers of legerdemain.

199 *mere*: pure, complete.

SIR FREDERICK. Faith I have engaged to dine with my dear Lucy; poor girl, I have lately given her occasion to suspect my kindness; yet for your sake I'll venture to break my word, upon condition you'll excuse my errors; you know my conversation has not been amongst ceremonious ladies.

BEAUFORT. All modest freedom you will find allowed; formality is banished thence.

SIR FREDERICK. This virtue is enough to make me bear with all the inconveniences of honest company.

BEAUFORT. The freeness of your humour is your friend. I have such news to tell thee that I fear thou'lt find thy breast too narrow for thy joy.

SIR FREDERICK. Gently, my lord, lest I find the thing too little for my expectation.

BEAUFORT. Know that thy careless carriage has done more than all the skill and diligence of love could e'er effect.

SIR FREDERICK. What? the widow has some kind thoughts of my body.

BEAUFORT. She loves you, and dines on purpose at her brother's house this day, in hopes of seeing you.

SIR FREDERICK. Some women like fishes despise the bait, or else suspect it, whilst still it's bobbing at their mouths; but subtilly waved by the angler's hand, greedily hang themselves upon the hook. There are many so critically wise, they'll suffer none to deceive them but themselves.

BEAUFORT. Cousin, 'tis time you were preparing for your mistress.

SIR FREDERICK. Well, since 'tis my fortune, I'll about it. Widow, thy ruin lie on thy own head: faith, my lord, you can witness 'twas none of my seeking.

Exeunt.

---

203 *engaged*: promised.
207 *conversation*: range of acquaintance.
208 *ceremonious ladies*: ladies who precisely observe the decorums of respectable society.
212 *honest*: respectable.
213 *humour*: disposition.
218 *careless carriage*: carefree mode of behaviour.
227 *subtilly*: subtly.
229 *critically wise*: minutely circumspect.

SCENE III

Wheadle's lodging.

Enter WHEADLE *and* PALMER.

WHEADLE. Come, bear thy losses patiently.

PALMER. A pox confound all ordinaries, if ever I play in an ordinary again – (*Bites his thumb*)

WHEADLE. Thou'lt lose thy money: thou hast no power to forbear; I will as soon undertake to reclaim a horse from a hitch he has learned in his pace, or an old mastive from worrying of sheep.

PALMER. Ay, ay, there is nothing can do it but hemp.

WHEADLE. Want of money may do much.

PALMER. I protest I had rather still be vicious than owe my virtue to necessity. How commendable is chastity in an eunuch? I am grown more than half virtuous of late: I have laid the dangerous pad now quite aside; I walk within the purlieus of the law. Could I but leave this ordinary, this square, I were the most accomplished man in town.

---

s.d. *Palmer*: one who palms or conceals in the hand (e.g. a card or die in gambling), one who practices sleight of hand.

2 *ordinaries*: public eating-houses; these were also places where gambling was carried on (cf. *Man of Mode*, III ii 125).

3 s.d. *Bites his thumb*: This can be a sign of anger or vexation, which would be quite apt here, but it was also used as a sign of contempt, in which case the object of abuse would be either the ordinary or Palmer himself.

6 *a hitch*: a limp, a hobble.

6 *pace*: 'a particular movement which horses are taught, though some have it naturally, made by lifting the legs on the same side together' (Johnson).

7 *mastive*: mastiff.

8 *hemp*: i.e. the gallows.

9 *Want of money*: lack of money.

10 *vicious*: given over to vice.

10–11 *owe my virtue to necessity*: cf. the proverbial 'Make a virtue of necessity' (Tilley, V 73).

13 *pad*: highway robbery.

14 *purlieus*: permitted limits (*OED*: 'A place where one has the right to range at large.')

15 *this square*: to play 'upon the square' meant to gamble 'without trickery or deceit'; so perhaps Palmer's meaning here is 'this place where I play honestly (and am therefore more likely to lose)'.

WHEADLE. 'Tis pity, thou art master of thy art; such a nimble hand, such neat conveyance.

PALMER. Nay, I should have made an excellent juggler, faith.

WHEADLE. Come, be cheerful, I've lodged a deer shall make amends for all; I lacked a man to help me set my toils, and thou art come most happily.

PALMER. My dear Wheadle, who is it?

WHEADLE. My new friend and patron Sir Nicholas Cully.

PALMER. He's fat, and will say well, I promise you. Well, I'll do his business most dextrously, else let me ever lose the honour of serving a friend in the like nature.

WHEADLE. No more words, but haste, prepare for the design; habit yourself like a good thrifty countryman; get tools, dice, and money for the purpose, and meet me at the Devil about three exactly.

Enter BOY.

BOY. Sir, Sir Nicholas Cully is without.

WHEADLE. Desire him to walk in. [*Exit* BOY.] Here Palmer, the back way, quickly, and be sure –

PALMER. Enough, enough, I'll warrant thee.

Exit PALMER.

Enter SIR NICHOLAS CULLY.

---

17 *art*: skill, craft.
18 *neat conveyance*: skilful sleight of hand.
21 *lodged*: (in hunting) to discover the lodge or lair of a buck.
23 *toils*: traps.
23 *happily*: luckily, fortunately.
27 *fat*: (1) (of people) wealthy (2) (of animals) fatted, ready to kill (see following note).
27 *say well*: 'i.e. assay. The metaphor is from the breaking up of a deer, when the huntsman's knife tests how many fingers of fat the beast has on its ribs.' (Brett-Smith).
28 *dextrously*: craftily, deftly, cunningly (in Etherege, usually with an implication of deceitful practice).
29–30 *in the like nature*: in similar circumstances, or on a similar errand.
32 *design*: 'a scheme formed to the detriment of another' (Johnson).
32 *habit*: dress.
34 *the Devil*: a famous tavern in Fleet Street, near Temple Bar.

WHEADLE. Sir Nicholas, this visit is too great a favour; I intended one to you; how do you find yourself this morning?

SIR NICHOLAS. Faith much the drier for the last night's wetting.

WHEADLE. Like thirsty earth, which gapes the more for a small shower; we'll soak you throughly today.

SIR NICHOLAS. Excuse me, faith I am engaged.

WHEADLE. I am sorry for't; I meant you a share in my good fortune; but since it cannot be –

SIR NICHOLAS. What? what good fortune?

WHEADLE. Nay, 'twill but vex you to know it, since you have not leisure to pursue it.

SIR NICHOLAS. Dear Wheadle, prithee tell me.

WHEADLE. Now do I want power to keep it from you. Just as you came in at that door, went out at this a waiting-gentlewoman, sent with a civil message from her lady, to desire the happiness of my company this afternoon, where I should have the opportunity of seeing another lovely brisk woman, newly married to a foolish citizen, who will be apt enough to hear reason from one that can speak it better than her husband: I returned my humble thanks for the honour she did me, and that I could not do myself so great an injury to disobey her will; this is th'adventure; but since y'ave business –

SIR NICHOLAS. A pox on business, I'll defer't.

WHEADLE. By no means for a silly woman; our pleasures must be slaves to our affairs.

SIR NICHOLAS. Were it to take possession of an estate, I'd neglect it. Are the ladies Cavaliers?

WHEADLE. Oh, most loyal-hearted ladies!

SIR NICHOLAS. How merry will we be then!

WHEADLE. I say, mind your business.

---

58 *brisk*: sharp-witted, sprightly, lively.

59 *citizen*: 'a townsman; a man of trade; not a gentleman' (Johnson).

59–60 *hear reason*: i.e. respond to approaches.

64 *adventure*: piece of good fortune (see line 48).

66 *silly*: perhaps, foolish; but, more probably, insignificant.

67 *affairs*: serious business.

72 *mind your business*: attend to your more important concerns.

SIR NICHOLAS. I'll go and put it off immediately. Where shall I meet you in the afternoon?

WHEADLE. You'll find me at the Devil about three a clock, where I expect a second summons as she passes toward the city.

SIR NICHOLAS. Thither will I come without fail; be sure you wait for me. *Exit* SIR NICHOLAS.

WHEADLE. Wait for thee, as a cat does for a mouse she intends to play with, and then prey upon. How eagerly did this half-witted fellow chap up the bait! like a ravenous fish, that will not give the angler leave to sink his line, but greedily darts up and meets it half way. *Exit laughing.*

SCENE IV

The Lord Bevill's house.

Enter GRACIANA, *and* AURELIA *immediately after her, with a letter in her hand.*

GRACIANA. The sun's grown lazy; 'tis a tedious space
Since he set forth, and yet's not half his race.
I wonder Beaufort does not yet appear;
Love never loiters, love sure brings him here.

AURELIA. Brought on the wings of love, here I present
Presenting the letter.
His soul, whose body prisons yet prevent;
The noble Bruce, whose virtues are his crimes:
GRACIANA *rejects the letter.*
Are you as false and cruel as the times!
Will you not read the story of his grief?
But wilfully refuse to give relief?

GRACIANA. Sister, from you this language makes me start:
Can you suspect such vices in my heart?
His virtues I, as well as you, admire;
I never scorned, but pity much his fire.

---

82 *chap up*: gobble up.
2 *race*: daily course.
13 *admire*: view with wonder, marvel at.

AURELIA. If you did pity, you would not reject

GRACIANA *rejects the letter again.*

This messenger of love: this is neglect.

GRACIANA. 'Tis cruelty to gaze on wounds I'm sure,
When we want balsam to effect their cure.

AURELIA. 'Tis only want of will in you, you have
Beauty to kill, and virtue too to save.

GRACIANA. We of ourselves can neither love nor hate;
Heav'n does reserve the pow'r to guide our fate.

AURELIA. Graciana, –

Enter LORD BEVILL, LOVIS, *and the* WIDOW.

GRACIANA. Sister, forbear; my father's here.

LORD BEVILL. So girl; what, no news of your lover yet? Our dinner's ready, and I am afraid he will go nigh to incur the cook's anger.

WIDOW. I believe h'as undertook a hard task; Sir Frederick, they say, is no easy man to be persuaded to come among us women.

LOVIS. Sir.

LORD BEVILL. What now?

LOVIS *and* LORD BEVILL *whisper.*

WIDOW. (*to* GRACIANA) I am as impatient as thou art, girl; I long to see Sir Frederick here.

LORD BEVILL. Forbear, I charge you on my blessing; not one word more of Colonel Bruce.

LOVIS. You gave encouragement sir to his love;
The honour of our house now lies at stake.

LORD BEVILL. You find by your sister's inclinations heaven has decreed her otherwise.

LOVIS. But sir, –

LORD BEVILL. Forbear to speak, or else forbear the room.

LOVIS. This I can obey, but not the other. *Exit* LOVIS.

Enter FOOTBOY.

FOOTBOY. Sir, my Lord Beaufort's come.

LORD BEVILL. 'Tis well.

---

18 *balsam*: an aromatic preparation, for soothing pain and healing wounds.

21–2 *We of ourselves . . . our fate*: see Additional Note.

WIDOW. D'hear, are there not two gentlemen?

FOOTBOY. Yes madam, there is another proper handsome gentleman. *Exit* FOOTBOY.

LORD BEVILL. Come, let us walk in, and give them entertainment.

WIDOW. Now cousin for Sir Frederick, this man of men, there's nothing like him.

Exeunt all but AURELIA.

AURELIA. With curious diligence I still have strove
Holding the letter in her hand.
During your absence, Bruce, to breathe your love
Into my sister's bosom; but the fire
Wants force; fate does against my breath conspire:
I have obeyed, though I cannot fulfil,
Against myself, the dictates of your will:
My love to yours does yield; since you enjoined,
I hourly court my rival to be kind;
With passion too, as great as you can do,
Taught by those wounds I have received from you.
Small is the difference that's between our grief;
Yours finds no cure, and mine seeks no relief:
You unsuccessfully your love reveal;
And I for ever must my love conceal:
Within my bosom I'll your letter wear,
Putting the letter in her bosom.
It is a tomb that's proper for despair. *Exit.*

---

48 *proper*: (adverbial) thoroughly, finely.
51 *entertainment*: kind reception.
54 *curious*: solicitous, elaborate.
60 *enjoined*: prescribed this task.
61 *kind*: loving, fond.
64 *grief*: in addition to the obvious meaning of 'grief', there is a secondary sense of the word relevant here, i.e. 'physical pain from wounds' (cf. line 63).

ACT II

SCENE I

The Lord Bevill's house.

Enter CLARK *and* DUFOY.

CLARK. Methinks the wound your master gave you last night, makes you look very thin and wan, monsieur.

DUFOY. Begar you are mistaké, it be de voundé dat my metresse did give me long agoe.

CLARK. What? some pretty little English lady's crept into your heart?

DUFOY. No, but damned littel English whore is creepé into my bone begar, me could vish dat de *diable* vould také her vid allé my harté.

CLARK. You have managed your business ill, monsieur.

DUFOY. It vas de raskal cyrugin English dat did manage de businesse illé; me did putté my businessé into his haundé; he did stop de tapé, and de liquor did varké, varké, varké, up into de headé and de shoulder begar.

CLARK. Like soap clapped under a saddle.

DUFOY. Here come my matré, holdé your peacé.

Exit CLARK.

Enter SIR FREDERICK, WIDOW, *and* MAID.

---

11 *cyrugin*: surgeon (the *1664* spelling, preserved here, leaves one uncertain as to whether the English 'chirurgeon' or French 'chirurgien' is intended).

12 *my businessé*: Dufoy has a venereal disease, and the surgeon subjects him to the common seventeenth-century treatment for that malady – confinement in a sweating-tub.

13 *de tapé*: in the sense of 'a hollow or tubular plug through which liquid may be drawn, having some device for shutting off or governing the flow; used especially in drawing liquor from a cask' (*OED*).

13 *liquor*: liquid.

15 *Like soap clapped under a saddle*: identified as one of the 'pranks of ale, and hostelry' likely to be inflicted on visitors to inns in Ben Jonson's *The New Inn* (1629), III i 124–5 (*Works*, ed. C.H. Herford and Percy and Evelyn Simpson (Oxford, Clarendon Press, 1925–52), vol. 6, p. 448).

SIR FREDERICK. Whither, whither do you draw me, widow? What's your design?

WIDOW. To walk a turn in the garden, and then repose in a cool arbour.

SIR FREDERICK. Widow, I dare not venture myself in those amorous shades; you have a mind to be talking of love I perceive, and my heart's too tender to be trusted with such conversation.

WIDOW. I did not imagine you were so foolishly conceited; is it your wit or your person, sir, that is so taking?

SIR FREDERICK. Truly you are much mistaken, I have no such great thoughts of the young man you see; who ever knew a woman have so much reason to build her love upon merit? Have we not daily experience of great fortunes, that fling themselves into the arms of vain idle fellows? Can you blame me then for standing upon my guard? No, let us sit down here, have each on's a bottle of wine at our elbows; so prompted, I dare enter into discourse with you.

WIDOW. Would you have me sit and drink hand to fist with you, as if we were in the Fleece, or some other of your beloved taverns?

SIR FREDERICK. Faith I would have thee come as near as possible to something or other I have been used to converse with, that I may the better know how to entertain thee.

WIDOW. Pray which of those ladies you use to converse with, could you fancy me to look like? be merry, and tell me.

SIR FREDERICK. 'Twere too great a sin to compare thee to any of them; and yet th'ast so incensed me, I can hardly forbear to wish thee one of 'em. Ho, Dufoy! Widow, I stand in awe of this gentleman; I must have his advice before I dare keep you company

---

27 *taking*: alluring.
30–1 *to build*: i.e. as to build.
33 *idle*: worthless, trifling.
35 *on's*: of us.
37 *hand to fist*: i.e. side by side.
38 *the Fleece*: a well-known tavern in Covent Garden.
42 *converse with*: associate with.
43 *entertain*: deal with.

any further. – How do you approve the spending of my time with this lady?

DUFOY. Ver vel, begar; I could vish I had never spendé my time in de vorsé *compagnie.*

WIDOW. You look but ill, monsieur; have you been sick lately?

DUFOY. I havé de ver great affliction in my mindé, madam.

WIDOW. What is't?

DUFOY. Truly I havé de ver great passion vor dis jentelwoman, and she havé no compassion at all vor me; she do refusé me all my *amour* and my *adresse.*

WIDOW. Indeed Betty you are to blame.

BETTY. Out upon him for a French dissembler, he never spake to me in his life, madam.

DUFOY. You see, madam, she scorné me vor her *serviteur.*

BETTY. Pray, when did you make any of your French lové to mé?

DUFOY. It vil breké my hearté to remember de time ven you did refusé mé.

WIDOW. Will you permit me to serve you in this business, monsieur?

DUFOY. Madam, it be d'honour vor de King dé Francé.

WIDOW. Betty, whither run you?

BETTY. I'll not stay to be jeered by a sneaking *valet de chambre*: I'll be revenged if I live, monsieur.

Exit BETTY.

WIDOW. I'll take some other time.

DUFOY. Van you have de leisuré, madam.

SIR FREDERICK. By those lips, –

WIDOW. Nay, pray forbear, sir.

SIR FREDERICK. Who's conceited now, widow? could you imagine I was so fond to kiss them?

---

55 *compagnie*: company.

63 *all my amour and my addresse*: all my love and adroitness in courtship.

65 *Out upon him*: an expression of reproach and disapproval.

70 *lové to mé*: the *1664* accents, reproduced here, suggest that Betty mocks Dufoy's pronunciation.

77 *sneaking*: (1) paltry, contemptibly poor and lowly (2) stealthy, sly.

77–8 *valet de chambre*: gentleman's personal attendant.

84 *fond*: (1) affectionate, loving (2) foolish.

WIDOW. You cannot blame me for standing on my guard so near an enemy.

SIR FREDERICK. If you are so good at that, widow, let's see, what guard would you choose to be at should the trumpet sound a charge to this dreadful foe?

WIDOW. It is an idle question amongst experienced soldiers; but if we ever have a war, we'll never trouble the trumpet; the bells shall proclaim our quarrel.

SIR FREDERICK. It will be most proper; they shall be rung backwards.

WIDOW. Why so, sir?

SIR FREDERICK. I'll have all the helps that may be to allay a dangerous fire; widows must needs have furious flames; the bellows have been at work, and blown 'em up.

WIDOW. You grow too rude, sir: I will have my humour, a walk i' th' garden; and afterwards we'll take the air in the Park.

SIR FREDERICK. Let us join hands then, widow.

WIDOW. Without the dangerous help of a parson I do not fear it, sir.

Exeunt SIR FREDERICK *and* WIDOW.

DUFOY. Begar, I do no care two *sous* if de shambermaid ver hangé; be it not great deal better pretendé d'affection to her, dan to tellé de hole varldé I do take de medicine vor de clapé; begar it be de ver great deale better. *Exit* DUFOY.

SCENE II

A garden belonging to my Lord Bevill's house.

Enter BEAUFORT *and* GRACIANA.

---

91 *idle*: needless, unnecessary.

95 *rung backwards*: an emergency signal, as, for example, in case of fire (see Sir Frederick's next speech).

101 *humour*: whim.

103 *the Park*: either Hyde Park or St James's Park, both fashionable promenading-places.

110 *clapé*: venereal disease.

BEAUFORT. Graciana, why do you condemn your love?
Your beauty without that, alas! would prove
But my destruction, an unlucky star
Prognosticating ruin and despair.
GRACIANA. Sir, you mistake; 'tis not my love I blame,
But my discretion; (*Pointing to her breast*) here the active flame
Should yet a longer time have been concealed;
Too soon, too soon I fear it was revealed.
Our weaker sex glories in a surprise,
We boast the sudden conquests of our eyes;
But men esteem a foe that dares contend,
One that with noble courage does defend
A wounded heart; the victories they gain
They prize by their own hazard and their pain.
BEAUFORT. Graciana, can you think we take delight
To have our happiness against us fight;
Or that such goodness should us men displease
As does afford us heav'n with greater ease?

Enter LOVIS, *walking discontentedly.*

See where your brother comes;
His carr'age has been strange of late to me;
I never gave him cause of discontent;
He takes no notice of our being here:
I will salute him.
GRACIANA. By no means.
Some serious thoughts you see employ his mind.
BEAUFORT. I must be civil. Your servant, sir.
LOVIS. You are my sister's servant, sir; go fawn
Upon your mistress; fare-you-well. *Exit* LOVIS.
BEAUFORT. Fare-you-well, if you are no better company.

GRACIANA *weeps.*

Heavens! what is the matter?
What saucy sorrow dares approach your heart?
Waste not these precious tears; oh, weep no more!

---

3 *unlucky*: boding ill-luck.
9 *surprise*: an unexpected and sudden conquest.
20 *strange*: unfriendly, estranged.
28 *fare-you-well*: thus *1664*; perhaps to suggest an insolent, drawling manner of delivery?

Should heaven frown the world would be too poor,
(Robbed of the sacred treasure of your eyes)
To pay for mercy one fit sacrifice.

GRACIANA. My brother, sir, is growing mad, I fear.

BEAUFORT. Your brother is a man whose noble mind
Was to severest virtue still inclined;
He in the school of honour has been bred,
And all her subtle laws with heed has read:
There is some hidden cause, I fain would know
From whence these strange disorders in him flow.
Graciana, shall I beg you to dispel
These mists which round my troubled reason dwell.

GRACIANA. It is a story I could wish you'd learn
From one whom it does not so much concern;
I am th'unhappy cause of what y'ave seen;
My brother's passion does proceed from mine.

BEAUFORT. This does confound me more! it cannot be;
You are the joy of all your family:
Dares he condemn you for a noble love
Which honour and your duty both approve.

GRACIANA. My lord, those errors merit our excuse
Which an access of virtue does produce.

BEAUFORT. I know that envy is too base a guest
To have a lodging in his gen'rous breast;
'Tis some extreme of honour, or of love,
Or both, that thus his indignation move.

GRACIANA. Ere I begin, you my sad story end;
You are a rival to his dearest friend.

BEAUFORT. Graciana, though you have so great a share
Of beauty, all that see you rivals are;
Yet during this small space I did proclaim
To you, and to the world, my purer flame,

---

40 *school*: lore, doctrines.

41 *read*: studied.

42 *fain*: gladly.

50 *confound*: confuse, perplex, amaze.

55 *access*: see Additional Note.

56 *envy*: the modern sense ('jealousy') is possible, but, in the seventeenth century, the word had more extended and general meanings which may be dominant here, i.e. 'malice, ill-will, spirit of mischief' (cf. *She Would*, II ii 158).

57 *gen'rous*: of noble lineage, high-born; and, therefore, possessing the virtues appropriate to such, i.e. 'gallant, magnanimous'.

I never saw the man that durst draw near,
With his ambitious love t'assault your ear.
What providence has kept us thus asunder?

GRACIANA. When I have spoke you'll find it is no wonder.
He has a mistress more renowned than me,
Whom he does court, his dearer loyalty;
He on his legs does now her favours wear;
He is confined by her foul ravisher:
You may not know his person; but his name
Is strange to none that have conversed with fame.
'Tis Bruce.

BEAUFORT. The man indeed I ne'er did see,
But have heard wonders of his gallantry.

GRACIANA. This gallant man my brother ever loved;
But his heroic virtues so improved
In time those seeds of love which first were sown,
That to the highest friendship they are grown.
This friendship first, and not his love to me,
Sought an alliance with our family.
My sister and myself were newly come
From learning how to live, to live at home;
When barren of discourse one day, and free
With's friend, my brother chanced to talk of me;
Unlucky accident! his friend replied,
He long had wished their blood might be allied;
Then pressed him that they might my father move
To give an approbation to his love:
His person and his merits were so great,
He granted faster than they could entreat;
He wished the fates which govern hearts would be
So kind to him to make our hearts agree;
But told them he had made a sacred vow,
Never to force what love should disallow.

---

70 *He has a mistress more renowned than me*: see Additional Note.

72 *favours*: something worn as a mark of favour (i.e. in love-matters, a glove, a ribbon, etc.); here applied to the prison fetters Bruce wears as the consequence of his loyalty to the Stuart cause.

75 *conversed with fame*: are familiar with matters of public reputation.

Enter SIR FREDERICK *and* WIDOW.

But see, Sir Frederick and my aunt.
My lord, some other time I will relate
The story of his love, and of its fate.

SIR FREDERICK. How now my lord? so grave a countenance in the presence of your mistress? Widow, what would you give your eyes had power to make me such another melancholy gentleman?

WIDOW. I have seen e'en as merry a man as yourself, Sir Frederick, brought to stand with folded arms, and with a tristful look tell a mournful tale to a lady.

Enter a FOOTBOY, *and whispers* SIR FREDERICK.

SIR FREDERICK. The devil owes some men a shame; the coach is ready; widow, I know you are ambitious to be seen in my company.

WIDOW. My lord, and cousin, will you honour me with yours to the Park? that may take off the scandal of his.

Enter AURELIA *and* LETITIA.

BEAUFORT. Madam, we'll wait upon you; but we must not leave this lady behind us.

WIDOW. Cousin Aurelia –

AURELIA. Madam, I beg you will excuse me, and you, my lord; I feel a little indisposition, and dare not venture into so sharp an air.

BEAUFORT. Your servant, madam.

Exeunt all but AURELIA *and* LETITIA.

AURELIA. Retire; I would not have you stay with me,
I have too great a train of misery.
[LETITIA *walks aside.*]
If virtuous love in none be cause of shame,

---

106 *stand with folded arms*: in contemporary portraits an emblem of the doleful lover.

107 *tristful*: sorrowful, dreary.

108 *The devil owes some men a shame*: cf. the proverbial 'The Devil owed him a shame and now he has paid it' (Tilley, D 261).

122 *train*: retinue.

Why should it be a crime to own the flame?
But we by custom, not by nature led,
Must in the beaten paths of honour tread.
I love thee, Bruce; but heav'n, what have I done!
Letitia, did I not command you hence?
LETITIA. Madam, I hope my care is no offence:
I am afflicted thus to see you take
Delight to keep your miseries awake.
AURELIA. Since you have heard me, swear you will be true;
Letitia, none must know I love but you.
LETITIA. If I at any time your love declare,
May I of heav'n and serving you despair.
Though I am young, yet I have felt this smart;
Love once was busy with my tender heart.
AURELIA. Wert thou in love?
LETITIA. I was.
AURELIA. Prithee, with whom?
LETITIA. With one that like myself did newly bloom:
Methoughts his actions were above his years.
She weeps.
AURELIA. Letitia, you confirm me by your tears;
Now I believe you loved; did he love you?
LETITIA. That had been more than to my love was due;
He was so much above my humble birth,
My passion had been fitter for his mirth.
AURELIA. And does your love continue still the same?
LETITIA. Some sparks remain, but time has quenched the flame;
I hope 'twill prove as kind to you, and cure
These greater griefs which (madam) you endure.
AURELIA. Time to my bleeding heart brings no relief;
Death there must heal the fatal wounds of grief:
Letitia, come, within this shady bow'r
We'll join our mournful voices, and repeat
The saddest tales we ever learned of love.
AURELIA *and* LETITIA *walk into an arbour, and sing this song in parts.*

---

124 *own*: admit to.
154 s.d. *into an arbour*: see Additional Note.

SONG.

'When Phillis watched her harmless sheep
Not one poor lamb was made a prey;
Yet she had cause enough to weep,
   Her silly heart did go astray:
Then flying to the neighb'ring grove,
She left the tender flock to rove,
And to the winds did breathe her love.
      She sought in vain
      To ease her pain;
The heedless winds did fan her fire;
      Venting her grief
      Gave no relief;
But rather did increase desire.
Then sitting with her arms across,
Her sorrows streaming from each eye;
She fixed her thoughts upon her loss,
And in despair resolved to die.'

AURELIA. Why should you weep, Letitia, whilst we sing? *Walking out of the arbour.*
Tell me from whence those gentle currents spring.
Can yet your faded love cause such fresh show'rs?
This water is too good for dying flow'rs.

LETITIA. Madam, it is such love commands this dew
As cannot fade; it is my love to you.

AURELIA. Letitia, I am weary of this place;
And yet I know not whither I should go.

LETITIA. Will you be pleased to try if you can sleep?
That may deceive you of your cares awhile.

AURELIA. I will: there's nothing here does give me ease,
But in the end will nourish my disease.

Exeunt.

---

155 *harmless*: innocent, inoffensive; but probably also, free from harm.
158 *silly*: helpless; frail; foolish.
181 *deceive you of*: make you forget.

SCENE III

A tavern.

Enter WHEADLE, *and immediately after him a* FOOTBOY.

WHEADLE. The hour is come; where's your master, sirrah?

FOOTBOY. He'll be here immediately, sir.

WHEADLE. Is he neatly dressed?

FOOTBOY. In the very suit he won th'other day of the Buckinghamshire grazier.

WHEADLE. Take this letter, and give it me when you perceive me talking with Sir Nicholas Cully, with recommendations from a lady; lurk in some secret place till he's come, that he may not perceive you at his entrance. Oh, here's Palmer.

Exit FOOTBOY.

Enter PALMER.

Tom, what's the price of a score of fat wethers?

PALMER. Do they not well become me, boy?

WHEADLE. Nature doubtless intended thee for a rogue, she has so well contrived thee for disguises. Here comes Sir Nicholas.

Enter SIR NICHOLAS.

Sir Nicholas, come, come; this is an honest friend and countryman of mine.

SIR NICHOLAS. Your servant, sir; is not the lady come by yet?

WHEADLE. I expect her every moment, – ho, here's her boy.

Enter FOOTBOY.

Well, what news?

---

4 *neatly*: smartly.
9 *recommendations*: compliments.
15 *contrived*: designed.
18 *countryman*: i.e. a man from the same part of the country.

FOOTBOY. My lady presents her service to you, sir, and has sent you this. (*Delivers a letter*)

WHEADLE *reads, and seems much displeased.*

SIR NICHOLAS. What is the matter, man?

WHEADLE. Read read; I want patience to tell you. (*Gives* SIR NICHOLAS *the letter*) Fortune still jades me in all my expectations.

SIR NICHOLAS. (*reading the letter*) 'The citizen's wife forced to go to Greenwich with her husband; will meet some time next week.' Come, come, Wheadle, another time will do; be not so passionate, man.

WHEADLE. I must abuse my friend upon an idle woman's words!

SIR NICHOLAS. Pish, 'tis an accident: come, let us drink a glass of wine, to put these women out of our heads.

PALMER. Women? ho boys, women, where are the women?

WHEADLE. Here's your merry countryman.

PALMER. (*sings*)
'He took her by the apron,
To bring her to his beck;
But as he wound her to him
The apron-strings did break.'

Enter DRAWER *with wine* [*and exits.*]

SIR NICHOLAS. A merry man indeed. Sir, my service to you. (*Drinks to* PALMER)

PALMER. Thank you, sir. Come Mr Wheadle, remembering my landlord, i'faith; would he were e'en among us now. Come, be merry man. (*To* SIR NICHOLAS) Lend me your hand, sir; you look like an honest man; here's a good health to all that are so: tope – here pledge me. (*Drinks; gives* SIR NICHOLAS *the glass*)

SIR NICHOLAS. Mr Wheadle, to you. (*Drinks, and leaves some in the glass*)

---

28 *jades*: fools.
45 s.d. *Drawer*: tapster or waiter at a tavern.
52 *tope*: a drinking toast, a relatively recent coinage (*OED*'s earliest example is from 1651).
53 *pledge me*: 'to pledge' is 'to drink in reply to a health proposed by another'.

PALMER. I'll not abate you an ace. 'Slid, y'are not so honest as I took you for.

SIR NICHOLAS *drinks up the rest.*

PALMER. (*sings*)

'If any man balk his liquor
Let him never balk the gallows,
But sing a psalm there wi' th' vicar,
Or die in a dirty alehouse.'

Enter DRAWER.

DRAWER. There's a countryman below desires to speak with his master Palmer.

PALMER. So, so, thank thee lad; it is my man, I appointed him to call here; h'as sold the cattle I'll warrant you: I'll wait upon you again presently, gentlemen. *Exit* PALMER.

WHEADLE. Is not this a very pleasant fellow?

SIR NICHOLAS. The pleasant'st I ever met with; what is he?

WHEADLE. He's a Buckinghamshire grazier, very rich; he has the fat oxen, and fat acres in the vale: I met him here by chance, and could not avoid drinking a glass o' wine with him. I believe he's gone down to receive money; 'twere an excellent design to bubble him.

SIR NICHOLAS. How 'twould change his merry note; will you try him?

WHEADLE. Do you: I cannot appear in't, because he takes me for his friend.

SIR NICHOLAS. How neatly I could top upon him!

---

55 *I'll not abate you an ace*: make the slightest abatement, i.e. allow him to drink less than a full glass.
57 *balk*: refuse, jib at.
58 *balk*: avoid; disappoint.
59 *wi' th'*: 'with' ' (*1664a*); 'wi'th' ' (*1664b*).
59 *wi' th' vicar*: condemned men were accompanied to the gallows by a clergyman.
64 *appointed*: gave him orders.
65 *presently*: immediately.
67 *pleasant*: (1) good-humoured (2) jocular, facetious (3) hilarious or excited from drink.
71 *fat acres*: i.e. yielding rich returns.
74 *bubble*: swindle.
80 *top upon him*: cheat him.

WHEADLE. All things will pass upon him; I'll go your half: talk of dice, you'll perceive if he's coming. What money have you about you?

SIR NICHOLAS. Ten pieces.

WHEADLE. I have about that quantity too, here, take it. If he should run us out of our ready money be sure you set him deep upon tick, if he'll be at you, that we may recover it; for we'll not pay a farthing of what we lose that way. Hush, here he comes.

Enter PALMER *with a bag of money under his arm, and flings it upon the table.*

PALMER. All my fat oxen and sheep are melted to this, gentlemen.

WHEADLE. Their grease is well tried, sir.

SIR NICHOLAS. Come, sir, for all your riches, you are in arrear here. (*Offers him a glass*)

PALMER. I'll be soon out of your debts: my hearty love to you, sir. (*Drinks*) Would I had you both in Buckinghamshire, and a pipe of this canary in my cellar; we'd roast an ox before we parted; should we not, boy?

PALMER. (*sings*)
'We'd sing, and we'd laugh, and we'd drink all the day;
Our reason we'd banish, our senses should sway;
And every pleasure our wills should obey.'

PALMER. Come, drink to me a brimmer if you dare now.

SIR NICHOLAS. Nay, if you provoke me you'll find me a bold man: give me a bigger glass, boy: so, this is fit

---

81 *pass upon him*: impose upon him, gain credit with him.
81–2 *go your half*: be your partner, share the expenses.
82 *coming*: inclined to yield to temptation.
84 *pieces*: gold coins worth about twenty shillings.
86 *run us out of*: exhaust.
87 *set him deep on tick*: get him to play heavily on credit ('on tick' was another recent usage; *OED*'s first example is from 1642).
92 *Their grease is well tried*: 'to try' means 'to extract (oil) from blubber or fat by heat; to melt down (blubber, etc.) to obtain the oil'.
97 *pipe*: large cask.
97 *canary*: a light sweet wine from the Canaries.
103 *brimmer*: goblet filled to the brim.

for men of worship: hang your retail drinkers; have at thee, my brave countryman. (*Drinks*)

PALMER. I'll do all I can for my guts to pledge thee. Ho, brave boys! that's he, that's he, i'faith; how I could hug thee now! Mr Wheadle, to you.

WHEADLE. I protest, gentlemen, you'll fright me out of your company. Sir Nicholas, shall we have th'other round?

SIR NICHOLAS. Let's pause a while. What say you, gentlemen, if, to pass away the time, and to refresh us, we should have a box and dice, and fling a merry main among ourselves in sport?

WHEADLE. 'Twill spoil good company; by no means, Sir Nicholas.

PALMER. Hang play among friends; let's have a wench: (*Sings*)

'And Jenny was all my joy,
She had my heart at her will;
But I left her and her toy
When once I had got my fill.'

What say you, shall we have her?

SIR NICHOLAS. We are not drunk enough for a wench.

PALMER. Let's sing a catch then.

WHEADLE.
SIR NICHOLAS. } Agreed, agreed.

WHEADLE. Begin, Mr Palmer.

PALMER *sings, standing in the middle, with a glass of wine in his hand.*

PALMER. 'I have no design here,
But drinking good wine here.

WHEADLE. Nor I, boy.

SIR NICHOLAS. Nor I, boy.

WHEADLE. Th'art my boy.

SIR NICHOLAS. Th'art my boy.

---

107 *worship*: good standing, high repute.
107 *retail drinkers*: those who consume their drink in small instalments.
118 *main*: a hand at dice.
121 *play*: gambling.
124 *toy*: knick-knack, trifle (with an obvious innuendo).
128 *catch*: 'a song sung in succession, where one catches it from another' (Johnson).

ALL THREE. Our heads are too airy for plots:
Let us hug then all three,
Since our virtues agree,
We'll hollow and cast up our hats.'

They hollow whilst PALMER *drinks, and then change till it has gone round.*

SIR NICHOLAS. Enough, enough.

PALMER. Very good boys all, very good boys all. Give me a glass of wine there; fill a brimmer: Sir Nicholas, your lady.

SIR NICHOLAS. Pray, sir, forbear; I must be forced to leave your company else. Prithee, Wheadle, let's have a box and dice.

WHEADLE. We shall grow dull. Mr Palmer, what say you to the business?

PALMER. I do not understand dice: I understand good pasture and drink. – Hang the devil's bones.

WHEADLE *whispers* SIR NICHOLAS *to send for dice.*
SIR NICHOLAS *whispers the* DRAWER.

PALMER. (*sings*)
'He that leaves his wine for boxes and dice,
Or his wench for fear of mishaps,
May he beg all his days, cracking of lice,
And die in conclusion of claps.'

Enter DRAWER *with dice.*

PALMER. Come, come, gentlemen, this is the harmlesser sport of the two; a merry glass round.

SIR NICHOLAS. Excuse me, sir; I'll pledge you here. (*Takes dice*) Come, come, sir, on six; six is the main.

PALMER. The main? what's the main?

SIR NICHOLAS. Do not you understand hazard?

PALMER. I understand dice, or hap-hazard!

SIR NICHOLAS. Can you play at passage?

---

137 *airy*: light, full of mirth, without solidity.
137 *plots*: i.e. royalist plots on behalf of Charles II. See Additional Note.
151 *devil's bones*: dice.
159 *main*: in the game of hazard, a number (from five to nine inclusive) called by the caster before the dice are thrown.
161 *hazard*: a dice game in which the chances are complicated by a number of arbitrary rules. See Additional Note.
163 *passage*: a dice game, played with three dice, in which the thrower 'passes' or wins when he throws above ten.

PALMER. You pass my understanding: I can fling most at a throw, for a shot, or a glass of wine.

SIR NICHOLAS. Passage is easily learned: the caster wins if he fling above ten with doublets upon three dice.

PALMER. How doublets?

SIR NICHOLAS. Two of a sort; two cinques, two treys, or the like.

PALMER. Ho, ho; I have you.

SIR NICHOLAS. Come, set then.

PALMER. I set you this bottle.

SIR NICHOLAS. Nay, nay, set money!

PALMER. Is it a fair play Mr Wheadle? I trust to you.

WHEADLE. Upon my word a very fair square play; but this table is so wet, there's no playing upon it.

DRAWER. Will you be pleased to remove into the next room, gentlemen?

SIR NICHOLAS. I think 'twill not be amiss.

WHEADLE. Much better. Come Mr Palmer.

PALMER. I'll follow, sir. (*Sings*)
'If she be not as kind as fair,
But peevish and unhandy,
Leave her, she's only worth the care
Of some spruce jack-a-dandy.
I would not have thee such an ass,
Hadst thou ne'er so much leisure,
To sigh and whine for such a lass
Whose pride's above her pleasure.'

SIR NICHOLAS. Ho brave boy!

PALMER. March on, march on. (*Sings*)
'Make much of e'ry buxom girl,
Which needs but little courting;
Her value is above the pearl,
That takes delight in sporting.'

Exeunt omnes.

164–5 *most at a throw*: highest score on a single throw.
165 *for a shot*: for one's share of the tavern bill.
167 *doublets*: i.e. the same number turning up on two dice at a single throw.
170 *cinques, treys*: (in dice games) fives, threes.
173 *set*: wager.
185 *unhandy*: not easy to handle or manage.
194 *buxom*: comely and vigorous; but also, tractable, obliging.
197 *sporting*: amorous play.

ACT III

SCENE I

A tavern.

Enter SIR NICHOLAS, WHEADLE, PALMER, *and* DRAWER.

PALMER. Nay, Sir Nicholas, for all your haste, I must have a note under your hand for the thousand pounds you owe me.

WHEADLE. This must not be among friends, Mr Palmer; Sir Nicholas shall not pay the money.

SIR NICHOLAS. I had been a madman to play at such a rate if I had ever intended to pay.

PALMER. Though I am but a poor countryman I scorn to be choused; I have friends in town.

WHEADLE. But hark you, Mr Palmer.

PALMER. Hark me no harks; I'll have my money.

SIR NICHOLAS. Drawer, take your reckoning.

WHEADLE. (*laughing*) Farewell, sir; haste into the country to mind your cattle.

PALMER. But hark you, gentlemen; are you in earnest?

WHEADLE. Ay indeed; fare you well, sir.

PALMER. I took you for my friend, Mr Wheadle; but now I perceive what you are. (*To* SIR NICHOLAS) Your ear, sir.

WHEADLE. Never fear him; he dares not to go into the field, without it be among his sheep.

SIR NICHOLAS. Agreed; tomorrow, about eight in the morning, near Pancridge.

WHEADLE. I will have the honour to serve you, Sir Nicholas. Provide yourself a second, Mr Palmer.

---

2 *a note under your hand*: i.e. a written promise (signed by you) to pay at a specified time.

9 *choused*: cheated.

12 *reckoning*: money owed for the tavern bill.

21 *without*: unless.

23 *Pancridge*: St Pancras; a rather unsalubrious area of London in this period.

Exeunt SIR NICHOLAS *and* WHEADLE *laughing.*

PALMER. So, laugh: this is the sheep that I must fleece.

Exit.

SCENE II

Covent Garden.

Enter SIR FREDERICK FROLLICK, *with* FIDDLERS *before him, and six or eight* LINK-BOYS, *dancing and singing.*

SIR FREDERICK. Here, here, this is the window; range yourselves here.

Enter the BELLMAN.

BELLMAN. Good-morrow, gentlemen.

SIR FREDERICK. Honest bellman, prithee lend me thy bell.

BELLMAN. With all my heart, master.

SIR FREDERICK *rings the bell, and then repeats these verses.*

SIR FREDERICK. You widow, that do sleep dog-sleep,
And now for your dead husband weep,
Perceiving well what want you have
Of that poor worm has eat in grave;
Rise out of bed, and ope the door;
Here's that will all your joys restore.
Good-morrow, my mistress dear, good-morrow.
Good-morrow, widow. (*He rings the bell again*)

The CHAMBERMAID [BETTY] *comes to the window unlaced, holding her petticoats in her hand.*

BETTY. Who's that that comes at this unseasonable hour, to disturb my lady's quiet?

---

26 *fleece*: 'fleece' already had the colloquial meaning of 'to cheat' in the seventeenth century.

2 s.d. *Bellman*: night-watchman who called the hours, ringing a bell.

7 *dog-sleep*: light, fitful, easily interrupted sleep.

10 *that*: i.e. that which.

SIR FREDERICK. An honest bellman, to mind her of her frailty.

BETTY. Sir Frederick, I wonder you will offer this; you will lose her favour for ever.

SIR FREDERICK. Y'are mistaken; now's the time to creep into her favour.

BETTY. I'm sure y'ave waked me out of the sweetest sleep. Hey ho –

SIR FREDERICK. Poor girl! let me in, I'll rock thee into a sweeter.

BETTY. I hear a stirring in my mistress's chamber; I believe y'ave frighted her. *Exit* BETTY.

SIR FREDERICK. Sound a fresh alarm; the enemy's at hand.

FIDDLERS *play.*

The WIDOW *comes to the window in her night-gown.*

WIDOW. Whose insolence is this, that dares affront me thus?

SIR FREDERICK. (*in a canting tone*)
If there be insolence in love, 'tis I
Have done you this unwilling injury.

WIDOW. What pitiful rhyming fellow's that? he speaks as if he were prompted by the fiddlers.

SIR FREDERICK. Alas, what pains I take thus to unclose
Those pretty eyelids which locked up my foes!

WIDOW. A godly book would become that tone a great deal better: he might get a pretty living by reading Mother Shipton's prophecies, or some pious exhor-

---

18 *frailty*: (1) liability to err or yield to temptation (2) mortality (for the use of a bellman to put condemned prisoners 'in minde of their mortalitie' at Newgate and Tyburn, see John Webster, *The Duchess of Malfi*, ed. John Russell Brown (London, Methuen & Co. 1964), note to IV ii 173).

29 *alarm*: a call to arms, warning note.

33 s.d. *canting tone*: Johnson defines 'cant' as 'a corrupt dialect used by beggars and vagabonds'.

41 *Mother Shipton's prophecies*: allegedly an early sixteenth-century prophetess; but she may never have existed. Prophecies attributed to her were published in 1641 and reprinted thereafter.

tation at the corner of a street: his mournful voice, I vow, has moved my compassion.

SIR FREDERICK. Ay, ay, we should have a fellow-feeling of one another indeed, widow.

WIDOW. Sir Frederick, is it you?

SIR FREDERICK. Yes truly; and can you be angry, lady? Have not your quarters been beaten up at these most seasonable hours before now?

WIDOW. Yes; but it has been by one that has had a commission for what he did: I'm afraid should it once become your duty, you would soon grow weary of the employment.

SIR FREDERICK. Widow, I hate this distance; 'tis not the English fashion: prithee let's come to't hand to fist.

WIDOW. I give no entertainment to such lewd persons. Farewell, sir. *Exit* WIDOW.

SIR FREDERICK. I'll fetch thee again, or conjure the whole Garden up. Sing the catch I taught you at the Rose.

FIDDLERS *sing.*

SONG.

'He that will win a widow's heart
Must bear up briskly to her:
She loves the lad that's free and smart,

44–5 *fellow-feeling of*: sympathy for the feelings of (with an obvious innuendo).

48 *quarters . . . beaten up*: visited unceremoniously, disturbed (again with a clear double-meaning). The term is military in origin, meaning 'a pinprick sally against enemy positions by night, designed to undermine the latter's morale and resolution'.

50–1 *commission*: (1) legal authority, as her husband; but also (2) playing (cf. previous note) on the meaning, 'a military commission'.

55–6 *hand to fist*: he is mockingly recalling the Widow's earlier use of the phrase (II i 37).

59–60 *conjure . . . up*: summon up, as if by magic.

60–1 *the Rose*: a well-known tavern in Russell Street, Covent Garden.

64 *free*: plain-spoken, frank.

64 *smart*: vigorous, brisk, good at repartee.

But hates the formal wooer.'

WIDOW *runs to the window again, with her* MAID.

WIDOW. Hold, hold, Sir Frederick; what do you imagine the neighbours will think?

SIR FREDERICK. So ill, I hope, of thee, thou'lt be forced to think the better of me.

WIDOW. I am much beholden to you for the care you have of my reputation.

SIR FREDERICK. Talk no more, but let the door be opened; or else fiddlers –

WIDOW. Pray hold; what security shall I have for your good behaviour?

SIR FREDERICK. My sobriety.

WIDOW. That's pawned at the tavern from whence you came.

SIR FREDERICK. Thy own honesty then; is that engaged?

WIDOW. I think that will go nigh to secure me. Give 'em entrance, Betty.

Exeunt WIDOW, *and her* MAID.

Enter PALMER, *with a* LINK *before him.*

SIR FREDERICK. Ha! who goes there?

PALMER. An humble creature of yours, sir.

SIR FREDERICK. Palmer in a disguise! What roguery hast thou been about?

PALMER. Out of my local inclinations doing service to his majesty.

SIR FREDERICK. What? a-plotting?

PALMER. How to destroy his enemies, Mr Wheadle and I are very vigilant.

SIR FREDERICK. In bubbling of somebody, on my life.

PALMER. We do not use to boast our services, nor do we seek rewards; good actions recompense themselves

SIR FREDERICK. Ho, the door opens; farewell, sirrah. Gentlemen, wait you without, and be ready when I

---

65 *formal*: 'not irregular; not sudden; not extemporaneous' (Johnson).

80 *engaged*: pawned.

82 s.d. *Link*: i.e. a link-boy (see note to I ii 45–6).

84 *creature*: dependent, indebted servant.

94 *good actions recompense themselves*: cf. the proverbial 'Virtue is its own reward' (Tilley, V 81).

call. Honest bellman, drink this. (*Gives the* BELLMAN *money*)

BELLMAN. Thank you, noble master. *Exit* BELLMAN

SIR FREDERICK. (*entering*) Here's something to stop thy mouth too.

The MAID *shrieks.*

BETTY. Out upon you, Sir Frederick; you'll never leave your old tricks.

Exeunt.

SCENE III

The Widow's house.

Enter SIR FREDERICK, *leading the* WIDOW, *followed by her* MAID.

SIR FREDERICK. Little did I think I should ever have been brought to this pass: love never had the power to rob me of my rest before.

WIDOW. Alas, poor gentleman! he has not been used to these late hours.

SIR FREDERICK. Widow, do not you be peevish now; 'tis dangerous jesting with my affection; 'tis in its infancy, and must be humoured.

WIDOW. Pray teach me how, sir.

SIR FREDERICK. Why, with kisses, and such pretty little dalliances; thus, thus. (*Kisses her*)

WIDOW. Hold, hold, sir; if it be so froward, put it out to nurse; I am not so fond of it as you imagine; pray how have you disposed of your brave camarades? Have you left them to the mercy of the beadle?

SIR FREDERICK. No, you must be acquainted with their virtues. Enter, gentlemen.

Enter the FIDDLERS, *and a masque of the* LINK-BOYS, *who are dancing-masters, disguised for the frolic.*

---

6 *peevish*: refractory, obstinate; skittish.
12 *froward*: ungovernable, hard to please.
14 *camarades*: fellows, playmates.
17 s.d. *a masque . . . frolic*: i.e. the dancing-masters perform a dance in their disguise as link-boys.

WIDOW. (*after the masque*) These are men of skill.

SIR FREDERICK. I disguised 'em for your entertainment.

WIDOW. Well, sir, now I hope you'll leave me to my rest.

SIR FREDERICK. Can you in conscience turn a young man out of doors at this time o' th' night, widow? Fie, fie, the very thought on't will keep you waking.

WIDOW. So pretty, so well-favoured a young man; one that loves me.

SIR FREDERICK. Ay, one that loves you.

WIDOW. Truly 'tis a very hard-hearted thing. (*She sighs*)

SIR FREDERICK. Come, come, be mollified. (*To the* MASQUERS) You may go, gentlemen, and leave me here; you may go.

WIDOW. You may stay, gentlemen; you may stay, and take your captain along with you: you'll find good quarters in some warm hay-loft.

SIR FREDERICK. Merciless woman! Do but lend me thy maid; faith I'll use her very tenderly and lovingly, even as I'd use thyself, dear widow, if thou wouldst but make proof of my affection.

WIDOW. If the constable carry your suspicious person to the Compter, pray let me have notice of it; I'll send my tailor to be your bail.

SIR FREDERICK. Go, go to bed, and be idle, widow; that's worse than any misfortune I can meet with. Strike up, and give notice of our coming. Farewell, widow; I pity thy solitary condition.

Exeunt, FIDDLERS *playing.*

---

25 *well-favoured*: good-looking.

40 *Compter*: 'Compters, or Counters, were city prisons for debt and minor offences' (Brett-Smith).

41 *tailor*: i.e. someone rather lowly in status (thus reflecting her sense of Sir Frederick's importance); but, since tailors were proverbially reputed to be especially lecherous, she is also implying that Sir Frederick is not her only potential source of sexual solace.

SCENE IV

Sir Frederick's lodging.

Enter DUFOY, *and* CLARK.

CLARK. I wonder Sir Frederick stays out so late.

DUFOY. Dis is noting; six, seven a clock in de morning is ver good houre.

CLARK. I hope he does not use these hours often.

DUFOY. Some six, seven time a veeke; no oftiner.

CLARK. My lord commanded me to wait his coming.

DUFOY. Matré Clark, to divertise you, I vil tell you how I did get be acquainted vid dis bedlam matre.

Enter a FOOTBOY.

About two, tree year ago me had for my conveniance dischargé my self from attending as *maître d'hôtel* to a person of condition in Parie; it hapen after de dispatch of my littel affairé –

FOOTBOY. That is, after h'ad spent his money, sir.

DUFOY. *J'en foutrai* de lacque; me vil have de vip and de belle vor your breeck, rogue.

FOOTBOY. Sir, in a word, he was Jack Pudding to a

---

7 *divertise*: divert, amuse.

10 *maître d'hôtel*: head domestic, steward or butler.

11 *condition*: rank, social eminence.

14 *J'en foutrai de lacque*: 'Jan foutré de Lacque' (*1664*, Verity, Brett-Smith). It seems to be a blending of two French idioms – (1) 'Je m'en fous (foutrai)' ('I don't (won't) give a damn') and (2) 'Je foutrai le lacquais à la porte' ('I will throw the lackey out.') (It is also impossible to be certain whether the French '*laquais*' or English 'lackey' is intended.)

14–15 *de vip and de belle vor your breeck*: although Dufoy is clearly threatening the Footboy with a beating, the phrase 'a whip and a bell' usually has a more general meaning, i.e. 'something that detracts from one's comfort or pleasure'.

16 *Jack Pudding*: a buffoon, clown, merry-andrew. Dufoy's subsequent anxiety to account for the fact that he was eating a custard is illuminated by a reference in the prologue to John Lacy's *The Old Troop; Or, Monsieur Raggou* (London, [1672]): 'you that laugh aloud with wide-mouth'd grace, / To see Jack Pudding's Custard thrown in's face'.

mountebank, and turned off for want of wit; my master picked him up before a puppet-show, mumbling a halfpenny custard, to send him with a letter to the post.

DUFOY. *Morbleu*, see, see de insolance of de foot-boy English, *bougre* rascale, you lye, begar I vil cutté your troaté.

Exit FOOTBOY.

CLARK. He's a rogue; on with your story, monsieur.

DUFOY. Matré Clark, I am your ver humble *serviteur*; but begar me have no patience to be abusé. As I did say, after de dispatché of my affairé, van day being idelé, vich does producé de mellanchollique, I did valké over de new bridge in Parie, and to devertise de time, and my more serious toughté, me did look to see de marrioneté and de Jack-puddingé, vich did play hundred pretty triké, time de collation vas come; and vor I had no companie, I vas unvilling to go to de *cabaret*, but did buy a *dariole*, littel custardé vich did satisfie my apetite ver vel: in dis time young Monsieur de Grandvil (a jentelman of ver great quallity, van dat vas my ver good friendé, and has don me ver great and *insignal faveur*) come by in his caroché, vid dis Sir Frollick, who did *pension* at de same academy, to

---

17 *mountebank*: itinerant quack who from a platform appealed to his audience by means of stories, tricks, juggling, and the like, often with the assistance of a professional clown.

17 *turned off*: dismissed.

19 *mumbling*: chewing or biting softly (as with toothless gums).

21 *Morbleu*: 'The devil!' A comic oath, often given to French characters by seventeenth-century dramatists.

22 *bougre*: blackguard.

29 *de new bridge*: the Pont Neuf.

31 *marrioneté*: puppet (the word seems to have begun to enter English from French in the first half of the seventeenth century).

32 *time de collation*: time for a snack.

34 *cabaret*: inn, eating-house.

34 *dariole*: custard-tart.

36 *quallity*: rank.

38 *insignal faveur*: more properly, *faveur insigne*, a signal favour.

38 *caroché*: a coach of a stately or luxurious kind.

39 *pension*: pay for lodging.

39 *academy*: see Additional Note.

learn de language, de *bonne mine*, de great horse, and many oder triké; monsieur seeing me did make de bowé, and did beken, beken me come to him; he did tellé me dat de Englis jentelman had de letré vor de posté, and did entreaté me (if I had de oppertunity) to see de letré deliver; he did tellé me too, it vold be ver great obligation: de memory of de *faveur* I had receive from his famelyé, beside de inclination I naturally have to servé de strangeré, made me retourné de complemen vid ver great civility, and so I did take de letré, and see it deliveré. Sir Frollick perceiving (by de managment of dis affairé) dat I vas man *d'esprit*, and of vitté, did entreaté me to be his *serviteur*; me did take d'affection to his personé, and vas contenté to live vid him, to counsel and to advisé him. You see now de lye of de *bougre* dé lacque Englishé, *morbleu*.

Enter a FOOTMAN.

FOOTMAN. Monsieur, the apothecary is without.

DUFOY. Dat news be no ver velcome, begar. Matré Clarke, go and sit you down; I vil but swal my breakface, and be vid you again presant. *Morbleu* l'apothecaré.

Exeunt.

SCENE V

A field.

Enter WHEADLE *and* SIR NICHOLAS.

SIR NICHOLAS. Dear Wheadle, this is too dangerous a testimony of thy kindness.

WHEADLE. I should be angry with you if you thought so: what makes you so serious?

---

40 *bonne mine*: niceties of dress and personal appearance.

40 *great horse*: i.e. he was learning to ride the exceptionally large and powerful war horses which were managed according to fixed rules (a traditional part of an aristocratic education).

52 *esprit*: understanding.

SIR NICHOLAS. I am sorry I did not provide for both our safeties.

WHEADLE. How so?

SIR NICHOLAS. Colonel Hewson is my neighbour, and very good friend; I might have acquainted him with the business, and got him with a file of musketeers to secure us all.

WHEADLE. But this would not secure your honour. What would the world have judged?

SIR NICHOLAS. Let the world have judged what it would: have we not had many precedents of late, and the world knows not what to judge?

WHEADLE. But you see there was no need to hazard your reputation; here's no enemy appears.

SIR NICHOLAS. We have done our duty, let's be going then.

WHEADLE. We ought to wait a while.

SIR NICHOLAS. The air is so bleak, I vow I can no longer endure it.

WHEADLE. Have a little patience, methinks I see two making towards us in the next close.

SIR NICHOLAS. Where, where? 'tis them.

WHEADLE. Bear up bravely now like a man.

SIR NICHOLAS. I protest I am the worst dissembler in cases of this nature.

WHEADLE. *Allons*; look like a man of resolution. Whither, whither go you?

SIR NICHOLAS. But to the next house to make my will, for fear of the worst; tell them I'll be here again presently.

WHEADLE. By no means; if you give 'em the least occasion to suspect you, they'll appear like lions.

---

8 *Colonel Hewson*: see Additional Note.

11 *secure us all*: (1) arrest us (for duelling) and (2) thus ensure our safety.

25 *close*: 'a piece of Ground hedged, or fenced about' (Edward Phillips, *The New World of Words*, ed. J.K. (7th edition: London, 1720)).

30 *Allons*: 'let us go on' (he is encouraging his companion). *1664* reads 'Alon', and early eighteenth-century editions emend to 'Along'; but Brett-Smith plausibly defended the reading followed here.

SIR NICHOLAS. Well, 'tis but giving security for the money; that will bring me off at last.

Enter PALMER *and his* SECOND.

PALMER. I see you ride the fore-horse, gentlemen.

All strip but SIR NICHOLAS, *who fumbles with his doublet.*

WHEADLE. Good-morrow, sir.

SECOND. (*to* WHEADLE) Come, sir, let us match the swords.

WHEADLE. With all my heart.

They match the swords.

PALMER. (*sings*)

'He had and a good right Bilbo blade,
Wherewith he used to vapour;
Full many a stubborn foe had made
To wince and cut a caper.'

SECOND. (*to* PALMER) Here's your sword, sir.

PALMER. (*to* SIR NICHOLAS) Come, sir, are you ready for this sport?

SIR NICHOLAS. By and by, sir; I will not rend the buttons from my doublet for no man's pleasure.

WHEADLE. Death, y'ave spoiled all; make haste.

SIR NICHOLAS. Hang 'em, the devil eggs 'em on; they will fight.

PALMER. What, will you never have done fumbling?

SECOND. This is a shame; fight him with his doublet on; there's no foul play under it.

PALMER. Come, sir, have at you. (*Making to* SIR NICHOLAS)

SECOND. (*to* WHEADLE) Here, here, sir.

WHEADLE. I am for you, sir.

---

39 *ride the fore-horse*: 'to ride the fore-horse' is 'to be early or ahead of someone else'.

43 s.d. *match the swords*: i.e. check that the relative size, etc. of the swords does not give one of the duellists an unfair advantage.

44 *Bilbo blade*: a sword noted for the excellence of its temper, made originally at Bilbao in Spain; hence used colloquially for the sword of a bully or a swashbuckler.

45 *vapour*: swagger, show off.

47 *cut a caper*: i.e. jump in the air ('a caper' being 'a frolicsome leap in dancing').

58 *no foul play under it*: i.e. no protective clothing or armour.

WHEADLE *and the* SECOND *seem to fight.*

SIR NICHOLAS. Hold, hold, I beseech you, Mr Palmer, hear me, hear me.

WHEADLE. What's the matter?

SIR NICHOLAS. My conscience will not let me fight in a wrong cause; I will pay the money, I have fairly lost it.

WHEADLE. How contemptible is man, overcome by the worst of passions, fear! it makes him as much below beasts as reason raises him above them. I will myself fight you both; come on, if you dare. –

SIR NICHOLAS. Prithee, dear Wheadle, do but hear me.

WHEADLE. I disown all the kindness I ever had for you: where are these men of valour, which owe their virtue to this man's vice? let me go, I will chastise their insolence myself.

SIR NICHOLAS *holds him.*

SIR NICHOLAS. Dear Wheadle, bear with the frailties of thy friend.

WHEADLE. Death, what would you have me do? can I serve you with anything more dear than my life?

SIR NICHOLAS. Let us give them security.

WHEADLE. Do you know what it is you would do? have you considered what a thousand pounds is? 'tis a fortune for any one man.

SIR NICHOLAS. I will pay it all; thou shalt be no loser.

WHEADLE. Do you hear, shepherd? how do you expect this money?

PALMER. I expect such security for it as my friend shall advise.

SECOND. A warrant to confess a judgment from you both.

WHEADLE. You shall be damned first; you shall have nothing.

PALMER.
SECOND. } We'll have your bloods.

They proffer to fight;
SIR NICHOLAS *holds* WHEADLE.

WHEADLE. Let me go.

---

90 *a warrant to confess a judgment*: a document assigning to us property of yours as a security against the non-payment of the debt.

SIR NICHOLAS. Dear Wheadle, let it be so. You shall have a judgment, gentlemen.

WHEADLE. I will take care hereafter with whom I engage.

The SECOND *pulls papers out of his pocket.*

What? you have your tackling about you.

SECOND. We have articles for peace, as well as weapons for war.

WHEADLE. Dispatch, dispatch then, put me to no more torment with delays.

SECOND. Come Sir Nicholas to the book; you see we are favourable, we grant you the benefit of your clergy.

SIR NICHOLAS *subscribes on* PALMER*'s back, and then* WHEADLE.

Your helping hand, good Mr Wheadle, to finish the work.

WHEADLE. Take that into the bargain. (*Kicks him*)

PALMER. You shall have another, if you please, at the price.

SECOND. We seldom quarrel under a thousand pounds.

PALMER. SECOND. } We wish you merry, gentlemen.

PALMER. (*sings*)

'Come, let's to the tavern scape,
And drink whilst we can stand;
We thirst more for the blood o' th' grape
Than for the blood of man.'

Exeunt PALMER *and* SECOND.

WHEADLE. Do you see now what men of mighty prowess these are?

SIR NICHOLAS. I was to blame, indeed.

WHEADLE. I am in such a passion I know not what to do: let us not stand gazing here; I would not have this known for a kingdom.

SIR NICHOLAS. No, nor I neither.

Exeunt.

---

100 *tackling*: (ironically) weapons; accoutrements.

106 *favourable*: well-disposed, willing to concede what is asked.

106 *benefit of your clergy*: 'the privilege of exemption from the sentence, which, in the case of certain offences, might be pleaded on his first conviction by everyone who could read' (*OED*). It is, however, Sir Nicholas's ability to sign his name which saves him here.

SCENE VI

The Lord Bevill's house.

Enter my LORD BEVILL *and* LOVIS.

LOVIS. 'Tis yet within your pow'r, sir, to maintain
Our honour, and prevent this threat'ning stain.
LORD BELVILL. Forbear this wicked insolence: once more
I charge you think on your obedience.
Exit LORD BEVILL.
LOVIS. Beauty, what art thou, we so much admire!
Thou art no real, but a seeming fire,
Which, like the glow-worm, only cast'st a light
To them whose reason passion does benight.
Thou art a meteor, which but blazing dies,
Made of such vapours as from us arise.
Within thy guilty beams lurk cruel fates,
To peaceful families, and warring states.
Unhappy friend, to dote on what we know –

Enter a SERVANT.

SERVANT. Sir, Colonel Bruce, unexpectedly released from his imprisonment, is come to wait upon you.
Exit SERVANT.
LOVIS. What shall I do! Ye pow'rs above be kind,
Some counsel give to my distracted mind:
Friendship and shame within me so contend,
I know not how to shun or meet my friend.

Enter BRUCE.

BRUCE. Where is my gen'rous friend? Oh noble youth,
They embrace.
How long have I been robbed of this content?
Though deprivation be the greatest pain,
When heav'n restores our happiness again,
It makes amends by our increase of joy,
Perfecting that which it did once destroy.
Dear friend, my love does now exact its due;
Graciana must divide my heart with you:

---

6 *real*: pronounced as two syllables.

Conduct me to your sister, where I may
Make this my morn of joy a glorious day.
What means this sad astonishment!
LOVIS. How can we choose but with confusion greet,
When I your joys with equal sorrows meet?
BRUCE. Oh heav'n! must my afflictions have no end!
I scaped my foe, to perish by my friend.
What strange disaster can produce this grief!
Is Graciana dead? Speak, speak; be brief.
LOVIS. She lives; but I could wish her dead.
BRUCE. Rash man! why should your envy swell so high,
To wish the world this great calamity?
Wish the whole frame of nature were dissolved;
That all things to a chaos were revolved.
There is more charity in this desire;
Since with our loss, our sorrows would expire.

Enter AURELIA.

LOVIS. Here comes Aurelia, sent for my relief;
Heav'n knows her tongue can best express this grief:
Examine her, and you shall find ere long
I can revenge, though not relate your wrong.
BRUCE. For pity haste, Aurelia, and declare
Kisses her hand.
The reasons of your brother's frighting care:
My soul is racked with doubts, until I know.
(*After a pause*) Your silence and your looks, Aurelia, show
As if your kindness made you bear a part
Of those great sorrows that afflict his heart.
AURELIA. His passion is so noble and so just,
No gen'rous soul can know it but it must
Lay claim unto a portion, as its due:
He can be thus concerned for none but you.
BRUCE. Kind maid, reveal what my misfortunes are;
Friendship must not engross them, though it share.
I would not willingly my love suspect;
And yet I fear 'tis answered with neglect.
AURELIA. My sister, by unlucky stars misled,
From you and from her happiness is fled;

---

41 *revolved*: i.e. returned to its original state.
59 *engross*: monopolize.

Unskilful in the way, by passion pressed,
She has took shelter in another's breast.

BRUCE. Fate, thou hast done thy worst, thy triumph sing;
Now thou hast stung so home, th'ast lost thy sting.
(*After a pause*) I have not pow'r, Graciana, to exclaim
Against your fault; indeed you are to blame.

LOVIS. Tell me, did she her promise plight, or give
Your love encouragement enough to live?

BRUCE. It was her pity sure, and not her love,
That made her seem my passion to approve:
My story was unpleasant to her ear
At first; but time had made her apt to hear
My love: she told me that it grew her grief,
As much as mine, my pain found no relief;
Then promised she'd endeavour the decrease
Of that in her which warred against my peace.
'Twas in this joyful spring of love that I
Was ravished from her by our enemy:
My hopes grew strong, I banished all despair:
These glowing sparks I then left to the care
Of this fair maid, thinking she might inspire
My passion, and blow up the kindling fire.

LOVIS. Alas! she, to my knowledge, has been true;
Sh'as spoke and sighed all that she could for you.

AURELIA. When you were forced to end, I did proceed,
And with success the catching fire did feed;
Till noble Beaufort, one unlucky day,
A visit to our family did pay;
Newly arrived from foreign courts, and fraught
With all those virtues that in courts are taught:
He with his am'rous tales so charmed her ear,
That she of love from none but him would hear.

BRUCE. That heart which I so long with toil and pain
Besieged, and used all stratagems to gain,

---

64 *unskilful in the way*: ignorant of the right path.

66 *sing*: celebrate.

81 *ravished*: seized, snatched.

84 *inspire*: playing on the literal meaning of 'inspire', i.e. breathe or blow upon or into (cf. the following line).

97 *stratagems*: continuing Bruce's military imagery; the word's primary meaning remained 'an act of generalship; usually, an artifice or trick designed to surprise or outwit the enemy'.

Enter a SERVANT, *and whispers with* LOVIS.

Is now become within a trice we see
The triumph of another's victory.
There is a fate in love, as well as war;
Some though less careful more successful are.

LOVIS. Do not this opportunity withstand;
These lovers now are walking hand in hand
I' th' garden; fight him there, and sacrifice
His heart to that false woman's cruel eyes:
If fate be so unjust to make thee fall,
His blood or mine shall wait thy funeral.

BRUCE. Young man, this rashness must have my excuse,
Since 'tis your friendship does your fault produce;
If pow'rs above did not this passion sway,
But that our love our reason did obey,
Your sister I with justice might accuse,
Nor would I this occasion then refuse.

LOVIS. Does Bruce resolve thus tamely to decline
His int'rest, and like foolish women pine?
Can that great heart which in your breast does dwell
Let your fond griefs above your courage swell?

BRUCE. My passions grow unruly, and I find
Too soon they'll raise a tempest in my mind.
Graciana, like fond parents, y'are to blame
You did not in its youth correct my flame;
'Tis now so headstrong, and so wild a fire,
I fear to both our ruins 'twill conspire:
I grow impatient, friend, come lead me where
I may to her my injured love declare.
Graciana, yet your heart shall be my prize,
Or else my heart shall be your sacrifice.
Despair's the issue of ignoble minds,
And but with cowards entertainment finds.

Exeunt LOVIS *and* BRUCE.

AURELIA. Heav'n grant some moderation to this rage,
That reason their swelled passions may assuage.
Oh, Bruce! thou little think'st the fates in me
Have to the full revenged thy injury. *Exit.*

---

98 *within a trice*: in an instant.
99 *triumph*: i.e. object of triumph.
107 *wait*: attend upon.
114–15 *decline / His int'rest*: abandon his claim.

SCENE VII

A garden belonging to my Lord Bevill's house.

Enter BEAUFORT *and* GRACIANA.

BEAUFORT. Madam, what you have told so much must move
All that have sense of honour or of love,
That for my rival I could shed a tear,
If grief had any pow'r when you are near.
GRACIANA. Leave this discourse; your mistress you neglect,
And to your rival all your thoughts direct.

Enter BRUCE *and* LOVIS, *and stand undiscovered.*

BEAUFORT. Forgive me, dear Graciana, I have been
By my compassion soothed into a sin.
The holiest man that to the altar bows
With wand'ring thoughts too often stains his vows.
BRUCE. Graciana, you are altered much, I find; *Surprising her by the hand.*
Since I was here y'ave learned how to be kind.
The god of love, which subtly let you sway,
Has stol'n your heart, and taught it to obey.
GRACIANA. Heav'ns! what strange surprise is this!
BRUCE. Hither I'm come to make my lawful claim;
You are my mistress, and must own my flame.
BEAUFORT. Forbear, bold man, and do not tempt thy fate; *Taking her by the other hand.*
Thou hast no right, her love does right create:
Thy claim must to my title here give place;
'Tis not who loves, but whom she's pleased to grace.
GRACIANA. Hear me but speak; Bruce, you divide my care;
Though not my love, you my compassion share;
My heart does double duty; it does mourn
For you brave Bruce; for you brave Beaufort burn.

---

17 *own*: acknowledge as approved or accepted by her.

BRUCE. Your pity but destroys; if you would save,
It is your love, Graciana, I must have.
BEAUFORT. Her love is mine, she did it now declare;
Name it no more, but vanish and despair.
BRUCE. Death, do you think to conjure me away!
I am no devil that am forced t'obey:
If y'are so good at that, here are such charms
Laying his hand on his sword.
Can fright y'into the circle of her arms.
BEAUFORT. Here is a sword more fit for my defence;
This is not courage, Bruce, but insolence.
GRACIANA *takes* BEAUFORT *in her arms.*
Graciana, let me go, my heart wants room.
GRACIANA. My arms till now were ne'er thought troublesome.
BRUCE. Beaufort, I hope y'ave courage to appear,
Where sacred sanctuary is not near.
I'll leave you now within that happy state
Which does provoke my fury and my hate.
Exeunt BRUCE *and* LOVIS.
GRACIANA. You must not meet him in the field, to prove
A doubtful combat for my certain love.
Beside, your heart is mine; will you expose
The heart you gave me to its raging foes?
Those men want honour who stake that at play
Which to their friends their kindness gave away.
BEAUFORT. Graciana, why did you confine me so
Within your arms? you should have let me go:
We soon had finished this our hot debate,
Which now must wait a longer time on fate.
GRACIANA. None, in combustions blame such as desire
To save their precious goods from raging fire.
Banish this passion now, my lord, and prove
Your anger cannot overcloud your love.
BEAUFORT. Your glorious presence can this rage control,

30 *conjure me away*: remove (dismiss) by incantation.
32–3 *charms . . . circle*: see note to I ii 192.
42 *prove*: undergo.
43 *doubtful*: (1) uncertain (in opposition to 'certain love') (2) to be feared or dreaded.

And make a calm in my tempestuous soul;
But yet there must be time; the sun does bear
A while with the fierce tempests of the air,
Before he make those stormy conflicts cease,
And with his conqu'ring beams proclaims a peace.
Exeunt.

ACT IV

SCENE I

Enter BEAUFORT *and* LOVIS.

LOVIS. Farewell, my lord, I'll to my friend declare
How gen'rous you in your acceptance were.
BEAUFORT. My honour is as forward as my love,
On equal wings of jealousy they move:
I to my rival will in neither yield;
I've won the chamber, and will win the field.
LOVIS. Your emulation, sir, is swol'n so high,
You may be worthy of his victory:
You'll meet with honour blown, not in the bud,
Whose root was fed with vast expense of blood.
Exit LOVIS.

Enter SIR FREDERICK.

SIR FREDERICK. What, my lord, as studious as a country vicar on a Saturday in the afternoon? I thought you had been ready for the pulpit.

BEAUFORT. I am not studying of speeches for my mistress; 'tis action that I now am thinking on, wherein there's honour to be gained; and you, cousin, are come luckily to share it.

SIR FREDERICK. On my life a prize to be played for your mistress: I had notice of your quarrel, which brought me hither so early with my sword to serve

4 *jealousy*: rivalry.
9 *blown*: in bloom.
18 *prize*: contest, match.

you. But dares so zealous a lover as your lordship break the commandment of your mistress? I heard, poor lady, she wept, and charged you to sleep in a whole skin; but young men never know when th'are well.

BEAUFORT. Cousin, my love to her cannot make me forget my duty to my family.

SIR FREDERICK. Pray whose body must I exercise my skill upon?

BEAUFORT. You met the man; Graciana's brother.

SIR FREDERICK. An expert gentleman, and I have not fenced of late, unless it were with my widow's maids; and they are e'en too hard for me at my own weapon.

BEAUFORT. Cousin, 'tis time we were preparing for the field.

SIR FREDERICK. I wait to serve you, sir.

BEAUFORT. But yet with grief, Graciana, I must go,
Since I your brother there shall meet my foe:
My fate too near resembles theirs where he
Did wound himself that hurt his enemy.

Exeunt.

SCENE II

Enter WHEADLE, *and* PALMER *dressed like the* LORD BEVILL.

WHEADLE. So, my Proteus, exactly dressed! Dextrous rogue! Is Grace ready in her gears, and settled in my Lady Daubwell's house?

PALMER. Every trap is baited.

WHEADLE. I'll warrant thee then we catch our Cully: he's gone to put himself into a fantastic garb, in imitation of Sir Frederick Frollick; he's almost frantic

---

39–40 *My fate . . . enemy*: see Additional Note.
1 *Proteus*: a sea-god, fabled to assume various shapes; hence used for someone adept at altering their appearance.
1 *exactly*: to perfection; accurately.
2 *gears*: accoutrements.
3 *Lady Daubwell's house*: an apt place for them, since 'to daub' meant (1) 'to put on a false show' (2) 'to cover with finery or ornaments in a coarse, tasteless manner'.
6 *fantastic*: extravagant, grotesque.

with the very conceit of gaining the rich widow. But hark, I hear him coming; slip down the back way, and to your charge.

Exit PALMER.

Enter SIR NICHOLAS.

SIR NICHOLAS. Wheadle, and what think you of this habit? is it not very modish?

WHEADLE. As any man need wear: how did you furnish yourself so suddenly?

SIR NICHOLAS. Suddenly? I protest I was at least at sixteen brokers, before I could put myself exactly into the fashion; but now I defy Sir Frederick; I am as fine as he, and will be as mad as he, if that will carry the widow, I'll warrant thee.

WHEADLE. Is it not better pushing thus for a fortune, before your reputation's blasted with the infamous names of coward and gamester? And so become able to pay the thousand pounds without noise, than going into the country, selling your land, making a havoc among your woods, or mortgaging your estate to a scrupulous scrivener, that will whisper it into the ears of the whole town, by inquiring of your good behaviour?

SIR NICHOLAS. Excellent Wheadle! And will my Lord Bevill speak my commendations to his sister?

WHEADLE. She is impatient till she see you, sir; for in my hearing, upon the account I gave him of you, he told her you were the prettiest, wittiest, wildest

---

8 *conceit*: idea.
10 *your charge*: i.e. the part of the plot you have been allotted.
12 *modish*: a new word, the *OED*'s earliest examples date from the early 1660s.
16 *brokers*: dealers in second-hand apparel.
17 *defy*: challenge.
18 *mad*: extravagant in gaiety, wild.
21 *blasted*: blighted.
24–5 *making a havoc among your woods*: i.e. by selling off the timber.
26 *scrupulous*: minutely cautious.
26 *scrivener*: scriveners received money to place out at interest, and supplied those who wanted to raise money on security.
33 *prettiest*: a general epithet of admiration.
33 *wildest*: see note to *She Would*, I ii 47.

gentleman about the town, and a Cavalier in your heart; the only things that take her.

SIR NICHOLAS. Wheadle, come, I will go to the tavern, and swallow two whole quarts of wine instantly, and when I am drunk ride on a drawer's back to visit her.

WHEADLE. Some less frolic to begin with.

SIR NICHOLAS. I will cut three drawers over the pate then, and go with a tavern-lanthorn before me at noon-day. Come away.

Exeunt, SIR NICHOLAS *singing.*

SCENE III

Enter PALMER *and* GRACE.

PALMER. Do not I look like a very reverend lord, Grace?

GRACE. And I like a very fine lady, Mr Palmer?

PALMER. Yes in good faith, Grace; what a rogue is that Wheadle, to have kept such a treasure to himself, without communicating a little to his friends? (*Offers to kiss her*)

GRACE. Forbear; you'll be out in your part, my lord, when Sir Nicholas comes.

PALMER. The truth is, my lady, I am better prepared at this time to act a lover than a relation.

GRACE. That grave dress is very amorous indeed.

PALMER. My virtues, like those of plants in the winter, are retired; your warm spring would fetch 'em out with a vengeance.

Enter JENNY *in haste.*

JENNY. Mr Wheadle and Sir Nicholas are come.

PALMER. Away, away then, sister; expect your cue.

[*Exeunt* GRACE *and* JENNY.]

Enter WHEADLE, *and* SIR NICHOLAS, *kicking a tavern boy before him, who has three bottles of wine on a rope hanging at his back.*

SIR NICHOLAS. (*singing*) 'Then march along, boys;

---

41 *tavern-lanthorn*: tavern-lantern.

6 *communicating a little*: sharing a little with.

valiant and strong, boys.' So, lay down the bottles here.

WHEADLE. My lord, this is the worthy gentleman that I told you was ambitious to be your sister's servant.

SIR NICHOLAS. Hither I am come, my lord, to drink your sister's health, without offence, I hope.

PALMER. You are heartily welcome, sir.

SIR NICHOLAS. Here's a brimmer then to her, and all the fleas about her.

PALMER. Sir, I'll call herself to pledge it.

SIR NICHOLAS. Stay, stay, my lord, that you may be able to tell her you have drunk it.

PALMER *drinks and exit.*

SIR NICHOLAS. Wheadle, how do you like this? (*Draws his sword*) Shall I break the windows?

WHEADLE. Hold, hold; you are not in a house of evil reputation.

SIR NICHOLAS. Well admonished, Sir Frederick Frollick.

Enter PALMER *and* GRACE.

PALMER. This is Sir Nicholas, sister.

SIR NICHOLAS. Ay, madam, I am Sir Nicholas, and how do you like me?

GRACE. A pretty gentleman. Pray, sir, are you come a-house-warming, that you bring your wine with you?

SIR NICHOLAS. If you ask such pert questions, madam, I can stop your mouth. (*Kisses her*) Hither I am come to be drunk, that you may see me drunk; and here's a health to your flannel petticoat. (*Drinks*)

GRACE. Mr Wheadle, my service to you; a health to Sir Nicholas's great-grandfather's beard-brush.

She drinks part.

SIR NICHOLAS. Nay, pledge me; ha –

GRACE. You are not quarrelsome in your drink, I hope, sir.

SIR NICHOLAS. No, faith; I am wondrous loving. (*Hugs her*)

GRACE. You are a very bold lover.

32–3 *house of evil reputation*: brothel.
46 *beard-brush*: wench.

SIR NICHOLAS. Widow, let you and I go upon the ramble tonight.

GRACE. Do you take me for a night-walker, sir?

SIR NICHOLAS. Thou shalt be witness how many constables' staves I'll break about the watchmen's ears; how many bellmen I'll rob of their verses, to furnish a little apartment in the back-side of my lodging.

GRACE. I believe y'are an excellent man at quarterstaff, sir.

SIR NICHOLAS. The odds was on my head against any warrener in all our country; but I have left it off this two year. My lord, what say you, do you think your sister and I should not furnish a bedchamber as well as two soberer people? what think you, my lord?

GRACE. Ay, and a nursery too, I hope, sir.

SIR NICHOLAS. Well said, widow, i' faith; I will get upon thy body a generation of wild cats, children that shall waw, waw, scratch their nurses, and be drunk with their sucking-bottles.

WHEADLE. Brave Sir Nicholas.

SIR NICHOLAS. Wheadle, give me a brimmer; the widow shall drink it to our progeny. (*Exit* GRACE) Where, where is she gone?

PALMER. You have frighted her hence, sir.

SIR NICHOLAS. I'll fright her worse, if I find her in a corner. Ha, widow, I'll follow you; I'll follow you, ha.

[*Exit* SIR NICHOLAS.]

WHEADLE. The wine makes the rogue witty; he overacts the part I gave him; Sir Frederick is not half so mad: I will keep him thus elevated till he has married

---

53 *ramble*: cf. note to I ii 129.

54 *night-walker*: one who walks about by night, usually with an assumption of criminal intent (it was, for instance, used of thieves and prostitutes).

58 *little apartment*: privy.

60 *quarterstaff*: fighting (in earnest or for sport) with a lengthy pole (tipped with iron).

63 *warrener*: officer employed to watch over the game in a park or reserve.

63 *country*: neighbourhood, county.

70 *waw, waw*: cry (like a cat).

81 *elevated*: (1) elated (2) intoxicated.

Grace, and we have the best part of his estate at our mercy.

PALMER. Most ingenious Wheadle!

WHEADLE. I was not born to ease nor acres; industry is all my stock of living.

The WOMEN *shriek within.*

PALMER. Hark, he puts them to the squeak.

WHEADLE. We must go and take him off; he's as fierce as a bandog that has newly broke his chain.

Exeunt laughing.

SCENE IV

A field.

Enter BRUCE *and* LOVIS, *and traverse the stage.*
Then enter four or five MEN *in disguises.*

FIRST MAN. This way they went; be sure you kill the villain; let pity be a stranger to your breasts.

SECOND MAN. We have been bred, you know, unacquainted with compassion.

THIRD MAN. But why, colonel, should you so eagerly pursue his life? he has the report of a gallant man.

FIRST MAN. He murdered my father.

THIRD MAN. I have heard he killed him fairly in the field at Naseby.

FIRST MAN. He killed him, that's enough; and I myself was witness: I accused him to the Protector, and suborned witness to have taken away his life by form

---

84 *ingenious*: 'ingenious' and 'ingenuity' mostly have, in Etherege, overtones of 'expertise in trickery', presumably an ironic inversion of one of the words' common seventeenth-century meanings, 'freedom from dissimulation'.

86 *stock of living*: i.e. all I have to live on.

89 *bandog*: dog tied or chained up because of its ferocity.

6 *report*: reputation.

9 *Naseby*: this battle, in June 1645, was the most crucial of the defeats inflicted by Parliament's New Model Army on royalist forces during the first Civil War.

11 *Protector*: see note to I ii 178.

12 *witness*: testimony.

of law; but my plot was discovered, and he yesterday released; since which I've watched an opportunity, without the help of seeming justice, for my revenge. Strike home. –

THIRD MAN. We are your hired slaves; and since you'll have it so, we'll shed his blood, and never spare our own.

Exeunt, drawing their swords.

Enter BEAUFORT *and* SIR FREDERICK, *and traverse the stage.*
Enter BRUCE *and* LOVIS *at another door.*

BRUCE. Your friendship, noble youth, 's too prodigal;
For one already lost you venture all;
Your present happiness, your future joy;
You for the hopeless your great hopes destroy.
LOVIS. What can I venture for so brave a friend?
I have no hopes but what on you depend.
Should I your friendship and my honour rate
Below the value of a poor estate,
A heap of dirt! Our family has been
To blame, my blood must here atone the sin.

Enter the five VILLAINS *with drawn swords.*

Heav'ns! what is there an ambuscado laid!
Draw, dearest friend, I fear we are betrayed.

FIRST VILLAIN. Bruce, look on me, and then prepare to die. (*Pulling off his vizard*)

BRUCE. Oh treacherous villain!

FIRST VILLAIN. Fall on, and sacrifice his blood to my revenge.

LOVIS. More hearts than one shall bleed, if he must die.

They fight.

Enter BEAUFORT *and* SIR FREDERICK.

BEAUFORT. Heavens! what's this I see! Sir Frederick, draw; their blood's too good to grace such villains' swords. Courage, brave men; now we can match their force.

---

29 *must*: 'most' (*1664*).
30 *ambuscado*: ambush.
33 s.d. *vizard*: mask.

LOVIS. We'll make you, slaves, repent this treachery.
The VILLAINS *run.*
BEAUFORT. So.
BRUCE. They are not worth pursuit; we'll let them go.
Brave men! this action makes it well appear
'Tis honour and not envy brings you here.
BEAUFORT. We come to conquer, Bruce, and not to see
Such villains rob us of our victory.
Your lives our fatal swords claim as their due;
W'ad wronged ourselves had we not righted you.
BRUCE. Your gen'rous courage has obliged us so,
That to your succour we our safety owe.
LOVIS. Y'ave done what men of honour ought to do,
What in your cause we would have done for you.
BEAUFORT. You speak the truth, w'ave but our duty done;
Prepare: duty's no obligation.
He strips.
LOVIS *and* SIR FREDERICK *strip.*
BRUCE. My honour is dissatisfied; I must,
My lord, consider whether it be just
To draw my sword against that life which gave
Mine, but e'en now, protection from the grave.
BEAUFORT. None come into the field to weigh what's right;
This is no place for counsel, but for fight.
Dispatch.
BRUCE. I am resolved I will not fight.
BEAUFORT. Did I come hither then only to fright
A company of fearful slaves away;
My courage stoops not at so mean a prey:
Know, Bruce, I hither come to shed thy blood.
BRUCE. Open this bosom, and let out a flood.
BEAUFORT. I come to conquer bravely in the field,
Not to take poor revenge on such as yield.

---

46 *envy*: see note to II ii 56.

54 *in your cause*: i.e. in your behalf if you had faced similar danger.

56 *duty's no obligation*: i.e. our having performed what duty demanded does not place you under any obligation.

66 *stoops not*: (of a hawk or other bird of prey) swoops at, descends swiftly on.

Has nothing pow'r, too backward man, to move
Thy courage? Think on thy neglected love:
Think on the beauteous Graciana's eyes;
'Tis I have robbed thee of that glorious prize.

BRUCE. There are such charms in Graciana's name,

Strips hastily.

My scrup'lous honour must obey my flame:
My lazy courage I with shame condemn:
No thoughts have power streams of blood to stem.

SIR FREDERICK. Come, sir, out of kindness to our friends you and I must pass a small compliment on each other.

They all fight.

BEAUFORT *after many passes closes with* BRUCE; *they fall;* BEAUFORT *disarms him.*

BEAUFORT. Here, live. (*Giving* BRUCE *his sword again*)

BRUCE. My lord, y'ave gained a perfect victory;
Y'ave vanquished and obliged your enemy.

BEAUFORT. Hold, gallant men.

BRUCE *and* BEAUFORT *part* LOVIS *and* SIR FREDERICK.

LOVIS. Before we bleed! Do we here fight a prize,
Where handsome proffers may for wounds suffice?
I am amazed! What means this bloodless field?

BRUCE. The stoutest heart must to his fortune yield.
(*To* BEAUFORT) Brave youth! here honour did with
courage vie;
And both agree to grace your victory.
Heaven with such a conquest favours few:
'Tis easier to destroy than to subdue.
Our bodies may by brutish force be killed;
But noble minds alone to virtue yield.
My lord, I've twice received my life from you;
Much is to both those gen'rous actions due:
The noble giver I must highly prize,
Though I the gift, heav'n knows, as much despise.

---

71 *backward*: slow to respond or take action.
77 *lazy*: sluggish, dull.
77 *courage*: spirit, lustiness, vigour.
84 *obliged*: rendered indebted.
87 *proffers*: threats.

Can I desire to live, when all the joy
Of my poor life its ransom does destroy!
No, no, Graciana's loss I'll ne'er survive;
I pay too dear for this unsought reprieve.
Falls on his sword, and is desperately wounded.

BEAUFORT. Hold gallant man! Honour herself does bleed; *Running to him, takes him in his arms.*
All gen'rous hearts are wounded by this deed.

LOVIS. He does his blood for a lost mistress spend;
And shall not I bleed for so brave a friend?
LOVIS *offers to fall on his sword, but is hindered by* SIR FREDERICK.

SIR FREDERICK. Forbear, sir; the frolic's not to go round, as I take it.

BEAUFORT. 'Twere greater friendship to assist me here:
I hope the wound's not mortal, though I fear –

BRUCE. My sword, I doubt, has failed in my relief;
'T has made a vent for blood, but not for grief.
BRUCE *struggling,* LOVIS *and* SIR FREDERICK *help to hold him.*
Let me once more the unkind weapon try.
Will you prolong my pain? oh cruelty!

LOVIS. Ah, dearest Bruce, can you thus careless be
Of our great friendship, and your loyalty!
Look on your friend; your drooping country view;
And think how much they both expect from you.
You for a mistress waste that precious blood
Which should be spent but for our master's good.

SIR FREDERICK. Expense of blood already makes him faint; let's carry him to the next house, till we can procure a chair to convey him to my Lord Bevill's, the best place for accommodation.
They all take him up.

BEAUFORT. Honour has played an aftergame; this field
The conqu'ror does unto the conquered yield.
Exeunt.

---

112 *doubt*: fear.
125 *accommodation*: the supplying of what is necessary.
126 *aftergame*: a second game played in order to reverse or improve the issues of the first.

SCENE V

Enter GRACIANA *weeping.*

GRACIANA. Farewell all thoughts of happiness, farewell:
My fears together with my sorrows swell:
Whilst from my eyes there flows this crystal flood,
From their brave hearts there flows such streams of blood.
Here I am lost, while both for me contend;
With what success can this strange combat end!
Honour with honour fights for victory,
And love is made the common enemy.

Enter LORD BEVILL.

LORD BEVILL. (*weeping*) Ah, child! –
GRACIANA. Kill me not with expectation, sir.
LORD BEVILL. The generous Bruce has killed himself for you: being disarmed, and at his rival's mercy, his life and sword were given him by the noble youth; he made a brave acknowledgment for both; but then considering you were lost, he scorned to live; and falling on his sword, has given himself a mortal wound. *Exit* LORD BEVILL.

Enter AURELIA *weeping.*

AURELIA. Cruel Graciana, go but in and see
The fatal triumph of your victory.
The noble Bruce, to your eternal shame,
With his own blood has quenched his raging flame.
GRACIANA. (*weeping*) My carriage shall in these misfortunes prove
That I have honour too, as well as love.
AURELIA. (*aside*) Thy sorrows, sad Aurelia, will declare
At once, I fear, thy love and thy despair:
These streams of grief straight to a flood will rise;
I can command my tongue, but not my eyes.
Exit AURELIA.
GRACIANA. In what a maze, Graciana, dost thou tread!

---

6 *success*: upshot, termination.
19 *triumph*: victory procession.
24 *declare*: manifest, reveal.

Which is the path that doth to honour lead?
I in this lab'rinth so resolve to move,
That none shall judge I am misled by love.

Enter BEAUFORT.

BEAUFORT. Here conqu'rors must forget their victories,
And homage pay to your victorious eyes.
Graciana, hither your poor slave is come,
After his conquest to receive his doom;
Smile on his vict'ry; had he proved untrue
To honour, he had then proved false to you.
GRACIANA. Perfidious man, can you expect from me
An approbation of your treachery!
When I, distracted with prophetic fears,
Blasted with sighs, and almost drowned in tears,
Begged you to moderate your rage last night,
Did you not promise me you would not fight?
Go now and triumph in your victory;
Into the field you went my enemy,
And are returned the only man I hate,
The wicked instrument of my sad fate.
My love has but dissembled been to thee,
To try my gen'rous lover's constancy.
Exit GRACIANA.
BEAUFORT. Oh heav'n! how strange and cruel is my fate!
Preserved by love, to be destroyed by hate!
Exit BEAUFORT.

---

35 *doom*: judgment, sentence.
36–7 *had he . . . to you*: see Additional Note to II ii 70.
41 *Blasted*: stricken. See Additional Note.

SCENE VI

The Widow's house.

Enter BETTY *and* LETTICE, *the two chambermaids, severally.*

BETTY. Oh, Lettice, we have stayed for you.

LETTICE. What hast thou done to the Frenchman, girl? he lies yonder neither dead nor drunk; nobody knows what to make of him.

BETTY. I sent for thee to help make sport with him; he'll come to himself, never fear him: have you not observed how scurvily h'as looked of late?

LETTICE. Yes; and he protests it is for love of you.

BETTY. Out upon him, for a dissembling rascal; h'as got the foul disease; our coachman discovered it by a bottle of diet-drink he brought and hid behind the stairs, into which I infused a little opium.

LETTICE. What dost intend to do with him?

BETTY. You shall see.

Enter COACHMAN, *with a tub without a bottom, a shut at the top to be locked, and a hole to put one's head out at, made easy to be borne on one's shoulders.*

COACHMAN. Here's the tub; where's the Frenchman?

BETTY. He lies behind the stairs; haste and bring him in, that he may take quiet possession of this wooden tenement; for 'tis near his time of waking.

The COACHMAN *and another* SERVANT *bring in* DUFOY, *and put him into the tub.*

---

s.d. *Lettice*: thus *1664*. Verity emended to 'Letitia', thus identifying her with Aurelia's servant. I have followed the *1664* text, to leave open the possibility that this is, in fact, another character.

s.d. *severally*: separately.

7 *scurvily*: as if sick with scurvy.

11 *diet-drink*: a drink prepared and prescribed for medicinal purposes, used particularly for Dufoy's complaint.

14 s.d. *shut*: a locking-bar or bolt.

Is the fiddler at hand that used to ply at the blind ale-house?

COACHMAN. He's ready.

Enter a FIDDLER.

BETTY. Well, let's hear now what a horrible noise you can make to wake this gentleman.

FIDDLER *plays a tune.*

LETTICE. He wants a helping hand; his eyelids are sealed up; see how the wax sticks upon 'em. (DUFOY *begins to wake*) Let me help you, monsieur.

DUFOY. Vat aré you? Jernie! vat is dis! am I Jack in a boxé? begar, who did putté me here?

BETTY. Good-morrow, monsieur; will you be pleased to take your pills this morning?

DUFOY. Noé; but I vo'd have de *diable* take youé; it vas youé dat did abusé me duss, vas it noté? begar I vil killé ale de shamber-maid in Englandé.

LETTICE. Will you be pleased to drink, monsieur? There's a bottle of your diet-drink within.

DUFOY. Are youé de littel *diable* come to tormenté mé? *Morbleu*! vas ever man afronté in dis naturé!

BETTY. Methinks he has fer *bonne mine*, monsieur, now if you please to make your little *adresse*, and your *amour*, you will not find me so coy.

DUFOY. Begar I vill no marié de *cousin germain* of de *diable.*

LETTICE. What should he do with a wife? he has not house-room for her.

BETTY. Why do you not keep your head within doors, monsieur?

---

19 *ply*: from *1697* reprintings of the play tend to emend here to 'play', but 'ply' can mean 'to wait or attend regularly, to have one's stand at a certain place for hire or custom' and is therefore retained here.

19 *blind*: out of the way.

38 *fer bonne mine. monsieur*: 'ferbon, mine Monsieur' (*1664*). Verity emended to '*fort bonne mine*, monsieur'; but Brett-Smith defended 'fer' with the following note – 'a very good mien; Betty is mimicking Dufoy's pronunciation, which turns *very* into *ver*'.

39–40 *your little adresse, and your amour*: echoing Dufoy at II i 63.

41 *cousin germain*: first or full cousin.

LETTICE. Now there's such a storm abroad.

DUFOY. Why did not youé keep your maiden-headé vid in dooré? begar, tellé me daté.

COACHMAN. Have you any fine French commodities to sell, gloves and ribands? y'ave got a very convenient shop, monsieur.

DUFOY. I do hope you vil have de verié convenient halteré, begar. Jerny, can I not taré dis tingé in de pieces?

BETTY. You begin to sweat, monsieur; the tub is proper for you.

DUFOY. I have no more patiencé; I vil breaké dis prison, or I vil breaké my neké, and ye shall alé be hangé. (*Struggles to get out*)

LETTICE. He begins to rave: bless the poor man.

BETTY. Some music quickly, to compose his mind.

The music plays; and they dance about him. He walks with the tub on his back.

How prettily the snail carries his tenement on his back! I'm sorry I am but his mistress: if I had been your wife, monsieur, I had made you a complete snail; your horns should have appeared.

DUFOY. I vil have de patience, dere is no oder remedé; you be alé de raskalé whore; de *diable* take you alé; and I vil say no more, begar.

BETTY. This is a very fine vessel, and would swim well; let's to the horse-pond with him.

LETTICE. Come, come, he looks as sullenly as a hare in her form; let's leave him.

COACHMAN. Your *serviteur très* humble, monsieur.

Exeunt all but DUFOY.

DUFOY. *Bougre*, I canno hangé my selfé; begar I canno drowné my selfé; I vil go hidé my selfé, and starvé to dyé; I vil no be de laughé for every jackanapé Englishé. *Morbleu.* [*Exit.*]

---

51 *ribands*: ribbons, used decoratively on both ladies' and gentlemen's clothes (a fashion often alleged to be of French origin).

56–7 *You begin . . . proper for you*: see note to II i 12.

65 *your horns*: i.e. those of a cuckold.

69 *swim*: float.

SCENE VII

SIR FREDERICK *is brought in upon a bier, with a mourning cloth over him, attended by a* GENTLEMAN *in a mourning cloak: four* FIDDLERS *carry the corpse, with their instruments tucked under their cloaks. Enter the* WIDOW *weeping.*

MOURNER. Madam, you must expect a bloody consequence
When men of such prodigious courage fight.
The young Lord Beaufort was the first that fell,
After his sword too deeply had engaged
His rival not to stay behind him long.
Sir Fred'rick with your nephew bravely fought;
Death long did keep his distance, as if he
Had feared excess of valour; but when they,
O'erloaded with their wounds, began to faint,
He with his terrors did invade their breasts.
Fame soon brought many to the tragic place,
Where I found my dearest friend, Sir Fred'rick,
Almost as poor in breath as blood: he took
Me by the hand, and all the stock h'ad left
He spent, madam, in calling upon you.
He first proclaimed your virtues, then his love;
And having charged me to convey his corpse
Hither to wait on you, his latest breath
Expired with the command.
WIDOW. The world's too poor to recompense this loss.
Unhappy woman! why should I survive
The only man in whom my joys did live?
My dreadful grief!

The FIDDLERS *prepare.*

Enter DUFOY *in his tub.*

DUFOY. Oh my matré, my matré; who has kill my matré? *Morbleu*, I vil –

The WIDOW *shrieks, and runs out: all the* FIDDLERS *run out in a fright.* SIR FREDERICK *starts up, which frights* DUFOY.

Oh, de *diable*, de *diable*!

---

11 *Fame*: public report, rumour.
18 *latest*: last.

SIR FREDERICK. What devilish accident is this? or has the widow undermined me?

Enter the WIDOW *and her* MAID *laughing.*

SIR FREDERICK. I shall be laughed to death now indeed, by chambermaids; why, have you no pity, widow?

WIDOW. None at all for the living; ha, ha, ha. You see w'are provided for your frolic, sir; ha, ha.

SIR FREDERICK. Laugh but one minute longer I will forswear thy company, kill thy tabby cat, and make thee weep for ever after.

WIDOW. Farewell, sir; expect at night to see the old man, with his paper lanthorn and cracked spectacles, singing your woeful tragedy to kitchen-maids and cobblers' prentices.

WIDOW *offers to go,* SIR FREDERICK *holds her by the arm.*

SIR FREDERICK. Hark you, hark you, widow: by all those devils that have hitherto possessed thy sex –

WIDOW. No swearing, good Sir Frederick.

SIR FREDERICK. Set thy face then; let me not see the remains of one poor smile: so, now I will kiss thee, and be friends.

WIDOW *falls out a-laughing.*

Not all thy wealth shall hire me to come within smell of thy breath again. Jealousy, and, which will be worse for thee, widow, impotence light upon me, if I stay one moment longer with thee. (*Offers to go*)

WIDOW. Do you hear, sir; can you be so angry with one that loves you so passionately she cannot survive you?

SIR FREDERICK. Widow, may the desire of man keep thee waking till thou art as mad as I am.

Exit SIR FREDERICK.

WIDOW. How lucky was this accident! How he would have insulted over my weakness else!

27–8 *or has the widow undermined me?*: i.e. did she arrange this reversal herself?
37–8 *old man*: the bellman (see notes to III ii 1 s.d., 18).
39 *tragedy*: doleful tale.
46 s.d. *falls out a-laughing*: bursts out laughing.
56 *insulted*: exulted contemptuously, glorified.

Sir Fred'rick, since I've warning, you shall prove
More subtle ways, before I own my love.
Exeunt.

ACT V

SCENE I

The Lord Bevill's house.

Enter LOVIS, *a* CHIRURGEON, SERVANTS, *carrying* BRUCE *in a chair.*

CHIRURGEON. Courage, brave sir; do not mistrust my art.

BRUCE. Tell me, didst thou e'er cure a wounded heart?
Thy skill, fond man, thou here employ'st in vain;
The ease thou giv'st does but increase my pain.

LOVIS. Dear Bruce, my life does on your life depend;
Though you disdain to live, yet save your friend.

BRUCE. Do what you please; but are not those unkind
That ease the body, to afflict the mind?
The CHIRURGEON *dresses him.*
Oh cruel love! thou shoot'st with such strange skill,
The wounds thou mak'st will neither heal nor kill:
Thy flaming arrows kindle such a fire
As will not waste thy victims, nor expire!

Enter AURELIA.

LOVIS. (*to the* CHIRURGEON) Is the wound mortal? tell me; or may we cherish hopes of his recovery?

CHIRURGEON. The danger is not imminent; yet my prognostic bodes a sad event: for though there be no

---

57 *prove*: make trial of.
s.d. *Chirurgeon*: surgeon.
1 *mistrust*: fail to have trust in.
1 *art*: skill.
16 *prognostic*: prognosis.
16 *event*: outcome.

great vessel dissected, yet I have cause to fear that the *parenchyma* of the right lobe of the lungs, near some large branch of the *asperia arteria*, is perforated.

LOVIS. Tell me in English, will he live or die?

CHIRURGEON. Truly I despair of his recovery.

Exit CHIRURGEON.

AURELIA. (*aside*) Forgive me, ladies, if excess of love
Me beyond rules of modesty does move,
And, against custom, makes me now reveal
Those flames my tortured breast did long conceal;
'Tis some excuse, that I my love declare
When there's no med'cine left to cure despair.

Weeps by the chair-side.

BRUCE. Oh heav'n! can fair Aurelia weep for me!
This is some comfort to my misery.
Kind maid, those eyes should only pity take
Of such as feel no wounds but what they make:
Who for another in your sight does mourn,
Deserves not your compassion, but your scorn.

AURELIA. I come not here with tears to pity you;
I for your pity with this passion sue.

BRUCE. My pity! tell me, what can be the grief,
That from the miserable hopes relief!

AURELIA. Before you know this grief, you feel the pain.

BRUCE. You cannot love, and not be loved again:
Where so much beauty does with love conspire,
No mortal can resist that double fire.

AURELIA. When proud Graciana wounded your brave heart,
On poor Aurelia's you revenged the smart:
Whilst you in vain did seek those wounds to cure,
With patience I their torture did endure.

BRUCE. My happiness has been so long concealed,
That it becomes my misery revealed:
That which should prove my joy, now proves my grief;

---

18 *parenchyma*: 'the special or proper substance of a gland or other organ of the body . . . as distinguished from the connective tissue or *stroma*, and from muscular tissue or *flesh* proper' (*OED*).

19 *asperia arteria*: windpipe.

39 *again*: in return.

47 *revealed*: i.e. when revealed.

And that brings pain, which, known, had brought relief.
Aurelia, why would you not let me know,
Whilst I had pow'r to pay, the debt I owe?
'Tis now too late; yet all I can I'll do;
I'll sigh away the breath I've left for you.
AURELIA. You yet have pow'r to grant me all I crave;
'Tis not your love I court, I court your grave.
I with my flame seek not to warm your breast,
But beg my ashes in your urn may rest:
For since Graciana's loss you scorned t'outlive,
I am resolved I'll not your death survive.
BRUCE. Hold, you too gen'rous are; yet I may live:
Heav'n for your sake may grant me a reprieve.
AURELIA. Oh, no; heav'n has decreed, alas, that we
Should in our fates, not in our loves agree.
BRUCE. (*to* LOVIS) Dear friend, my rashness I too late repent;
I ne'er thought death till now a punishment.

Enter GRACIANA.

GRACIANA. Oh, do not talk of death! the very sound
Once more will give my heart a mortal wound:
Here on my knees I've sinned I must confess
Against your love, and my own happiness;
I, like the child, whose folly proves his loss,
Refused the gold, and did accept the dross.
BRUCE. You have in Beaufort made so good a choice,
His virtue's such, he has his rival's voice;
Graciana, none but his great soul could prove
Worthy to be the centre of your love.
GRACIANA. You to another would such virtue give,
Brave sir, as in yourself does only live.
If to the most deserving I am due,
He must resign his weaker claim to you.
BRUCE. This is but flatt'ry; for I'm sure you can
Think none so worthy as that gen'rous man:
By honour you are his.
GRACIANA. Yet, sir, I know
How much I to your gen'rous passion owe;

73 *voice*: support, approval.

You bleed for me; and if for me you die,
Your loss I'll mourn with vowed virginity.
BRUCE. Can you be mindful of so small a debt,
And that which you to Beaufort owe forget?
That will not honour but injustice be;
Honour with justice always does agree.
This gen'rous pity which for me you show,
Is more than you to my misfortunes owe:
These tears, Graciana, which for me you shed,
O'erprize the blood which I for you have bled:
But now I can no more –
My spirits faint within my wearied breast.
LOVIS. Sister, 'tis fit you give him leave to rest.
Who waits?

Enter SERVANTS.

With care convey him to his bed.
BRUCE. Hold –
Dearest Aurelia, I will strive to live,
If you will but endeavour not to grieve.
LOVIS. Brave man! The wonder of this age thou'lt prove,
For matchless gratitude, and gen'rous love.
Exeunt all but GRACIANA.
GRACIANA. How strangely is my soul perplexed by fate!
The man I love I must pretend to hate;
And with dissembled scorn his presence fly,
Whose absence is my greatest misery!

Enter BEAUFORT.

BEAUFORT. Hear me, upon my knees I beg you'll hear.
She's gone.
Exit GRACIANA.
There was no need, false woman, to increase
My misery with hopes of happiness.
This scorn at first had to my love and me
But justice been; now it is cruelty.
Was there no way his constancy to prove,
But by your own inconstancy in love?
To try another's virtue could you be,

---

93 *O'erprize*: surpass in value.
95 *spirits*: vital power or energy.

Graciana, to your own an enemy?
Sure 'tis but passion which she thus does vent,
Blown up with anger and with discontent,
Because my honour disobeyed her will,
And Bruce for love of her his blood did spill.
I once more in her eyes will read my fate;
I need no wound to kill me, if she hate. [*Exit.*]

SCENE II

Enter SIR NICHOLAS *drunk, with a blind* FELLOW *led before him playing on a cymbal, followed by a number of* BOYS *hollowing, and persecuting him.*

SIR NICHOLAS. Villains, sons of unknown fathers, tempt me no more.

The BOYS *hout at him, he draws his sword.*

I will make a young generation of cripples, to succeed in Lincoln's Inn Fields and Covent Garden. The barbarous breeding of these London boys! (*Frights the* BOYS *away*)

BOY THAT LEADS THE CYMBAL. Whither do you intend to go, sir?

SIR NICHOLAS. To see the wealthy widow, Mrs Rich.

BOY. Where does she dwell, sir?

SIR NICHOLAS. Hereabouts; enquire; I will serenade her at noonday.

Exeunt.

Enter the WIDOW *and her maid* BETTY.

WIDOW. Where is this poor Frenchman, girl? h'as done me good service.

BETTY. The butler has got him down into the cellar, madam, made him drunk, and laid him to sleep among his empty casks.

---

2 s.d. *hout*: hoot.

3 *to succeed*: i.e. to replace the current generation of beggars.

10 *serenade*: a serenade being, of course, properly a musical performance given in the open air at night (the word was a recent arrival from French; *OED*'s first example dates from 1649).

16 *casks*: 'Cask' (*1664*).

WIDOW. Pray, when he wakes let him be released of his imprisonment; Betty, you use your servant too severely.

The CYMBAL *plays without.*

Hark, what ridiculous noise is that? it sets my teeth an edge worse than the scraping of trenchers.

Enter a SERVANT.

SERVANT. Madam, a rude drunken fellow, with a cymbal before him, and his sword in his hand, is pressed into your house.

Enter SIR NICHOLAS *and* CYMBAL*; the* WOMEN *shriek.*

SIR NICHOLAS. Sirrah, play me a bawdy tune, to please the widow; have at thee, widow.

BETTY. 'Tis one of Oliver's knights, madam, Sir Nicholas Cully; his mother was my grandmother's dairy-maid.

Enter SERVANTS*; they lay hands on him, and take away his sword.*

SIR NICHOLAS. Let me go; I am not so drunk but I can stand without your help, gentlemen. Widow, here is music; send for a parson, and we will dance Barnaby within this half-hour.

WIDOW. I will send for a constable, sir.

SIR NICHOLAS. Hast a mind to see me beat him? how those rogues dread me! Did not Wheadle tell thee upon what conditions I would condescend to make thee my bedfellow, widow, speak?

WIDOW. This is some drunken mistake; away with him, thrust him out of door.

Enter a SERVANT*: clashing of swords and noise without.*

SERVANT. Help, help, for Sir Frederick.

---

18 *servant*: gallant, lover.
19 s.d. *Cymbal*: i.e. the cymbal player.
21 *an edge*: on edge.
21 *trenchers*: wooden plates or platters.
27 *Oliver's knights*: see note to I ii 178.
32 *Barnaby*: 'an old dance to a quick movement' (Brett-Smith).

WIDOW. What's the matter?

SERVANT. He is fighting, madam, with a company of bailiffs, that would arrest him at the door.

WIDOW. Haste everyone, and rescue him quickly.

Exeunt all but SIR NICHOLAS.

SIR NICHOLAS. Widow, come back, I say, widow; I will not stir one foot after thee: come back, I say, widow. (*Falls down and sleeps*)

Enter DUFOY.

DUFOY. Vat de *diable* be de matré? here is de ver strange varké in dis house; de vemen day do cry, ha, ha, ha; de men day do run, day do take de batton, de dung-vorké, and de vire-vorké: vat is here, van killé? (*Looking on* SIR NICHOLAS)

Enter BETTY.

BETTY. You are a trusty servant, indeed; here you are locked up, while your poor master is arrested, and dragged away by unmerciful bailiffs.

DUFOY. My matré? Jernie! Metres Bet, letté me go; begar I vil kill allé de *bougre* de bailié, and recover my matré. *Bougre* de bailié.

BETTY. So, make all the haste you can. (*She helps him out of the tub*)

DUFOY. *Morbleu*! *bougre* de baylié! I vil go prepare to killé a tousand baylié begar: *bougre* de baylié. *Exit.*

Enter the WIDOW *and* SERVANT *severally.*

WIDOW. Well, what news?

SERVANT. Madam, they have arrested him upon an execution for two hundred pounds, and carried him to a bailiff's house hard by.

WIDOW. If that be all, Betty, take my key, and give him the money in gold; do you content the bailiffs, but let Sir Frederick know nothing of it; and then let

---

51 *batton*: a baton, i.e. a stick used as a weapon, a cudgel.

52 *vire-vorké*: Dufoy's attempt to pronounce 'firework'?

64 *execution*: the enforcement of the judgment of a court, most frequently (as here) the seizure of the goods or person of a debtor in default of payment.

them bring him to my house as their prisoner: dispatch.

Exeunt BETTY *and* SERVANT.

Enter a FOOTBOY.

FOOTBOY. Pray, madam, is there not a stray gentleman here, misled by drink?

WIDOW. There lies the beast you look for; you had best remove him quickly, or I shall cause him to be put into the pound. *Exit* WIDOW.

FOOTBOY. If I do not get this fool clear off before he comes to himself, our plot is quite spoiled: this summer-livery may chance to hover over my shivering limbs next winter. Yonder sits honest Palmer, my poor master, in a coach, quaking for fear; all that see him in that reverend disguise, will swear he has got the palsy. Ho, Sir Nicholas. (*Pulls him*)

SIR NICHOLAS. I will drink three beer-glasses to the widow's health before I go.

FOOTBOY. The widow stays for you, to wait upon her to the Exchange.

SIR NICHOLAS. Let her go into her bedchamber and meditate; I am not drunk enough to be seen in her company.

FOOTBOY. I must carry him away upon my back; but, since things may go ill, 'tis good to make sure of something; I'll examine his pockets first: so, for this I thank my own ingenuity; in this way of plain dealing I can live without the help of my master.

Enter a SERVANT.

Pray, sir, will you help me up with my burden.

SERVANT. I am sure your master has his load already.

They lift him up.

---

75 *pound*: (1) enclosure for the detention of stray or trespassing cattle (cf. the preceding line) (2) prison.

86 *the Exchange*: a large arcaded area of fashionable shops, south of the Strand.

93 *plain dealing*: subjected to the same ironic inversion of its normal meaning as 'ingenuity' (see note to IV iii 84).

96 *his load*: i.e. of drink.

SIR NICHOLAS. Carry me to my widow, boy: where is my music?

Enter SIR FREDERICK *with the* BAILIFFS, *who are fiddlers disguised, with their fiddles under their coats, at one door; and the* WIDOW *at another.*

FOOTBOY. There is no hopes now; I'll shift for myself.

Exit FOOTBOY.

SIR FREDERICK. Widow, these are old acquaintance of mine, bid them welcome: I was coming to wait upon you before; but meeting them by the way, they pressed me to drink –

SIR NICHOLAS *reels against* SIR FREDERICK.

SIR NICHOLAS. Sir Frederick! Widow, bid him welcome; he is a very good friend of mine, and as mad a fellow as myself. Kiss, kiss the widow, man; she has a plump under-lip, and kisses smartly.

SIR FREDERICK. What's here? Cully drunk, transformed into a gallant, and acquainted with the spring and proportion of the widow's lips!

SIR NICHOLAS. Ay, I am drunk, sir; am I not widow? I scorn to be soberer than yourself, sir; I will drink with you, swear with you, break windows with you, and so forth.

SIR FREDERICK. Widow, is this your champion?

WIDOW. You have no exceptions against him, I hope; he has challenged you at your own weapons.

SIR NICHOLAS. Widow, Sir Frederick shall be one of our bridemen; I will have none but such mad fellows at our wedding; but before I marry thee I will consider upon it. (*He sits down and sleeps*)

SIR FREDERICK. Pray, widow, how long have you been acquainted with this mirror of knighthood?

WIDOW. Long enough you hear, sir, to treat of marriage.

SIR FREDERICK. What? You intend me for a reserve then? You will have two strings to your bow, widow;

---

107 *smartly*: vigorously.
109 *spring*: vigour.
116 *exceptions*: objections.
123 *mirror*: exemplar, model.
124 *treat of*: discuss.

I perceive your cunning; and faith I think I shall do the heartier service, if thou employ'st me by the by.

WIDOW. You are an excellent gallant indeed; shake off these lousy companions; come carry your mistress to the Park, and treat her at the Mulberry Garden this glorious evening.

SIR FREDERICK. Widow, I am a man of business, that ceremony's to be performed by idle fellows.

WIDOW. What would you give to such a friend as should dispatch this business now, and make you one of those idle fellows?

SIR FREDERICK. Faith pick and choose; I carry all my wealth about me; do it, and I am all at thy service, widow.

WIDOW. Well, I have done it, sir; you are at liberty, and a leg now will satisfy me.

SIR FREDERICK. Good faith, thou art too reasonable, dear widow; modesty will wrong thee.

WIDOW. Are you satisfied?

FIDDLERS. Yes, madam.

Enter DUFOY, *with a helmet on his head, and a great sword in his hand.*

DUFOY. Vare are de *bougre* de baylié? *Tête-blue, bougre* rogue. (*He falls upon the* FIDDLERS)

FIDDLERS. Help, help, Sir Frederick, murder, murder! alas, sir, we are not bailiffs; you may see we are men of an honester vocation. (*They show their instruments*)

SIR FREDERICK. Hold, hold, thou mighty man-at-arms.

DUFOY. *Morbleu*, de fidler! and is my matré at liberty?

---

128 *by the by*: only from time to time.
130 *lousy*: mean, sorry, contemptible; though the Widow also means the word literally.
131 *Mulberry Garden*: a garden of mulberry trees (now the site of Buckingham Palace), a fashionable meeting- and promenading-place.
138 *pick and choose*: i.e. make your choice with care.
142 *a leg*: a bow of thanks.
147 *Tête-bleu*: *bleu* is a euphemism for *Dieu*; therefore, 'by God's head'.

play me de trichaté, or de jegg Englishé, quicklie, or I vil make you all dance vidout your fiddle; quiké.

WIDOW. I am overreached, I perceive.

DUFOY *dances a jig.*

SIR FREDERICK. Kind widow, thank thee for this release. (*Shakes his pockets*) Laugh, widow; ha, ha, ha: where is your counter-plot, widow? Ha, ha, ha. Laugh at her, Dufoy. Come, be not so melancholy; we'll to the Park: I care not if I spend a piece or two upon thee in tarts and cheesecakes. Pish, widow, why so much out of humour? 'Tis no shame to love such a likely young fellow.

WIDOW. I could almost find in my heart to punish myself, to afflict thee, and marry that drunken sot I never saw before.

SIR FREDERICK. How came he hither?

WIDOW. Enquire elsewhere; I will not answer thee one question; nor let thee see me out of a mask any more this fortnight.

SIR FREDERICK. Go, go into thy closet, look over thy old receipts, and talk wantonly now and then with thy chambermaid: I shall not trouble thee much till this is spent; (*Shakes his pockets*) and by that time thy foolish vow will be near over.

WIDOW. I want patience to endure this insolence. Is my charity rewarded thus?

SIR FREDERICK. Pious widow, call you this charity? 'twill get thee little hereafter; thou must answer for every sin it occasions: here is wine and women in abundance. (*Shakes his pockets*)

WIDOW. Avoid my house, and never more come near me.

SIR FREDERICK. But hark you, hark you, widow; do you think this can last always?

WIDOW. Ungrateful man! *Exit* WIDOW.

---

154 *trichaté*: thus *1664* and subsequent editions; he is clearly demanding that the fiddlers play a dance-tune, and John Playford's *The Dancing Master* (3rd edition: London, 1657) lists in an appendix of French airs 'Trickettes (Tricotets)'. (I owe this reference to the kindness of Dr John Buttrey.)

156 *overreached*: outwitted.

172 *closet*: small, private inner room.

173 *receipts*: (1) records of moneys received or (2) recipes.

180 *hereafter*: i.e. in another world.

SIR FREDERICK. She's gone; impatience for these two hours possess her, and then I shall be pretty well revenged.

DUFOY. Begar, matré, have you not de ver faithful *serviteur*? you do never take notice of my merit.

SIR FREDERICK. Dufoy, thou art a man of courage, and hast done bravely; I will cast off this suit a week sooner than I intended, to reward thy service.

DUFOY. Begar I have several time given you ver dangerous testimonié of my affection.

Enter a SERVANT, *and takes up* SIR NICHOLAS *in his arms.*

SIR FREDERICK. Whither do you carry him?

SERVANT. Sir, there is an old gentleman below in a coach, very like my Lord Bevill, who, hearing what a condition Sir Nicholas was in, desired me to bring him to him in my arms.

SIR NICHOLAS. Let me go; where is the widow?

SIR FREDERICK. What widow?

SIR NICHOLAS. Mrs Rich; she is to be my wife.

SIR FREDERICK. But do you hear, Sir Nicholas? how long have you courted this widow?

SIR NICHOLAS. Mr Wheadle can tell you: trouble me not with idle questions. Sir Frederick, you shall be welcome at any time; she loves men that will roar, and drink, and serenade her.

SIR FREDERICK. This is some strange mistake; sure Wheadle, intending to chouse him, has showed him some counterfeit widow; and he, being drunk, has been misguided to the true widow's house. The fellow in the coach may discover all; I will step and see who it is: hold him here, Dufoy, till I return: gentlemen, come you with me.

Exeunt SIR FREDERICK *and* FIDDLERS.

SIR NICHOLAS. Where is my mistress?

DUFOY. Vat metres?

SIR NICHOLAS. The widow.

DUFOY. She be de metres of my matré.

---

193 *cast off*: it was one of a servant's perks to inherit their employers' discarded clothing.

209 *roar*: behave in a noisy, riotous manner.

SIR NICHOLAS. You lie, sirrah.

DUFOY. Begar you be de jackanape to tellé me I do lyea.

SIR NICHOLAS. You are a French rascal, and I will blow your nose without a handkerchief. (*He pulls* DUFOY *by the nose*)

DUFOY. Helpé, helpé me; *morbleu*! I vil beat you vid my fisté and my footé, tellé you aské me de pardon; take dat and daté; aské me de pardon.

SIR NICHOLAS *falls down, and* DUFOY *beats him.*

SIR NICHOLAS. I ask you pardon, sirrah?

DUFOY. Sirrah? *Tête-bleu.* (*Offers to strike*)

Enter SIR FREDERICK *and* FIDDLERS, *leading in* PALMER *trembling.*

SIR FREDERICK. Hold, hold, Dufoy.

DUFOY. Begar he do merite to be beaté; he swaré he vil marré youré metres.

PALMER. I beseech you, Sir Frederick.

SIR NICHOLAS. My Lord Bevill!

SIR FREDERICK. So, he takes him for my Lord Bevill; now the plot will out. 'Tis fit this rascal should be cheated; but these rogues will deal too unmercifully with him: I'll take compassion upon him, and use him more favourably myself.

SIR NICHOLAS. My lord, where is the mad wench your sister?

SIR FREDERICK *pulls off* PALMER*'s disguise.*

SIR FREDERICK. Look you, Sir Nicholas, where is my Lord Bevill now?

SIR NICHOLAS. My merry countryman, Mr Palmer! I thought you had been in Buckinghamshire. (*Sings*)
'And he took her by the apron
To bring her to his beck.'
Never a catch now, my merry countryman? Sir Frederick, I owe this gentleman a thousand pounds.

SIR FREDERICK. How so?

SIR NICHOLAS. He won it of me at dice, Wheadle went my halfs; and we have given him a judgment for it.

SIR FREDERICK. This was the roguery you had been about the other night, when I met you in disguise, Palmer: you'll never leave your cheating and your

230 *Sirrah*: see note to I ii 58.

robbing, how many robberies do I know of your committing?

PALMER. The truth is, sir, you know enough to hang me; but you are a worthy gentleman, and a lover of ingenuity.

SIR FREDERICK. This will not pass: produce the judgment.

PALMER. Alas, sir, Mr Wheadle has it.

SIR FREDERICK. Produce it, or – fetch the constable, boy.

PALMER. Sir Frederick, be merciful to a sorrowful rascal: here is a copy of the judgment, as it is entered.

SIR FREDERICK. Well, who is this counterfeit widow? confess.

PALMER. Truly 'twas Wheadle's contrivance; a pox on him: never no good comes on't when men are so unconscionable in their dealings.

SIR NICHOLAS. What, am I cheated, Sir Frederick? Sirrah, I will have you hanged.

SIR FREDERICK. Speak, who is this widow?

PALMER. 'Tis Grace, sir, Wheadle's mistress, whom he has placed in my Lady Daubwell's house: I am but a poor instrument, abused by that rascal.

SIR FREDERICK. You see, Sir Nicholas, what villains these are; they have cheated you of a thousand pounds, and would have married you to a wench, had I not discovered their villainy.

SIR NICHOLAS. I am beholden to you, Sir Frederick; they are rogues, villainous rogues: but where is the widow?

SIR FREDERICK. Why, you saw the true widow here a little while ago.

SIR NICHOLAS. The truth is, methoughts she was something comelier than my mistress: but will not this widow marry me?

SIR FREDERICK. She is my mistress.

SIR NICHOLAS. I will have none of her then.

SIR FREDERICK. Well, I have discovered this cheat,

---

262 *This will not pass*: see note to II iii 81.
271 *contrivance*: plot.
279 *instrument*: agent employed by Wheadle.
282 *wench*: someone else's mistress.

kept you from marrying a wench, and will save you the thousand pounds too. Now, if you have a mind to marry, what think you of my sister? She is a plain brown girl, and has a good portion; but not out twenty thousand pounds: this offer proves I have a perfect kindness for you.

SIR NICHOLAS. I have heard she is a very fine gentlewoman; I will marry her forthwith, and be your brother-in-law.

SIR FREDERICK. Come then, I'll carry you where you may see her, and ask her consent. Palmer, you must along with us, and by the way assign this judgment to me. (*To the* FIDDLERS) Do you guard him, gentlemen.

SIR FREDERICK. Come, Sir Nicholas.

SIR NICHOLAS. How came I hither?

SIR FREDERICK. You will be satisfied in that hereafter.

PALMER. What cursed accident was this? what mischievous stars have the managing of my fortune? Here's a turn with all my heart, like an aftergame at Irish!

DUFOY. *Allons marchez*, shentelmen sheté; *marchez*: you make de mouthé of de honest shentelmen: begar you vil make de wry mouthé ven you be hangé.

Exeunt.

SCENE III

A garden.

Enter GRACIANA *and* LETITIA *severally;* LETITIA *with a nosegay in her hand.*

GRACIANA. Letitia, what hast thou been doing here?

---

298 *out*: more than.
306 *assign this judgment*: i.e. make him the payee.
314–15 *an aftergame at Irish*: 'Irish' was a card game resembling backgammon; but for 'aftergame' see note to IV iv 126.
316 *marchez*: onwards!
316 *sheté*: i.e. cheat.
317 *make de mouthé*: deride with a grimace.
s.d. *nosegay*: a bunch of sweet-smelling flowers.

LETITIA. Cropping the beauty of the youthful year.

GRACIANA. How innocently dost thou spend thy hours,
Selecting from the crowd the choicest flow'rs!
Where is thy mistress?

LETITIA. Madam, she's with the wounded colonel.

GRACIANA. Come then into this arbour, girl, and there
With thy sweet voice refresh my wearied soul.

They walk into an arbour.

LETITIA. (*sings*)

SONG

'Ladies, though to your conqu'ring eyes
Love owes his chiefest victories,
And borrows those bright arms from you
With which he does the world subdue,
Yet you yourselves are not above
The empire nor the griefs of love.

Then wrack not lovers with disdain,
Lest love on you revenge their pain;
You are not free because y'are fair;
The boy did not his mother spare.
Beauty's but an offensive dart;
It is no armour for the heart.'

GRACIANA. Dear girl, thou art my little confident;
I oft to thee have breathed my discontent;
And thy sweet voice as oft has eased my care;
But now thy breath is like infectious air;

Enter BEAUFORT.

It feeds the secret cause of my disease,
And does enrage what it did use t'appease.

BEAUFORT. (*starting*) Hark, that was Graciana's voice.

GRACIANA. Oh Beaufort!

BEAUFORT. She calls on me, and does advance this way;
I will conceal myself within this bow'r; she may
The secret causes of my grief betray.

---

18 *The boy did not his mother spare*: the boy is Cupid who wounded Venus with his arrow and caused her to fall in love with Adonis.

21 *confident*: i.e. confidante.

BEAUFORT *goes into an arbour, and* GRACIANA *and* LETITIA *come upon the stage.*

GRACIANA. Too rigidly my honour I pursue;
Sure something from me to my love is due:
Within these private shades for him I'll mourn,
Whom I in public am obliged to scorn.

LETITIA. Why should you, madam, thus indulge your grief?
Love never yet in sorrow found relief:
These sighs, like northern winds to th'early spring,
Destruction to your blooming beauty bring.

GRACIANA. Letitia, peace; my beauty I despise:
Would you have me preserve these fatal eyes?

LETITIA. Had you less beauteous been, y'ad known less care;
Ladies are happiest moderately fair:
But now should you your beauty waste, which way
Could you the debt it has contracted pay?

GRACIANA. Beaufort, didst thou but know I weep for thee,
Thou wouldst not blame my scorn, but pity me.

LETITIA. When honour first made you your love decline,
You from the centre drew a crooked line;
You were to Beaufort too severe, I fear,
Lest to your love you partial might appear.

GRACIANA. I did what I in honour ought to do;
I yet to Beaufort and my love am true;
And if his rival live, I'll be his bride,
Joy shall unite whom grief does now divide;
But if for love of me brave Bruce does die,
I am contracted to his memory.
Oh, Beaufort!

BEAUFORT. Oh, Graciana! here am I
(By what I've heard) fixed in an ecstasy.

GRACIANA. We are surprised; unlucky accident!
Fresh sorrow's added to my discontent.

---

42 *care*: sorrow.
44 *waste*: lay waste.
48 *decline*: deflect (from a straight course).
59 *ecstasy*: the state of being 'beside oneself' with astonishment.
60 *surprised*: taken by surprise, come upon unawares.

Exeunt GRACIANA *and* LETITIA *leisurely.*

BEAUFORT *enters.*

BEAUFORT. Graciana, stay, you can no more contend,
Since fortune joins with love to be my friend;
There is no fear of Bruce his death; the wound
By abler chir'geons is not mortal found.
She will not stay:
My joys, like waters swelled into a flood,
Bear down whate'er their usual streams withstood.

Exit BEAUFORT.

SCENE IV

My Lady Daubwell's house.

Enter WHEADLE *and* GRACE.

WHEADLE. I wonder we have yet no tidings of our knight, nor Palmer, – fortune still crosses the industrious, girl. When we recover him you must begin to lie at a little opener ward; 'tis dangerous keeping the fool too long at bay, lest some old woodman drop in by chance, and discover th'art but a rascal deer. I have counterfeited half a dozen mortgages, a dozen bonds, and two scriveners to vouch all; that will satisfy him in thy estate: he has sent into the country for his writings: but see, here he comes.

Enter SIR NICHOLAS.

Sir Nicholas, I must chide you, indeed I must; you neglect your duty here: nay, madam, never blush; faith I'll reveal all. Y'are the happiest, the luckiest man –

---

61 s.d. *leisurely*: at a slow pace.
64 *Bruce his death*: i.e. Bruce's death.
4 *lie at a little opener ward*: be less reserved.
5 *old woodman*: experienced huntsman.
6 *rascal deer*: young, lean or inferior deer of a herd.
8 *bonds*: deeds by which the signatory binds himself to make payment to another.
10 *writings*: financial documents (especially those relating to a marriage settlement).

Enter SIR FREDERICK.

W'are betrayed; death, what makes him here? (*To* SIR FREDERICK) Sir Frederick, your humble servant; y'are come in the luckiest time for mirth; will you but lend me your ear? do not you see Sir Nicholas and Grace yonder? look, look.

SIR FREDERICK. Yes.

WHEADLE. I am persuading him to keep her; she's a pretty deserving girl; faith let us draw off a while, and laugh among ourselves, for fear of spoiling the poor wench's market; let us, let us.

SIR FREDERICK. With all my heart.

BAILIFFS *meet* WHEADLE *at the door, and arrest him.*

BAILIFFS. We arrest you, sir.

WHEADLE. Arrest me? Sir Frederick, Sir Nicholas.

SIR FREDERICK. We are not provided for a rescue at present, sir.

WHEADLE. At whose suit?

BAILIFFS. At Sir Frederick Frollick's.

WHEADLE. Sir Frederick Frollick's? I owe him never a farthing.

SIR FREDERICK. Y'are mistaken, sir; you owe me a thousand pounds: look you, do you know Mr Palmer's hand? He has assigned such a small debt over to me.

Enter PALMER *and* JENNY.

WHEADLE. How was I bewitched to trust such a villain! Oh rogue, dog, coward, Palmer!

PALMER. Oh thou unconscionable Wheadle; a thousand pounds was too small a bubble!

SIR FREDERICK. Away with him, away with him.

WHEADLE. Nay, Sir Frederick, 'tis punishment enough to fall from my expectation: do not ruin a young man.

GRACE. I beseech you, sir.

SIR FREDERICK. Thou hast moved me, Grace; do not

---

15 *what makes him here?*: 'what brings him here?', or 'what is he doing here?'

24 *market*: business transaction.

28 *rescue*: the forcible taking of a person out of legal custody.

tremble, chuck; I love thy profession too well to harm thee. Look you, sir, what think you of a rich widow? (*Proffering him the whore*) Was there no lady to abuse, Wheadle, but my mistress? No man to bubble but your friend and patron, Sir Nicholas? But let this pass; Sir Nicholas is satisfied; take Grace here, marry her, we are all satisfied: she's a pretty deserving girl, and a fortune now in earnest; I'll give her a thousand pounds.

WHEADLE. Pray, sir, do but consider –

SIR FREDERICK. No consideration; dispatch, or to limbo.

WHEADLE. Was there ever such a dilemma? I shall rot in prison. Come hither, Grace; I did but make bold, like a young heir, with his estate, before it come into his hands: little did I think, Grace, that this pasty, (*Stroking her belly*) when we first cut it up, should have been preserved for my wedding feast.

SIR NICHOLAS. You are the happiest, the luckiest man, Mr Wheadle.

PALMER. Much joy, Mr Wheadle, with your rich widow.

WHEADLE. Sir Frederick, shall that rogue Palmer laugh at me?

SIR FREDERICK. No, no; Jenny, come hither; I'll make thee amends, as well as thy mistress, for the injury I did thee th'other night: here is a husband for thee too: Mr Palmer, where are you?

PALMER. Alas, Sir Frederick, I am not able to maintain her.

SIR FREDERICK. She shall maintain you, sir. Do not you understand the mystery of stipony, Jenny?

JENNY. I know how to make democuana, sir.

---

47 *chuck*: dearest.
58 *limbo*: prison.
77 *mystery*: art (or trade) of making.
77 *stipony*: a kind of raisin wine, made from raisins with lemon-juice and sugar added.
78 *democuana*: Brett-Smith printed a learned note from Dr Henry Bradley who believed the word to be 'an adoption of the Spanish *damajuana* = demijohn' and surmised 'that sailors may have brought the word from some Spanish country, transferring the application from the vessel to the liquor contained in it'.

SIR FREDERICK. Thou art richly endowed, i' faith: here, here, Palmer; no 'Shall I, shall I?'; this or that, which you deserve better.

PALMER. This is but a short reprieve; the gallows will be my destiny.

SIR FREDERICK. Sir Nicholas, now we must haste to a better solemnity; my sister expects us. Gentlemen, meet us at the Rose; I'll bestow a wedding dinner upon you, and there release your judgment, Mr Wheadle. Bailiffs, wait upon them thither.

SIR NICHOLAS. I wish you much joy with your fair brides, gentlemen.

WHEADLE. A pox on your assignment, Palmer.

PALMER. A pox on your rich widow, Wheadle: come, spouse, come.

Exeunt.

SCENE V

The Lord Bevill's house.

Enter LORD BEVILL, BRUCE *led in,* LOVIS, BEAUFORT, GRACIANA *and* AURELIA.

BRUCE. Graciana, I have lost my claim to you,
And now my heart's become Aurelia's due;
She all this while within her tender breast
The flame of love has carefully suppressed,
Courting for me, and striving to destroy
Her own contentment, to advance my joy.

AURELIA. I did no more than honour pressed me to;
I wish I'd wooed successfully for you.

BRUCE. You so excel in honour and in love,
You both my shame and admiration move.
Aurelia, here, accept that life from me,
Which heav'n so kindly has preserved for thee.

---

79 *endowed*: possessed of a dowry.
85 *solemnity*: celebration of nuptials.
91 *assignment*: i.e. having assigned the judgment to Sir Frederick.
4 *carefully*: (1) sorrowingly (2) painstakingly.

(*To* LORD BEVILL) My lord, I hope you will my choice allow,
And with your approbation seal our vow.

LORD BEVILL. In gen'rous minds this to the world will prove
That gratitude has pow'r to conquer love.
It were, brave man, impiety in me
Not to approve that which the heav'ns decree.

BRUCE. Graciana, on my gen'rous rival you
Must now bestow what to his merit's due.

GRACIANA. Since you recov'ring, Bruce, your claim decline,
To him with honour I my heart resign.

BEAUFORT. Such honour and such love as you have shown
Are not in the records of virtue known.
(*To* LORD BEVILL) My lord, you must assist us here once more;
The god of love does your consent implore.

LORD BEVILL. May love in you still feed your mutual fire. *Joining their hands.*

BEAUFORT. And may that flame but with our breaths expire.

LOVIS. My lord, our quarrel now is at an end;
You are not Bruce's rival, but his friend.

BEAUFORT. In this brave strife your friendship soared above
The active flames of our aspiring love.

BRUCE. Dear friend, thy merits fame cannot express.

LOVIS. They are rewarded in your happiness.

BRUCE. Come all into my arms before I rest;
Let's breathe our joys into each other's breast:
Thus mariners rejoice when winds decrease,
And falling waves seem wearied into peace.

Enter SIR FREDERICK *and* DUFOY *at one door, and the* WIDOW *and* BETTY *at another.*

SIR FREDERICK. Haste, Dufoy, perform what I commanded you.

---

13 *allow*: give your approval to.
21 *decline*: give up.
24 *records*: cf. note to Prologue, line 24.

DUFOY. I vil be ver quick begar; I am more den half de Mercurié. [*Exit* DUFOY.]

SIR FREDERICK. Ho, widow! the noise of these nuptials brought you hither; I perceive your mouth waters.

WIDOW. Were I in a longing condition I should be apt enough to put myself upon you, sir.

SIR FREDERICK. Nay, I know th'art spiteful, and wouldst fain marry me in revenge; but so long as I have these guardian angels about me, I defy thee and all thy charms; do skilful faulkners thus reward their hawks before they fly the quarry?

WIDOW. When your gorge is empty you'll come to the lure again.

SIR FREDERICK. After I have had a little more experience of the vanity of this world, in a melancholy humour I may be careless of myself.

WIDOW. And marry some distressed lady, that has had no less experience of that vanity.

SIR FREDERICK. Widow, I profess the contrary; I would not have the sin to answer for of debauching any from such worthy principles: let me see; if I should be good-natured now, and consent to give thee a title to thy own wealth again, you would be stubborn, and not esteem the favour, widow.

WIDOW. Is it possible you can have thoughts of gratitude? Do you imagine me so foolish as yourself, who often venture all at play, to recover one inconsiderable parcel?

SIR FREDERICK. I told you how 'twould be, widow: less providence attend thee, else I shall do no good upon thee: fare-well.

---

42 *Mercurié*: Mercury, the messenger of the Roman gods.
43 *noise*: report.
49 *wouldst fain*: are eager to.
50 *angels*: gold coins worth about ten shillings (the money the Widow had provided for his release).
51 *faulkners*: falconers.
52 *fly*: attack.
53 *gorge*: throat.
53–4 *come to the lure*: see note to *She Would*, I i 30–1.
69 *parcel*: small sum.
71 *less providence attend thee*: i.e. you will have to become less cautious.

WIDOW. Stay, sir; let us shake hands at parting.

SIR FREDERICK. Nay, if thou once art acquainted with my constitution, thou't never let me go; widow, here, examine, examine. (*Holding out his hand*)

LORD BEVILL. Sister, I long have known your inclinations; give me leave to serve you. Sir Frederick, here, take her; and may you make each other happy.

WIDOW. Now I have received you into my family, I hope you will let my maids go quietly about their business, sir.

SIR FREDERICK. Upon condition there be no twits of the good man departed; no prescription pleaded for evil customs on the wedding night. Widow, what old doings will be anon! I have coupled no less than a pair-royal myself. This day, my lord, I hope you'll excuse the liberty I have taken to send for them; the sight will much increase your mirth this joyful day.

LORD BEVILL. I should have blamed you, sir, if you had restrained your humour here. – These must needs be pleasant matches that are of his making.

Enter DUFOY.

SIR FREDERICK. What, are they come?

DUFOY. Day be all at de dooré, begar; every man vid his pret metres, brid, whore. *Entrez*, jentelmen, vid your lady, *entrez* vid your great fortune: ha, ha, ha.

Enter SIR NICHOLAS *and his* BRIDE, WHEADLE *and his* BRIDE, PALMER *and his* BRIDE.

SIR NICHOLAS. Brother, do you see how sneakingly Wheadle looks yonder, with his rich widow?

83–4 *twits of the good man departed*: taunting references to (or comparisons with) your late husband.

84 *prescription*: 'rules produced and authorised by long custom; custom continued till it has the force of law' (Johnson).

87 *pair-royal*: a set of three of the same kind.

87 *This day*: Brett-Smith emended to make this the conclusion of the preceding sentence. But it reads perfectly well as it stands; Sir Frederick means that the liberty he has taken will be excused because it is appropriate to this day of betrothals and festivity.

95 *Entrez*: enter.

WIDOW. Brother! is this fellow your brother?

SIR NICHOLAS. Ay, that I am.

SIR FREDERICK. No, no, Sir Nicholas.

SIR NICHOLAS. Did not I marry your sister, sir?

SIR FREDERICK. Fie, fie, Sir Nicholas; I thought y'ad been a modester man.

SIR NICHOLAS. Is my wife no kin to you, sir?

SIR FREDERICK. Not your wife; but your son and heir may, if it prove so. (*To* LUCY) Joy be with thee, old acquaintance. Widow, resolving to lead a virtuous life, and keep house altogether with thee, I have disposed of my own household-stuff, my dear Mrs Lucy, to this gentleman.

WHEADLE. } PALMER. } We wish you joy with your fair bride, Sir Nicholas.

SIR NICHOLAS. I will go and complain, and have you all clapped up for a plot immediately.

SIR FREDERICK. Hold, hold, Sir Nicholas; there are certain catchpoles without; you cannot scape, without y'ave a thousand pounds in your pocket: carry her into the country, come; your neighbours' wives will visit her, and vow she's a virtuous well-bred lady: and, give her her due, faith she was a very honest wench to me, and I believe will make a very honest wife to you.

SIR NICHOLAS. If I discover this I am lost; I shall be ridiculous, even to our own party.

SIR FREDERICK. You are in the right: come, take her, make much of her, she shall save you a thousand pounds.

SIR NICHOLAS. Well, Lucy, if thou canst but deceive my old mother, and my neighbours in the country, I shall bear my fortune patiently.

SIR FREDERICK. I'll warrant you, sir, women so skilled in vice can dissemble virtue.

---

109 *altogether*: uninterruptedly, without deviation.
110 *household-stuff*: household-furnishings.
115 *clapped up*: arrested.
115 *for a plot*: see note to II iii 137.
117 *catchpoles*: sheriff's officers who arrest for debt.

DUFOY. Fy, fy, maké de much of your lady, shentelmen; begar you vil find dem ver civil.

SIR FREDERICK. Dufoy, I had almost forgot thee.

DUFOY. Begar my merit is ver seldome in your memorié.

SIR FREDERICK. Now I will reward thy services; here, enjoy thy mistress.

DUFOY. Ver vel, begar; you vill give me two tree oldé gowné vor all my diligence.

BETTY. Marry come up! Is that a despicable portion for your greasy pantaloons?

DUFOY. Peace, peace, Metres Bett; ve vil be ver good friend upon occasion; but ve vil no marrié: dat be ver much beter, begar.

SIR FREDERICK. Did you bring the bailiffs with you?

DUFOY. Day be vidout: begar, shentelmen, you have bin made ver sad; and now you shall be made ver mer vid de fidler.

WHEADLE. Ha! cozened with fiddlers for bailiffs! I durst have sworn false dice might as soon have passed upon me.

SIR FREDERICK. Bid them strike up; we will have a dance. Widow, to divert these melancholy gentlemen.

They dance.

LORD BEVILL. (*after the dance*)
Sir Frederick, you shall command my house this day;
Make all those welcome that are pleased to stay.

SIR FREDERICK. Sir Nicholas, and Mr Wheadle, I release you both of your judgment, and will give it you under my hand at any time. Widow, for all these bloody preparations, there will be no great massacre of maidenheads among us here. Anon I will make you all laugh with the occasion of these weddings.
On what small accidents depends our fate,
Whilst chance, not prudence, makes us fortunate.

[*Exeunt.*]

---

140 *vill*: 'will' (*1664a*); 'vill' (*1664b*). The latter seeming apter to Dufoy's speech-habits, I have followed Brett-Smith's precedent in adopting it.

142 *Marry come up*: a phrase expressing indignation or amused surprise or contempt.

143 *pantaloons*: see Additional Note.

155 *Widow, to divert these melancholy gentlemen*: he is inviting her to dance.

163 *the occasion of*: i.e. what occasioned.

EPILOGUE

Spoke by the WIDOW.

Sir Fred'rick, now I am revenged on you;
For all your frolic wit, y'are cozened too:
I have made over all my wealth to these
Honest gentlemen; they are my trustees.
Yet, gentlemen, if you are pleased, you may
Supply his wants, and not your trust betray.

Spoke by WHEADLE.

Poor Wheadle hopes h'as gi'n you all content;
Here he protests 'tis that he only meant:
If y'are displeased w'are all crossbit today,
And he has wheedled us that writ the play.

EPILOGUE

Like pris'ners, conscious of th'offended law,
When juries after th'evidence withdraw;
So waits our author between hope and fear,
Until he does your doubtful verdict hear.
Men are more civil than in former days;
Few now in public hiss or rail at plays;
He bid me therefore mind your looks with care,
And told me I should read your sentence there;
But I, unskilled in faces, cannot guess
By this first view, what is the play's success;
Nor shall I ease the author of his fear,
Till twice or thrice, at least, I've seen you here.

5 *gentlemen*: of the audience.
9 *crossbit*: deceived, gulled.
1 *conscious*: guiltily aware.
4 *doubtful*: (1) as yet in doubt (2) to be feared.

SHE WOULD IF SHE COULD

INTRODUCTORY NOTE

As was the case with *The Comical Revenge*, no definite source has been established for any part of the play.

Its first performance (again by the Duke's Company at the theatre in Lincoln's Inn Fields) was on 6 February 1668. Downes (pp. 28–9) once more provides a cast-list and a comment: '*Courtall*, Acted by Mr. *Smith*: *Freeman*, Mr. *Young*: Sir *Joslin*, Mr. *Harris*: Sir *Oliver*, Mr. *Nokes*: *Ariana*, Mrs. *Jenning*: *Gatty*, Mrs. *Davies*: Lady *Cockwood*, Mrs. *Shadwell*. It took well, but Inferior to Love in a Tub.'

Pepys described the first performance:

my wife being gone before, I to the Duke of York's playhouse, where a new play of Etheriges called *She would if she could*. And though I was there by 2 a-clock, there was 1000 people put back that could not have room in the pit; and I at last, because my wife was there, made shift to get into the 18*d* box – and there saw; but Lord, how full was the house and how silly the play, there being nothing in the world good in it and few people pleased in it. The King was there; but I sat mightily behind, and could see but little and hear not all. The play being done, I into the pit to look my wife; . . . and among the rest, here was the Duke of Buckingham today openly sat in the pit; and there I found him with my Lord Buckhurst and Sidly and Etherige the poett – the last of whom I did hear mightily find fault with the Actors, that they were out of humour and had not their parts perfect, and that Harris did do nothing, nor could so much as sing a Ketch in it, and so was mightily concerned: while all the rest did through the whole pit blame the play as a silly, dull thing, though there was something very roguish and witty; but the design of the play, and end, mighty insipid.

In the preface to *The Humorists* (1671), Thomas Shadwell offered a higher estimate of the play and further comment on that first performance:

The last (*viz.*) imperfect Action, had like to have destroy'd *She would if she could*, which I think (and I have the Authority of some of the best Judges in *England* for't) is the best Comedy that has been written since the Restauration of the Stage: And even that, for the imperfect representation of it at first, received such prejudice, that, had it not been for the favour of the *Court*, in all probability it had never got up again, and it suffers for it; in a great measure to this very day (*Complete*

Works, ed. Montague Summers (London, The Fortune Press, 1927), vol. 1, p. 183).

Though never as popular as its predecessor, the play did not lack for performances. Its last recorded eighteenth-century appearance was on 7 January 1751. It has had some attention from amateurs in modern times (including a production co-directed by the present editor at York Arts Centre in March 1976), but it has still to find the professional director and cast who can give it the kind of performance its merits deserve. A production by Jonathan Miller at the Greenwich Theatre, London, in April 1979 fell sadly short on all counts.

Its first appearance in print was in 1668, and there were subsequent quartos in 1671, 1693, 1710 and *c.* 1711.

DRAMATIS PERSONAE

SIR OLIVER COCKWOOD and SIR JOSLIN JOLLY } two country knights

MR COURTALL and MR FREEMAN } two honest gentlemen of the town

My LADY COCKWOOD

ARIANA and GATTY } two young ladies, kinswomen of Sir Joslin Jolly's

MRS SENTRY, my Lady Cockwood's gentlewoman

MRS GAZETTE and MRS TRINKET } two Exchange-women

MR RAKEHELL, a knight of the industry

THOMAS, Sir Oliver Cockwood's man

A SERVANT belonging to Mr Courtall

WAITERS, FIDDLERS and other ATTENDANTS

---

5 *honest*: (1) holding an honourable position, but also (2) possessing those qualities (of wit, good manners, easy politeness, etc.) necessary for social relations (cf. the French concepts of *l'honnêteté* and *l'honnête homme* and the definitions of them cited by John G. Hayman, 'Dorimant and the comedy of a man of mode', *Modern Language Quarterly*, 30 (1969), 185–97).

10 *Gatty*: an abbreviation of Gertrude.

15 *knight of the industry*: cf. the French *chevalier d'industrie*, one who lives by his wits, a sharper.

SHE WOULD IF SHE COULD: A COMEDY

ACT I

SCENE I

A dining-room.

Enter COURTALL *and* FREEMAN, *and a* SERVANT *brushing* COURTALL.

COURTALL. So, so, 'tis well: let the coach be made ready.

SERVANT. It shall, sir. *Exit* SERVANT.

COURTALL. Well, Frank, what is to be done today?

FREEMAN. Faith, I think we must e'en follow the old trade; eat well, and prepare ourselves with a bottle or two of good Burgundy, that our old acquaintance may look lovely in our eyes; for, for ought as I see, there is no hopes of new.

COURTALL. Well! this is grown a wicked town, it was otherwise in my memory; a gentleman should not have gone out of his chamber, but some civil officer or other of the game would have been with him, and have given him notice where he might have had a course or two in the afternoon.

FREEMAN. Truly a good motherly woman of my acquaintance t'other day, talking of the sins of the times, told me, with tears in her eyes, that there are a company of higgling rascals, who partly for themselves, but more especially for some secret friends,

---

6 *trade*: manner of life, habitual course of action.

12 *civil*: see note to *Comical Revenge*, I ii 62 (in addition, 'civil officer', i.e. 'a civilian soldier', is presumably a deliberate oxymoron).

12–13 *officer . . . of the game*: pimp.

15 *course*: hunt, chase, gallop.

16 *motherly*: Freeman is playing on the seventeenth-century slang meaning of 'mother', 'a female bawd'.

19 *higgling*: haggling.

19 *rascals*: low fellows (in contrast to the 'gentlemen' later in the sentence); see note to *Comical Revenge*, I ii 103.

daily forestall the markets; nay, and that many gentlemen who formerly had been persons of great worth and honour, are of late, for some private reasons, become their own purveyors, to the utter decay and disencouragement of trade and industry.

COURTALL. I know there are some wary merchants, who never trust their business to a factor; but for my part, I hate the fatigue, and had rather be bound to back my own colts, and man my own hawks, than endure the impertinencies of bringing a young wench to the lure.

Enter SERVANT.

SERVANT. Sir, there is a gentlewoman below desires to speak with you.

COURTALL. Ha, Freeman, this may be some lucky adventure.

SERVANT. She asked me, if you were alone.

COURTALL. And did not you say ay?

SERVANT. I told her, I would go see.

COURTALL. Go, go down quickly, and tell her I am. [*Exit* SERVANT.] Frank, prithee let me put thee into this closet a while.

FREEMAN. Why, may not I see her?

COURTALL. On my life thou shalt have fair play, and go halfs, if it be a purchase that may with honour be divided; you may overhear all: but for decency sake, in, in man.

FREEMAN. Well, good fortune attend thee.

[*Exit* FREEMAN.]

---

21 *forestall the markets*: anticipate or prevent sales at the public markets by buying the goods beforehand.

24 *purveyors*: (another trading term) one who supplies or procures something for another.

27 *factor*: a merchant's agent, one who buys or sells for another.

28 *fatigue*: wearying labour, 'trouble'.

29 *back*: tame, break.

29 *man*: accustom them to the presence of men, hence render them tame and tractable.

30–1 *bringing . . . to the lure*: a lure is an apparatus containing food used by falconers to recall their hawks; hence, 'bringing to the lure' means 'training the hawks to respond to such enticement'.

41 *closet*: see note to *Comical Revenge*, V ii 172.

44 *purchase*: prize, booty.

Enter MRS SENTRY.

COURTALL. Mrs Sentry, this is a happiness beyond my expectation.

SENTRY. Your humble servant, sir.

COURTALL. I hope your lady's come to town?

SENTRY. Sir Oliver, my lady, and the whole family: well! we have had a sad time in the country; my lady's so glad she's come to enjoy the freedom of this place again, and I dare say longs to have the happiness of your company.

COURTALL. Did she send you hither?

SENTRY. Oh no, if she should but know that I did such a confident trick, she would think me a good one i'faith; the zeal I have to serve you, made me venture to call in my way to the Exchange, to tell you the good news, and to let you know our lodgings are in James Street at the Black Posts, where we lay the last summer.

COURTALL. Indeed it is very obligingly done.

SENTRY. But I must needs desire you to tell my lady, that you came to the knowledge of this by some lucky chance or other; for I would not be discovered for a world.

COURTALL. Let me alone, I warrant thee.

Enter SERVANT.

SERVANT. Sir Oliver Cockwood, sir, is come to wait on you.

SENTRY. Oh heaven! my master! my lady, and myself are both undone, undone –

COURTALL. 'Sdeath, why did you not tell him I was busy?

---

52 *family*: household; cf. II ii 161.

59 *confident*: presumptuous.

63 *James Street*: Brett-Smith quotes an almost contemporary description of it as 'a spacious street, with very good houses, well inhabited by gentry' and notes that Waller, the poet so favoured by Etherege's Dorimant, had a house there from 1660 until his death in 1687.

63 *lay*: lodged.

70 *Let me alone*: You can rely on me.

75 *'Sdeath*: an oath, an abbreviation of 'God's death'.

SENTRY. For heaven's sake, Mr Courtall, what shall I do?

COURTALL. Leave, leave trembling, and creep into the wood-hole here.

She goes into the wood-hole.

Enter SIR OLIVER.

COURTALL. Sir Oliver Cockwood! (*Embraces him*)

SIR OLIVER. Honest Ned Courtall, by my troth I think thou tak'st me for a pretty wench, thou hug'st me so very close and heartily.

COURTALL. Only my joy to see you, Sir Oliver, and to welcome you to town.

SIR OLIVER. Methinks, indeed, I have been an age absent, but I intend to redeem the time; and how, and how stand affairs, prithee now? is the wine good? are the women kind? Well, faith, a man had better be a vagabond in this town, than a justice of peace in the country: I was e'en grown a sot for want of gentleman-like recreations; if a man do but rap out an oath, the people start as if a gun went off; and if one chance but to couple himself with his neighbour's daughter, without the help of the parson of the parish, and leave a little testimony of his kindness behind him, there is presently such an uproar, that a poor man is fain to fly his country: as for drunkenness, 'tis true, it may be used without scandal, but the drink is so abominable, that a man would forbear it, for fear of being made out of love with the vice.

COURTALL. I see, Sir Oliver, you continue still your

---

80 *wood-hole*: a covered recess for the storage of firewood.

88 *to redeem the time*: to make amends for wasted time. The phrase is biblical in origin (Ephesians 5, verse 16: 'Redeeming the time, because the days are evil'), but it was often used (as here) in decidedly profane contexts.

89 *affairs*: throughout the comedy play is made with two meanings of the word – (1) matters of professional and public concern (2) amorous intrigues.

91 *vagabond*: vagrant, itinerant beggar.

98 *presently*: immediately.

99 *fain*: obliged.

99 *country*: neighbourhood, district.

old humour, and are resolved to break your sweet lady's heart.

SIR OLIVER. You do not think me sure so barbarously unkind, to let her know all this; no, no, these are secrets fit only to be trusted to such honest fellows as thou art.

COURTALL. Well may I, poor sinner, be excused, since a woman of such rare beauty, such incomparable parts, and of such an unblemished reputation, is not able to reclaim you from these wild courses, Sir Oliver.

SIR OLIVER. To say the truth, she is a wife that no man need be ashamed of, Ned.

COURTALL. I vow, Sir Oliver, I must needs blame you, considering how tenderly she loves you.

SIR OLIVER. Ay, ay, the more is her misfortune, and mine too Ned: I would willingly give thee a pair of the best coach-horses in my stable, so thou couldst but persuade her to love me less.

COURTALL. Her virtue and my friendship sufficiently secure you against that, Sir Oliver.

SIR OLIVER. I know thou wert never married; but has it never been thy misfortune to have a mistress love thee thus entirely?

COURTALL. It never has been my good fortune, Sir Oliver. But why do you ask this question?

SIR OLIVER. Because then, perchance, thou might'st have been a little sensible what a damned trouble it is.

COURTALL. As how, Sir Oliver?

SIR OLIVER. Why look thee thus: for a man cannot be altogether ungrateful, sometimes one is obliged to kiss, and fawn, and toy, and lie fooling an hour or two, when a man had rather, if it were not for the disgrace sake, stand all that while in the pillory paulted with rotten eggs and oranges.

COURTALL. This is a very hard case indeed, Sir Oliver.

---

104 *humour*: mood, temper.
107 *unkind*: certainly, lacking in kindness; but perhaps also, unnatural.
131 *sensible*: aware of, conscious of.
135 *toy*: indulge in amorous play.
138 *paulted*: pelted.

SIR OLIVER. And then the inconvenience of keeping regular hours; but above all, that damned fiend jealousy does so possess these passionate lovers, that I protest, Ned, under the rose be it spoken, if I chance to be a little prodigal in my expense on a private friend or so, I am called to so strict an account at night, that for quietness' sake I am often forced to take a dose of cantharides to make up the sum.

COURTALL. Indeed, Sir Oliver, everything considered, you are not so much to be envied as one may rashly imagine.

SIR OLIVER. Well, a pox of this tying man and woman together, for better, for worse! upon my conscience it was but a trick that the clergy might have a feeling in the cause.

COURTALL. I do not conceive it to be much for their profit, Sir Oliver, for I dare lay a good wager, let 'em but allow Christian liberty, and they shall get ten times more by christenings, than they are likely to lose by marriages.

SIR OLIVER. Faith, thou hast hit it right, Ned; and now thou talk'st of Christian liberty, prithee let us dine together today, and be swingingly merry, but with all secrecy.

COURTALL. I shall be glad of your good company, Sir Oliver.

SIR OLIVER. I am to call on a very honest fellow, whom I left here hard by making a visit, Sir Joslin Jolly, a kinsman of my wife's, and my neighbour in the country; we call brothers, he came up to town with me, and lodgeth in the same house; he has brought up a couple of the prettiest kinswomen, heiresses of a very good fortune: would thou hadst the instructing of 'em a little; faith, if I am not very

---

143 *under the rose*: i.e. *sub rosa*, in confidence.

147 *cantharides*: Spanish Fly, believed to be an aphrodisiac.

154–5 *a feeling in the cause*: some profit from the proceedings ('cause' being used in the sense of 'affair, business'). 'Feeling', however, suggests that the profits aspired to are as much sexual as financial.

158 *Christian liberty*: see Additional Note.

163 *swingingly*: hugely, immensely.

much mistaken, they are very prone to the study of the mathematics.

COURTALL. I shall be beholding to you for so good an acquaintance.

SIR OLIVER. This Sir Joslin is in great favour with my lady, one that she has an admirable good opinion of, and will trust me with him anywhere; but to say truth, he is as arrant a sinner as the best of us, and will boggle at nothing that becomes a man of honour. We will go and get leave of my lady; for it is not fit I should break out so soon without her approbation, Ned.

COURTALL. By no means, Sir Oliver.

SIR OLIVER. Where shall we meet about an hour hence?

COURTALL. At the French house or the Bear.

SIR OLIVER. At the French house by all means.

COURTALL. Agreed, agreed.

SIR OLIVER. Would thou couldst bring a fourth man.

COURTALL. What think you of Frank Freeman?

SIR OLIVER. There cannot be a better – well – servant, Ned, servant, Ned! *Exit* SIR OLIVER.

COURTALL. Your servant, Sir Oliver. Mrs Sentry!

SENTRY. (*in the hole*) Is he gone?

COURTALL. Ay, ay! you may venture to bolt now.

SENTRY. (*crawling out*) Oh heavens! I would not endure such another fright.

COURTALL. Come, come, prithee be composed.

SENTRY. I shall not be myself again this fortnight; I

---

176 *mathematics*: 'the particular branch of this science which Sir Oliver had in mind was, no doubt, Multiplication' (Brett-Smith) – a fact which alerts us to Sir Oliver's punning use of the word 'prone'.

182 *arrant*: downright, unmitigated.

183 *boggle at*: hesitate to commit.

189 *French house*: presumably Chatelin's, a well-known eating-house in Covent Garden.

189 *the Bear*: another famous eating-house, in Drury Lane. Pepys (18 February 1668) described it as 'an excellent ordinary after the French manner, but of Englishmen'.

never was in such a taking all the days of my life. To have been found false, and to one who to say truth, has been always very kind and civil to me; but above all, I was concerned for my lady's honour –

COURTALL. Come, come – there's no harm done.

SENTRY. Ah! Mr Courtall, you do not know Sir Oliver so well as I do, he has strange humours sometimes, and has it enough in's nature to play the tyrant, but that my lady and myself awe him by our policy.

COURTALL. Well, well, all's well; did you not hear what a tearing blade Sir Oliver is?

SENTRY. Ah! 'tis a vile dissembling man; how fairly he carries it to my lady's face! but I dare not discover him for fear of betraying myself.

COURTALL. Well, Mrs Sentry, I must dine with 'em, and after I have entered them with a beer-glass or two, if I can I will slip away, and pay my respects to your lady.

SENTRY. You need not question your welcome, I assure you, sir – your servant, sir.

COURTALL. Your servant, Mrs Sentry, I am very sensible of this favour, I assure you.

SENTRY. I am proud it was in my power to oblige you, sir. *Exit* SENTRY.

COURTALL. Freeman! come, come out of thy hole; [*Enter* FREEMAN] how hast thou been able to contain?

FREEMAN. Faith much ado, the scene was very pleasant; but above all, I admire thy impudence, I

---

203 *taking*: disturbed or agitated state of mind.
203 *all the days of my life*: 'days of my life' (*1668*). The version printed here was also preferred by the early eighteenth-century editions and by Verity and Brett-Smith; although one modern edition (Davison) has adhered to the *1668* version, some addition on these lines seems indispensable to reclaim the sense.
209 *humours*: temporary states of mind.
211 *policy*: cunning contrivance.
213 *tearing blade*: roistering, swaggering gallant.
214–15 *how fairly he carries it*: how unblemished and gentle is his behaviour.
218 *entered them*: started them drinking.
231 *admire*: am astonished by, view with wonder.

could never have had the face to have wheedled the poor knight so.

COURTALL. Pish, pish, 'twas both necessary and honest; we ought to do all we can to confirm a husband in the good opinion of his wife.

FREEMAN. Pray how long, if without offence a man may ask you, have you been in good grace with this person of honour? I never knew you had that commendable quality of secrecy before.

COURTALL. You are mistaken, Freeman, things go not as you wickedly imagine.

FREEMAN. Why, hast thou lost all sense of modesty? Dost thou think to pass these gross wheedles on me too? come, come, this good news should make thee a little merrier: faith, though she be an old acquaintance, she has the advantage of four or five months' absence. 'Slid, I know not how proud you are, but I have thought myself very spruce ere now in an old suit, that has been brushed and laid up a while.

COURTALL. Freeman, I know in cases of this nature thou art an infidel; but yet methinks the knowledge thou hast of my sincere dealing with my friends should make thee a little more confiding.

FREEMAN. What devilish oath could she invent to fright thee from a discovery?

COURTALL. Wilt thou believe me if I swear, the preservation of her honour has been my fault, and not hers?

FREEMAN. This is something.

COURTALL. Why then, know that I have still been as careful to prevent all opportunities, as she has been to contrive 'em; and still have carried it so like a gentleman, that she has not had the least suspicion of

---

232 *wheedled*: coaxed, cajoled (but with a strong overtone of trickery, see note to *Comical Revenge*, I ii 172).
236 *the good opinion of his wife*: the good opinion which he has of his wife.
252 *infidel*: unbeliever, sceptic.
254 *confiding*: trusting.
256 *discovery*: revelation.
260 *This is something*: i.e. remarkable, difficult to credit.
264 *that she has*: 'that there has' (*1668*). This was emended to 'that she has' in *1693*, and this version has, as here, been preferred by editors from Verity onwards.

unkindness: she is the very spirit of impertinence, so foolishly fond and troublesome, that no man above sixteen is able to endure her.

FREEMAN. Why did you engage thus far then?

COURTALL. Some conveniences which I had by my acquaintance with the sot her husband, made me extraordinary civil to her, which presently by her ladyship was interpreted after the manner of the most obliging women: this wench came hither by her commission today.

FREEMAN. With what confidence she denied it!

COURTALL. Nay, that's never wanting, I assure you; now is it expected I should lay by all other occasions, and watch every opportunity to wait upon her; she would by her good will give her lover no more rest, than a young squire that has newly set up a coach, does his only pair of horses.

FREEMAN. Faith, if it be as thou say'st, I cannot much blame the hardness of thy heart: but did not the oaf talk of two young ladies?

COURTALL. Well remembered, Frank, and now I think on't, 'twill be very necessary to carry on my business with the old one, that we may the better have an opportunity of being acquainted with them. Come, let us go and bespeak dinner, and by the way consider of these weighty affairs.

FREEMAN. Well, since there is but little ready money stirring, rather than want entertainment, I shall be contented to play a while upon tick.

COURTALL. And I, provided they promise fair, and we find there's hopes of payment hereafter.

FREEMAN. Come along, come along.

Exeunt.

---

265 *impertinence*: see Additional Note.
277 *lay by all other occasions*: set aside all other commitments.
279 *by her good will*: with her consent.
293 *tick*: cf. note to *Comical Revenge*, II iii 89.
294 *promise fair*: give us grounds for hope.

SCENE II

Sir Oliver Cockwood's lodging.

Enter LADY COCKWOOD.

LADY COCKWOOD. 'Tis too late to repent: I sent her, but yet I cannot but be troubled to think she stays so long; sure if she has so little gratitude to let him, he has more honour than to attempt anything to the prejudice of my affection – oh – Sentry, are you come?

Enter SENTRY.

SENTRY. Oh madam! there has been such an accident!

LADY COCKWOOD. Prithee do not fright me, wench –

SENTRY. As I was discoursing with Mr Courtall, in came Sir Oliver.

LADY COCKWOOD. Oh! – I'm ruined – undone for ever!

SENTRY. You'll still be sending me on these desperate errands.

LADY COCKWOOD. I am betrayed, betrayed – by this false – what shall I call thee?

SENTRY. Nay, but madam – have a little patience –

LADY COCKWOOD. I have lost all patience, and will never more have any –

SENTRY. Do but hear me, all is well –

LADY COCKWOOD. Nothing can be well, unfortunate woman.

SENTRY. Mr Courtall thrust me into the wood-hole.

LADY COCKWOOD. And did not Sir Oliver see thee?

SENTRY. He had not the least glimpse of me –

LADY COCKWOOD. Dear Sentry – and what good news?

SENTRY. He intends to wait upon you in the afternoon, madam –

LADY COCKWOOD. I hope you did not let him know I sent you.

4–5 *to the prejudice of my affection*: i.e. which would prejudice my affection for him.

13 *desperate*: reckless, involving serious risk.

SENTRY. No, no, madam – I'll warrant you I did everything much to the advantage of your honour.

LADY COCKWOOD. Ah Sentry! if we could but think of some lucky plot now to get Sir Oliver out of the way.

SENTRY. You need not trouble yourself about that, madam, he has engaged to dine with Mr Courtall at the French house, and is bringing Sir Joslin Jolly to get your good will; when Mr Courtall has fixed 'em with a beer-glass or two, he intends to steal away, and pay his devotion to your ladyship.

LADY COCKWOOD. Truly he is a person of much worth and honour.

SENTRY. Had you but been there, madam, to have overheard Sir Oliver's discourse, he would have made you bless yourself; there is not such another wild man in the town; all his talk was of wenching, and swearing, and drinking, and tearing.

LADY COCKWOOD. Ay, ay, Sentry, I know he'll talk of strange matters behind my back; but if he be not an abominable hypocrite at home, and I am not a woman easily to be deceived, he is not able to play the spark abroad thus, I assure you.

Enter SIR OLIVER, *and* SIR JOSLIN, SIR JOSLIN *singing.*

My dearest dear, this is kindly done of thee to come home again thus quickly.

SIR OLIVER. Nay, my dear, thou shalt never have any just cause to accuse me of unkindness.

LADY COCKWOOD. Sir Joslin, now you are a good man, and I shall trust you with Sir Oliver again.

SIR JOSLIN. Nay, if I ever break my word with a lady, I will be delivered bound to Mrs Sentry here, and she shall have leave to carve me for a capon.

SENTRY. Do you think I have a heart cruel enough for such a bloody execution?

---

47 *wild man*: see Additional Note.

54 *spark*: gallant.

54 *abroad*: away from home (cf. line 84).

63 *carve me for a capon*: castrate me, 'a capon' being 'a castrated cock'.

65 *such a . . . execution*: the carrying out of such a deed.

SIR JOSLIN. Kindly spoke i'faith, girl, I'll give thee a buss for that. (*Kisses her*)

LADY COCKWOOD. Fie, fie, Sir Joslin, this is not seemly in my presence.

SIR JOSLIN. We have all our failings, lady, and this is mine: a right bred greyhound can as well forbear running after a hare when he sees her, as I can mumbling a pretty wench when she comes in my way.

LADY COCKWOOD. I have heard indeed you are a parlous man, Sir Joslin.

SIR JOSLIN. I seldom brag, lady, but for a true cock of the game, little Joslin dares match with the best of 'em.

SIR OLIVER. Sir Joslin's merry, my dear.

LADY COCKWOOD. Ay, ay, if he should be wicked, I know thou art too much a gentleman to offer an injury to thine own dear lady.

SIR JOSLIN. Faith, madam, you must give my brother Cockwood leave to dine abroad today.

LADY COCKWOOD. I protest, Sir Joslin, you begin to make me hate you too; well, you are e'en grown as bad as the worst of 'em, you are still robbing me of the sweet society of Sir Oliver.

SIR JOSLIN. Come, come, your discipline is too severe, i'faith lady.

LADY COCKWOOD. Sir Oliver may do what he pleases, sir, he knows I have ever been his obedient lady.

SIR OLIVER. Prithee, my dear, be not angry, Sir Joseph was so earnest in his invitation, that none but a clown could have refused him.

SIR JOSLIN. Ay, ay, we dine at my uncle Sir Joseph Jolly's, lady.

LADY COCKWOOD. Will you be sure now to be a good dear, and not drink, nor stay out late?

---

67 *buss*: kiss.
73 *mumbling*: fondling with the lips.
75 *parlous*: risky to deal with.
76–7 *cock of the game*: a cock of the breed used in cock-fighting; therefore, ready for anything.
77 *match*: contend with, meet in combat with.
88 *society*: companionship.
94 *clown*: peasant, boor.

SIR JOSLIN. I'll engage for all, and if there be no harm in a merry catch or a waggish story –

Enter ARIANA *and* MRS GATTY.

Ha, ha! Sly-girl and Mad-cap, are you got up? I know what you have been meditating on; but never trouble your heads, let me alone to bring you consolation.

GATTY. We have often been beholding to you, sir; for every time he's drunk, he brings us home a couple of fresh servants.

SIR OLIVER. Well, farewell my dear, prithee do not sigh thus, but make thee ready, visit, and be merry.

LADY COCKWOOD. I shall receive most satisfaction in my chamber.

SIR JOSLIN. Come, come along, brother: farewell one and all, lady and Sly-girl, Sly-girl and Mad-cap, your servant, your servant –

Exeunt SIR OLIVER *and* SIR JOSLIN *singing.*

LADY COCKWOOD. (*to* SENTRY *aside*) Sentry, is the new point I bought come home, and is everything in a readiness?

SENTRY. Everything, madam.

LADY COCKWOOD. Come, come up quickly then, girl, and dress me.

Exeunt LADY COCKWOOD *and* SENTRY.

ARIANA. Dost not thou wonder, Gatty, she should be so strangely fond of this coxcomb?

GATTY. Well, if she does not dissemble, may I still be discovered when I do; didst thou not see how her countenance changed, as soon as ever their backs were turned, and how earnestly she whispered with her woman? there is some weighty affair in hand, I warrant thee: my dear Ariana, how glad am I we are in this town again.

ARIANA. But we have left the benefit of the fresh air, and the delight of wandering in the pleasant groves.

GATTY. Very pretty things for a young gentlewoman

---

101 *catch*: see note to *Comical Revenge*, II iii 128.
107 *servants*: gallants, lovers.
116 *point*: a piece of thread lace (made wholly with a needle) used as a kerchief or the like.

to bemoan the loss of indeed, that's newly come to a relish of the good things of this world.

ARIANA. Very good, sister!

GATTY. Why, hast not thou promised me a thousand times, to leave off this demureness?

ARIANA. But you are so quick.

GATTY. Why, would it not make anyone mad to hear thee bewail the loss of the country? speak but one grave word more, and it shall be my daily prayers thou may'st have a jealous husband, and then you'll have enough of it I warrant you.

ARIANA. It may be, if your tongue be not altogether so nimble, I may be conformable; but I hope you do not intend we shall play such mad reaks as we did last summer?

GATTY. 'Slife, dost thou think we come here to be mewed up, and take only the liberty of going from our chamber to the dining-room, and from the dining-room to our chamber again? and like a bird in a cage, with two perches only, to hop up and down, up and down?

ARIANA. Well, thou art a mad wench.

GATTY. Wouldst thou never have us go to a play but with our grave relations, never take the air but with our grave relations? to feed their pride, and make the world believe it is in their power to afford some gallant or other a good bargain?

ARIANA. But I am afraid we shall be known again.

GATTY. Pish! the men were only acquainted with our

---

134 *relish of*: liking for.
137 *demureness*: gravity, reservedness.
138 *quick*: hasty, impetuous.
142 *jealous husband*: the assumption being that a jealous husband would be anxious to deny his wife contact with the freer ways of life in the capital and would spirit her away to the more conservative and isolated world of the country.
145 *conformable*: tractable, compliant.
146 *reaks*: pranks.
149 *mewed up*: confined, cooped up (used of birds, see line 151).
154 *mad*: impulsive, reckless; cf. Sir Joslin's nickname of 'Madcap' for Gatty.

vizards and our petticoats, and they are wore out long since: how I envy that sex! well! we cannot plague 'em enough when we have it in our power for those privileges which custom has allowed 'em above us.

ARIANA. The truth is, they can run and ramble here, and there, and everywhere, and we poor fools rather think the better of 'em.

GATTY. From one playhouse, to the other playhouse, and if they like neither the play nor the women, they seldom stay any longer than the combing of their periwigs, or a whisper or two with a friend; and then they cock their caps, and out they strut again.

ARIANA. But whatsoever we do, prithee now let us resolve to be mighty honest.

GATTY. There I agree with thee.

ARIANA. And if we find the gallants like lawless subjects, who the more their princes grant, the more they impudently crave –

GATTY. We'll become absolute tyrants, and deprive 'em of all the privileges we gave 'em –

ARIANA. Upon these conditions I am contented to trail a pike under thee – march along girl.

Exeunt.

---

162 *vizards*: masks.

162 *petticoats*: women's skirts were usually open in front, showing the petticoat or under-skirt; the latter were often richly decorated.

166 *ramble*: see note to *Comical Revenge*, I ii 129.

171–2 *combing of their periwigs*: see Additional Note.

173 *cock their caps*: a fashionable knack, in the intricacies of which Rakehell begins to instruct Sir Oliver, III iii 154–5. Pepys (3 June 1667) notes seeing 'a brisk young fellow (with his hat cocked like a fool behind, as the present fashion among the blades is)'.

175 *honest*: respectable.

182–3 *trail a pike*: serve as a soldier.

ACT II

SCENE I

The Mulberry Garden.

Enter COURTALL *and* FREEMAN.

COURTALL. Was there ever a couple of fops better matched than these two knights are?

FREEMAN. They are harp and violin, nature has so tuned 'em, as if she intended they should always play the fool in consort.

COURTALL. Now is Sir Oliver secure, for he dares not go home till he's quite drunk, and then he grows valiant, insults, and defies his sweet lady; for which with prayers and tears he's forced to feign a bitter repentance the next morning.

FREEMAN. What do we here idling in the Mulberry Garden? Why do not we make this visit then?

COURTALL. Now art thou as mad upon this trail, as if we were upon a hot scent.

FREEMAN. Since we know the bush, why do we not start the game?

COURTALL. Gently, good Frank; first know that the laws of honour prescribed in such nice cases, will not allow me to carry thee along with me; and next, hast thou so little wit to think, that a discreet lady that has had the experience of so much human frailty, can

s.d. *Mulberry Garden*: see note to *Comical Revenge*, V ii 131.
1 *fops*: fools, buffoons (not yet used exclusively or necessarily to mean a dandy).
5 *in consort*: i.e. together ('consort' meaning 'the accord of two or more instruments making music together', here 'harp and violin').
6 *secure*: secured, i.e. no danger to Courtall's plans.
8 *insults*: probably, 'exults contemptuously' (i.e. intransitive use of the verb) rather than 'abuses' (transitive); cf. II ii 50.
13 *mad*: carried away by enthusiasm, wildly excited.
16 *start the game*: (in hunting) force an animal to leave its lair or resting-place.
18 *nice*: delicate, needing tactful handling.

have so good an opinion of the constancy of her servant, as to lead him into temptation?

FREEMAN. Then we must not hope her ladyship should make us acquainted with these gentlewomen.

COURTALL. Thou may'st as reasonably expect, that an old rook should bring a young snap acquainted with his bubble; but advantages may be hereafter made, by my admission into the family.

FREEMAN. What is to be done then?

COURTALL. Why, look you, thus I have contrived it: Sir Oliver, when I began to grow resty, that he might incline me a little more to drunkenness, in my ear discovered to me the humour of his dear friend Sir Joslin: he assured me, that when he was in that good-natured condition, to requite their courtesy, he always carried the good company home with him, and recommended them to his kinswomen.

FREEMAN. Very good!

COURTALL. Now after the fresh air has breathed on us a while, and expelled the vapours of the wine we have drunk, thou shalt return to these two sots, whom we left at the French house, according to our promise, and tell 'em, I am a little stayed by some unlucky business, and will be with 'em presently; thou wilt find 'em tired with long fight, weak and unable to observe their order; charge 'em briskly, and in a moment thou shalt rout 'em, and with little or no damage to thyself gain an absolute victory.

FREEMAN. Very well!

COURTALL. In the meantime I will make my visit to the longing lady, and order my business so handsomely, that I will be with thee again immediately, to make an experiment of the good humour of Sir Joslin.

FREEMAN. Let's about it.

---

27 *rook*: swindler.
27 *snap*: cheat.
28 *bubble*: dupe.
28 *advantages*: chances, opportunities.
32 *resty*: sluggish, disinclined for action (here, drinking).
38 *recommended*: (1) introduced (2) commended.
44 *stayed*: delayed.
47 *order*: battle-formation.
54 *make an experiment of*: put to the test.

COURTALL. 'Tis yet too early, we must drill away a little time here, that my excuses may be more probable, and my persecution more tolerable.

Enter ARIANA *and* GATTY *with vizards, and pass nimbly over the stage.*

FREEMAN. Ha, ha – how wantonly they trip it! there is temptation enough in their very gait, to stir up the courage of an old alderman: prithee let us follow 'em.

COURTALL. I have been so often balked with these vizard-masks, that I have at least a dozen times forsworn 'em; they are a most certain sign of an ill face, or what is worse, an old acquaintance.

FREEMAN. The truth is, nothing but some such weighty reason, is able to make women deny themselves the pride they have to be seen.

COURTALL. The evening's fresh and pleasant, and yet there is but little company.

FREEMAN. Our course will be the better, these deer cannot herd: come, come man, let's follow.

COURTALL. I find it is a mere folly to forswear anything, it does but make the devil the more earnest in his temptation.

They go after the WOMEN.

Enter WOMEN *again, and cross the stage.*

ARIANA. Now if these should prove two men-of-war that are cruising here, to watch for prizes.

GATTY. Would they had courage enough to set upon us; I long to be engaged.

ARIANA. Look, look yonder, I protest they chase us.

---

59 *wantonly*: playfully, unrestrainedly.
59 *trip*: move lightly and nimbly.
61 *courage*: vigour, spirit, lustiness.
62 *balked*: disappointed.
63 *vizard-masks*: ladies of pleasure, perhaps prostitutes.
71 *course*: see note to I i 15.
72 *herd*: i.e. join a herd; thus, derive protection from the company of others.
73 *a mere*: utter, complete.
77 *prizes*: ships captured at sea in virtue of the rights of war (part of a sequence of words drawn from naval combat, e.g. 'men-at-war', 'set upon', 'engaged', 'bear away', etc.).

GATTY. Let us bear away then; if they be truly valiant they'll quickly make more sail, and board us.

The WOMEN *go out, and go about behind the scenes to the other door.*

Enter COURTALL *and* FREEMAN.

FREEMAN. 'Sdeath, how fleet they are! whatsoever faults they have, they cannot be broken-winded.

COURTALL. Sure, by that little mincing step they should be country fillies that have been breathed at course-a-park, and barley-break: we shall never reach 'em.

FREEMAN. I'll follow directly, do thou turn down the cross-walk and meet 'em.

[*Exeunt* COURTALL *and* FREEMAN.]

Enter the WOMEN, *and after 'em* COURTALL *at the lower door, and* FREEMAN *at the upper on the contrary side.*

COURTALL. By your leave, ladies –

GATTY. I perceive you can make bold enough without it.

FREEMAN. Your servant, ladies –

ARIANA. Or any other ladies' that will give themselves the trouble to entertain you.

FREEMAN. 'Slife, their tongues are as nimble as their heels.

COURTALL. Can you have so little good nature to dash

---

82 s.d. *behind the scenes to the other door*: there were doors in the proscenium arch on either side of the stage in contemporary playhouses.

84 *broken-winded*: broken wind is an incurable disease of horses, caused by the rupture of the air-cells, which disables them from bearing fatigue.

86 *breathed*: exercised briskly, to improve breathing.

87 *course-a-park*: a country-game in which a girl called out a boy to chase her.

87 *barley-break*: another country-game involving hard running, played by six persons (three of each sex) in couples; one couple had to catch the other, who were allowed to 'break', and change partners, when hard pressed.

96 *entertain*: receive addresses from, respond amiably to.

97 *'Slife*: a petty oath, an abbreviation of 'God's life'.

a couple of bashful young men out of countenance, who came out of pure love to tender you their service?

GATTY. 'Twere pity to balk 'em, sister.

ARIANA. Indeed methinks they look as if they never had been slipped before.

FREEMAN. Yes faith, we have had many a fair course in this paddock, have been very well fleshed, and dare boldly fasten.

They kiss their hands with a little force.

ARIANA. Well, I am not the first unfortunate woman that has been forced to give her hand, where she never intends to bestow her heart.

GATTY. Now, do you think 'tis a bargain already?

COURTALL. Faith, would there were some lusty earnest given, for fear we should unluckily break off again.

FREEMAN. Are you so wild that you must be hooded thus?

COURTALL. Fie, fie, put off these scandals to all good faces.

GATTY. For your reputation's sake we shall keep 'em on: 'slife we should be taken for your relations, if we durst show our faces with you thus publicly.

ARIANA. And what a shame that would be to a couple of young gallants! methinks you should blush to think on't.

COURTALL. These were pretty toys, invented, first, merely for the good of us poor lovers to deceive the jealous, and to blind the malicious; but the proper use is so wickedly perverted, that it makes all honest men hate the fashion mortally.

---

104 *slipped*: released (as a greyhound, etc.) from a leash or slip.
106 *paddock*: a course in a park, for hounds to run matches.
106 *fleshed*: to flesh a hound was to give it a taste of the flesh of the game killed in order to incite it to the chase.
107 *fasten*: close (hands, teeth) with a firm grip.
112 *lusty*: vigorous, pleasing.
113 *earnest*: money in part-payment, especially for the purpose of binding a bargain; therefore, a foretaste or pledge.
115 *hooded*: a hood was a cover put over the head of a hawk to keep her quiet while not in pursuit of game (the reference here, of course, is to the vizard-masks).
125 *toys*: trifles, knick-knacks.
127 *jealous*: suspicious.

FREEMAN. A good face is as seldom covered with a vizard-mask, as a good hat with an oiled case: and yet on my conscience, you are both handsome.

COURTALL. Do but remove 'em a little, to satisfy a foolish scruple.

ARIANA. This is a just punishment you have brought upon yourselves, by that unpardonable sin of talking.

GATTY. You can only brag now of your acquaintance with a farendon gown, and a piece of black velvet.

COURTALL. The truth is, there are some vain fellows whose loose behaviour of late has given great discouragement to the honourable proceedings of all virtuous ladies.

FREEMAN. But I hope you have more charity, than to believe us of the number of the wicked.

ARIANA. There's not a man of you to be trusted.

GATTY. What a shame is it to your whole sex, that a woman is more fit to be a privy-counsellor, than a young gallant a lover?

COURTALL. This is a pretty kind of fooling, ladies, for men that are idle; but you must bid a little fairer, if you intend to keep us from our serious business.

GATTY. Truly you seem to be men of great employment, that are every moment rattling from the eating-houses to the playhouses, from the playhouses to the Mulberry Garden, that live in a perpetual hurry, and have little leisure for such an idle entertainment.

COURTALL. Now would not I see thy face for the world; if it should but be half so good as thy humour, thou wouldst dangerously tempt me to dote upon thee, and forgetting all shame, become constant.

FREEMAN. I perceive, by your fooling here, that wit and good humour may make a man in love with a blackamoor. That the devil should contrive it so, that we should have earnest business now.

---

136 *talking*: i.e. revealing the secrets of love-affairs.
138 *farendon*: farandine, a fabric made of silk, wool and hair.
138 *a piece of black velvet*: used to make the vizard-mask.
150 *bid a little fairer*: give us a little more encouragement.
163 *blackamoor*: dark complexions not being favourably regarded by contemporary notions of beauty.
164 *earnest*: demanding serious, urgent attention.

COURTALL. Would they would but be so kind to meet us here again tomorrow.

GATTY. You are full of business, and 'twould but take you off of your employments.

ARIANA. And we are very unwilling to have the sin to answer for, of ruining a couple of such hopeful young men.

FREEMAN. Must we then despair?

ARIANA. The ladies you are going to, will not be so hard-hearted.

COURTALL. (*to* FREEMAN) On my conscience, they love us, and begin to grow jealous already.

FREEMAN. Who knows but this may prove the luckier adventure of the two?

COURTALL. Come, come, we know you have a mind to meet us: we cannot see you blush, speak it out boldly.

GATTY. Will you swear then, not to visit any other women before that time?

ARIANA. Not that we are jealous, but because we would not have you tired with the impertinent conversation of our sex, and come to us dull and out of humour.

COURTALL. Invent an oath, and let it be so horrid 'twould make an atheist start to hear it.

FREEMAN. And I will swear it readily, that I will not so much as speak to a woman, till I speak to you again.

GATTY. But are you troubled with that foolish scruple of keeping an oath?

FREEMAN. Oh most religiously!

COURTALL. And may we not enlarge our hopes upon a little better acquaintance?

ARIANA. You see all the freedom we allow.

GATTY. It may be we may be entreated to hear a fiddle, or mingle in a country dance, or so.

COURTALL. Well! we are in too desperate a condition

167–8 *take you off of your employments*: distract you from your business.

178 *adventure*: see note to *Comical Revenge*, I iii 64.

184–5 *conversation*: society, companionship (but the word could also mean 'sexual intimacy').

197 *entreated*: prevailed upon.

198 *mingle in*: take part in.

to stand upon articles, and are resolved to yield on any terms.

FREEMAN. Be sure you be punctual now!

ARIANA. Will you be sure?

COURTALL. Or else may we become a couple of credulous coxcombs, and be jilted ever after. – Your servants, ladies.

Exeunt MEN.

ARIANA. I wonder what they think of us!

GATTY. You may easily imagine; for they are not of a humour so little in fashion, to believe the best: I assure you the most favourable opinion they can have, is that we are still a little wild, and stand in need of better manning.

ARIANA. Prithee, dear girl, what dost think of 'em?

GATTY. Faith so well, that I'm ashamed to tell thee.

ARIANA. Would I had never seen 'em!

GATTY. Ha! Is it come to that already?

ARIANA. Prithee, let's walk a turn or two more, and talk of 'em.

GATTY. Let us take care then we are not too particular in their commendations, lest we should discover we intrench upon one another's inclinations, and so grow quarrelsome.

Exeunt.

SCENE II

Sir Oliver's lodgings.

Enter LADY COCKWOOD *and* SENTRY.

SENTRY. Dear madam, do not afflict yourself thus unreasonably; I dare lay my life, it is not want of devotion, but opportunity that stays him.

---

200 *stand upon articles*: argue about the details of the surrender terms.

212 *manning*: see note to I ii 29.

219–20 *too particular in their commendations*: i.e. praise qualities belonging to only one of them (thus revealing the speaker's preferences).

LADY COCKWOOD. Ingrateful man! to be so insensible of a lady's passion!

SENTRY. If I thought he were so wicked, I should hate him strangely – but, madam –

LADY COCKWOOD. Do not speak one word in his behalf, I am resolved to forget him; perfidious mortal, to abuse so sweet an opportunity!

SENTRY. Hark, here is somebody coming upstairs.

LADY COCKWOOD. Peace, he may yet redeem his honour.

Enter COURTALL.

COURTALL. Your humble servant, madam.

LADY COCKWOOD. (*starting*) Mr Courtall, for heaven sake how came you hither?

COURTALL. Guided by my good fortune, madam – your servant, Mrs Sentry.

SENTRY. Your humble servant, sir; I protest you made me start too, to see you come in thus unexpectedly.

LADY COCKWOOD. I did not imagine it could be known I was in town yet.

COURTALL. Sir Oliver did me the favour to make me a visit, and dine with me today, which brought me to the knowledge of this happiness, madam; and as soon as I could possibly, I got the freedom to come hither and enjoy it.

LADY COCKWOOD. You have ever been extreme obliging, sir.

SENTRY. (*aside*) 'Tis a worthy gentleman, how punctual he is to my directions!

LADY COCKWOOD. Will you be pleased to repose, sir? Sentry, set some chairs.

Exit SENTRY.

COURTALL. With much difficulty, madam, I broke out of my company, and was forced by the importunity of one Sir Joslin Jolly, I think they call him, to engage my honour I would return again immediately.

LADY COCKWOOD. You must not so soon rob me of so sweet a satisfaction.

---

7 *strangely*: extremely, in an uncommon or exceptional degree.
30–1 *punctual . . . to*: precisely observant of.
37 *engage my honour*: promise.

COURTALL. No consideration, madam, could take me from you, but that I know my stay at this time must needs endanger your honour; and how often I have denied myself the greatest satisfaction in the world, to keep that unblemished, you yourself can witness.

LADY COCKWOOD. Indeed I have often had great trials of your generosity, in those many misfortunes that have attended our innocent affections.

COURTALL. Sir Oliver, madam, before I did perceive it, was got near that pitch of drunkenness, which makes him come reeling home, and unmanfully insult over your ladyship; and how subject he is then to injure you with an unjust suspicion, you have often told me; which makes me careful not to be surprised here.

LADY COCKWOOD. Repose yourself a little, but a little, dear sir: these virtuous principles make you worthy to be trusted with a lady's honour: indeed Sir Oliver has his failings; yet I protest, Mr Courtall, I love him dearly, but cannot be altogether unsensible of your generous passion.

COURTALL. (*aside*) Ay, ay, I am a very passionate lover! – Indeed this escape has only given me leisure to look upon my happiness.

LADY COCKWOOD. Is my woman retired?

COURTALL. Most dutifully, madam.

LADY COCKWOOD. Then let me tell you, sir – yet we may make very good use of it.

COURTALL. (*aside*) Now am I going to be drawn in again.

LADY COCKWOOD. If Sir Oliver be in that indecent condition you speak of, tomorrow he will be very submissive, as it is meet for so great a misdemeanour; then can I, feigning a desperate discontent, take my own freedom without the least suspicion.

COURTALL. This is very luckily and obligingly thought on, madam.

---

45 *trials*: examples, evidence.
46 *generosity*: nobility of conduct; cf. note to *Comical Revenge*, II ii 57.
59 *generous*: see note to line 46.
74 *obligingly*: pleasingly.

LADY COCKWOOD. Now if you will be pleased to make an assignation, sir.

COURTALL. Tomorrow about ten a clock in the lower walk of the New Exchange, out of which we can quickly pop into my coach.

LADY COCKWOOD. But I am still so pestered with my woman, I dare not go without her; on my conscience she's very sincere, but it is not good to trust our reputations too much to the frailty of a servant.

COURTALL. I will bring my chariot, madam, that will hold but two.

LADY COCKWOOD. Oh most ingeniously imagined, dear sir! for by that means I shall have a just excuse to give her leave to see a relation, and bid her stay there till I call her.

COURTALL. It grieves me much to leave you so soon, madam; but I shall comfort myself with the thoughts of the happiness you have made me hope for.

LADY COCKWOOD. I wish it were in my power eternally to oblige you, dear sir.

COURTALL. Your humble servant, madam.

LADY COCKWOOD. Your humble servant, sweet sir.

Exit COURTALL.

Sentry – why Sentry – where are you?

Enter SENTRY.

SENTRY. Here, madam.

LADY COCKWOOD. What a strange thing is this! will you never take warning, but still be leaving me alone in these suspicious occasions?

SENTRY. I was but in the next room, madam.

LADY COCKWOOD. What may Mr Courtall think of my innocent intentions? I protest if you serve me so again, I shall be strangely angry: you should have more regard to your lady's honour.

---

77 *assignation*: a new and fashionable use of the word (*OED*'s earliest examples date from the early 1660s).

79 *New Exchange*: see note to *Comical Revenge*, V ii 86.

81 *pestered with*: encumbered with, embarrassed by the presence of.

85 *chariot*: a light four-wheeled carriage with only back seats.

102 *suspicious occasions*: circumstances which might breed suspicion.

SENTRY. [*aside*] If I stay in the room, she will not speak kindly to me in a week after; and if I go out, she always chides me thus: this is a strange infirmity she has, but I must bear with it; for on my conscience, custom has made it so natural, she cannot help it.

LADY COCKWOOD. Are my cousins come home yet?

SENTRY. Not yet, madam.

LADY COCKWOOD. Dost thou know whither they went this evening?

SENTRY. I heard them say they would go take the air, madam.

LADY COCKWOOD. Well, I see it is impossible with virtuous counsel to reclaim them; truly they are so careless of their own, I could wish Sir Joslin would remove 'em, for fear they should bring an unjust imputation on my honour.

SENTRY. Heavens forbid, madam!

Enter ARIANA *and* GATTY.

LADY COCKWOOD. Your servant, cousins.

AMBO. Your servant, madam.

LADY COCKWOOD. How have you spent the cool of the evening?

GATTY. As the custom is, madam, breathing the fresh air in the Park and Mulberry Garden.

LADY COCKWOOD. Without the company of a relation, or some discreet body to justify your reputations to the world – you are young, and may be yet insensible of it; but this is a strange censorious age, I assure you.

Noise of music without.

ARIANA. Hark! what music's this?

GATTY. I'll lay my life my uncle's drunk, and hath picked us up a couple of worthy servants, and brought them home with him in triumph.

Enter the MUSIC *playing,* SIR OLIVER *strutting, and swaggering,* SIR JOSLIN *singing, and dancing with* MR COURTALL, *and* MR

---

120 *reclaim*: restrain.
126 s.d. *Ambo*: both (Latin); i.e. Gatty and Ariana reply together.
130 *the Park*: see note to *Comical Revenge*, II i 103.
138 *triumph*: victory procession.

FREEMAN *in each hand:* GATTY *and* ARIANA *seeing* COURTALL *and* FREEMAN *shriek and exeunt.*

SIR JOSLIN. Hey-day! I told you they were a couple of skittish fillies, but I never knew 'em boggle at a man before; I'll fetch 'em again I warrant you, boys.

Exit after them.

FREEMAN. (*to* COURTALL) These are the very self-same gowns and petticoats.

COURTALL. Their surprise confirms us it must be them.

FREEMAN. 'Slife, we have betrayed ourselves very pleasantly.

COURTALL. Now am I undone to all intents and purposes, for they will innocently discover all to my lady, and she will have no mercy.

SIR OLIVER. (*strutting*) Dan, dan, da ra, dan, &c. Avoid my presence, the very sight of that face makes me more impotent than an eunuch.

LADY COCKWOOD. (*offering to embrace him*) Dear Sir Oliver!

SIR OLIVER. Forbear your conjugal clippings, I will have a wench, thou shalt fetch me a wench, Sentry.

SENTRY. Can you be so inhuman to my dear lady?

SIR OLIVER. Peace, Envy, or I will have thee executed for petty treason; thy skin flayed off, stuffed and hung up in my hall in the country, as a terror to my whole family.

---

139 *Hey-day*: an exclamation of surprise.

140 *skittish*: of horses (fillies): apt to start or be unruly without sufficient cause.

140 *boggle at*: shy away from, start with fright at.

146 *pleasantly*: ridiculously.

150 *Dan, dan, da ra, dan*: cf. John Tatham, *The Rump* (London, 1660), p. 41: 'I espy'd a very fine fellow, some Officer no doubt, he did Ran Dan so!' (*OED* lists the noun, 'randan', from *c.* 1710 onwards, as 'riotous or disorderly behaviour'.)

155 *clippings*: embraces.

158 *Envy*: see note to *Comical Revenge*, II ii 56.

159 *petty treason*: usually applied to the murder of one to whom the murderer owes allegiance, as of a master by his servant or a husband by his wife. Sir Oliver, however, uses it more generally to signify any insurrectionary act against a master of a household by one of his underlings.

161 *family*: see note to I i 52.

COURTALL. What crime can deserve this horrid punishment?

SIR OLIVER. I'll tell thee, Ned: 'twas my fortune t'other day to have an intrigue with a tinker's wife in the country, and this malicious slut betrayed the very ditch where we used to make our assignations, to my lady.

FREEMAN. She deserves your anger indeed, Sir Oliver: but be not so unkind to your virtuous lady.

SIR OLIVER. Thou dost not know her, Frank; I have had a design to break her heart ever since the first month that I had her, and 'tis so tough, that I have not yet cracked one string on't.

COURTALL. You are too unmerciful, Sir Oliver.

SIR OLIVER. Hang her, Ned, by wicked policy she would usurp my empire, and in her heart is a very Pharaoh; for every night she's a-putting me upon making brick without straw.

COURTALL. I cannot see a virtuous lady so afflicted, without offering her some consolation: (*Aside to her*) dear madam, is it not as I told you?

LADY COCKWOOD. (*to* COURTALL *aside*) The fates could not have been more propitious, and I shall not be wanting to the furthering of our mutual happiness.

Enter SIR JOSLIN, *with* ARIANA *and* GATTY *in each hand, dancing and singing.*

CATCH.

'This is sly and pretty,
And this is wild and witty;
If either stayed
Till she died a maid,
I'faith 'twould be great pity.'

SIR JOSLIN. Here they are, boys, i'faith, and now little Joslin's a man of his word. Heuk! Sly-girl and Mad-

---

165 *intrigue*: in the sense of 'sexual liaison' another recent, fashionable coinage. *OED* cites Walter Charleton in 1668 speaking of 'an Intrigue (as they now adays call it)'.

167 *assignations*: see note to line 77.

177 *empire*: absolute sway.

179 *brick without straw*: see Exodus 5, verses 6–19.

192 *Heuk*: presumably, like 'alou', a hunting-cry.

cap, to 'em, to 'em, to 'em, boys, alou! (*Flings 'em to* COURTALL *and* FREEMAN, *who kiss their hands*) What's yonder, your lady in tears, brother Cockwood? Come, come, I'll make up all breaches. (*He sings*) 'And we'll all be merry and frolic.' Fie, fie, though man and wife are seldom in good humour alone, there are few want the discretion to dissemble it in company.

SIR JOSLIN, SIR OLIVER, *and* LADY COCKWOOD *stand talking together.*

FREEMAN. I knew we should surprise you, ladies.

COURTALL. Faith I thought this conjuring to be but a mere jest till now, and could not believe the astrological rascal had been so skilful.

FREEMAN. How exactly he described 'em, and how punctual he was in his directions to apprehend 'em!

GATTY. Then you have been with a conjurer, gentlemen.

COURTALL. You cannot blame us, ladies, the loss of our hearts was so considerable, that it may well excuse the indirect means we took to find out the pretty thieves that stole 'em.

ARIANA. Did not I tell you what men of business these were, sister?

GATTY. I vow I innocently believed they had some pre-engagement to a scrivener or a surgeon, and wished 'em so well, that I am sorry to find 'em so perfidious.

FREEMAN. Why, we have kept our oaths, ladies.

ARIANA. You are much beholding to providence.

GATTY. But we are more, sister; for had we once been deluded into an opinion they had been faithful, who knows into what inconveniences that error might have drawn us?

---

195 *make up all breaches*: cure (settle) all quarrels.

196 *frolic*: mirthful.

201–3 *conjuring . . . astrological rascal*: they are pretending to have traced the girls with the aid of an astrologer.

205 *punctual*: exactly accurate.

205 *apprehend*: find; but also, lay hold of (the gallants may still be holding the ladies' hands).

214 *a scrivener or a surgeon*: i.e. experts able to help repair the depredations wrought upon their finances and bodies by their style of life (for the scriveners' talents, see note to *Comical Revenge*, IV ii 26).

220 *inconveniences*: mischiefs, harm.

COURTALL. Why should you be so unreasonable, ladies, to expect that from us, we should scarce have hoped for from you? fie, fie, the keeping of one's word is a thing below the honour of a gentleman.

FREEMAN. A poor shift! fit only to uphold the reputation of a paltry citizen.

SIR JOSLIN. Come, come, all will be well again, I warrant you, lady.

LADY COCKWOOD. These are insupportable injuries, but I will bear 'em with an invincible patience, and tomorrow make him dearly sensible how unworthy he has been.

SIR JOSLIN. Tomorrow my brother Cockwood will be another man – so, boys, and how do you like the flesh and blood of the Jollies – heuk, Sly-girl – and Mad-cap, hey – come, come, you have heard them exercise their tongues a while; now you shall see them ply their feet a little: this is a clean-limbed wench, and has neither spavin, splinter, nor wind-gall; tune her a jig, and play't roundly, you shall see her bounce it away like a nimble frigate before a fresh gale – hey, methinks I see her under sail already.

GATTY *dances a jig.*

SIR JOSLIN. Hey my little Mad-cap – here's a girl of the true breed of the Jollies, i'faith – but hark you, hark you, a consultation, gentlemen – bear up, brother Cockwood, a little: what think you, if we pack these idle huswives to bed now, and retire into a room by ourselves, and have a merry catch, and a bottle or two of the best, and perfect the good work we have so unanimously carried on today?

SIR OLIVER. A most admirable intrigue – tan, dan, da, ra, dan; come, come, march to your several quarters:

---

226 *shift*: expedient.
227 *citizen*: see note to *Comical Revenge*, I iii 59.
239 *ply*: exercise.
239 *clean-limbed*: shapely of limb.
240 *spavin*: disease of horse's hock-joint.
240 *splinter*: disease in horse's foreleg.
240 *wind-gall*: soft tumour on horse's fetlock-joint.
241 *roundly*: fluently, smartly.
248 *huswives*: pert women or girls.

go, we have sent for a civil person or two, and are resolved to fornicate in private.

LADY COCKWOOD. This is a barbarous return of all my kindness.

FREEMAN.
COURTALL. } Your humble servant, madam.

Exeunt LADY COCKWOOD *and* SENTRY.

COURTALL. Hark you! hark you! ladies, do not harbour too ill an opinion of us, for faith, when you have had a little more experience of the world, you'll find we are no such abominable rascals.

GATTY. We shall be so charitable to think no worse of you, than we do of all mankind for your sakes, only that you are perjured, perfidious, inconstant, ingrateful.

FREEMAN. Nay, nay, that's enough in all conscience ladies, and now you are sensible what a shameful thing it is to break one's word, I hope you'll be more careful to keep yours tomorrow.

GATTY. Invent an oath, and let it be so horrid –

COURTALL. Nay, nay, it is too late for raillery, i'faith, ladies.

GATTY.
ARIANA. } Well, your servant then.

FREEMAN.
COURTALL. } Your servant, ladies.

[*Exeunt* GATTY *and* ARIANA.]

SIR OLIVER. Now the enemy's marched out –

SIR JOSLIN. Then the castle's our own boys – hey.

[*Sings*]

'And here and there I had her,
And every where I had her,
Her toy was such, that every touch
Would make a lover madder.'

FREEMAN.
COURTALL. } Hey brave Sir Joslin!

SIR OLIVER. Ah my dear little witty Joslin, let me hug thee.

---

271 *Invent . . . horrid*: an echo of Courtall's speech at II i 186.

275 s.d. [*Exeunt Gatty and Ariana*]: No separate exit is marked for them in *1668*, but this seems the aptest moment for their departure.

SIR JOSLIN. Strike up you obstreperous rascals, and march along before us.

Exeunt singing and dancing.

ACT III

SCENE I

The New Exchange.

MRS TRINKET *sitting in a shop, people passing by as in the Exchange.*

MRS TRINKET. What d'ye buy? what d'ye lack, gentlemen? Gloves, ribbons, and essences; ribbons, gloves, and essences?

Enter MR COURTALL.

Mr Courtall! I thought you had a quarrel to the Change, and were resolved we should never see you here again.

COURTALL. Your unkindness indeed, Mrs Trinket, had been enough to make a man banish himself for ever.

Enter MRS GAZETTE.

TRINKET. Look you, yonder comes fine Mrs Gazette, thither you intended your visit, I am sure.

GAZETTE. Mr Courtall! your servant.

COURTALL. Your servant, Mrs Gazette.

GAZETTE. This happiness was only meant to Mrs Trinket, had it not been my good fortune to pass by, by chance, I should have lost my share on't.

---

1 *what d'ye lack*: a standard seventeenth-century street-vendors' cry.

2 *ribbons*: see note to *Comical Revenge*, IV vi 51.

2 *essences*: perfumes.

5 *Change*: i.e. the New Exchange.

8 s.d. *Gazette*: a news-sheet; therefore, derivatively, a news-monger (cf. Fr. *gazette*).

COURTALL. This is too cruel, Mrs Gazette, when all the unkindness is on your side, to rally your servant thus.

GAZETTE. I vow this tedious absence of yours made me believe you intended to try an experiment on my poor heart, to discover that hidden secret, how long a despairing lover may languish without the sight of the party.

COURTALL. You are always very pleasant on this subject, Mrs Gazette.

GAZETTE. And have not you reason to be so too?

COURTALL. Not that I know of.

GAZETTE. Yes, you hear the good news.

COURTALL. What good news?

GAZETTE. How well this dissembling becomes you! But now I think better on't, it cannot concern you, you are more a gentleman, than to have an amour last longer than an Easter Term with a country lady; and yet there are some I see as well in the country as in the city, that have a pretty way of huswifing a lover, and can spin an intrigue out a great deal farther, than others are willing to do.

COURTALL. What pretty art have they, good Mrs Gazette?

GAZETTE. When tradesmen see themselves in an ill condition, and are afraid of breaking, can they do better than to take in a good substantial partner, to help to carry on their trading?

COURTALL. Sure you have been at riddle me, riddle me, lately, you are so wondrous witty.

GAZETTE. And yet I believe my Lady Cockwood is so haughty, she had rather give over the vanity of an intrigue, than take in a couple of young handsome kinswomen to help to maintain it.

---

17 *rally*: banter, make fun of.

32 *Easter Term*: one of the four law-terms; the sitting of the courts brought many to London from the country on legal and other business, and the length of term was thus the natural span for many a visit to the capital.

34 *huswifing*: managing.

40 *breaking*: going bankrupt.

41 *substantial*: well-to-do, wealthy.

43–4 *at riddle me, riddle me*: playing at riddles.

44 *witty*: subtle in expression, therefore difficult to follow (see the beginning of Courtall's next speech).

COURTALL. I knew it would out at last; indeed it is the principle of most good women that love gaming, when they begin to grow a little out of play themselves, to make an interest in some young gamester or other, in hopes to rook a favour now and then: but you are quite out in your policy, my Lady Cockwood is none of these, I assure you – hark you, Mrs Gazette, you must needs bestir yourself a little for me this morning, or else heaven have mercy on a poor sinner.

GAZETTE. I hope this wicked woman has no design upon your body already: alas! I pity your tender conscience.

COURTALL. I have always made thee my confident, and now I come to thee as to a faithful counsellor.

GAZETTE. State your case.

COURTALL. Why, this ravenous kite is upon wing already, is fetching a little compass, and will be here within this half hour to swoop me away.

GAZETTE. And you would have me your scarecrow?

COURTALL. Something of that there is in't; she is still your customer?

GAZETTE. I have furnished her and the young ladies with a few fashionable toys since they came to town, to keep 'um in countenance at a play, or in the Park.

COURTALL. I would have thee go immediately to the

---

50 *gaming*: amorous sport, as in 'officer of the game' (I i 12–13); but also playing, here and subsequently, on another meaning, 'gambling'.
51 *out of play*: (1) out of action, unemployed (2) lacking in luck as a gambler.
52 *make an interest*: (1) make an investment in (2) associate themselves with.
53 *rook*: steal for herself.
53 *favour*: of a sexual kind.
54 *you are quite out in your policy*: your cunning interpretation is quite wrong.
62 *confident*: confidante.
64 *case*: picking up the legal meaning ('legal advocate') played upon in Courtall's use of 'counsellor'.
65 *ravenous*: (of animals) given to seizing in order to devour.
65 *kite*: a bird of prey.
66 *fetching a little compass*: going a roundabout way.
73 *keep 'um in countenance*: keep them from being abashed.

young ladies, and by some device or other entice 'em hither.

GAZETTE. I came just now from taking measure of 'em for a couple of handkerchiefs.

COURTALL. How unlucky's this!

GAZETTE. They were calling for their hoods and scarfs, and are coming hither to lay out a little money in ribbons and essences: I have recommended them to Mrs Trinket's shop here.

COURTALL. This falls out more luckily than what I had contrived myself, or could have done; for here will they be busy just before the door, where we have made our appointment: but if this long-winged devil should chance to truss me before they come.

GAZETTE. I will only step up and give some directions to my maid, about a little business that is in haste, and come down again and watch her; if you are snapped, I'll be with you presently, and rescue you I warrant you, or at least stay you till more company come: she dares not force you away in my sight; she knows I am great with Sir Oliver, and as malicious a devil as the best of 'em – your servant, sir.

Exit GAZETTE.

Enter FREEMAN.

COURTALL. Freeman! 'tis well you are come.

FREEMAN. Well! what counter-plot? what hopes of dis-appointing the old, and of seeing the young ladies? I am ready to receive your orders.

COURTALL. Faith, things are not so well contrived as I could have wished 'em, and yet I hope by the help of Mrs Gazette to keep my word, Frank.

FREEMAN. Nay, now I know what tool thou hast made

---

85 *contrived*: plotted, devised.
87 *long-winged*: birds used for falconry were divided into short-winged (used for smaller game) and long-winged (including kites).
88 *truss*: (of a bird of prey) seize upon its prey and carry it off.
92 *snapped*: seized (as by a bird of prey).
95 *great with*: intimate, friendly with.
98–9 *dis-appointing*: the *1668* spelling reproduced here suggests that Freeman is punning on the meaning, 'depriving of the benefits of an appointment'.

choice of, I make no question but the business will go well forward; but I am afraid this last unlucky business has so distasted these young trouts, they will not be so easily tickled as they might have been.

COURTALL. Never fear it; whatsoever women say, I am sure they seldom think the worse of a man, for running at all, 'tis a sign of youth and high mettle, and makes them rather *piqué*, who shall tame him: that which troubles me most, is, we lost the hopes of variety, and a single intrigue in love is as dull as a single plot in a play, and will tire a lover worse, than t'other does an audience.

FREEMAN. We cannot be long without some underplots in this town, let this be our main design, and if we are anything fortunate in our contrivance, we shall make it a pleasant comedy.

COURTALL. Leave all things to me, and hope the best: be gone, for I expect their coming immediately; walk a turn or two above, or fool a while with pretty Mrs Anvil, and scent your eyebrows and periwig with a little essence of oranges, or jessamine; and when you see us all together at Mrs Gazette's shop, put in as it were by chance: I protest yonder comes the old haggard, to your post quickly: 'sdeath, where's Gazette and these young ladies now?

Exit FREEMAN.

Enter LADY COCKWOOD, *and* SENTRY.

Oh madam, I have waited here at least an hour, and time seems very tedious, when it delays so great a happiness as you bring with you.

LADY COCKWOOD. I vow, sir, I did but stay to give Sir

---

107 *distasted*: displeased; but perhaps also, robbed of their taste (for such adventures).

108 *tickled*: a way of catching trout and other fish by hand.

112 *piqué*: more eagerly competitive.

118 *design*: (1) schemes (2) plan of action for a comedy (the same double meaning is played upon in 'contrivance').

125 *essence of oranges*: perfume extracted from the orange-flower.

125 *jessamine*: perfume derived from the climbing shrub called jasmine.

128 *haggard*: untamed adult (female) hawk.

Oliver his due correction for those unseemly injuries he did me last night. Is your coach ready?

COURTALL. Yes, madam: but how will you dispose of your maid?

LADY COCKWOOD. My maid! for heaven's sake, what do you mean, sir? do I ever use to go abroad without her?

COURTALL. 'Tis upon no design, madam, I speak it, I assure you; but my glass-coach broke last night, and I was forced to bring my chariot, which can hold but two.

LADY COCKWOOD. Oh heaven! you must excuse me, dear sir, for I shall deny myself the sweetest recreations in the world, rather than yield to anything that may bring a blemish upon my spotless honour.

Enter GAZETTE.

GAZETTE. Your humble servant, madam. Your servant, Mr Courtall.

LADY COCKWOOD.
COURTALL. } Your servant, Mrs Gazette.

GAZETTE. I am extreme glad to see your ladyship here, I intended to send my maid to your lodgings this afternoon, madam, to tell you I have a parcel of new lace come in, the prettiest patterns that ever were seen; for I am very desirous so good a customer as your ladyship should see 'em first, and have your choice.

LADY COCKWOOD. I am much beholding to you, Mrs Gazette, I was newly come into the Exchange, and intended to call at your shop before I went home.

Enter ARIANA *and* GATTY, GAZETTE *goes to 'em.*

COURTALL. 'Sdeath, here are your cousins too! now there is no hope left for a poor unfortunate lover to comfort himself withal.

---

141 *design*: i.e. crafty intent.
142 *glass-coach*: a coach with glass windows (a recent innovation).

LADY COCKWOOD. Will fate never be more propitious?

ARIANA. }
GATTY. } Your servant, madam.

LADY COCKWOOD. I am newly come into the Exchange, and by chance met with Mr Courtall here, who will needs give himself the trouble, to play the gallant, and wait upon me.

GATTY. Does your ladyship come to buy?

LADY COCKWOOD. A few trifles; Mrs Gazette says she has a parcel of very fine new laces, shall we go look upon 'em?

ARIANA. We will only fancy a suit of knots or two at this shop, and buy a little essence, and wait upon your ladyship immediately.

GATTY. Mrs Gazette, you are skilled in the fashion, pray let our choice have your approbation.

GAZETTE. Most gladly, madam.

All go to the shop to look upon ware, but COURTALL *and* LADY COCKWOOD.

COURTALL. 'Sdeath, madam, if you had made no ceremony, but stepped into the coach presently, we had escaped this mischief.

LADY COCKWOOD. My over-tenderness of my honour, has blasted all my hopes of happiness.

COURTALL. To be thus unluckily surprised in the height of all our expectation, leaves me no patience.

LADY COCKWOOD. Moderate your passion a little, sir, I may yet find out a way.

COURTALL. Oh 'tis impossible, madam, never think on't now you have been seen with me; to leave 'em upon any pretence will be so suspicious, that my concern for your honour will make me so feverish and disordered, that I shall lose the taste of all the happiness you give me.

165–6 *Will fate never be more propitious?*: of the early texts only *1668* includes this speech.

176 *fancy*: examine with a view to buying (but cf. line 246 and note).

176 *a suit of knots*: a group of bows of ribbon worn as an ornament on a dress.

186 *blasted*: blighted.

LADY COCKWOOD. Methinks you are too scrupulous, heroic sir.

COURTALL. Besides the concerns I have for you, madam, you know the obligations I have to Sir Oliver, and what professions of friendship there are on both sides; and to be thought perfidious and ingrateful, what an affliction would that be to a generous spirit!

LADY COCKWOOD. Must we then unfortunately part thus?

COURTALL. Now I have better thought on't, that is not absolutely necessary neither.

LADY COCKWOOD. These words revive my dying joys, dear sir, go on.

COURTALL. I will by and by, when I see it most convenient, beg the favour of your ladyship, and your young kinswomen, to accept of a treat and a fiddle; you make some little difficulty at first, but upon earnest persuasion comply, and use your interest to make the young ladies do so too: your company will secure their reputations, and their company take off from you all suspicion.

LADY COCKWOOD. The natural inclination they have to be jigging, will make them very ready to comply: but what advantage can this be to our happiness, dear sir?

COURTALL. Why, first, madam, if the young ladies, or Mrs Gazette, have any doubts upon their surprising us together, our joining company will clear 'em all; next, we shall have some satisfaction in being an afternoon together, though we enjoy not that full freedom we so passionately desire.

LADY COCKWOOD. Very good, sir.

COURTALL. But then lastly, madam, we gain an opportunity to contrive another appointment tomorrow, which may restore us unto all those joys we have been so unfortunately disappointed of today.

LADY COCKWOOD. This is a very prevailing argument indeed; but since Sir Oliver believes I have conceived

---

212 *a treat and a fiddle*: an entertainment of food and drink, with music.

212 *and a fiddle*: 'and a A Fiddle' (*1668*).

so desperate a sorrow, 'tis fit we should keep this from his knowledge.

COURTALL. Are the young ladies secret?

LADY COCKWOOD. They have the good principles not to betray themselves, I assure you.

COURTALL. Then 'tis but going to a house that is not haunted by the company, and we are secure, and now I think on't, the Bear in Drury Lane is the fittest place for our purpose.

LADY COCKWOOD. I know your honour, dear sir, and submit to your discretion –

To them ARIANA, GATTY, *and* GAZETTE *from the shop.*

Have you gratified your fancies, cousins?

ARIANA. We are ready to wait upon you, madam.

GATTY. I never saw colours better mingled.

GAZETTE. How lively they set off one another, and how they add to the complexion!

LADY COCKWOOD. Mr Courtall, your most humble servant.

COURTALL. Pray, madam, let me have the honour to wait upon you and these young ladies, till I see you in your coach.

LADY COCKWOOD. Your friendship to Sir Oliver would engage you in an unnecessary trouble.

ARIANA. Let not an idle ceremony take you from your serious business, good sir.

GATTY. I should rather have expected to have seen you, sir, walking in Westminster Hall, watching to make a match at tennis, or waiting to dine with a Parliament man, than to meet you in such an idle place as the Exchange is.

---

241 *haunted by the company*: frequented by those we know.
246 *fancies*: judgment in matters of art or fashion (cf. *Man of Mode*, I i 392).
258 *idle*: trifling.
261 *Westminster Hall*: the seat of the law courts, and a place where an ambitious young man might make valuable contacts.
262 *match at tennis*: Charles II was deeply enthusiastic about real tennis, and demonstrating one's skill at the game might be a plausible way of catching his eye.

COURTALL. Methinks, ladies, you are well acquainted with me upon the first visit.

ARIANA. We received your character before, you know, sir, in the Mulberry Garden upon oath.

COURTALL. (*aside*) 'Sdeath, what shall I do? Now out comes all my roguery.

GATTY. Yet I am apt to believe, sister, that was some malicious fellow that wilfully perjured himself, on purpose to make us have an ill opinion of this worthy gentleman.

COURTALL. Some rash men would be apt enough to enquire him out, and cut his throat, ladies, but I heartily forgive him whosoever he was; for on my conscience 'twas not so much out of malice to me, as out of love to you he did it.

GAZETTE. He might imagine Mr Courtall was his rival.

COURTALL. Very likely, Mrs Gazette.

LADY COCKWOOD. Whosoever he was, he was an unworthy fellow I warrant him; Mr Courtall is known to be a person of worth and honour.

ARIANA. We took him for an idle fellow, madam, and gave but very little credit to what he said.

COURTALL. 'Twas very obliging, lady, to believe nothing to the disadvantage of a stranger – [*Aside*] what a couple of young devils are these?

LADY COCKWOOD. Since you are willing to give yourself this trouble –

COURTALL. I ought to do my duty, madam.

Exeunt all but ARIANA *and* GATTY.

ARIANA. How he blushed, and hung down his head!

GATTY. A little more had put him as much out of countenance, as a country clown is when he ventures to compliment his attorney's daughter.

They follow.

---

267 *your character*: a detailed report of your qualities.
295 *country clown*: see note to I ii 94.

SCENE [II]

Sir Oliver's dining-room.

Enter SIR JOSLIN *and* SERVANT *severally.*

SIR JOSLIN. How now old boy! where's my brother Cockwood today?

SERVANT. He desires to be in private, sir.

SIR JOSLIN. Why? what's the matter, man?

SERVANT. This is a day of humiliation, sir, with him for last night's transgression.

SIR JOSLIN. I have business of consequence to impart to him, and must and will speak with him – so, ho! brother Cockwood!

SIR OLIVER. (*without*) Who's that, my brother Jolly?

SIR JOSLIN. The same, the same, come away, boy.

SIR OLIVER. (*without*) For some secret reasons I desire to be in private, brother.

SIR JOSLIN. I have such a design on foot as would draw Diogenes out of his tub to follow it; therefore I say, come away, come away.

SIR OLIVER. (*entering in a nightgown and slippers*) There is such a strange temptation in thy voice, never stir.

SIR JOSLIN. What in thy gown and slippers yet! why, brother, I have bespoke dinner, and engaged Mr Rakehell, the little smart gentleman I have often promised thee to make thee acquainted withal, to bring a whole bevy of damsels in sky, and pink, and flame-coloured taffetas. Come, come, dress thee quickly, there's to be Madam Rampant, a girl that

---

s.d. *severally*: separately.

15 *Diogenes*: the Cynic philosopher (died 324 B.C.), who chose a tub as his house and place of repose. Alexander the Great paid him a visit there.

21 *Rakehell*: debauchee, rake, thorough scoundrel or rascal.

24 *taffetas*: prostitutes wore taffeta petticoats; for parallel references, see the note to I ii 10 in the New Arden edition of Shakespeare's *Henry IV Part I*, ed. A.R. Humphreys.

25 *Rampant*: lustful.

shines, and will drink at such a rate, she's a mistress for Alexander, were he alive again.

SIR OLIVER. How unluckily this falls out! Thomas, what clothes have I to put on?

SERVANT. None but your penitential suit, sir, all the rest are secured.

SIR OLIVER. Oh unspeakable misfortune! that I should be in disgrace with my lady now!

SIR JOSLIN. Come, come, never talk of clothes, put on anything, thou hast a person and a mine will bear it out bravely.

SIR OLIVER. Nay, I know my behaviour will show I am a gentleman; but yet the ladies will look scurvily upon me, brother.

SIR JOSLIN. That's a jest i'faith! he that has *terra firma* in the country, may appear in anything before 'em. [*Sings*]

'For he that would have a wench kind,
Ne'er smugs up himself like a ninny;
But plainly tells her his mind,
And tickles her first with a guinea.'
Hey boy –

SIR OLIVER. I vow thou hast such a bewitching way with thee!

SIR JOSLIN. How lovely will the ladies look when they have a beer-glass in their hands!

SIR OLIVER. I now have a huge mind to venture; but if this should come to my lady's knowledge.

SIR JOSLIN. I have bespoke dinner at the Bear, the privat'st place in town: there will be no spies to

---

27 *Alexander*: for Alexander the Great's capacities as a drinker, see Plutarch, *Moralia* (Loeb edition), vol. 8, pp. 69–71. Plutarch, however, reports that Alexander's devotion to this pastime made him a lazy lover (cf. III iii 434–5).

35 *mine*: mien.

35–6 *bear it out*: carry it off.

36 *bravely*: handsomely.

38 *scurvily*: sourly.

40 *terra firma*: estates, property.

43 *smugs up*: smartens up his appearance, makes trim or gay.

45 *tickles*: see note to III i 108.

50 *beer-glass*: used during heavy drinking to consume wine in large quantities.

betray us, if Thomas be but secret, I dare warrant thee, brother Cockwood.

SIR OLIVER. I have always found Thomas very faithful; but faith 'tis too unkind, considering how tenderly my lady loves me.

SIR JOSLIN. Fie, fie, a man, and kept so much under correction by a busk and a fan!

SIR OLIVER. Nay, I am in my nature as valiant as any man, when once I set out; but i'faith I cannot but think how my dear lady will be concerned when she comes home and misses me.

SIR JOSLIN. A pox upon these qualms.

SIR OLIVER. Well, thou hast seduced me; but I shall look so untowardly.

SIR JOSLIN. Again art thou at it? in, in, and make all the haste that may be, Rakehell and the ladies will be there before us else.

SIR OLIVER. Well, thou art an errant devil – hey – for the ladies, brother Jolly.

SIR JOSLIN. Hey for the ladies, brother Cockwood.

Exeunt singing, 'For he that would', &c.

SCENE III

The Bear.

[SERVANT.] (*without*) Ho Francis, Humphrey, show a room there!

Enter COURTALL, FREEMAN, LADY COCKWOOD, ARIANA, GATTY *and* SENTRY.

COURTALL. Pray, madam, be not so full of apprehension; there is no fear that this should come to Sir Oliver's knowledge.

LADY COCKWOOD. I were ruined if it should, sir! Dear, how I tremble! I never was in one of these houses before.

---

61 *a busk*: a strip of wood, whalebone or other material to stiffen and support a corset.

68 *untowardly*: unseemly, unbecoming.

72 *errant*: unmitigated.

SENTRY. (*aside*) This is a bait for the young ladies to swallow; she has been in most of the eating-houses about town, to my knowledge.

COURTALL. Oh Francis!

Enter WAITER.

WAITER. Your worship's welcome, sir; but I must needs desire you to walk into the next room, for this is bespoke.

LADY COCKWOOD. Mr Courtall, did not you say, this place was private?

COURTALL. I warrant you, madam. What company dines here, Francis?

WAITER. A couple of country knights, Sir Joslin Jolly and Sir Oliver Cockwood, very honest gentlemen.

LADY COCKWOOD. Combination to undo me!

COURTALL. Peace, madam, or you'll betray yourself to the waiter.

LADY COCKWOOD. I am distracted! Sentry, did not I command thee to secure all Sir Oliver's clothes, and leave nothing for him to put on, but his penitential suit, that I might be sure he could not stir abroad today?

SENTRY. I obeyed you in everything, madam; but I have often told you this Sir Joslin is a wicked seducer.

ARIANA. If my uncle sees us, sister, what will he think of us?

GATTY. We come but to wait upon her ladyship.

FREEMAN. You need not fear, you chickens are secure under the wings of that old hen.

COURTALL. Is there to be nobody, Francis, but Sir Oliver and Sir Joslin?

WAITER. Faith, sir, I was enjoined secrecy; but you have an absolute power over me: coming lately out of the country, where there is but little variety, they have a design to solace themselves with a fresh girl or two, as I understand the business. *Exit* WAITER.

LADY COCKWOOD. Oh Sentry! Sir Oliver disloyal! My misfortunes come too thick upon me.

---

39 *enjoined*: prescribed.
42 *solace*: provide some amusement for.

COURTALL. (*aside*) Now is she afraid of being disappointed on all hands.

LADY COCKWOOD. I know not what to do, Mr Courtall, I would not be surprised here myself, and yet I would prevent Sir Oliver from prosecuting his wicked and perfidious intentions.

ARIANA. Now shall we have admirable sport, what with her fear and jealousy.

GATTY. I lay my life she routs the wenches.

Enter WAITER.

WAITER. I must needs desire you to step into the next room; Sir Joslin and Sir Oliver are below already.

LADY COCKWOOD. I have not power to move a foot.

FREEMAN. We will consider what is to be done within, madam.

COURTALL. Pray, madam, come; I have a design in my head which shall secure you, surprise Sir Oliver, and free you from all your fears.

LADY COCKWOOD. It cannot be, sir.

COURTALL. Never fear it: Francis, you may own Mr Freeman and I are in the house, if they ask for us; but not a word of these ladies, as you tender the wearing of your ears.

Exeunt.

Enter SIR JOSLIN, SIR OLIVER, *and* WAITER.

SIR JOSLIN. Come, brother Cockwood, prithee be brisk.

SIR OLIVER. I shall disgrace myself for ever, brother.

SIR JOSLIN. Pox upon care, never droop like a cock in moulting time; thou art spark enough in all conscience.

SIR OLIVER. But my heart begins to fail me when I think of my lady.

SIR JOSLIN. What, more qualms yet?

SIR OLIVER. Well, I will be courageous: but it is not

---

61 *surprise*: take by surprise; cf. line 49.
66 *tender*: hold dear.
68 *brisk*: cheery, lively.
76 *courageous*: lively, lusty, vigorous; see note to II i 61.

necessary these strangers should know this is my penitential suit, brother.

SIR JOSLIN. They shall not, they shall not. Hark you old boy, is the meat provided? is the wine and ice come? and are the melodious rascals at hand I spoke for?

WAITER. Everything will be in a readiness, sir.

SIR JOSLIN. If Mr Rakehell, with a coach full or two of vizard-masks and silk petticoats, call at the door, usher 'em up to the place of execution.

WAITER. You shall be obeyed, sir. *Exit* WAITER.

Enter RAKEHELL.

SIR JOSLIN. Ho, here's my little Rakehell come! Brother Cockwood, let me commend this ingenious gentleman to your acquaintance; he is a knight of the industry, has many admirable qualities, I assure you.

SIR OLIVER. I am very glad, sir, of this opportunity to know you.

RAKEHELL. I am happy, sir, if you esteem me your servant. Hark you, Sir Joslin, is this Sir Oliver Cockwood in earnest?

SIR JOSLIN. In very good earnest I assure you; he is a little fantastical now and then, and dresses himself up in an odd fashion: but that's all one among friends, my little Rakehell.

SIR OLIVER. Where are the damsels you talked of, brother Jolly? I hope Mr Rakehell has not forgot 'em.

RAKEHELL. They are arming for the rancounter.

SIR JOSLIN. What, tricking and trimming?

RAKEHELL. Even so, and will be here immediately.

SIR OLIVER. They need not make themselves so full of temptation; my brother Jolly and I can be wicked enough without it.

SIR JOSLIN. The truth is, my little Rakehell, we are

81–2 *spoke for*: ordered.
89 *ingenious*: cf. note to *Comical Revenge*, IV iii 84.
90–1 *knight of the industry*: see note to *Dramatis Personae*, line 15.
98 *fantastical*: capricious, fanciful.
99 *odd*: editions from *1671* to *1735* read 'old' here.
103 *rancounter*: skirmish.
104 *tricking and trimming*: adorning and prettifying themselves.

both mighty men-at-arms, and thou shalt see us charge anon to the terror of the ladies.

RAKEHELL. Methinks that dress Sir Oliver is a little too rustical for a man of your capacity.

SIR OLIVER. I have an odd humour, sir, now and then; but I have wherewithal at home to be as spruce as any man.

RAKEHELL. Your periwig is too scandalous, Sir Oliver, your black cap and border is never wore but by a fiddler or a waiter.

SIR JOSLIN. Prithee, my little Rakehell, do not put my brother Cockwood out of conceit of himself; methinks your calot is a pretty ornament, and makes a man look both polite and politic.

RAKEHELL. I will allow you, 'tis a grave ware, and fit for men of business, that are every moment bending of their brows, and scratching of their heads, every project would claw out another periwig; but a lover had better appear before his mistress with a bald pate: 'twill make the ladies apprehend a savour, stop their noses, and avoid you: 'slife, love in a cap is more ridiculous than love in a tub, or love in a pipkin.

SIR OLIVER. I must confess your whole head is now in

---

113 *rustical*: rustic.
113 *capacity*: character, social station.
117 *periwig*: the prevailing fashion; large French wigs (also called 'perukes') made up of a mass of irregular curls framing the face and falling round the shoulders (see C. Willett and Phillis Cunnington, *Handbook of English Costume in the Seventeenth Century* (London, Faber, 1955), pp. 163–4).
117 *scandalous*: inappropriate to, unworthy of, your rank.
118 *border*: of hair, worn round the forehead with the cap.
122 *calot*: a plain skull-cap.
122 *ornament*: article of dress, adornment.
123 *polite*: well-bred, modish, elegant.
123 *politic*: shrewd, sagacious, prudent.
128–9 *a bald pate*: an unfortunate side-effect of one contemporary treatment for venereal disease.
129 *apprehend*: anticipate fearfully.
129 *savour*: smell.
131 *love in a tub*: echoing the sub-title of his first comedy, with its allusion to the sweating-tub treatment (see note to *Comical Revenge*, II i 12).
131 *love in a pipkin*: a playful variation on 'love in a tub', 'a pipkin' being 'a small earthenware pot'.
132 *whole head*: full periwig.

fashion; but there was a time when your calot was not so despicable.

RAKEHELL. Here's a peruke, sir.

SIR OLIVER. A very good one.

RAKEHELL. A very good one? 'tis the best in England. Pray, Sir Joslin, take him in your hand, and draw a comb through him, there is not such another frizz in Europe.

SIR JOSLIN. 'Tis a very fine one indeed.

RAKEHELL. Pray, Sir Oliver, do me the favour to grace it on your head a little.

SIR OLIVER. To oblige you, sir.

RAKEHELL. You never wore anything became you half so well in all your life before.

SIR JOSLIN. Why, you never saw him in your life before.

RAKEHELL. That's all one, sir, I know 'tis impossible. Here's a beaver, Sir Oliver, feel him; for fineness, substance, and for fashion, the court of France never saw a better; I have bred him but a fortnight, and have him at command already. Clap him on boldly, never hat took the fore-cock and the hind-cock at one motion so naturally.

SIR OLIVER. I think you have a mind to make a spark of me before I see the ladies.

RAKEHELL. Now you have the mien of a true cavalier, and with one look may make a lady kind, and a hector humble: and since I named a hector, here's a sword, sir: sa, sa, sa, try him, Sir Joslin, put him to't, cut through the staple, run him through the door, beat him to the hilts, if he breaks, you shall have liberty to break my pate, and pay me never a groat of the ten for't.

---

135 *peruke*: see note to line 117.
139 *frizz*: a wig of crisp curls.
150 *beaver*: hat made of beaver's fur.
152 *bred*: trained.
154 *the fore-cock and the hind-cock*: see note to I ii 173.
160 *hector*: blusterer, bully.
161 *sa, sa, sa*: Fr. *ça, ça*, used by fencers when delivering a thrust.
162 *staple*: iron clasp on door-post for fastening door.
164 *groat*: a coin, worth about four pence.
164–5 *of the ten*: i.e. the ten groats it is worth.

SIR JOSLIN. 'Tis a very pretty weapon indeed, sir.

RAKEHELL. The hilt is true French-wrought, and *dorée* by the best workman in France. This sword and this castor, with an embroidered button and loop, which I have to vary him upon occasion, were sent me out of France for a token by my elder brother, that went over with a handsome equipage, to take the pleasure of this *campagne*.

SIR OLIVER. Have you a mind to sell these things, sir?

RAKEHELL. That is below a gentleman; yet if a person of honour or a particular friend, such as I esteem you, Sir Oliver, take at any time a fancy to a band, a cravat, a velvet coat, a vest, a ring, a flageolet, or any other little toy I have about me, I am good-natured, and may be easily persuaded to play the fool upon good terms.

Enter FREEMAN.

SIR JOSLIN. Worthy Mr Freeman!

SIR OLIVER. Honest Frank, how cam'st thou to find us out, man?

FREEMAN. By mere chance, sir; Ned Courtall is without writing a letter, and I came in to know whether you had any particular engagements, gentlemen.

---

167 *dorée*: gilded.
169 *castor*: beaver-hat.
169 *button and loop*: used for securing the hat in one of the fashionable positions (see note to I ii 173).
171 *token*: something given as a mark of affection.
172 *equipage*: outfit for an expedition or journey.
173 *campagne*: see Additional Note.
174 *sell these things*: taverns and eating-houses were, in fact, commonly used as places for bartering and selling (see, for example, Pepys, 24 June 1660).
177 *band*: neck-band or collar of a shirt.
178 *vest*: a sleeveless garment of some length worn by men beneath the coat. It was a fashion recently initiated by Charles II (see Pepys, 8 October and 15 October 1666).
178 *flageolet*: small wind instrument.
180 *play the fool*: act like a fool, i.e. in parting with them.
180–1 *upon good terms*: probably, 'quite cheaply' (though the opposite is also possible, i.e. 'but the price has to be right').
185–6 *without*: outside.

SIR OLIVER. We resolved to be in private; but you are men without exception.

FREEMAN. Methinks you intended to be in private indeed, Sir Oliver. 'Sdeath, what disguise have you got on? are you grown grave since last night, and come to sin incognito?

SIR OLIVER. Hark you in your ear, Frank, this is my habit of humiliation, which I always put on the next day after I have transgressed, the better to make my pacification with my incensed lady –

FREEMAN. Ha, ha, ha –

RAKEHELL. Mr Freeman, your most humble servant, sir.

FREEMAN. Oh my little dapper officer! are you here?

SIR JOSLIN. Ha, Mr Freeman, we have bespoke all the jovial entertainment that a merry wag can wish for, good meat, good wine, and a wholesome wench or two; for the digestion, we shall have Madam Rampant, the glory of the town, the brightest she that shines, or else my little Rakehell is not a man of his word, sir.

RAKEHELL. I warrant you she comes, Sir Joslin.

SIR JOSLIN. (*sings*)

'And if she comes, she shall not scape,
If twenty pounds will win her;
Her very eye commits a rape,
'Tis such a tempting sinner.'

Enter COURTALL.

COURTALL. Well said, Sir Joslin, I see you hold up still, and bate not an ace of your good humour.

SIR JOSLIN. Noble Mr Courtall!

COURTALL. Bless me, Sir Oliver, what, are you going

---

189 *without exception*: i.e. against whom no objection can be made.
195 *habit*: dress.
197 *pacification*: treaty of peace.
201 *officer*: i.e. of the game; see note to I i 12–13.
204 *wholesome*: (1) promoting or conducive to health (2) sound, free from disease (see line 273).
214 *bate not an ace of*: make not the slightest reduction in.

to act a droll? how the people would throng about you, if you were but mounted on a few deal-boards in Covent Garden now!

SIR OLIVER. Hark you, Ned, this is the badge of my lady's indignation for my last night's offense; do not insult over a poor sober man in affliction.

COURTALL. Come, come, send home for your clothes; I hear you are to have ladies, and you are not to learn at these years, how absolutely necessary a rich vest and a peruke are to a man that aims at their favours.

SIR OLIVER. A pox on't, Ned, my lady's gone abroad in a damned jealous melancholy humour, and has commanded her woman to secure 'em.

COURTALL. Under lock and key?

SIR OLIVER. Ay, ay, man, 'tis usual in these cases, out of pure love in hopes to reclaim me, and to keep me from doing myself an injury by drinking two days together.

COURTALL. What a loving lady 'tis!

SIR OLIVER. There are sots that would think themselves happy in such a lady, Ned; but to a true-bred gentleman all lawful solace is abomination.

RAKEHELL. Mr Courtall, your most humble servant, sir.

COURTALL. Oh! my little knight of the industry, I am glad to see you in such good company.

FREEMAN. Courtall, hark you, are the masking-habits which you sent to borrow at the playhouse come yet?

COURTALL. Yes, and the ladies are almost dressed: this design will add much to our mirth, and give us the benefit of their meat, wine, and music for our entertainment.

FREEMAN. 'Twas luckily thought of.

Music.

SIR OLIVER. Hark, the music comes.

SIR JOSLIN. Hey, boys – let 'em enter, let 'em enter.

---

217 *a droll*: farce (the word was used for the short entertainments carved out of full-length plays for surreptitious performance during the closing of the theatres between 1642 and 1660).

217 *the people*: i.e. the common people (the presumption is that the audience for such an entertainment would be fairly lowly).

218 *a few deal-boards*: i.e. an improvised stage.

232 *reclaim*: see note to II ii 120.

Enter WAITER.

WAITER. An't please your worships, there is a mask of ladies without, that desire to have the freedom to come in and dance.

SIR JOSLIN. Hey! boys –

SIR OLIVER. Did you bid 'em come *en masquerade*, Mr Rakehell?

RAKEHELL. No; but Rampant is a mad wench, she was half a dozen times a-mumming in private company last Shrovetide, and I lay my life she has put 'em all upon this frolic.

COURTALL. They are mettled girls, I warrant them, Sir Joslin, let 'em be what they will.

SIR JOSLIN. Let 'em enter, let 'em enter, ha boys –

Enter MUSIC *and the* LADIES *in an antic, and then they take out, my* LADY COCKWOOD SIR OLIVER, *the* YOUNG LADIES COURTALL *and* FREEMAN, *and* SENTRY SIR JOSLIN, *and dance a set dance.*

SIR OLIVER. Oh my little rogue! have I got thee? How I will turn and wind, and fegue thy body!

SIR JOSLIN. Mettle on all sides, mettle on all sides, i'faith; how swimmingly would this pretty little ambling filly carry a man of my body! (*Sings*)

'She's so bonny and brisk,
How she'd curvet and frisk,
If a man were once mounted upon her!
Let me have but a leap

---

251 *An't*: if it.
251–2 *a mask of ladies*: a set of masked ladies.
255 *en masquerade*: see Additional Note.
257 *mad*: see note to I ii 154.
258 *a-mumming*: i.e. in disguise.
259 *Shrove-tide*: the period immediately preceding Lent, a time for merrymaking and carnival.
261 *mettled*: mettlesome.
263 s.d. *antic*: fancy dress.
263 s.d. *take out*: select partners for a dance.
265 *fegue*: 'do for'.
267 *swimmingly*: glidingly, fluently.
268 *ambling*: graceful, smooth and easy in movement.
270 *curvet*: leap, frisk; 'carvet' (*1668*).
272 *leap*: a 'leaping-house' was one name for a brothel.

Where 'tis wholesome and cheap,
And a fig for your person of honour.'

SIR OLIVER. 'Tis true, little Joslin, i'faith.

COURTALL. They have warmed us, Sir Oliver.

SIR OLIVER. Now am I as rampant as a lion, Ned, and could love as vigorously as a seaman that is newly landed after an East India voyage.

COURTALL. Take my advice, Sir Oliver, do not in your rage deprive yourself of your only hope of an accommodation with your lady.

SIR OLIVER. I had rather have a perpetual civil war, than purchase peace at such a dishonourable rate. A poor fiddler, after he has been three days persecuted at a country wedding, takes more delight in scraping upon his old squeaking fiddle, than I do in fumbling on that domestic instrument of mine.

COURTALL. Be not so bitter, Sir Oliver, on your own dear lady.

SIR OLIVER. I was married to her when I was young, Ned, with a design to be balked, as they tie whelps to the bell-wether; where I have been so butted, 'twere enough to fright me, were I not pure mettle, from ever running at sheep again.

COURTALL. That's no sure rule, Sir Oliver; for a wife's a dish, of which if a man once surfeit, he shall have a better stomach to all others ever after.

SIR OLIVER. What a shape is here, Ned! so exact and tempting, 'twould persuade a man to be an implicit sinner, and take her face upon credit.

SIR JOSLIN. Come, brother Cockwood, let us get 'em to lay aside these masking fopperies, and then we'll fegue 'em in earnest: give us a bottle, waiter.

FREEMAN. Not before dinner, good Sir Joslin –

---

274 *honour*: rank.

277 *rampant*: (1) lustful, as in Madam Rampant (2) (of a lion) rearing or standing with the fore-paws in the air.

292 *balked*: held in check.

292–3 *tie whelps to the bell-wether*: young dogs were tied to the head sheep of a flock in order to break them of bothering the sheep.

298 *stomach*: appetite.

300–1 *implicit sinner*: a play on the theological term, 'implicit faith', which meant acceptance of a doctrine on the authority of another person and without question.

SIR OLIVER. Lady, though I have out of drollery put myself into this contemptible dress at present, I am a gentleman, and a man of courage, as you shall find anon by my brisk behaviour.

RAKEHELL. Sir Joslin! Sir Oliver! these are none of our ladies, they are just come to the door in a coach, and have sent for me down to wait upon 'em up to you.

SIR JOSLIN. Hey – boys, more game, more game! Fetch 'em up, fetch 'em up.

SIR OLIVER. Why, what a day of sport will here be, Ned!

Exit RAKEHELL.

SIR JOSLIN. They shall all have fair play, boys.

SIR OLIVER. And we will match ourselves, and make a prize on't, Ned Courtall and I, against Frank Freeman and you brother Jolly, and Rakehell shall be judge for gloves and silk stockings, to be bestowed as the conqueror shall fancy.

SIR JOSLIN. Agreed, agreed, agreed.

COURTALL.
FREEMAN. } A match, a match.

SIR OLIVER. Hey, boys!

LADY COCKWOOD *counterfeits a fit.*

SENTRY. (*pulling off her mask*) Oh heavens! my dear lady! help, help!

SIR OLIVER. What's here? Sentry and my lady! 'Sdeath, what a condition am I in now, brother Jolly! You have brought me into this premunire: for heaven's sake run down quickly, and send the rogue and whores away. Help, help! oh help! dear madam, sweet lady!

Exit SIR JOSLIN, SIR OLIVER *kneels down by her.*

---

318 *match*: set up a contest between.

319 *prize*: contest, match.

330 *into this premunire*: into this predicament, difficulty. Given the subsequent talk of 'disloyal actions' (lines 344–5) and 'abominable treason' (line 349), however, the term's original meaning is relevant; a 'premunire' was 'an act in contempt of the royal prerogative, especially the prosecuting in a foreign court of a suit cognizable by the law of England'. Here, Lady Cockwood is the royal personage whose prerogative has been slighted, and for 'foreign court' one should read 'Madam Rampant'.

SENTRY. Oh she's gone, she's gone!

FREEMAN. Give her more air.

COURTALL. Fetch a glass of cold water, Freeman.

SIR OLIVER. Dear madam speak, sweet madam speak.

SENTRY. Out upon thee for a vile hypocrite! thou art the wicked author of all this; who but such a reprobate, such an obdurate sinner as thou art, could go about to abuse so sweet a lady?

SIR OLIVER. Dear Sentry, do not stab me with thy words, but stab me with thy bodkin rather, that I may here die a sacrifice at her feet, for all my disloyal actions.

SENTRY. No, live, live, to be a reproach and a shame to all rebellious husbands; ah, that she had but my heart! but thou hast bewitched her affections; thou shouldst then dearly smart for this abominable treason.

GATTY. So, now she begins to come to herself.

ARIANA. Set her more upright, and bend her a little forward.

LADY COCKWOOD. Unfortunate woman! let me go, why do you hold me? would I had a dagger at my heart, to punish it for loving that ungrateful man.

SIR OLIVER. Dear madam, were I but worthy of your pity and belief.

LADY COCKWOOD. Peace, peace, perfidious man, I am too tame and foolish – were I every day at the plays, the Park, and Mulberry Garden, with a kind look secretly to indulge the unlawful passion of some young gallant; or did I associate myself with the gaming madams, and were every afternoon at my Lady Brief's and my Lady Meanwell's at ombre and quebas, pretending ill luck to borrow money of a

---

343 *bodkin*: a long pin used by women to fasten up their hair.

363 *madams*: used as a generally contemptuous term, perhaps 'hussies'.

364 *Brief's*: the lady's name suggests her character; 'a brief' was a cheating-device at cards.

364 *ombre*: a card game played by three persons with forty cards; its popularity was of recent origin (*OED* cites from 1661 a reference to 'Hombre, the new game at cards now in fashion at court'). 'Umbre' (*1668*).

365 *quebas*: 'some kind of a game' (*OED*); presumably another card game.

friend, and then pretending good luck to excuse the plenty to a husband, my suspicious demeanour had deserved this; but I who out of a scrupulous tenderness to my honour, and to comply with thy base jealousy, have denied myself all those blameless recreations, which a virtuous lady might enjoy, to be thus inhumanly reviled in my own person, and thus unreasonably robbed and abused in thine too!

COURTALL. Sure she will take up anon, or crack her mind, or else the devil's in't.

LADY COCKWOOD. Do not stay and torment me with thy sight; go, graceless wretch, follow thy treacherous resolutions, do, and waste that poor stock of comfort which I should have at home, upon those your ravenous cormorants below: I feel my passion begin to swell again. (*She has a little fit again*)

COURTALL. Now will she get an absolute dominion over him, and all this will be my plague in the end.

SIR OLIVER. (*running up and down*) Ned Courtall, Frank Freeman, cousin Ariana, and dear cousin Gatty, for heaven's sake join all, and moderate her passion – ah Sentry! forbear thy unjust reproaches, take pity on thy master! thou hast a great influence over her, and I have always been mindful of thy favours.

SENTRY. You do not deserve the least compassion, nor would I speak a good word for you, but that I know for all this, 'twill be acceptable to my poor lady. Dear madam, do but look up a little, Sir Oliver lies at your feet an humble penitent.

ARIANA. How bitterly he weeps! how sadly he sighs!

GATTY. I dare say he counterfeited his sin, and is real in his repentance.

COURTALL. Compose yourself a little, pray, madam; all this was mere raillery, a way of talk, which Sir Oliver being well-bred, has learned among the gay people of the town.

FREEMAN. If you did but know, madam, what an odious thing it is to be thought to love a wife in good company, you would easily forgive him.

---

374 *take up*: stop.
380 *cormorants*: large, voracious sea-birds; hence, insatiably greedy people (in this case, the whores below).

LADY COCKWOOD. No, no, 'twas the mild correction which I gave him for his insolent behaviour last night, that has encouraged him again thus to insult over my affections.

COURTALL. Come, come, Sir Oliver, out with your bosom-secret, and clear all things to your lady; is it not as we have said?

SIR OLIVER. Or may I never have the happiness to be in her good grace again; and as for the harlots, dear madam, here is Ned Courtall and Frank Freeman, that have often seen me in company of the wicked; let 'em speak, if they ever knew me tempted to a disloyal action in their lives.

COURTALL. On my conscience, madam, I may more safely swear, that Sir Oliver has been constant to your ladyship, than that a girl of twelve years old has her maidenhead this warm and ripening age.

Enter SIR JOSLIN.

SIR OLIVER. Here's my brother Jolly too can witness the loyalty of my heart, and that I did not intend any treasonable practice against your ladyship in the least.

SIR JOSLIN. Unless feguing 'em with a beer-glass be included in the statute. Come, Mr Courtall, to satisfy my lady, and put her in a little good humour, let us sing the catch I taught you yesterday, that was made by a country vicar on my brother Cockwood and me.

They sing.

'Love and wenching are toys,
Fit to please beardless boys,
Th'are sports we hate worse than a leaguer;
When we visit a miss,
We still brag how we kiss,
But 'tis with a bottle we fegue her.'

SIR JOSLIN. Come, come, madam, let all things be forgot; dinner is ready, the cloth is laid in the next

---

432 *leaguer*: military camp; siege (the song seems to be a rather cowardly variation on those lyrics from the Cavalier defeat which turned their back on the war and looked to the pleasures of the flesh for consolation – see, for instance, Alexander Brome, *Songs And Other Poems* (London, 1661), p. 48).

433 *miss*: kept mistress or whore.

room, let us in and be merry; there was no harm meant as I am true little Joslin.

LADY COCKWOOD. Sir Oliver knows I can't be angry with him, though he plays the naughty man thus; but why, my dear, would y'expose yourself in this ridiculous habit, to the censure of both our honours?

SIR OLIVER. Indeed I was to blame to be over-persuaded; I intended dutifully to retire into the pantry, and there civilly to divert myself at back-gammon with the butler.

SIR JOSLIN. Faith, I must ev'n own, the fault was mine, I enticed him hither, lady.

SIR OLIVER. How the devil, Ned, came they to find us out here!

COURTALL. No bloodhound draws so sure as a jealous woman.

SIR OLIVER. I am afraid Thomas has been unfaithful: prithee, Ned, speak to my lady, that there may be a perfect understanding between us, and that Sentry may be sent home for my clothes, that I may no longer wear the marks of her displeasure.

COURTALL. Let me alone, Sir Oliver. (*He goes to my* LADY COCKWOOD) How do you find yourself, madam, after this violent passion?

LADY COCKWOOD. This has been a lucky adventure, Mr Courtall; now am I absolute mistress of my own conduct for a time.

COURTALL. Then shall I be a happy man, madam: [*aside*] I knew this would be the consequence of all, and yet could not I forbear the project.

SIR OLIVER. (*to* SIR JOSLIN) How didst thou shuffle away Rakehell and the ladies brother?

SIR JOSLIN. I have appointed 'em to meet us at six a clock at the new Spring Garden.

SIR OLIVER. Then will we yet, in spite of the stars that

---

441 *naughty*: a stronger term of disapproval in the seventeenth century than now.
444–5 *over-persuaded*: persuaded against my own judgment.
446 *divert myself*: entertain myself.
452 *draws*: follows a scent.
456 *understanding*: agreement, peace-treaty.
471 *Spring Garden*: pleasure gardens at Vauxhall.

have crossed us, be in conjunction with Madam Rampant, brother.

COURTALL. Come, gentlemen, dinner is on the table.

SIR JOSLIN. Ha! Sly-girl and Mad-cap, I'll enter you, i'faith; since you have found the way to the Bear, I'll fegue you. (*Sings*)

'When we visit a miss,
We still brag how we kiss;
But 'tis with a bottle we fegue her.'

Exeunt singing.

ACT IV

SCENE I

A dining-room.

Enter LADY COCKWOOD.

LADY COCKWOOD. A lady cannot be too jealous of her servant's love, this faithless and inconstant age: his amorous carriage to that prating girl today, though he pretends it was to blind Sir Oliver, I fear will prove a certain sign of his revolted heart; the letters I have counterfeited in these girls' name will clear all; if he accept of that appointment, and refuses mine, I need not any longer doubt.

Enter SENTRY.

Sentry, have the letters and message been delivered, as I directed?

SENTRY. Punctually, madam; I knew they were to be found at the latter end of a play, I sent a porter first

473 *conjunction*: playing upon the astrological meaning of the word (cf. 'the stars', line 472), i.e. the apparent proximity of two planets or other heavenly bodies.
476 *enter*: initiate.
11 *Punctually*: cf. note to II ii 30.

with the letter to Mr Courtall, who was at the King's House, he sent for him out by the door-keeper, and delivered it into his own hands.

LADY COCKWOOD. Did you keep on your vizard, that the fellow might not know how to describe you?

SENTRY. I did, madam.

LADY COCKWOOD. And how did he receive it?

SENTRY. Like a traitor to all goodness, with all the signs of joy imaginable.

LADY COCKWOOD. Be not angry, Sentry, 'tis as my heart wished it: what did you do with the letter to Mr Freeman? for I thought fit to deceive 'em both, to make my policy less suspicious to Courtall.

SENTRY. The porter found him at the Duke's House, madam, and delivered it with like care.

LADY COCKWOOD. Very well.

SENTRY. After the letters were delivered, madam, I went myself to the playhouse, and sent in for Mr Courtall, who came out to me immediately; I told him your ladyship presented your humble service to him, and that Sir Oliver was going into the city with Sir Joslin, to visit his brother Cockwood, and that it would add much more to your ladyship's happiness, if he would be pleased to meet you in Gray's Inn Walks this lovely evening.

LADY COCKWOOD. And how did he entertain the motion?

SENTRY. Bless me! I tremble still to think upon it! I could not have imagined he had been so wicked; he counterfeited the greatest passion, railed at his fate, and swore a thousand horrid oaths, that since he came into the playhouse he had notice of a business that concerned both his honour and fortune; and that he was an undone man, if he did not go about it presently; prayed me to desire your ladyship to

---

13–14 *King's House*: the Theatre Royal near Drury Lane, at which the King's Company acted.

26 *Duke's House*: the theatre in Lincoln's Inn Fields, at which the Duke's Company played. It was there that *She Would* was performed.

36–7 *Gray's Inn Walks*: a fashionable promenading-place.

38–9 *entertain the motion*: receive the proposal.

excuse him this evening, and that tomorrow he would be wholly at your devotion.

LADY COCKWOOD. Ha, ha, ha! he little thinks how much he has obliged me.

SENTRY. I had much ado to forbear upbraiding him with his ingratitude to your ladyship.

LADY COCKWOOD. Poor Sentry! be not concerned for me, I have conquered my affection, and thou shalt find it is not jealousy has been my counsellor in this. Go, let our hoods and masks be ready, that I may surprise Courtall, and make the best advantage of this lucky opportunity.

SENTRY. I obey you, madam. *Exit* SENTRY.

LADY COCKWOOD. How am I filled with indignation! To find my person and my passion both despised, and what is more, so much precious time fooled away in fruitless expectation: I would poison my face, so I might be revenged on this ingrateful villain.

Enter SIR OLIVER.

SIR OLIVER. My dearest!

LADY COCKWOOD. My dearest dear! prithee do not go into the city tonight.

SIR OLIVER. My brother Jolly is gone before, and I am to call him at counsellor Trott's chamber in the Temple.

LADY COCKWOOD. Well, if you did but know the fear I have upon me when you are absent, you would not seek occasions to be from me thus.

SIR OLIVER. Let me comfort thee with a kiss; what shouldst thou be afraid of?

LADY COCKWOOD. I cannot but believe that every woman that sees thee must be in love with thee, as I am; do not blame my jealousy.

SIR OLIVER. I protest I would refuse a countess rather than abuse thee, poor heart.

LADY COCKWOOD. And then you are so desperate upon the least occasion, I should have acquainted you else with something that concerns your honour.

---

68 *the city*: the business or trading part of the city of London.

70 *the Temple*: a centre for the legal profession in London; the name refers to two of the Inns of Court, which stand on the site of the buildings once occupied by the Knights Templar.

SIR OLIVER. My honour! you ought in duty to do it.

LADY COCKWOOD. Nay, I knew how passionate you would be presently; therefore you shall never know it.

SIR OLIVER. Do not leave me in doubt, I shall suspect everyone I look upon; I will kill a Common Council-man or two before I come back, if you do not tell me.

LADY COCKWOOD. Dear, how I tremble! will you promise me you will not quarrel then? if you tender my life and happiness, I am sure you will not.

SIR OLIVER. I will bear anything rather than be an enemy to thy quiet, my dear.

LADY COCKWOOD. I could wish Mr Courtall a man of better principles, because I know you love him, my dear.

SIR OLIVER. Why, what has he done?

LADY COCKWOOD. I always treated him with great respects, out of my regard to your friendship; but he, like an impudent man as he is, today misconstruing my civility, in most unseemly language, made a foul attempt upon my honour.

SIR OLIVER. Death, and hell, and furies, I will have my pumps, and long sword!

LADY COCKWOOD. Oh, I shall faint! did not you promise me you would not be so rash?

SIR OLIVER. Well, I will not kill him, for fear of murdering thee, my dear.

LADY COCKWOOD. You may decline your friendship, and by your coldness give him no encouragement to visit our family.

SIR OLIVER. I think thy advice the best for this once indeed; for it is not fit to publish such a business: but if he should be ever tempting or attempting, let me know it, prithee, my dear.

LADY COCKWOOD. If you moderate yourself accord-

88–9 *Common Council-man*: elected member of the city government of London.

91 *tender*: regard with kindness, treat with proper regard.

100 *your friendship*: i.e. the friendship you felt for him.

105 *pumps*: light shoes appropriate for duelling.

105 *long sword*: Sir Oliver is once again behind the times, since short swords were now the fashionable wear.

114 *publish*: make publicly known.

117 *moderate yourself*: become less violent.

ing to my directions now, I shall never conceal anything from you, that may increase your just opinion of my conjugal fidelity.

SIR OLIVER. Was ever man blessed with such a virtuous lady! (*aside*) yet cannot I forbear going a-ranging again. Now must I to the Spring Garden to meet my brother Jolly and Madam Rampant.

LADY COCKWOOD. Prithee, be so good to think how melancholy I spend my time here; for I have joy in no company but thine, and let that bring thee home a little sooner.

SIR OLIVER. Thou hast been so kind in this discovery, that I am loth to leave thee.

LADY COCKWOOD. I wish you had not been engaged so far.

SIR OLIVER. Ay, that's it: farewell, my virtuous dear.

Exit SIR OLIVER.

LADY COCKWOOD. Farewell, my dearest dear. I know he has not courage enough to question Courtall; but this will make him hate him, increase his confidence of me, and justify my banishing that false fellow our house; it is not fit a man that has abused my love, should come hither, and pry into my actions: besides, this will make his access more difficult to that wanton baggage.

Enter ARIANA *and* GATTY *with their hoods and masks.*

Whither are you going, cousins?

GATTY. To take the air upon the water, madam.

ARIANA. And for variety, to walk a turn or two in the new Spring Garden.

LADY COCKWOOD. I heard you were gone abroad with Mr Courtall and Mr Freeman.

GATTY. For heaven's sake, why should your ladyship have such an ill opinion of us?

LADY COCKWOOD. The truth is, before I saw you, I believed it merely the vanity of that prating man; Mr Courtall told Mrs Gazette this morning, that you were

---

122 *a-ranging*: roving sexually.

143–5 *upon the water . . . Spring Garden*: a popular way of going to the Spring Garden was by river.

so well acquainted already, that you would meet him and Mr Freeman anywhere, and that you had promised 'em to receive and make appointment by letters.

GATTY. Oh impudent man!

ARIANA. Now you see the consequence, sister, of our rambling; they have raised this false story from our innocent fooling with 'em in the Mulberry Garden last night.

GATTY. I could almost forswear ever speaking to a man again.

LADY COCKWOOD. Was Mr Courtall in the Mulberry Garden last night?

ARIANA. Yes, madam.

LADY COCKWOOD. And did he speak to you?

GATTY. There passed a little harmless raillery betwixt us; but you amaze me, madam.

ARIANA. I could not imagine any man could be thus unworthy.

LADY COCKWOOD. He has quite lost my good opinion too: in duty to Sir Oliver, I have hitherto showed him some countenance; but I shall hate him hereafter for your sakes. But I detain you from your recreations, cousins.

GATTY. We are very much obliged to your ladyship for this timely notice.

ARIANA.
GATTY. } Your servant, madam.

Exeunt ARIANA *and* GATTY.

LADY COCKWOOD. Your servant, cousins – in the Mulberry Garden last night! when I sat languishing, and vainly expecting him at home: this has incensed me so, that I could kill him. I am glad these girls are gone to the Spring Garden, it helps my design; the letters I have counterfeited, have appointed Courtall and Freeman to meet them there, they will produce 'em, and confirm all I have said: I will daily poison these girls with such lies as shall make their quarrel to Courtall irreconcileable, and render Freeman only suspected; for I would not have him thought equally

159 *rambling*: a word more usually applied to male excursions; see note to *Comical Revenge*, I ii 129.

guilty: he secretly began to make an address to me at the Bear, and this breach shall give him an opportunity to pursue it.

Enter SENTRY.

SENTRY. Here are your things, madam.

LADY COCKWOOD. That's well: oh Sentry! I shall once more be happy; for now Mr Courtall has given me an occasion, that I may without ingratitude check his unlawful passion, and free myself from the trouble of an intrigue, that gives me every day such fearful apprehensions of my honour.

Exeunt LADY COCKWOOD *and* SENTRY.

SCENE II

New Spring Garden.

Enter SIR JOSLIN, RAKEHELL, *and* WAITER.

WAITER. Will you be pleased to walk into an arbour, gentlemen?

SIR JOSLIN. By and by, good sir.

RAKEHELL. I wonder Sir Oliver is not come yet.

SIR JOSLIN. Nay, he will not fail I warrant thee, boy; but what's the matter with thy nose, my little Rakehell?

RAKEHELL. A foolish accident; jesting at the Fleece this afternoon, I mistook my man a little, a dull rogue that could not understand raillery, made a sudden repartee with a quart-pot, Sir Joslin.

SIR JOSLIN. Why didst not thou stick him to the wall, my little Rakehell?

RAKEHELL. The truth is, Sir Joslin, he deserved it; but look you, in case of a doubtful wound, I am unwilling to give my friends too often the trouble to bail me; and if it should be mortal, you know a younger

---

8 *the Fleece*: see note to *Comical Revenge* II i 38.
15 *doubtful wound*: i.e. a wound that might prove mortal.

brother has not wherewithal to rebate the edge of a witness, and mollify the hearts of a jury.

SIR JOSLIN. This is very prudently considered indeed.

RAKEHELL. 'Tis time to be wise, sir; my courage has almost run me out of a considerable annuity. When I lived first about this town, I agreed with a surgeon for twenty pounds a quarter to cure me of all the knocks, bruises, and green wounds I should receive, and in one half year the poor fellow begged me to be released of his bargain, and swore I would undo him else in lint and balsam.

Enter SIR OLIVER.

SIR JOSLIN. Ho! here's my brother Cockwood come –

SIR OLIVER. Ay, brother Jolly, I have kept my word, you see; but 'tis a barbarous thing to abuse my lady, I have had such a proof of her virtue, I will tell thee all anon. But where's Madam Rampant, and the rest of the ladies, Mr Rakehell?

RAKEHELL. Faith, sir, being disappointed at noon, they were unwilling any more to set a certainty at hazard: 'tis term-time, and they have severally betook themselves, some to their chamber-practice, and others to the places of public pleading.

SIR OLIVER. Faith, brother Jolly, let us ev'n go into an arbour, and then fegue Mr Rakehell.

SIR JOSLIN. With all my heart, would we had Madam Rampant. (*Sings*)

'She's as frolic and free,
As her lovers dare be,
Never awed by a foolish punctilio;

---

18 *rebate*: blunt.
25 *green*: fresh, unhealed.
28 *balsam*: see note to *Comical Revenge*, I iv 18.
37 *term-time*: therefore, London is crowded (see note to III i 32), and the whores, like the lawyers, find it easy to pick up clients.
38 *chamber-practice*: playing on 'chamber' as (1) lawyers' chambers (2) bedchamber.
39 *public pleading*: (1) lawyers' advocacy (2) sexual solicitation.
41 *fegue*: presumably with a beer-glass, cf. III iii 435.
44 *frolic*: full of sportive tricks.
46 *punctilio*: 'a small nicety of behaviour; a nice point of exactness' (Johnson).

She'll not start from her place,
Though thou nam'st a black ace,
And will drink a beer-glass to spudilio.'
Hey, boys! Come, come, come! let's in, and delay our sport no longer.

Exeunt singing, 'She'll not start from her', &c.

Enter COURTALL *and* FREEMAN *severally.*

COURTALL. Freeman!

FREEMAN. Courtall, what the devil's the matter with thee? I have observed thee prying up and down the walks like a citizen's wife that has dropped her holy-day pocket-handkercher.

COURTALL. What unlucky devil has brought thee hither?

FREEMAN. I believe a better-natured devil than yours, Courtall, if a leveret be better meat than an old puss, that has been coursed by most of the young fellows of her country: I am not working my brain for a counter-plot, a disappointment is not my business.

COURTALL. You are mistaken, Freeman: prithee be gone, and leave me the garden to myself, or I shall grow as testy as an old fowler that is put by his shoot, after he has crept half a mile upon his belly.

FREEMAN. Prithee be thou gone, or I shall take it as unkindly as a chymist would, if thou shouldst kick down his limbeck in the very minute that he looked for projection.

COURTALL. Come, come, you must yield, Freeman, your business cannot be of such consequence as mine.

FREEMAN. If ever thou hadst a business of such conse-

---

49 *spudilio*: the ace of spades in ombre and quadrille (but the context suggests that both this word and 'black ace' are codes for some activity in Madam Rampant's line).
55–6 *holy-day*: holiday (the latter still falling largely on holy days).
60 *leveret . . . old puss*: young hare . . . old hare.
66 *put by*: prevented from making.
69 *chymist*: alchemist.
70 *limbeck*: alembic, an apparatus used for distilling.
71 *projection*: in alchemy, the casting of the powder of the philosopher's stone upon a metal in fusion in order to transmute it into gold or silver (often used, as here, as a synonym for 'sexual climax').

quence in thy life as mine is, I will condescend to be made incapable of affairs presently.

COURTALL. Why, I have an appointment made me, man, without my seeking, by a woman for whom I would have mortgaged my whole estate to have had her abroad but to break a cheesecake.

FREEMAN. And I have an appointment made me without my seeking too, by such a she, that I will break the whole ten commandments, rather than disappoint her of her breaking one.

COURTALL. Come, you do but jest, Freeman, a forsaken mistress could not be more malicious than thou art: prithee be gone.

FREEMAN. Prithee do thou be gone.

COURTALL. 'Sdeath! the sight of thee will scare my woman for ever.

FREEMAN. 'Sdeath! the sight of thee will make my woman believe me the falsest villain breathing.

COURTALL. We shall stand fooling till we are both undone, and I know not how to help it.

FREEMAN. Let us proceed honestly like friends, discover the truth of things to one another, and if we cannot reconcile our business, we will draw cuts, and part fairly.

COURTALL. I do not like that way; for talk is only allowable at the latter end of an intrigue, and should never be used at the beginning of an amour, for fear of frighting a young lady from her good intentions – yet I care not, though I read the letter, but I will conceal the name.

FREEMAN. I have a letter too, and am content to do the same.

COURTALL. (*reads*) 'Sir, in sending you this letter, I proceed against the modesty of our sex – '

FREEMAN. 'Sdeath, this begins just like my letter.

COURTALL. Do you read on then –

FREEMAN. (*reads*) 'But let not the good opinion I have conceived of you, make you too severe in your censuring of me – '

COURTALL. Word for word.

---

75 *condescend*: agree.
97 *draw cuts*: draw lots (with sticks of differing lengths).

FREEMAN. Now do you read again.

COURTALL. (*reads*) 'If you give yourself the trouble to be walking in the new Spring Garden this evening, I will meet you there, and tell you a secret, which I have reason to fear, because it comes to your knowledge by my means, will make you hate your humble servant.'

FREEMAN. Verbatim my letter, hey-day!

COURTALL. Prithee let's compare the hands.

They compare 'em.

FREEMAN. 'Sdeath, the hand's the same.

COURTALL. I hope the name is not the same too –

FREEMAN. If it be, we are finely jilted, faith.

COURTALL. I long to be undeceived; prithee do thou show first, Freeman.

FREEMAN. No – but both together, if you will.

COURTALL. Agreed.

FREEMAN. Ariana.

COURTALL. Gatty – ha, ha, ha.

FREEMAN. The little rogues are masculine in their proceedings, and have made one another confidents in their love.

COURTALL. But I do not like this altogether so well, Frank; I wish they had appointed us several places: for though 'tis evident they have trusted one another with the bargain, no woman ever seals before witness.

FREEMAN. Prithee how didst thou escape the snares of the old devil this afternoon?

COURTALL. With much ado; Sentry had set me; if her ladyship had got me into her clutches, there had been no getting off without a rescue, or paying down the money; for she always arrests upon execution.

FREEMAN. You made a handsome lie to her woman.

COURTALL. For all this, I know she's angry; for she thinks nothing a just excuse in these cases, though it were to save the forfeit of a man's estate, or reprieve the life of her own natural brother.

---

123 *hands*: handwriting.
137 *several*: different.
139 *seals*: i.e. 'the bargain'.
144–5 *rescue . . . execution*: see notes to *Comical Revenge*, V iv 28 and V ii 64.

FREEMAN. Faith, thou hast not done altogether like a gentleman with her; thou shouldst fast thyself up to a stomach now and then, to oblige her; if there were nothing in it, but the hearty welcome, methinks 'twere enough to make thee bear sometimes with the homeliness of the fare.

COURTALL. I know not what I might do in a camp, where there were no other woman; but I shall hardly in this town, where there is such plenty, forbear good meat, to get myself an appetite to horseflesh.

FREEMAN. This is rather an aversion in thee, than any real fault in the woman; if this lucky business had not fallen out, I intended with your good leave to have outbid you for her ladyship's favour.

COURTALL. I should never have consented to that, Frank; though I am a little resty at present, I am not such a jade, but I should strain if another rid against me; I have ere now liked nothing in a woman that I have loved at last in spite only, because another had a mind to her.

FREEMAN. Yonder are a couple of vizards tripping towards us.

COURTALL. 'Tis they, i'faith.

FREEMAN. We need not divide, since they come together.

COURTALL. I was a little afraid when we compared letters, they had put a trick upon us; but now I am confirmed they are mighty honest.

Enter ARIANA *and* GATTY.

ARIANA. We cannot avoid 'em.

GATTY. Let us dissemble our knowledge of their business a little, and then take 'em down in the height of their assurance.

COURTALL.
FREEMAN. } Your servant, ladies.

ARIANA. I perceive it is as impossible, gentlemen, to

---

157 *camp*: military camp.
166 *resty*: see note to II i 32.
167 *jade*: sorry, worn-out horse.
167 *strain*: stretch myself to the utmost.
181 *take 'em down*: humble, humiliate them.

walk without you, as without our shadows; never were poor women so haunted by the ghosts of their self-murdered lovers.

GATTY. If it should be our good fortunes to have you in love with us, we will take care you shall not grow desperate, and leave the world in an ill humour.

ARIANA. If you should, certainly your ghosts would be very malicious.

COURTALL. 'Twere pity you should have your curtains drawn in the dead of the night, and your pleasing slumbers interrupted by anything but flesh and blood, ladies.

FREEMAN. Shall we walk a turn?

ARIANA. By yourselves, if you please.

GATTY. Our company may put a constraint upon you; for I find you daily hover about these gardens, as a kite does about a back-side, watching an opportunity to catch up the poultry.

ARIANA. Woe be to the daughter or wife of some merchant-tailor, or poor felt-maker now; for you seldom row to Fox Hall without some such plot against the city.

FREEMAN. You wrong us, ladies, our business has happily succeeded, since we have the honour to wait upon you.

GATTY. You could not expect to see us here.

COURTALL. Your true lover, madam, when he misses his mistress, is as restless as a spaniel that has lost his master; he ranges up and down the plays, the Park, and all the gardens, and never stays long, but where he has the happiness to see her.

GATTY. I suppose your mistress, Mr Courtall, is always the last woman you are acquainted with.

COURTALL. Do not think, madam, I have that false measure of my acquaintance, which poets have of their verses, always to think the last best, though I esteem you so, in justice to your merit.

---

201 *back-side*: rear of premises (birds of prey were a common presence in seventeenth-century towns).

205 *Fox Hall*: Vauxhall (spelt Fox Hall until about 1700), the location of the Spring Gardens.

206 *the city*: see note to IV i 68.

217 *last*: most recent.

GATTY. Or if you do not love her best, you always love to talk of her most; as a barren coxcomb that wants discourse, is ever entertaining company out of the last book he read in.

COURTALL. Now you accuse me most unjustly, madam; who the devil, that has common sense, will go a-birding with a clack in his cap?

ARIANA. Nay, we do not blame you, gentlemen, every one in their way; a huntsman talks of his dogs, a falconer of his hawks, a jockey of his horse, and a gallant of his mistress.

GATTY. Without the allowance of this vanity, an amour would soon grow as dull as matrimony.

COURTALL. Whatsoever you say, ladies, I cannot believe you think us men of such abominable principles.

FREEMAN. For my part, I have ever held it as ingrateful to boast of the favours of a mistress, as to deny the courtesies of a friend.

COURTALL. A friend that bravely ventures his life in the field to serve me, deserves but equally with a mistress that kindly exposes her honour to oblige me, especially when she does it as generously too, and with as little ceremony.

FREEMAN. And I would no more betray the honour of such a woman, than I would the life of a man that should rob on purpose to supply me.

GATTY. We believe you men of honour, and know it is below you to talk of any woman that deserves it.

ARIANA. You are so generous, you seldom insult after a victory.

GATTY. And so vain, that you always triumph before it.

COURTALL. 'Sdeath! what's the meaning of all this?

GATTY. Though you find us so kind, Mr Courtall, pray do not tell Mrs Gazette tomorrow, that we came hither on purpose this evening to meet you.

COURTALL. I would as soon print it, and fee a fellow to post it up with the playbills.

---

228 *clack*: rattle to scare away birds (worked by the wind).
259 *playbills*: playbills were displayed outside the theatres and on posts in the streets.

GATTY. You have reposed a great deal of confidence in her, for all you pretend this ill opinion of her secrecy now.

COURTALL. I never trusted her with the name of a mistress, that I should be jealous of, if I saw her receive fruit, and go out of the playhouse with a stranger.

GATTY. For ought as I see, we are infinitely obliged to you, sir.

COURTALL. 'Tis impossible to be insensible of so much goodness, madam.

GATTY. What goodness, pray, sir?

COURTALL. Come, come, give over this raillery.

GATTY. You are so ridiculously unworthy, that 'twere a folly to reprove you with a serious look.

COURTALL. On my conscience, your heart begins to fail you now we are coming to the point, as a young fellow's that was never in the field before.

GATTY. You begin to amaze me.

COURTALL. Since you yourself sent the challenge, you must not in honour fly off now.

GATTY. Challenge! Oh heavens! this confirms all: were I a man, I would kill thee for the injuries thou hast already done me.

FREEMAN. (*to* ARIANA) Let not your suspicion of my unkindness make you thus scrupulous; was ever city ill treated, that surrendered without assault or summons?

ARIANA. Dear sister, what ill spirit brought us hither? I never met with so much impudence in my life.

COURTALL. (*aside*) Hey jilts! they are as good at it already, as the old one i'faith.

FREEMAN. Come, ladies, you have exercised your wit enough; you would not venture letters of such consequence for a jest only.

GATTY. Letters! bless me, what will this come to?

COURTALL. To that none of us shall have cause to repent I hope, madam.

ARIANA. Let us fly 'em, sister, they are devils, and not men, they could never be so malicious else.

---

260 *confidence*: confidential information.
285 *scrupulous*: over-cautious and troubled about niceties.

Enter LADY COCKWOOD *and* SENTRY.

LADY COCKWOOD. Your servant, cousins.

COURTALL. (*starting*) Ho my Lady Cockwood! my ears are grown an inch already.

ARIANA. My lady! she'll think this an appointment, sister.

FREEMAN. This is Madam Machiavil, I suspect, Courtall.

COURTALL. Nay, 'tis her plot doubtless: now am I as much out of countenance, as I should be if Sir Oliver should take me making bold with her ladyship.

LADY COCKWOOD. Do not let me discompose you, I can walk alone, cousins.

GATTY. Are you so uncharitable, madam, to think we have any business with 'em?

ARIANA. It has been our ill fortune to meet 'em here, and nothing could be so lucky as your coming, madam, to free us from 'em.

GATTY. They have abused us in the grossest manner.

ARIANA. Counterfeited letters under our hands.

LADY COCKWOOD. Never trouble yourselves, cousins, I have heard this is a common practice with such unworthy men: did they not threaten to divulge them, and defame you to the world?

GATTY. We cannot believe they intend anything less, madam.

LADY COCKWOOD. Doubtless, they had such a mean opinion of your wit and honour, that they thought to fright you to a base compliance with their wicked purposes.

ARIANA. I hate the very sight of 'em.

GATTY. I could almost wish myself a disease, to breathe infection upon 'em.

COURTALL. Very pretty! we have carried on our designs very luckily against these young ladies.

FREEMAN. We have lost their good opinion for ever.

301–2 *my ears are grown an inch already*: thus making clear his resemblance to an ass.

305 *Machiavil*: unscrupulous schemer (i.e. one who acts on what were popularly believed to be the principles of the Florentine statesman, Machiavelli).

309 *discompose*: disturb (i.e. take you away from your gallants).

320 *divulge*: make publicly known.

LADY COCKWOOD. I know not whether their folly or their impudence be greater, they are not worth your anger, they are only fit to be laughed at, and despised.

COURTALL. A very fine old devil this!

LADY COCKWOOD. Mr Freeman, this is not like a gentleman, to affront a couple of young ladies thus; but I cannot blame you so much, you are in a manner a stranger to our family: but I wonder how that base man can look me in the face, considering how civilly he has been treated at our house.

COURTALL. The truth is, madam, I am a rascal; but I fear you have contributed to the making me so: be not as unmerciful as the devil is to a poor sinner.

SENTRY. Did you ever see the like? never trust me, if he has not the confidence to make my virtuous lady accessary to his wickedness.

LADY COCKWOOD. Ay Sentry! 'tis a miracle if my honour escapes, considering the access which his greatness with Sir Oliver has given him daily to me.

FREEMAN. Faith, ladies, we did not counterfeit these letters, we are abused as well as you.

COURTALL. I received mine from a porter at the King's playhouse, and I will show it you, that you may see if you know the hand.

LADY COCKWOOD. Sentry, are you sure they never saw any of your writing?

COURTALL. 'Sdeath! I am so discomposed, I know not where I have put it.

SENTRY. Oh madam! now I remember myself, Mrs Gatty helped me once to indite a letter to my sweet-heart.

LADY COCKWOOD. Forgetful wench! then I am undone.

COURTALL. Oh here it is – hey, who's here?

As he has the letter in hand, enter SIR JOSLIN, SIR OLIVER, *and* RAKEHELL, *all drunk, with music.*

They sing.

---

348 *confidence*: presumption, impudence.
352 *greatness*: intimacy.

'She's no mistress of mine
That drinks not her wine,
Or frowns at my friends' drinking motions;
If my heart thou wouldst gain,
Drink thy bottle of champagne.
'Twill serve thee for paint and love-potions.'

SIR OLIVER. Who's here? Courtall, in my lady's company! I'll dispatch him presently; help me, brother Jolly. (*He draws*)

LADY COCKWOOD. For heaven's sake, Sir Oliver!

COURTALL. (*drawing*) What do you mean, sir?

SIR OLIVER. I'll teach you more manners, than to make your attempts on my lady, sir.

LADY COCKWOOD. }
SENTRY. } Oh! murder! murder! (*They shriek*)

LADY COCKWOOD. Save my dear Sir Oliver, oh my dear Sir Oliver!

The YOUNG LADIES *shriek and run out, they all draw to part 'em, they fight off the stage,* LADY COCKWOOD *shrieks and runs out.*

ACT V

SCENE I

Sir Oliver's dining-room.

Enter LADY COCKWOOD, *table, and carpet.*

LADY COCKWOOD. I did not think he had been so desperate in his drink; if they had killed one another, I had then been revenged, and freed from all my fears –

Enter SENTRY.

Sentry, your carelessness and forgetfulness some time

370 *drinking motions*: proposals that we should drink.
373 *paint and love-potions*: make-up and aphrodisiacs.
s.d. *carpet*: a table-cloth, made of thick fabric (commonly, wool).

or other will undo me; had not Sir Oliver and Sir Joslin came so luckily into the garden, the letters had been discovered, and my honour left to the mercy of a false man, and two young fleering girls: did you speak to Mr Freeman unperceived in the hurry?

SENTRY. I did, madam, and he promised me to disengage himself as soon as possibly he could, and wait upon your ladyship with all secrecy.

LADY COCKWOOD. I have some reason to believe him a man of honour.

SENTRY. Methinks indeed his very look, madam, speaks him to be much more a gentleman than Mr Courtall; but I was unwilling before now to let your ladyship know my opinion, for fear of offending your inclinations.

LADY COCKWOOD. I hope by his means to get these letters into my own hands, and so prevent the inconveniencies they may bring upon my honour.

SENTRY. I wonder, madam, what should be Sir Oliver's quarrel to Mr Courtall.

LADY COCKWOOD. You know how apt he is to be suspicious in his drink; 'tis very likely he thought Mr Courtall betrayed him at the Bear today.

SENTRY. Pray heaven he be not jealous of your ladyship, finding you abroad so unexpectedly; if he be, we shall have a sad hand of him when he comes home, madam.

LADY COCKWOOD. I should have apprehended it much myself, Sentry, if his drunkenness had not unadvisedly engaged him in his quarrel; as soon as he grows a little sober, I am sure his fear will bring him home, and make him apply himself to me with all humility and kindness; for he is ever underhand fain to use my interest and discretion to make friends to

---

9 *fleering*: jeering.
31 *a sad hand of*: a difficult situation with.
35 *unadvisedly*: rashly.
38 *underhand fain*: covertly eager.
39 *interest*: influence.

compound these businesses, or to get an order for the securing his person and his honour.

SENTRY. I believe verily, Mr Courtall would have been so rude to have killed him, if Mr Freeman and the rest had not civilly interposed their weapons.

LADY COCKWOOD. Heavens forbid! though he be a wicked man, I am obliged in duty to love him: whither did my cousins go after we came home, Sentry?

SENTRY. They are at the next door, madam, laughing and playing at lantreloo, with my old Lady Loveyouth and her daughters.

LADY COCKWOOD. I hope they will not come home then to interrupt my affairs with Mr Freeman: (*Knocking without*) hark! somebody knocks, it may be him, run down quickly.

SENTRY. I fly, madam. *Exit* SENTRY.

LADY COCKWOOD. Now if he has a real inclination for my person, I'll give him a handsome opportunity to reveal it.

Enter SENTRY *and* FREEMAN.

FREEMAN. Your servant, madam.

LADY COCKWOOD. Oh Mr Freeman! this unlucky accident has robbed me of all my quiet; I am almost distracted with thinking of the danger Sir Oliver's dear life is in.

FREEMAN. You need not fear, madam, all things will be reconciled again tomorrow.

SENTRY. You would not blame my lady's apprehensions, did you but know the tenderness of her affections.

LADY COCKWOOD. Mr Courtall is a false and merciless man.

FREEMAN. He has always owned a great respect for

---

40 *compound*: bring to a peaceful conclusion.

40–1 *order for the securing his person and his honour*: i.e. Sir Oliver wishes Lady Cockwood to forbid his taking the matter further, so that he can then plead his wife's wishes as an honourable excuse for avoiding the perils of a duel.

43 *rude*: barbarous.

50 *lantreloo*: the older name of the card game later called loo.

your ladyship, and I never heard him mention you with the least dishonour.

LADY COCKWOOD. He cannot without injuring the truth, heaven knows my innocence: I hope you did not let him know, sir, of your coming hither.

FREEMAN. I should never merit the happiness to wait upon you again, had I so abused this extraordinary favour, madam.

LADY COCKWOOD. If I have done anything unbeseeming my honour, I hope you will be just, sir, and impute it to my fear; I know no man so proper to compose this unfortunate difference as yourself, and if a lady's tears and prayers have power to move you to compassion, I know you will employ your utmost endeavour to preserve me my dear Sir Oliver.

FREEMAN. Do not, madam, afflict yourself so much, I dare engage my life, his life and honour shall be both secure.

LADY COCKWOOD. You are truly noble, sir; I was so distracted with my fears, that I cannot well remember how we parted at the Spring Garden.

FREEMAN. We all divided, madam: after your ladyship and the young ladies were gone together, Sir Oliver, Sir Joslin, and the company with them, took one boat, and Mr Courtall and I another.

LADY COCKWOOD. Then I need not apprehend their meeting again tonight.

FREEMAN. You need not, madam; I left Mr Courtall in his chamber, wondering what should make Sir Oliver draw upon him, and fretting and fuming about the trick that was put upon us with the letters today.

LADY COCKWOOD. Oh! I had almost forgot myself; I assure you, sir, those letters were sent by one that has no inclination to be an enemy of yours. (*Knocking below*) Somebody knocks.

Exit SENTRY.

If it be Sir Oliver, I am undone, he will hate me mortally, if he does but suspect I use any secret means to hinder him from justifying his reputation honourably to the world.

---

84 *compose*: settle, end.

Enter SENTRY.

SENTRY. Oh madam! here is Mr Courtall below in the entry, discharging a coachman; I told him your ladyship was busy, but he would not hear me, and I find, do what I can, he will come up.

LADY COCKWOOD. I would not willingly suspect you, sir.

FREEMAN. I have deceived him, madam, in my coming hither, and am as unwilling he should find me here, as you can be.

LADY COCKWOOD. He will not believe my innocent business with you, but will raise a new scandal on my honour, and publish it to the whole town.

SENTRY. Let him step into the closet, madam.

LADY COCKWOOD. Quick, sir, quick, I beseech you, I will send him away again immediately.

[*Exit* FREEMAN.]

Enter COURTALL.

LADY COCKWOOD. Mr Courtall! have you no sense of honour nor modesty left? after so many injuries, to come into our house, and without my approbation rudely press upon my retirement thus?

COURTALL. Pray, madam, hear my business.

LADY COCKWOOD. Thy business is maliciously to pursue my ruin; thou comest with a base design to have Sir Oliver catch thee here, and destroy the only happiness I have.

COURTALL. I come, madam, to beg your pardon for the fault I did unwillingly commit, and to know of you the reason of Sir Oliver's quarrel to me.

LADY COCKWOOD. Thy guilty conscience is able to tell thee that, vain and ungrateful man!

COURTALL. I am innocent, madam, of all things that may offend him; and I am sure, if you would but hear me, I should remove the justice of your quarrel too.

LADY COCKWOOD. You are mistaken, sir, if you think I am concerned for your going to the Spring Garden this evening; my quarrel is the same with Sir Oliver,

---

146 *with Sir Oliver*: as Sir Oliver's.

and is so just, that thou deserv'st to be poisoned for what thou hast done.

COURTALL. Pray, madam, let me know my fault.

LADY COCKWOOD. I blush to think upon't: Sir Oliver, since we came from the Bear, has heard something thou hast said concerning me; but what it is, I could not get him to discover: he told me 'twas enough for me to know he was satisfied of my innocence.

COURTALL. This is mere passion, madam.

LADY COCKWOOD. This is the usual revenge of such base men as thou art, when they cannot compass their ends, with their venomous tongues to blast the honour of a lady.

COURTALL. This is a sudden alteration, madam; within these few hours you had a kinder opinion of me.

LADY COCKWOOD. 'Tis no wonder you brag of favours behind my back, that have the impudence to upbraid me with kindness to my face; dost thou think I could ever have a good thought of thee, whom I have always found so treacherous in thy friendship to Sir Oliver?

Knock at the door.

Enter SENTRY.

SENTRY. Oh madam! here is Sir Oliver come home.

LADY COCKWOOD. Oh heavens! I shall be believed guilty now, and he will kill us both.

COURTALL. I warrant you, madam, I'll defend your life. (*He draws*)

LADY COCKWOOD. Oh! there will be murder, murder; for heaven's sake, sir, hide yourself in some corner or other.

COURTALL. I'll step into that closet, madam.

SENTRY. Hold, hold, sir, by no means; his pipes and his tobacco-box lie there, and he always goes in to fetch 'em.

LADY COCKWOOD. Your malice will soon be at an end: heaven knows what will be the fatal consequence of your being found here.

SENTRY. Madam, let him creep under the table, the carpet is long enough to hide him.

LADY COCKWOOD. Have you good nature enough to save the life and reputation of a lady?

COURTALL. Anything to oblige you, madam. (*He goes under the table*)

LADY COCKWOOD. (*running to the closet*) Be sure you do not stir, sir, whatsoever happens.

COURTALL. Not unless he pulls me out by the ears.

SENTRY. Good! he thinks my lady speaks to him.

Enter SIR OLIVER.

LADY COCKWOOD. My dear Sir Oliver –

SIR OLIVER. I am unworthy of this kindness, madam.

LADY COCKWOOD. Nay, I intend to chide you for your naughtiness anon; but I cannot choose but hug thee, and kiss thee a little first; I was afraid I should never have had thee alive within these arms again.

SIR OLIVER. Your goodness does so increase my shame, I know not what to say, madam.

LADY COCKWOOD. Well, I am glad I have thee safe at home, I will lock thee up above in my chamber, and will not so much as trust thee downstairs, till there be an end of this quarrel.

SIR OLIVER. I was so little myself, I knew not what I did, else I had not exposed my person to so much danger before thy face.

SENTRY. 'Twas cruelly done, sir, knowing the killing concerns my lady has for you.

LADY COCKWOOD. If Mr Courtall had killed thee, I was resolved not to survive thee; but before I had died, I would have dearly revenged thy murder.

SIR OLIVER. As soon as I had recollected myself a little, I could not rest till I came home to give thee this satisfaction, that I will do nothing without thy advice and approbation, my dear: I know thy love makes thy life depend upon mine, and it is unreasonable I should upon my own rash head hazard that, though it be for the justification of thy honour. Uds me I have let fall a China orange that was

---

217 *upon my own rash head*: in rashly venturing my own life.

219 *Uds*: a common oath (a foreshortening either of 'God's' or 'God save').

219 *China orange*: a sweet orange, so called because originally brought from China; in the 1660s, most were imported from France.

recommended to me for one of the best that came over this year; 'slife light the candle, Sentry, 'tis run under the table.

Knock.

LADY COCKWOOD. Oh, I am not well!

SENTRY *takes up the candle, there is a great knocking at the door, she runs away with the candle.*

SENTRY. Oh heaven! who's that that knocks so hastily?

SIR OLIVER. Why, Sentry! bring back the candle; are you mad to leave us in the dark, and your lady not well? how is it, my dear?

LADY COCKWOOD. For heaven's sake run after her, Sir Oliver, snatch the candle out of her hand, and teach her more manners.

SIR OLIVER. I will, my dear. [*Exit* SIR OLIVER.]

LADY COCKWOOD. What shall I do? was ever woman so unfortunate in the management of affairs!

COURTALL. What will become of me now?

LADY COCKWOOD. It must be so, I had better trust my honour to the mercy of them two, than be betrayed to my husband: Mr Courtall, give me your hand quickly, I beseech you.

COURTALL. Here, here, madam, what's to be done now?

LADY COCKWOOD. I will put you into the closet, sir.

COURTALL. He'll be coming in for his tobacco-box and pipes.

LADY COCKWOOD. Never fear that, sir.

FREEMAN. (*out of the closet-door*) Now shall I be discovered; pox on your honourable intrigue, would I were safe at Gifford's.

LADY COCKWOOD. Here, here, sir, this is the door, whatsoever you feel, be not frighted; for should you make the least disturbance, you will destroy the life, and what is more, the honour of an unfortunate lady.

COURTALL. So, so, if you have occasion to remove again, make no ceremony, madam.

[*Exit* COURTALL.]

247 *Gifford's*: a well-known London brothel.

Enter SIR OLIVER, SENTRY, ARIANA, GATTY.

SIR OLIVER. Here is the candle, how dost thou, my dear?

LADY COCKWOOD. I could not imagine, Sentry, you had been so ill-bred, to run away, and leave your master and me in the dark.

SENTRY. I thought there had been another candle upon the table, madam.

LADY COCKWOOD. Good! you thought! you are always excusing of your carelessness; such another misdemeanour –

SIR OLIVER. Prithee, my dear, forgive her.

LADY COCKWOOD. The truth is, I ought not to be very angry with her at present, 'tis a good-natured creature; she was so frighted, for fear of thy being mischiefed in the Spring Garden, that I verily believe she scarce knows what she does yet.

SIR OLIVER. Light the candle, Sentry, that I may look for my orange.

LADY COCKWOOD. You have been at my Lady Loveyouth's, cousins, I hear.

ARIANA. We have, madam.

GATTY. She charged us to remember her service to you.

SIR OLIVER. So, here it is, my dear, I brought it home on purpose for thee.

LADY COCKWOOD. 'Tis a lovely orange indeed! thank you, my dear; I am so discomposed with the fright I have had, that I would fain be at rest.

SIR OLIVER. Get a candle, Sentry: will you go to bed, my dear?

LADY COCKWOOD. With all my heart, Sir Oliver: 'tis late, cousins, you had best retire to your chamber too.

GATTY. We shall not stay long here, madam.

SIR OLIVER. Come, my dear.

LADY COCKWOOD. Good night, cousins.

GATTY.
ARIANA. } Your servant, madam.

---

268 *mischiefed*: injured, harmed.
275 *remember her service*: deliver her compliments.

Exeunt SIR OLIVER, LADY COCKWOOD, *and* SENTRY.

ARIANA. I cannot but think of those letters, sister.

GATTY. That is, you cannot but think of Mr Freeman, sister, I perceive he runs in thy head as much as a new gown uses to do in the country, the night before 'tis expected from London.

ARIANA. You need not talk, for I am sure the losses of an unlucky gamester are not more his meditation, than Mr Courtall is yours.

GATTY. He has made some slight impression on my memory, I confess; but I hope a night will wear him out again, as it does the noise of a fiddle after dancing.

ARIANA. Love, like some stains, will wear out of itself, I know, but not in such a little time as you talk of, sister.

GATTY. It cannot last longer than the stain of a mulberry at most; the next season out that goes, and my heart cannot be long unfruitful, sure.

ARIANA. Well, I cannot believe they forged these letters; what should be their end?

GATTY. That you may easily guess at; but methinks they took a very improper way to compass it.

ARIANA. It looks more like the malice or jealousy of a woman, than the design of two witty men.

GATTY. If this should prove a fetch of her ladyship's now, that is a-playing the loving hypocrite above with her dear Sir Oliver.

ARIANA. How unluckily we were interrupted, when they were going to show us the hand!

GATTY. That might have discovered all: I have a small suspicion, that there has been a little familiarity between her ladyship and Mr Courtall.

ARIANA. Our finding of 'em together in the Exchange, and several passages I observed at the Bear, have almost made me of the same opinion.

GATTY. Yet I would fain believe the continuance of it is more her desire, than his inclination: that which makes me mistrust him most, is her knowing we made

---

312 *fetch*: trick, contrivance.

321 *passages*: incidents, exchanges between Lady Cockwood and Courtall.

'em an appointment.

ARIANA. If she were jealous of Mr Courtall, she would not be jealous of Mr Freeman too; they both pretend to have received letters.

GATTY. There is something in it more than we are able to imagine; time will make it out, I hope, to the advantage of the gentlemen.

ARIANA. I would gladly have it so; for I believe, should they give us a just cause, we should find it a hard task to hate them.

GATTY. How I love the song I learnt t'other day, since I saw them in the Mulberry Garden! (*She sings*)

'To little or no purpose I spent many days,
In ranging the Park, th' Exchange, and th'plays;
For ne'er in my rambles till now did I prove
So lucky to meet with the man I could love.
Oh! how I am pleased when I think on this man,
That I find I must love, let me do what I can!

How long I shall love him, I can no more tell,
Than had I a fever, when I should be well.
My passion shall kill me before I will show it,
And yet I would give all the world he did know it;
But oh how I sigh, when I think should he woo me,
I cannot deny what I know would undo me!'

ARIANA. Fie, sister, thou art so wanton.

GATTY. I hate to dissemble when I need not; 'twould look as affected in us to be reserved now w'are alone, as for a player to maintain the character she acts in the tiring-room.

ARIANA. Prithee sing a good song.

GATTY. Now art thou for a melancholy madrigal, composed by some amorous coxcomb, who swears in all companies he loves his mistress so well, that he would not do her the injury, were she willing to grant him

---

328 *pretend*: claim.
331 *make it out*: decipher it, unravel it.
350 *wanton*: (of speech) unrestrained, impetuous.
354 *tiring-room*: dressing-room in a theatre.
356 *madrigal*: used loosely in colloquial speech to mean a song of any kind.

the favour, and it may be is sot enough to believe he would oblige her in keeping his oath too.

ARIANA. Well, I will reach thee thy guitar out of the closet, to take thee off of this subject.

GATTY. I'd rather be a nun, than a lover at thy rate; devotion is not able to make me half so serious as love has made thee already.

ARIANA *opens the closet,* COURTALL *and* FREEMAN *come out.*

COURTALL. Ha, Freeman! is this your business with a lawyer? here's a new discovery, i'faith!

ARIANA *and* GATTY *shriek and run out.*

FREEMAN. Peace, man, I will satisfy your jealousy hereafter; since we have made this lucky discovery, let us mind the present businesses.

COURTALL *and* FREEMAN *catch the* LADIES, *and bring them back.*

COURTALL. Nay, ladies, now we have caught you, there is no escaping till w'are come to a right understanding.

Enter LADY COCKWOOD *and* SIR OLIVER *and* SENTRY.

FREEMAN. Come, never blush, we are as loving as you can be for your hearts, I assure you.

COURTALL. Had it not been our good fortunes to have been concealed here, you would have had ill nature enough to dissemble with us at least a fortnight longer.

LADY COCKWOOD. What's the matter with you here? Are you mad, cousins? bless me, Mr Courtall and Mr Freeman in our house at these unseasonable hours!

SIR OLIVER. Fetch me down my long sword, Sentry, I lay my life Courtall has been tempting the honour of the young ladies.

LADY COCKWOOD. Oh my dear! (*She holds him*)

GATTY. We are almost scared out of our wits; my sister went to reach my guitar out of the closet, and found 'em both shut up there.

LADY COCKWOOD. Come, come, this will not serve

---

362 *guitar*: especially among the upper classes, the guitar was gradually displacing the lute in popularity.

your turn; I am afraid you had a design secretly to convey 'em into your chamber: well, I will have no more of these doings in my family, my dear; Sir Joslin shall remove these girls tomorrow.

FREEMAN. You injure the young ladies, madam; their surprise shows their innocence.

COURTALL. If anybody be to blame, it is Mrs Sentry.

SENTRY. What mean you, sir? Heaven knows I know no more of their being here –

COURTALL. Nay, nay, Mrs Sentry, you need not be ashamed to own the doing of a couple of young gentlemen such a good office.

SENTRY. Do not think to put your tricks upon me, sir.

COURTALL. Understanding by Mrs Sentry, madam, that these young ladies would very likely sit and talk in the dining-room an hour before they went to bed, of the accidents of the day, and being impatient to know whether that unlucky business which happened in the Spring Garden, about the letters, had quite destroyed our hopes of gaining their esteem; for a small sum of money Mr Freeman and I obtained the favour of her to shut us up where we might overhear 'em.

LADY COCKWOOD. Is this the truth, Sentry?

SENTRY. I humbly beg your pardon, madam.

LADY COCKWOOD. A lady's honour is not safe, that keeps a servant so subject to corruption; I will turn her out of my service for this.

SIR OLIVER. (*aside*) Good! I was suspicious their businesses had been with my lady at first.

LADY COCKWOOD. [*aside*] Now will I be in charity with him again, for putting this off so handsomely.

SIR OLIVER. Hark you my dear, shall I forbid Mr Courtall my house?

LADY COCKWOOD. Oh! by no means, my dear; I had forgot to tell thee, since I acquainted thee with that business, I have been discoursing with my Lady Love-youth, and she blamed me infinitely for letting thee know it, and laughed exceedingly at me, believing Mr Courtall intended thee no injury, and told me 'twas

417–18 *in charity with*: on good terms with.

only a harmless gallantry, which his French breeding has used him to.

SIR OLIVER. Faith, I am apt enough to believe it; for on my conscience, he is a very honest fellow. Ned Courtall! how the devil came it about that thee and I fell to sa, sa, in the Spring Garden?

COURTALL. You are best able to resolve yourself that, Sir Oliver.

SIR OLIVER. Well, the devil take me, if I had the least unkindness for thee – prithee let us embrace and kiss, and be as good friends as ever we were, dear rogue.

COURTALL. I am so reasonable, Sir Oliver, that I will ask no other satisfaction for the injury you have done me.

FREEMAN. Here's the letter, madam.

ARIANA. Sister, look here, do you know this hand?

GATTY. 'Tis Sentry's.

LADY COCKWOOD. Oh heavens! I shall be ruined yet.

GATTY. She has been the contriver of all this mischief.

COURTALL. Nay, now you lay too much to her charge in this; she was but my lady's secretary, I assure you, she has discovered the whole plot to us.

SENTRY. What does he mean?

LADY COCKWOOD. Will he betray me at last?

COURTALL. My lady being in her nature severely virtuous, is, it seems, offended at the innocent freedom you take in rambling up and down by yourselves; which made her, out of a tenderness to your reputations, counterfeit these letters, in hopes to fright you to that reservedness which she approves of.

LADY COCKWOOD. (*aside*) This has almost redeemed my opinion of his honour. – Cousins, the little regard you had to the good counsel I gave you, puts me upon this business.

GATTY. Pray, madam, what was it Mrs Gazette told you concerning us?

LADY COCKWOOD. Nothing, nothing, cousins: what I told you of Mr Courtall, was mere invention, the better to carry on my design for your good.

COURTALL. Freeman! pray what brought you hither?

FREEMAN. A kind summons from her ladyship.

COURTALL. Why did you conceal it from me?

FREEMAN. I was afraid thy peevish jealousy might have destroyed the design I had of getting an opportunity to clear ourselves to the young ladies.

COURTALL. Fortune has been our friend in that beyond expectation. (*To the* LADIES) I hope, ladies, you are satisfied of our innocence now.

GATTY. Well, had you been found guilty of the letters, we were resolved to have counterfeited two contracts under your hands, and have suborned witnesses to swear 'em.

ARIANA. That had been a full revenge; for I know you would think it as great a scandal to be thought to have an inclination for marriage, as we should to be believed willing to take our freedom without it.

COURTALL. The more probable thing, ladies, had been only to pretend a promise; we have now and then courage enough to venture so far for a valuable consideration.

GATTY. The truth is, such experienced gentlemen as you are, seldom mortgage your persons without it be to redeem your estates.

COURTALL. 'Tis a mercy we have scaped the mischief so long, and are like to do penance only for our own sins; most families are a wedding behindhand in the world, which makes so many young men fooled into wives, to pay their fathers' debts: all the happiness a gentleman can desire, is to live at liberty, till he be forced that way to pay his own.

FREEMAN. Ladies, you know we are not ignorant of the good intentions you have towards us; pray let us treat a little.

GATTY. I hope you are not in so desperate a condition, as to have a good opinion of marriage, are you?

ARIANA. 'Tis to as little purpose to treat with us of anything under that, as it is for those kind ladies, that have obliged you with a valuable consideration, to challenge the performance of your promise.

SIR OLIVER. Well, and how, and how, my dear Ned, goes the business between you and these ladies? are you like to drive a bargain?

COURTALL. Faith, Sir Oliver, we are about it.

SIR OLIVER. And cannot agree, I warrant you; they

485–6 *consideration*: reward.
499 *treat*: negotiate.

are for having you take a lease for life, and you are for being tenants at will, Ned, is it not so?

GATTY. These gentlemen have found it so convenient lying in lodgings, they'll hardly venture on the trouble of taking a house of their own.

COURTALL. A pretty country-seat, madam, with a handsome parcel of land, and other necessaries belonging to't, may tempt us; but for a town-tenement that has but one poor conveniency, we are resolved we'll never deal.

A noise of music without.

SIR OLIVER. Hark! my brother Jolly's come home.

ARIANA. Now, gentlemen, you had best look to yourselves, and come to an agreement with us quickly; for I'll lay my life, my uncle has brought home a couple of fresh chapmen, that will outbid you.

Enter SIR JOSLIN *with music.*

Dance.

SIR JOSLIN. Hey boys! (*Sings*)

'A catch and a glass,
A fiddle and a lass,
What more would an honest man have?
Hang your temperate sot,
Who would seem what he's not;
'Tis I am wise, he's but grave.'

SIR JOSLIN. What's here? Mr Courtall and Mr Freeman!

SIR OLIVER. Oh man! here has been the prettiest, the luckiest discovery on all sides! we are all good friends again.

SIR JOSLIN. Hark you brother Cockwood, I have got Madam Rampant; Rakehell and she are without.

SIR OLIVER. Oh heavens! dear brother Jolly, send her

---

517 *parcel*: portion.

517 *necessaries*: 'things needful for Humane Life' (Edward Phillips, *The New World of Words*, ed. J.K. (7th edition: London, 1720)) (the slang meaning of a 'necessary', however, was a 'bedfellow', cf. note to 'conveniency', line 519).

518–19 *town-tenement*: town-house, -dwelling.

519 *conveniency*: (1) material arrangement conducive to personal comfort (2) (slang) wife.

520 *deal*: do business.

525 *chapmen*: traders.

away immediately, my lady has such an aversion to a naughty woman, that she will swound if she does but see her.

SIR JOSLIN. Faith, I was hard put to't, I wanted a lover, and rather than I would break my old wont, I dressed up Rampant in a suit I bought of Rakehell; but since this good company's here, I'll send her away.

Enter RAKEHELL.

My little Rakehell, come hither; you see here are two powerful rivals; therefore for fear of kicking, or a worse disaster, take Rampant with you, and be going quickly.

RAKEHELL. Your humble servant, sir.

Exit RAKEHELL.

COURTALL. You may hereafter spare yourself this labour, Sir Joslin; Mr Freeman and I have vowed ourselves humble servants to these ladies.

FREEMAN. I hope we shall have your approbation, sir.

SIR JOSLIN. Nay, if you have a mind to commit matrimony, I'll send for a canonical sir shall dispatch you presently.

FREEMAN. You cannot do better.

COURTALL. What think you of taking us in the humour? Consideration may be your foe, ladies.

ARIANA. Come, gentlemen, I'll make you a fair proposition; since you have made a discovery of our inclinations, my sister and I will be content to admit you in the quality of servants.

GATTY. And if after a month's experience of your good behaviour, upon serious thoughts, you have courage

---

541 *swound*: swoon.

543 *wanted*: lacked.

552 s.d. *Exit Rakehell*: *1668* reads '*Ex.* Rake-hell *and* Rampant' here, but it provides no entrance for Rampant. Brett-Smith and Davison simply copy this, Taylor makes her enter with Rakehell, and Verity omits her altogether. The last seems preferable to me; after all the build-up it is much funnier if she never arrives on stage, and this was how we played it in the 1976 York production.

558 *canonical sir*: clergyman.

566 *in the quality of servants*: as suitors.

enough to engage further, we will accept of the challenge, and believe you men of honour.

SIR JOSLIN. Well spoke i'faith, girls; and is it a match, boys?

COURTALL. If the heart of man be not very deceitful, 'tis very likely it may be so.

FREEMAN. A month is a tedious time, and will be a dangerous trial of our resolutions; but I hope we shall not repent before marriage, whate'er we do after.

SIR JOSLIN. How stand matters between you and your lady, brother Cockwood? is there peace on all sides?

SIR OLIVER. Perfect concord, man: I will tell thee all that has happened since I parted from thee, when we are alone, 'twill make thee laugh heartily. Never man was so happy in a virtuous and a loving lady!

SIR JOSLIN. Though I have led Sir Oliver astray this day or two, I hope you will not exclude me the Act of Oblivion, madam.

LADY COCKWOOD. The nigh relation I have to you, and the respect I know Sir Oliver has for you, makes me forget all that has passed, sir; but pray be not the occasion of any new transgressions.

SENTRY. I hope, Mr Courtall, since my endeavours to serve you, have ruined me in the opinion of my lady, you will intercede for a reconciliation.

COURTALL. Most willingly, Mrs Sentry – faith, madam, since things have fallen out so luckily, you must needs receive your woman into favour again.

LADY COCKWOOD. Her crime is unpardonable, sir.

SENTRY. Upon solemn protestations, madam, that the gentlemen's intentions were honourable, and having reason to believe the young ladies had no aversion to their inclinations, I was of opinion I should have been ill-natured, if I had not assisted 'em in the removing those difficulties that delayed their happiness.

---

585 *exclude me*: i.e. exclude me from.

585–6 *Act of Oblivion*: alluding to the Act of Indemnity and Oblivion of 1660, which exempted (apart from named exceptions) all those who had taken arms or acted against Charles I and Charles II from legal punishment for their deeds. Lady Cockwood is once again being compared to an offended monarch – cf. note to III iii 330.

SIR OLIVER. Come, come, girl, confess how many guineas prevailed upon your easy nature.

SENTRY. Ten, an't please you, sir.

SIR OLIVER. 'Slife, a sum able to corrupt an honest man in office! faith you must forgive her, my dear.

LADY COCKWOOD. If it be your pleasure, Sir Oliver, I cannot but be obedient.

SENTRY. If Sir Oliver, madam, should ask me to see this gold, all may be discovered yet.

LADY COCKWOOD. If he does, I will give thee ten guineas out of my cabinet.

SENTRY. [*aside*] I shall take care to put him upon't; 'tis fit, that I who have bore all the blame, should have some reasonable reward for't.

COURTALL. I hope, madam, you will not envy me the happiness I am to enjoy with your fair relation.

LADY COCKWOOD. Your ingenuity and goodness, sir, have made a perfect atonement for you.

COURTALL. Pray, madam, what was your business with Mr Freeman?

LADY COCKWOOD. Only to oblige him to endeavour a reconciliation between you and Sir Oliver; for though I was resolved never to see your face again, it was death to me to think your life was in danger.

SENTRY. What a miraculous come-off is this, madam!

LADY COCKWOOD. It has made me so truly sensible of those dangers to which an aspiring lady must daily expose her honour, that I am resolved to give over the great business of this town, and hereafter modestly confine myself to the humble affairs of my own family.

COURTALL. 'Tis a very pious resolution, madam, and the better to confirm you in it, pray entertain an able chaplain.

LADY COCKWOOD. Certainly fortune was never before so unkind to the ambition of a lady.

SIR JOSLIN. Come, boys, faith we will have a dance

---

614 *cabinet*: a case for the safe custody of jewels, money, etc.
628 *come-off*: conclusion; escape.
636 *entertain*: employ.
636–7 *an able chaplain*: for the innuendo, see *Man of Mode*, V i 211–12.

before we go to bed – Sly-girl and Mad-cap, give me your hands, that I may give 'em to these gentlemen, a parson shall join you ere long, and then you will have authority to dance to some purpose: brother Cockwood, take out your lady, I am for Mrs Sentry.
[*Sings*]
'We'll foot it and side it, my pretty little miss,
And when we are aweary, we'll lie down and kiss.'
Play away, boys.

They dance.

COURTALL. (*to* GATTY) Now shall I sleep as little without you, as I should do with you: madam, expectation makes me almost as restless as jealousy.

FREEMAN. Faith, let us dispatch this business; yet I never could find the pleasure of waiting for a dish of meat, when a man was heartily hungry.

GATTY. Marrying in this heat would look as ill as fighting in your drink.

ARIANA. And be no more a proof of love, than t'other is of valour.

SIR JOSLIN. Never trouble your heads further; since I perceive you are all agreed on the matter, let me alone to hasten the ceremony: come, gentlemen, lead 'em to their chambers; brother Cockwood, do you show the way with your lady. Ha Mrs Sentry! (*Sings*)
'I gave my love a green-gown
I' th' merry month of May,
And down she fell as wantonly,
As a tumbler does at play.'
Hey boys, lead away boys.

SIR OLIVER. Give me thy hand, my virtuous, my dear;
Henceforwards may our mutual loves increase,
And when we are abed, we'll sign the peace.

Exeunt omnes.

---

646 *foot it*: dance.

646 *side it*: move side by side (the uncorrected version of *1668* omits 'it' here).

654 *hungry*: *1668* (uncorrected) reads 'A hungry' here.

664 *gave my love a green-gown*: i.e. made her gown green by rolling her in the grass.

667 *tumbler*: acrobat; but the verb had sexual connotations – cf. Autolycus in Shakespeare's *The Winter's Tale*, IV iii 11–12: 'summer songs for me and my aunts, / While we lie tumbling in the hay'.

THE MAN OF MODE

INTRODUCTORY NOTE

The question of French sources for the play has often been raised, but never (apart from one brief passage, see the note to III iii 138–9) successfully established. The most ambitious attempt of this kind is Jean Auffret, 'Etherege à l'école de Molière', in Jean Jacquot (ed.), *Dramaturgie et Société* (Paris, Éditions du Centre National de la Recherche Scientifique, 1968), tome 1, pp. 397–407.

Another possibility often debated is that certain of the characters, and Dorimant above all, were modelled upon real-life originals. Gossip about this dates from early in the comedy's stage-history; but so many candidates for the various honours have been put forward that it is difficult to place trust in any one of them. Dorimant, for instance, has at various times been said to derive from Rochester, Dorset, Monmouth or Etherege himself.

The first recorded performance (it is not known whether it was the première) was given on 11 March 1676 by the Duke's Company at the Dorset Garden theatre. The cast-list according to Downes (p. 36) was: '*Dorimant*, by Mr. *Betterton*: *Medly*, Mr. *Harris*: Sir *Fopling*, by Mr. *Smith*: Old *Bellair*, Mr. *Leigh*: Young *Bellair*, Mr. *Jevon*: Mrs. *Lovit*, Mrs. *Barry*, *Bellinda*, Mrs. *Betterton*, Lady *Woodvil*, Mrs. *Leigh*, *Emilia*, Mrs. *Twiford*'. (Mrs Barry may, in fact, have taken over the role of Mrs Loveit later in the play's career.) The play was clearly enormously popular, and Downes wrote happily that 'This Comedy being well Cloath'd and well *Acted*, got a great deal of Money.' There was even an amateur performance at Brussels on 3 October 1679 (possibly before the Duke and Duchess of York), and on 7 December 1685 the Earl of Middleton wrote to Etherege in Ratisbon that 'Every weeke there are plays at Court. The last time, Sir Fopling appear'd with the usuall applause, and the King was pleas'd to tell me that he expected you shou'd put on your socks' and write another comedy (Bracher (ed.), *Letters of Sir George Etherege*, p. 269).

Towards the century's end the play became the object of another kind of attention, and the profanity of one passage of its dialogue caused the actor who spoke it to be successfully prosecuted by a stage reformer (Joseph Wood Krutch, *Comedy and Conscience after the Restoration* (New York, Columbia University Press, 1924), pp. 174–5). In *The Spectator*, no. 65 (15 May 1711), Steele mounted a more wholesale attack upon it, denouncing it as 'a perfect Contradiction to good Manners, good Sense, and common Honesty', and thus provoked from John Dennis an acerbic response which, in defending Etherege, impugned Steele's motives and literary perceptiveness (*A Defence of Sir Fopling Flutter* (1722), *Critical Works*, ed. E.N. Hooker (2 vols., Baltimore, Johns Hopkins Press, 1939–43)). Echoes of that quarrel are heard over the subsequent decades, and arguments on both sides are advanced with great confidence. Lady Mary Wortley Montagu, for instance, was confident that the play's influence was benign, since it taught young ladies a very useful lesson: 'You see there to what insults a Woman of Wit, Beauty, and Quality is expos'd that has been seduc'd by the artificial Tenderness of a Vain agreable Gallant; and I beleive that very comedy has given more checks to Ladys in persuit of present pleasures, so closely attended with shame and sorrow, than all the sermons they have ever heard in their Lives' (*Essays and Poems and 'Simplicity, A Comedy'*, ed. R. Halsband and Isobel Grundy (Oxford, Clarendon Press, 1977), p. 130).

The last known performance of the play in the eighteenth century was on 15 March 1766. There have in recent years been both amateur revivals and a professional production by the Prospect Theatre Company in 1965. The most significant production, however, was by Terry Hands for the Royal Shakespeare Company at the Aldwych Theatre in September 1971. The play was strongly cast (Alan Howard was Dorimant, Helen Mirren Harriet, John Wood Sir Fopling, and Vivien Merchant Mrs Loveit), but the performance did not attain the same level of convincing advocacy of the play's virtues as had previous Royal Shakespeare productions of *The Jew of Malta* and *The Revenger's Tragedy*.

The play was first published in 1676 and there were numerous subsequent quartos.

THE EPISTLE DEDICATORY

TO HER ROYAL HIGHNESS THE DUCHESS

Madam,

Poets however they may be modest otherwise, have always too good an opinion of what they write. The world when it sees this play dedicated to your Royal Highness, will conclude, I have more than my share of that vanity. But I hope the honour I have of belonging to you, will excuse my presumption. 'Tis the first thing I have produced in your service, and my duty obliges me to what my choice durst not else have aspired.

I am very sensible, madam, how much it is beholding to your indulgence, for the success it had in the acting, and your protection will be no less fortunate to it in the printing; for all are so ambitious of making their court to you, that none can be severe to what you are pleased to favour.

This universal submission and respect is due to the greatness of your rank and birth; but you have other illustrious qualities, which are much more engaging. Those would but dazzle, did not these really charm the eyes and understandings of all who have the happiness to approach you.

Authors on these occasions are never wanting to

Her . . . Duchess: Mary of Modena (1658–1718); she became Duchess of York in 1673. Of Etherege's being in her 'service' nothing is known. The Duke of York granted Etherege a pension in 1682 and, as James II, appointed him as envoy to Ratisbon in 1685.

10 *sensible*: conscious, aware.

11 *indulgence*: the favour you showed it.

publish a particular of their patron's virtues and perfections; but your Royal Highness's are so eminently known, that did I follow their examples, I should but paint those wonders here of which everyone already has the idea in his mind. Besides, I do not think it proper to aim at that in prose, which is so glorious a subject for verse; in which hereafter if I show more zeal than skill, it will not grieve me much, since I less passionately desire to be esteemed a poet, than to be thought,

Madam,

Your Royal Highness's

most humble, most obedient,

and most faithful servant,

GEORGE ETHEREGE.

23 *particular*: minute account or list.

PROLOGUE

By Sir Car Scroope Baronet

Like dancers on the ropes poor poets fare,
Most perish young, the rest in danger are;
This (one would think) should make our authors wary,
But gamester-like the giddy fools miscarry.
A lucky hand or two so tempts 'em on,
They cannot leave off play till they're undone.
With modest fears a muse does first begin,
Like a young wench newly enticed to sin:
But tickled once with praise by her good will,
The wanton fool would never more lie still.
'Tis an old mistress you'll meet here tonight,
Whose charms you once have looked on with delight.
But now of late such dirty drabs have known ye,
A muse o' th' better sort's ashamed to own you.
Nature well-drawn and wit must now give place
To gaudy nonsense and to dull grimace;
Nor is it strange that you should like so much
That kind of wit, for most of yours is such.
But I'm afraid that while to France we go,
To bring you home fine dresses, dance, and show;
The stage like you will but more foppish grow.
Of foreign wares why should we fetch the scum,
When we can be so richly served at home?
For heav'n be thanked 'tis not so wise an age,
But your own follies may supply the stage.
Though often ploughed, there's no great fear the soil
Should barren grow by the too frequent toil;
While at your doors are to be daily found,
Such loads of dunghill to manure the ground.
'Tis by your follies that we players thrive,
As the physicians by diseases live.
And as each year some new distemper reigns,
Whose friendly poison helps t'increase their gains:

Sir Car Scroope: courtier, poet and member of the Court Wit circle (1649–80).

1 *dancers on the ropes*: tightrope-walkers.

4 *miscarry*: come to grief.

9 *by her good will*: (1) with her consent (2) by her lover, Will.

13 *drabs*: slatterns; prostitutes.

14 *own*: acknowledge as an acquaintance.

22 *scum*: refuse.

So among you, there starts up every day,
Some new unheard-of fool for us to play.
Then for your own sakes be not too severe,
Nor what you all admire at home, damn here.
Since each is fond of his own ugly face,
Why should you, when we hold it, break the glass?

DRAMATIS PERSONAE

MR DORIMANT MR MEDLEY OLD BELLAIR YOUNG BELLAIR SIR FOPLING FLUTTER	gentlemen
LADY TOWNLEY EMILIA MRS LOVEIT BELLINDA LADY WOODVILL and HARRIET her daughter	gentlewomen
PERT and BUSY	waiting-women

A SHOEMAKER
An ORANGE WOMAN
Three SLOVENLY BULLIES
Two CHAIRMEN
MR SMIRK, a parson
HANDY, a *valet de chambre*
PAGES, FOOTMEN, &c.

THE MAN OF MODE, OR, SIR FOPLING FLUTTER: A COMEDY

ACT I

SCENE I

A dressing room, a table covered with a toilet, clothes laid ready.

Enter DORIMANT *in his gown and slippers, with a note in his hand made up, repeating verses.*

DORIMANT. 'Now for some ages had the pride of Spain,
Made the sun shine on half the world in vain.'
(*Then looking on the note*) 'For Mrs Loveit.' What a dull insipid thing is a billet doux written in cold blood, after the heat of the business is over? It is a tax upon good nature which I have here been labouring to pay, and have done it, but with as much regret, as

s.d. *toilet*: a cloth cover for a dressing-table.

s.d. *made up*: this would normally mean that the letter is closed and sealed; but see I i 202ff.

1–2 *Now for . . . in vain*: the opening couplet of Waller's 'Of a War with Spain, and a Fight at Sea' (*Poems*, ed. G. Thorn Drury (London, 1901), vol. 2, p. 23). John Dennis recorded that the original audiences, discerning in Dorimant 'several of the Qualities of *Wilmot* Earl of *Rochester*', took as one of these 'his repeating, on every occasion, the Verses of *Waller*, for whom that noble Lord had a very particular Esteem' (*A Defence of Sir Fopling Flutter* (1722), *Critical Works*, ed. E.N. Hooker (Baltimore, Johns Hopkins Press, 1939–43), vol. 2, p. 248). Though this testimony must be taken extremely seriously, it should be remembered that Dennis was writing almost half a century after the play's first performance.

4 *billet doux*: love letter (a recent importation; *OED*'s first example dates from 1673).

ever fanatic paid the Royal Aid, or church duties; 'twill have the same fate I know that all my notes to her have had of late, 'twill not be thought kind enough. Faith women are i' the right when they jealously examine our letters, for in them we always first discover our decay of passion. – Hey! – Who waits! –

Enter HANDY.

HANDY. Sir. –

DORIMANT. Call a footman.

HANDY. None of 'em are come yet.

DORIMANT. Dogs! will they ever lie snoring abed till noon.

HANDY. 'Tis all one, sir: if they're up, you indulge 'em so, they're ever poaching after whores all the morning.

DORIMANT. Take notice henceforward who's wanting in his duty, the next clap he gets, he shall rot for an example. What vermin are those chattering without?

HANDY. Foggy Nan the orange woman, and swearing Tom the shoemaker.

DORIMANT. Go; call in that overgrown jade with the flasket of guts before her, fruit is refreshing in a morning.

Exit HANDY.

'It is not that I love you less
Than when before your feet I lay.'

---

8 *fanatic*: an extreme Nonconformist, opposed to both the religious and the political status quo.

8 *Royal Aid*: a parliamentary grant of a subsidy or tax to the king for an extraordinary purpose.

8 *church duties*: levied locally for the services of the established church.

21 *poaching*: taking game illegally (cf. *She Would*, I i 12–13); but Barnard thinks there is also here 'a sexual pun on the meaning "poke" (from OF *pocher*, to thrust or dig out with the fingers)'.

23 *clap*: venereal disease.

25 *Foggy*: unwholesomely bloated, puffy.

27 *jade*: contemptuous name for an inferior horse, applied pejoratively to women.

28 *flasket*: basket, tub.

30–1 *It is not . . . I lay*: lines 1–2 from Waller's 'The Self-Banished' (*Poems*, ed. Thorn Drury, vol. 1, p. 101).

Enter ORANGE WOMAN.

How now double-tripe, what news do you bring?

ORANGE WOMAN. News! Here's the best fruit has come to town t'year, gad I was up before four a clock this morning, and bought all the choice i' the market.

DORIMANT. The nasty refuse of your shop.

ORANGE WOMAN. You need not make mouths at it, I assure you 'tis all culled ware.

DORIMANT. The citizens buy better on a holiday in their walk to Tot'nam.

ORANGE WOMAN. Good or bad 'tis all one, I never knew you commend anything, lord would the ladies had heard you talk of 'em as I have done: here bid your man give me an angel. (*Sets down the fruit*)

DORIMANT. Give the bawd her fruit again.

ORANGE WOMAN. Well, on my conscience, there never was the like of you. God's my life, I had almost forgot to tell you, there is a young gentlewoman lately come to town with her mother, that is so taken with you.

DORIMANT. Is she handsome?

ORANGE WOMAN. Nay, gad there are few finer women I tell you but so, and a hugeous fortune they say. Here eat this peach, it comes from the stone, 'tis better than any Newington y'have tasted.

DORIMANT. This fine woman I'll lay my life (*Taking the peach*) is some awkward ill-fashioned country toad, who not having above four dozen of black hairs on her head, has adorned her baldness with a large

---

32 *double-tripe*: enormously fat (literally, double-stomach).

38 *culled*: selected.

39–40 *citizens . . . Tot'nam*: Tottenham still lay separate from the capital proper and made a convenient place of holiday resort for those who worked in the trades of the city.

44 *angel*: cf. note to *Comical Revenge*, V v 50.

45 *bawd*: fruit-women were notorious as go-betweens.

54 *it comes from the stone*: presumably the peach is a freestone, a variety in which the flesh parts easily from the stone.

55 *Newington*: a town in Kent from which some varieties of peach took their name (Carnochan).

white fruz, that she may look sparkishly in the fore-front of the king's box, at an old play.

ORANGE WOMAN. Gad you'd change your note quickly if you did but see her.

DORIMANT. How came she to know me?

ORANGE WOMAN. She saw you yesterday at the Change, she told me you came and fooled with the woman at the next shop.

DORIMANT. I remember there was a mask observed me indeed. 'Fooled' did she say?

ORANGE WOMAN. Ay, I vow she told me twenty things you said too, and acted with head and with her body so like you –

Enter MEDLEY.

MEDLEY. Dorimant my life, my joy, my darling-sin; how dost thou.

ORANGE WOMAN. Lord what a filthy trick these men have got of kissing one another! (*She spits*)

MEDLEY. Why do you suffer this cartload of scandal to come near you, and make your neighbours think you so improvident to need a bawd?

ORANGE WOMAN. Good now, we shall have it, you did but want him to help you; come pay me for my fruit.

---

60 *fruz*: a wig of short curled hair.

60 *sparkishly*: elegantly, smartly.

61 *an old play*: i.e. when there would not be such great competition for the most prestigious and prominent seats (the king, of course, would not be present).

66 *the Change*: cf. note to *Comical Revenge*, V ii 86.

71 *with head*: this is the reading of the first three quartos, and a perfectly plausible one. From the 1704 *Works* onwards, however, most editions (Conaghan is an exception) have preferred 'with her head'.

76 *kissing one another*: Brett-Smith cited as a parallel from Shadwell's *The Sullen Lovers* (1668) a description of Woodcock as 'A Familiar loving Coxcomb, that embraces and kisses all men'.

77 *cartload*: i.e. heap.

80 *Good now, we shall have it*: This is the *1676* reading, which has frequently, in later editions, been emended to 'Good, now we shall have it'; but this is a completely unnecessary alteration, since the original yields perfectly good sense as it stands, 'Good now' being an interjection expressing expostulation, entreaty or slightly pained acquiescence.

81 *want*: lack, need.

MEDLEY. Make us thankful for it huswife, bawds are as much out of fashion as gentlemen ushers; none but old formal ladies use the one, and none but foppish old stagers employ the other, go you are an insignificant brandy bottle.

DORIMANT. Nay, there you wrong her, three quarts of canary is her business.

ORANGE WOMAN. What you please gentlemen.

DORIMANT. To him, give him as good as he brings.

ORANGE WOMAN. Hang him, there is not such another heathen in the town again, except it be the shoemaker without.

MEDLEY. I shall see you hold up your hand at the bar next sessions for murder, huswife; that shoemaker can take his oath you are in fee with the doctors to sell green fruit to the gentry, that the crudities may breed diseases.

ORANGE WOMAN. Pray give me my money.

DORIMANT. Not a penny, when you bring the gentlewoman hither you spoke of, you shall be paid.

ORANGE WOMAN. The gentlewoman! the gentlewoman may be as honest as your sisters for ought as I know. Pray pay me Mr Dorimant, and do not abuse me so, I have an honester way of living, you know it.

MEDLEY. Was there ever such a resty bawd?

DORIMANT. Some jade's tricks she has, but she makes amends when she's in good humour: come, tell me the lady's name, and Handy shall pay you.

ORANGE WOMAN. I must not, she forbid me.

DORIMANT. That's a sure sign she would have you.

---

82 *huswife*: hussy.
83 *gentlemen ushers*: attendants upon a person of rank.
85 *old stagers*: old hands, veterans.
87–8 *three quarts of canary*: a light sweet wine from the Canary Islands. Since 'canary' was also a slang-term for (1) a whore and (2) a gaol-bird, Dorimant's choice of intoxicant may hint at the orange-woman's characteristic habitat. Carnochan also notes that 'Visitors to the bawdy-houses of the day were usually put to the expense of a few bottles of wine.'
97 *crudities*: undigested (or indigestible) matter in the stomach.
103 *honest*: honourable, chaste.
106 *resty*: inactive, sluggish, intractable (an adjective frequently used of a stubborn horse or jade, hence Dorimant's following reference to the 'tricks' of the latter).

MEDLEY. Where does she live?

ORANGE WOMAN. They lodge at my house.

MEDLEY. Nay, then she's in a hopeful way.

ORANGE WOMAN. Good Mr Medley say your pleasure of me, but take heed how you affront my house, God's my life, in a hopeful way!

DORIMANT. Prithee peace, what kind of woman's the mother?

ORANGE WOMAN. A goodly grave gentlewoman, lord how she talks against the wild young men o' the town; as for your part she thinks you an arrant devil, should she see you, on my conscience she would look if you had not a cloven foot.

DORIMANT. Does she know me?

ORANGE WOMAN. Only by hearsay, a thousand horrid stories have been told her of you, and she believes 'em all.

MEDLEY. By the character, this should be the famous Lady Woodvill, and her daughter Harriet.

ORANGE WOMAN. The devil's in him for guessing I think.

DORIMANT. Do you know 'em?

MEDLEY. Both very well, the mother's a great admirer of the forms and civility of the last age.

DORIMANT. An antiquated beauty may be allowed to be out of humour at the freedoms of the present. This is a good account of the mother, pray what is the daughter?

MEDLEY. Why, first she's an heiress vastly rich.

DORIMANT. And handsome?

MEDLEY. What alteration a twelvemonth may have bred in her I know not, but a year ago she was the beautifullest creature I ever saw; a fine, easy, clean shape, light brown hair in abundance; her features regular, her complexion clear and lively, large wanton eyes, but above all a mouth that has made me kiss it a

---

122 *arrant*: (1) wandering, vagrant (2) notorious, manifest.

135 *forms and civility of the last age*: the manners and notions of social decorum favoured by those of the previous generation (i.e. those of the court of Charles I).

144 *easy*: graceful, attractive.

144 *clean*: well-built, shapely.

146 *wanton*: (sexually) playful, capricious, unrestrained.

thousand times in imagination, teeth white and even, and pretty pouting lips, with a little moisture ever hanging on them that look like the Provence rose fresh on the bush, ere the morning sun has quite drawn up the dew.

DORIMANT. Rapture, mere rapture!

ORANGE WOMAN. Nay, gad he tells you true, she's a delicate creature.

DORIMANT. Has she wit?

MEDLEY. More than is usual in her sex, and as much malice. Then she's as wild as you would wish her, and has a demureness in her looks that makes it so surprising.

DORIMANT. Flesh and blood cannot hear this, and not long to know her.

MEDLEY. I wonder what makes her mother bring her up to town, an old doting keeper cannot be more jealous of his mistress.

ORANGE WOMAN. She made me laugh yesterday, there was a judge came to visit 'em, and the old man she told me did so stare upon her, and when he saluted her smacked so heartily; who would think it of 'em?

MEDLEY. God-a-mercy judge.

DORIMANT. Do 'em right, the gentlemen of the long robe have not been wanting by their good examples to countenance the crying sin o' the nation.

MEDLEY. Come, on with your trappings, 'tis later than you imagine.

DORIMANT. Call in the shoemaker Handy.

ORANGE WOMAN. Good Mr Dorimant pay me, gad I

---

150 *Provence rose*: 'the Province rose' (*1676*); Carnochan emends to 'Provins rose', now used to describe *rosa gallica*. The Provence rose is the cabbage rose (*rosa centifolia*), a double red rose, with large round compact flowers.

153 *mere*: pure, sheer.

155 *delicate*: delightful, charming, pleasing to the palate.

158 *wild*: acting or moving freely, without constraint; resisting control or restraint, self-willed.

159 *demureness*: see note to *She Would*, I ii 137.

164 *keeper*: a man who keeps a mistress.

169 *smacked*: i.e. his lips.

170 *God-a-mercy*: 'God reward you', often used as an exclamation of thanks or applause (here, of course, ironically).

171–2 *gentlemen of the long robe*: members of the legal profession.

had rather give you my fruit than stay to be abused by that foul-mouthed rogue; what you gentlemen say it matters not much, but such a dirty fellow does one more disgrace.

DORIMANT. Give her ten shillings, and be sure you tell the young gentlewoman I must be acquainted with her.

ORANGE WOMAN. Now do you long to be tempting this pretty creature. Well, heavens mend you.

MEDLEY. Farewell bog. –

Exeunt ORANGE WOMAN *and* HANDY.

Dorimant, when did you see your *pis aller* as you call her, Mrs Loveit?

DORIMANT. Not these two days.

MEDLEY. And how stand affairs between you?

DORIMANT. There has been great patching of late, much ado, we make a shift to hang together.

MEDLEY. I wonder how her mighty spirit bears it.

DORIMANT. Ill enough on all conscience, I never knew so violent a creature.

MEDLEY. She's the most passionate in her love, and the most extravagant in her jealousy of any woman I ever heard of. What note is that?

DORIMANT. An excuse I am going to send her for the neglect I am guilty of.

MEDLEY. Prithee read it.

DORIMANT. No, but if you will take the pains you may.

MEDLEY. (*reads*) 'I never was a lover of business, but now I have a just reason to hate it, since it has kept me these two days from seeing you. I intend to wait upon you in the afternoon, and in the pleasure of your conversation, forget all I have suffered during

---

180 *dirty*: morally unclean, 'smutty' (as in the modern 'dirty story').

187 *bog*: *OED* (followed by Barnard) cites this use of the word as an instance of the meaning, 'a bugbear, a source of dread'; but the primary reference must surely be to the orange-woman's spongy fatness, and it is the *OED*'s other definition of the word (as a piece of ground 'too soft to bear the weight of any heavy body upon the surface') that gives the apter clue to its meaning here.

188 *pis aller*: last resort, makeshift.

208 *conversation*: see note to *She Would*, II i 184–5.

this tedious absence.' This business of yours Dorimant has been with a vizard at the playhouse, I have had an eye on you. If some malicious body should betray you, this kind note would hardly make your peace with her.

DORIMANT. I desire no better.

MEDLEY. Why, would her knowledge of it oblige you?

DORIMANT. Most infinitely; next to the coming to a good understanding with a new mistress, I love a quarrel with an old one, but the devil's in't, there has been such a calm in my affairs of late, I have not had the pleasure of making a woman so much as break her fan, to be sullen, or forswear herself these three days.

MEDLEY. A very great misfortune, let me see, I love mischief well enough, to forward this business myself, I'll about it presently, and though I know the truth of what y'ave done will set her a-raving, I'll heighten it a little with invention, leave her in a fit o' the mother, and be here again before y'are ready.

DORIMANT. Pray stay, you may spare yourself the labour, the business is undertaken already by one who will manage it with as much address, and I think with a little more malice than you can.

MEDLEY. Who i' the devil's name can this be!

DORIMANT. Why the vizard, that very vizard you saw me with.

MEDLEY. Does she love mischief so well, as to betray herself to spite another?

DORIMANT. Not so neither, Medley, I will make you comprehend the mystery; this mask for a farther confirmation of what I have been these two days swearing to her, made me yesterday at the playhouse make her a promise before her face, utterly to break off with Loveit, and because she tenders my reputation, and would not have me do a barbarous thing, has contrived a way to give me a handsome occasion.

MEDLEY. Very good.

DORIMANT. She intends about an hour before me, this

---

210 *vizard*: woman wearing a mask, often used of a prostitute.
224 *presently*: immediately.
226 *a fit o' the mother*: hysteria.
242 *tenders*: has tender feeling for.

afternoon, to make Loveit a visit, and (having the privilege by reason of a professed friendship between 'em to talk of her concerns) –

MEDLEY. Is she a friend?

DORIMANT. Oh, an intimate friend!

MEDLEY. Better and better, pray proceed.

DORIMANT. She means insensibly to insinuate a discourse of me, and artificially raise her jealousy to such a height, that transported with the first motions of her passion, she shall fly upon me with all the fury imaginable, as soon as ever I enter; the quarrel being thus happily begun, I am to play my part, confess and justify all my roguery, swear her impertinence and ill humour makes her intolerable, tax her with the next fop that comes into my head, and in a huff march away, slight her and leave her to be taken by whosoever thinks it worth his time to lie down before her.

MEDLEY. This vizard is a spark, and has a genius that makes her worthy of yourself, Dorimant.

Enter HANDY, SHOEMAKER, *and* FOOTMAN.

DORIMANT. You rogue there, who sneak like a dog that has flung down a dish, if you do not mend your waiting I'll uncase you, and turn you loose to the wheel of fortune. Handy, seal this and let him run with it presently.

Exeunt HANDY *and* FOOTMAN.

MEDLEY. Since y'are resolved on a quarrel, why do you send her this kind note?

DORIMANT. To keep her at home in order to the business. (*To the* SHOEMAKER) How now you drunken sot?

---

248 *professed*: openly acknowledged, mutually declared; but also, alleged, pretended.
253 *insensibly*: imperceptibly.
254 *artificially*: artfully.
264 *spark*: a woman of great wit.
264 *genius*: prevailing character or disposition.
268 *uncase you*: strip you (of livery), i.e. dismiss you.
270 s.d. *Exeunt Handy and Footman*: Handy exits here, but returns at some unmarked point in the following conversation.
273 *in order to*: for the sake of.

SHOEMAKER. 'Zbud, you have no reason to talk, I have not had a bottle of sack of yours in my belly this fortnight.

MEDLEY. The orange woman says, your neighbours take notice what a heathen you are, and design to inform the bishop, and have you burned for an atheist.

SHOEMAKER. Damn her, dunghill, if her husband does not remove her, she stinks so, the parish intend to indict him for a nuisance.

MEDLEY. I advise you like a friend, reform your life, you have brought the envy of the world upon you, by living above yourself. Whoring and swearing are vices too genteel for a shoemaker.

SHOEMAKER. 'Zbud, I think you men of quality will grow as unreasonable as the women; you would engross the sins o' the nation; poor folks can no sooner be wicked, but th'are railed at by their betters.

DORIMANT. Sirrah, I'll have you stand i' the pillory for this libel.

SHOEMAKER. Some of you deserve it, I'm sure, there are so many of 'em, that our journeymen nowadays instead of harmless ballads, sing nothing but your damned lampoons.

DORIMANT. Our lampoons you rogue?

SHOEMAKER. Nay, good master, why should not you write your own commentaries as well as Caesar?

---

276 *'Zbud*: 'Sblood, i.e. 'God's blood'.

277 *sack*: a general name for a class of white wines formerly imported from Spain and the Canaries.

281–2 *burned for an atheist*: see Additional Note.

290 *men of quality*: gentlemen.

292 *engross*: monopolize.

298–9 *ballads . . . lampoons*: i.e. the city journeymen's taste has turned from their traditional liking for ballads to an enthusiasm for the scurrilous and lubricious verse satires (often against named individuals) which were produced in large quantities in the 1660s and 1670s. The Shoemaker (in many ways aptly) associates the production of the latter with such fashionable gentlemen as Dorimant and implies (see following note) that the lampoons contain a large element of autobiography.

302 *commentaries*: (1) memoirs, as in Caesar's writings on his own life (2) interpretative glosses.

MEDLEY. The rascal's read, I perceive.

SHOEMAKER. You know the old proverb, ale and history.

DORIMANT. Draw on my shoes, sirrah.

SHOEMAKER. Here's a shoe.

DORIMANT. Sits with more wrinkles than there are in an angry bully's forehead.

SHOEMAKER. 'Zbud, as smooth as your mistress's skin does upon her, so, strike your foot in home. 'Zbud if e'er a monsieur of 'em all make more fashionable ware, I'll be content to have my ears whipped off with my own paring knife.

MEDLEY. And served up in a ragout, instead of cocks-combs to a company of French shoemakers for a collation.

SHOEMAKER. Hold, hold, damn 'em caterpillars, let 'em feed upon cabbage; come master, your health this morning next my heart now.

DORIMANT. Go, get you home, and govern your family better; do not let your wife follow you to the ale-house, beat your whore, and lead you home in triumph.

SHOEMAKER. 'Zbud, there's never a man i' the town lives more like a gentleman, with his wife, than I do.

---

303 *read*: well-read, learned.

304–5 *ale and history*: 'Truth is in ale as in history' (Tilley, T 578). Doubts have been raised about whether Tilley was correct to list this as a proverb, but, in his note, Barnard cites evidence in support of Tilley.

309 *bully*: blustering gallant, swashbuckler.

315–16 *cockscombs*: 'Coxcombs' (*1676*). Barnard suggested the spelling used here and added the comment that 'cockscombs can be used in French cooking as a garnish or in a sauce' for such dishes as a 'ragout', i.e. a highly flavoured stew. There is, of course, also play here on 'coxcomb', originally, the cap worn by a professional fool, like a cock's comb in shape and colour – an emblem appropriate to the gallants' estimate of the Shoemaker's intelligence.

317 *collation*: a light repast.

318 *caterpillars*: extortioners, people who prey on society.

319–20 *your health this morning next my heart*: 'The shoemaker asks Dorimant for money to drink his health; *next my heart* may refer to a toast drunk with hand on heart' (Carnochan). The use of the latter phrase suits the deliberate impudence of his manner; cf. *Comical Revenge*, I ii 64 and note.

I never mind her motions, she never inquires into mine, we speak to one another civilly, hate one another heartily, and because 'tis vulgar to lie and soak together, we have each of us our several settle-bed.

DORIMANT. Give him half a crown.

MEDLEY. Not without he will promise to be bloody drunk.

SHOEMAKER. Tope's the word i' the eye of the world for my master's honour Robin.

DORIMANT. Do not debauch my servants, sirrah.

SHOEMAKER. I only tip him the wink, he knows an alehouse from a hovel. *Exit* SHOEMAKER.

DORIMANT. My clothes quickly.

MEDLEY. Where shall we dine today?

Enter YOUNG BELLAIR.

DORIMANT. Where you will; here comes a good third man.

YOUNG BELLAIR. Your servant gentlemen.

MEDLEY. Gentle sir; how will you answer this visit to your honourable mistress? 'tis not her interest you should keep company with men of sense, who will be talking reason.

YOUNG BELLAIR. I do not fear her pardon, do you but grant me yours, for my neglect of late.

MEDLEY. Though y'ave made us miserable by the want of your good company, to show you I am free from all resentment, may the beautiful cause of our misfortune, give you all the joys happy lovers have shared ever since the world began.

YOUNG BELLAIR. You wish me in heaven, but you believe me on my journey to hell.

---

327 *motions*: (1) movements (2) inward impulses, desires.
329 *vulgar*: plebeian.
330 *soak*: (1) sweat (2) drink heavily.
330 *several*: separate.
330–1 *settle-bed*: long wooden bench, used as a bed.
333 *without*: unless.
333 *bloody*: see Additional Note.
335–6 *Tope's the word i' the eye of the world for my master's honour Robin*: thus *1676*. See Additional Note.
345 *answer*: justify.

MEDLEY. You have a good strong faith, and that may contribute much towards your salvation. I confess I am but of an untoward constitution, apt to have doubts and scruples, and in love they are no less distracting than in religion; were I so near marriage, I should cry out by fits as I ride in my coach, 'Cuckold, cuckold', with no less fury than the mad fanatic does 'Glory' in Beth'lem.

YOUNG BELLAIR. Because religion makes some run mad, must I live an atheist?

MEDLEY. Is it not great indiscretion for a man of credit, who may have money enough on his word, to go and deal with Jews; who for little sums make men enter into bonds, and give judgments?

YOUNG BELLAIR. Preach no more on this text, I am determined, and there is no hope of my conversion.

DORIMANT. (*to* HANDY *who is fiddling about him*) Leave your unnecessary fiddling; a wasp that's buzzing about a man's nose at dinner, is not more troublesome than thou art.

HANDY. You love to have your clothes hang just, sir.

DORIMANT. I love to be well dressed sir: and think it no scandal to my understanding.

HANDY. Will you use the essence or orange-flower water?

DORIMANT. I will smell as I do today, no offence to the ladies' noses.

HANDY. Your pleasure sir.

DORIMANT. That a man's excellency should lie in neatly tying of a ribbond, or a cravat! how careful's

---

360 *untoward*: unruly, stubborn, awkward.
364 *the mad fanatic*: Oliver Cromwell's porter, Daniel; his religious delusions caused his imprisonment in the lunatic asylum more commonly known as Bedlam.
371 *bonds*: see note to *Comical Revenge*, V iv 8.
371 *judgments*: judicial assignment of chattels, hence certificates recording such a judgment as security.
377 *just*: in the correct manner.
380 *essence*: perfume, scent.
380–1 *orange-flower water*: scent or perfume extracted from the orange-flower.
386 *ribbond*: see note to *Comical Revenge*, IV vi 51.

nature in furnishing the world with necessary coxcombs!

YOUNG BELLAIR. That's a mighty pretty suit of yours Dorimant.

DORIMANT. I am glad 't has your approbation.

YOUNG BELLAIR. No man in town has a better fancy in his clothes than you have.

DORIMANT. You will make me have an opinion of my genius.

MEDLEY. There is a great critic I hear in these matters lately arrived piping hot from Paris.

YOUNG BELLAIR. Sir Fopling Flutter you mean.

MEDLEY. The same.

YOUNG BELLAIR. He thinks himself the pattern of modern gallantry.

DORIMANT. He is indeed the pattern of modern foppery.

MEDLEY. He was yesterday at the play, with a pair of gloves up to his elbows, and a periwig more exactly curled than a lady's head newly dressed for a ball.

YOUNG BELLAIR. What a pretty lisp he has!

DORIMANT. Ho that he affects in imitation of the people of quality of France.

MEDLEY. His head stands for the most part on one side, and his looks are more languishing than a lady's when she lolls at stretch in her coach, or leans her head carelessly against the side of a box i' the playhouse.

DORIMANT. He is a person indeed of great acquired follies.

MEDLEY. He is like many others, beholding to his education for making him so eminent a coxcomb; many a fool had been lost to the world, had their indulgent parents wisely bestowed neither learning nor good breeding on 'em.

YOUNG BELLAIR. He has been, as the sparkish word is, brisk upon the ladies already, he was yesterday at my Aunt Townley's, and gave Mrs Loveit a catalogue of his good qualities, under the character of a complete

---

387–8 *necessary coxcombs*: men who are by nature fools, who cannot be other than they are.

392 *fancy*: see note to *She Would*, III i 246.

421 *brisk*: sharp.

423 *under the character of*: in the form of a character-sketch of.

gentleman, who according to Sir Fopling, ought to dress well, dance well, fence well, have a genius for love letters, an agreeable voice for a chamber, be very amorous, something discreet, but not over-constant.

MEDLEY. Pretty ingredients to make an accomplished person.

DORIMANT. I am glad he pitched upon Loveit.

YOUNG BELLAIR. How so?

DORIMANT. I wanted a fop to lay to her charge, and this is as pat as may be.

YOUNG BELLAIR. I am confident she loves no man but you.

DORIMANT. The good fortune were enough to make me vain, but that I am in my nature modest.

YOUNG BELLAIR. Hark you Dorimant, with your leave Mr Medley, 'tis only a secret concerning a fair lady.

MEDLEY. Your good breeding sir gives you too much trouble, you might have whispered without all this ceremony.

YOUNG BELLAIR. (*to* DORIMANT) How stand your affairs with Bellinda of late?

DORIMANT. She's a little jilting baggage.

YOUNG BELLAIR. Nay, I believe her false enough, but she's ne'er the worse for your purpose; she was with you yesterday in a disguise at the play.

DORIMANT. There we fell out, and resolved never to speak to one another more.

YOUNG BELLAIR. The occasion?

DORIMANT. Want of courage to meet me at the place appointed. These young women apprehend loving, as much as the young men do fighting at first; but once entered, like them too, they all turn bullies straight.

Enter HANDY *to* YOUNG BELLAIR.

---

430 *pitched upon*: set his sights upon, selected.

446 *baggage*: according to the *OED*, from the early 1670s, the word was beginning to be used familiarly or playfully of any young woman, but an older sense ('a worthless good-for-nothing woman', 'a strumpet') was still active.

456 *entered*: initiated.

HANDY. Sir: your man without desires to speak with you.

YOUNG BELLAIR. Gentlemen, I'll return immediately.

Exit YOUNG BELLAIR.

MEDLEY. A very pretty fellow this.

DORIMANT. He's handsome, well-bred, and by much the most tolerable of all the young men that do not abound in wit.

MEDLEY. Ever well-dressed, always complaisant, and seldom impertinent; you and he are grown very intimate I see.

DORIMANT. It is our mutual interest to be so; it makes the women think the better of his understanding, and judge more favourably of my reputation; it makes him pass upon some for a man of very good sense, and I upon others for a very civil person.

MEDLEY. What was that whisper?

DORIMANT. A thing which he would fain have known, but I did not think it fit to tell him; it might have frighted him from his honourable intentions of marrying.

MEDLEY. Emilia, give her her due, has the best reputation of any young woman about the town, who has beauty enough to provoke detraction; her carriage is unaffected, her discourse modest, not at all censorious, nor pretending like the counterfeits of the age.

DORIMANT. She's a discreet maid, and I believe nothing can corrupt her but a husband.

MEDLEY. A husband?

DORIMANT. Yes, a husband; I have known many women make a difficulty of losing a maidenhead, who have afterwards made none of making a cuckold.

MEDLEY. This prudent consideration I am apt to think has made you confirm poor Bellair in the desperate resolution he has taken.

DORIMANT. Indeed the little hope I found there was of her, in the state she was in, has made me by my

---

464 *complaisant*: disposed to please, courteous, accommodating.
470 *pass upon . . . for*: see note to *Comical Revenge*, II iii 81.
479 *carriage*: behaviour, habitual conduct, deportment.

advice, contribute something towards the changing of her condition.

Enter YOUNG BELLAIR.

Dear Bellair, by heavens I thought we had lost thee; men in love are never to be reckoned on when we would form a company.

YOUNG BELLAIR. Dorimant, I am undone, my man has brought the most surprising news i' the world.

DORIMANT. Some strange misfortune is befallen your love.

YOUNG BELLAIR. My father came to town last night, and lodges i' the very house where Emilia lies.

MEDLEY. Does he know it is with her you are in love?

YOUNG BELLAIR. He knows I love, but knows not whom, without some officious sot has betrayed me.

DORIMANT. Your Aunt Townley is your confident, and favours the business.

YOUNG BELLAIR. I do not apprehend any ill office from her. I have received a letter, in which I am commanded by my father to meet him at my aunt's this afternoon; he tells me farther he has made a match for me, and bids me resolve to be obedient to his will, or expect to be disinherited.

MEDLEY. Now's your time, Bellair, never had lover such an opportunity of giving a generous proof of his passion.

YOUNG BELLAIR. As how I pray?

MEDLEY. Why hang an estate, marry Emilia out of hand, and provoke your father to do what he threatens; 'tis but despising a coach, humbling yourself to a pair of goloshoes, being out of countenance when you meet your friends, pointed at and pitied wherever you go by all the amorous fops that know you, and your fame will be immortal.

YOUNG BELLAIR. I could find in my heart to resolve not to marry at all.

DORIMANT. Fie, fie, that would spoil a good jest, and

---

508 *confident*: confidante.

517 *generous*: see notes to *She Would*, II ii 46, 49.

523 *goloshoes*: galoshes, 'rustic shoes or overshoes, usually with wooden soles' (Carnochan).

disappoint the well-natured town of an occasion of laughing at you.

YOUNG BELLAIR. The storm I have so long expected, hangs o'er my head, and begins to pour down upon me; I am on the rack, and can have no rest till I'm satisfied in what I fear; where do you dine?

DORIMANT. At Long's, or Locket's.

MEDLEY. At Long's let it be.

YOUNG BELLAIR. I'll run and see Emilia, and inform myself how matters stand; if my misfortunes are not so great as to make me unfit for company, I'll be with you. *Exit* YOUNG BELLAIR.

Enter a FOOTMAN *with a letter.*

FOOTMAN. (*to* DORIMANT) Here's a letter sir.

DORIMANT. The superscription's right; 'For Mr Dorimant'.

MEDLEY. Let's see, the very scrawl and spelling of a true-bred whore.

DORIMANT. I know the hand, the style is admirable I assure you.

MEDLEY. Prithee read it.

DORIMANT. (*reads*) 'I told a you you dud not love me, if you dud, you would have seen me again ere now; I have no money and am very mallicolly; pray send me a guynie to see the operies. Your servant to command, Molly.'

MEDLEY. Pray let the whore have a favourable answer, that she may spark it in a box, and do honour to her profession.

DORIMANT. She shall; and perk up i' the face of quality. Is the coach at door?

HANDY. You did not bid me send for it.

DORIMANT. Eternal blockhead! (HANDY *offers to go*) Hey sot. –

---

536 *Long's, or Locket's*: fashionable eating-places: Locket's was at Charing Cross, and the Long brothers ran two, in Covent Garden and the Haymarket.

553 *operies*: see note to II i 152.

558 *perk up*: behave impudently, struttingly; but presumably there is also a play on the meaning, 'to recover liveliness, as after a sickness or depression' (i.e. being 'very mallicolly').

HANDY. Did you call me, sir?

DORIMANT. I hope you have no just exception to the name, sir?

HANDY. I have sense, sir.

DORIMANT. Not so much as a fly in winter: – how did you come Medley?

MEDLEY. In a chair!

FOOTMAN. You may have a hackney coach if you please, sir.

DORIMANT. I may ride the elephant if I please, sir; call another chair, and let my coach follow to Long's. 'Be calm ye great parents', etc.

Exeunt, [DORIMANT] *singing.*

ACT II

SCENE I

Enter my LADY TOWNLEY, *and* EMILIA.

LADY TOWNLEY. I was afraid Emilia, all had been discovered.

EMILIA. I tremble with the apprehension still.

LADY TOWNLEY. That my brother should take lodgings i' the very house where you lie.

EMILIA. 'Twas lucky, we had timely notice to warn the people to be secret, he seems to be a mighty good-humoured old man.

---

564 *exception*: objection.

570 *hackney coach*: see note to *Comical Revenge*, I ii 45.

572 *elephant*: Barnard cites evidence that 'there are several contemporary references to elephants exhibited in London from 1675 to 1682'.

574 *'Be calm ye great parents', etc.*: Conaghan identified this as being from the song 'My Lord: Great *Neptune*, for my Sake' in the final scene of Shadwell's operatic version of *The Tempest* (1674). The relevant lines run: 'Be calm, ye great Parents of the Flouds and the Springs, / While each *Nereide* and *Triton* Plays, Revels and Sings' (*Complete Works*, ed. Montague Summers (London, Fortune Press, 1927), vol. 2, p. 266).

LADY TOWNLEY. He ever had a notable smirking way with him.

EMILIA. He calls me rogue, tells me he can't abide me; and does so bepat me.

LADY TOWNLEY. On my word you are much in his favour then.

EMILIA. He has been very inquisitive I am told about my family, my reputation, and my fortune.

LADY TOWNLEY. I am confident he does not i' the least suspect you are the woman his son's in love with.

EMILIA. What should make him then inform himself so particularly of me?

LADY TOWNLEY. He was always of a very loving temper himself; it may be he has a doting fit upon him, who knows?

EMILIA. It cannot be.

Enter YOUNG BELLAIR.

LADY TOWNLEY. Here comes my nephew. Where did you leave your father?

YOUNG BELLAIR. Writing a note within; Emilia, this early visit looks as if some kind jealousy would not let you rest at home.

EMILIA. The knowledge I have of my rival, gives me a little cause to fear your constancy.

YOUNG BELLAIR. My constancy! I vow –

EMILIA. Do not vow – our love is frail as is our life, and full as little in our power, and are you sure you shall outlive this day?

YOUNG BELLAIR. I am not, but when we are in perfect health, 'twere an idle thing to fright ourselves with the thoughts of sudden death.

LADY TOWNLEY. Pray what has passed between you and your father i' the garden?

YOUNG BELLAIR. He's firm in his resolution, tells me I must marry Mrs Harriet, or swears he'll marry himself, and disinherit me; when I saw I could not prevail with him to be more indulgent, I dissembled an obedience to his will, which has composed his passion, and will give us time, and I hope opportunity to deceive him.

Enter OLD BELLAIR, *with a note in his hand.*

LADY TOWNLEY. Peace, here he comes.

OLD BELLAIR. Harry, take this, and let your man carry it for me to Mr Fourbe's chamber, my lawyer i' the Temple. [*Exit* YOUNG BELLAIR.] (*To* EMILIA) Neighbour, a dod I am glad to see thee here, make much of her, sister, she's one of the best of your acquaintance; I like her countenance and her behaviour well, she has a modesty that is not common i' this age, a dod, she has.

LADY TOWNLEY. I know her value brother, and esteem her accordingly.

OLD BELLAIR. Advise her to wear a little more mirth in her face, a dod she's too serious.

LADY TOWNLEY. The fault is very excusable in a young woman.

OLD BELLAIR. Nay, a dod, I like her ne'er the worse, a melancholy beauty has her charms, I love a pretty sadness in a face which varies now and then, like changeable colours, into a smile.

LADY TOWNLEY. Methinks you speak very feelingly brother.

OLD BELLAIR. I am but five-and-fifty sister you know, an age not altogether unsensible! (*To* EMILIA) cheer up sweetheart; I have a secret to tell thee may chance to make thee merry, we three will make collation together anon, i' the meantime mum, I can't abide you, go I can't abide you –

Enter YOUNG BELLAIR.

Harry, come you must along with me to my Lady Woodvill's. I am going to slip the boy at a mistress.

YOUNG BELLAIR. At a wife sir, you would say.

OLD BELLAIR. You need not look so glum, sir, a wife

---

50 *Fourbe*: cheat, impostor (or trick, imposture), from the French.

51 *Temple*: see note to *She Would*, IV i 70.

52 *a dod*: an ejaculation, equivalent to 'egad', 'By God'.

66 *changeable colours*: as in some varieties of material (e.g. shot-silk) which, viewed from different angles, alter colour.

73 *mum*: two meanings are possible: (1) a colloquial contraction of 'madam', 'ma'am', or (2), more probably in this context, hush!

73–4 *i' the meantime mum, I can't abide you*: see Additional Note.

76 *slip*: see note to *She Would*, II i 104.

is no curse when she brings the blessing of a good estate with her, but an idle town flirt, with a painted face, a rotten reputation, and a crazy fortune, a dod is the devil and all, and such a one I hear you are in league with.

YOUNG BELLAIR. I cannot help detraction, sir.

OLD BELLAIR. Out, a pize o' their breeches, there are keeping fools enough for such flaunting baggages, and they are e'en too good for 'em. (*To* EMILIA) Remember night, go y'are a rogue, y'are a rogue; fare you well, fare you well; come, come, come along, sir.

Exeunt OLD *and* YOUNG BELLAIR.

LADY TOWNLEY. On my word the old man comes on apace; I'll lay my life he's smitten.

EMILIA. This is nothing but the pleasantness of his humour.

LADY TOWNLEY. I know him better than you, let it work, it may prove lucky.

Enter a PAGE.

PAGE. Madam, Mr Medley has sent to know whether a visit will not be troublesome this afternoon?

LADY TOWNLEY. Send him word his visits never are so.

[*Exit* PAGE.]

EMILIA. He's a very pleasant man.

LADY TOWNLEY. He's a very necessary man among us women; he's not scandalous i' the least, perpetually contriving to bring good company together, and always ready to stop up a gap at ombre, then he knows all the little news o' the town.

EMILIA. I love to hear him talk o' the intrigues, let 'em be never so dull in themselves, he'll make 'em pleasant i' the relation.

---

80 *idle*: worthless.

80 *flirt*: woman of loose character (the more modern meaning – one who flirts or plays at courtship – seems to be a mid-eighteenth-century development).

81 *crazy*: broken down, impaired.

85 *a pize*: an imprecation of uncertain meaning.

86 *keeping fools*: see note to I i 164.

101 *he's not scandalous*: i.e. it is not a cause of scandal for a woman to be seen in his company.

103 *ombre*: see note to *She Would*, III iii 364.

105 *intrigues*: see note to *She Would*, II ii 165.

LADY TOWNLEY. But he improves things so much one can take no measure of the truth from him. Mr Dorimant swears a flea or a maggot, is not made more monstrous by a magnifying glass, than a story is by his telling it.

EMILIA. Hold, here he comes.

Enter MEDLEY.

LADY TOWNLEY. Mr Medley.

MEDLEY. Your servant madam.

LADY TOWNLEY. You have made yourself a stranger of late.

EMILIA. I believe you took a surfeit of ombre last time you were here.

MEDLEY. Indeed I had my belly full of that termagant Lady Dealer; there never was so unsatiable a carder, an old gleeker never loved to sit to't like her; I have played with her now at least a dozen times, till she'as worn out all her fine complexion, and her tour would keep in curl no longer.

LADY TOWNLEY. Blame her not poor woman, she loves nothing so well as a black ace.

MEDLEY. The pleasure I have seen her in when she has had hope in drawing for a matadore.

EMILIA. 'Tis as pretty sport to her, as persuading masks off is to you to make discoveries.

LADY TOWNLEY. Pray where's your friend, Mr Dorimant?

MEDLEY. Soliciting his affairs, he's a man of great employment, has more mistresses now depending than the most eminent lawyer in England has causes.

EMILIA. Here has been Mrs Loveit, so uneasy and out of humour these two days.

---

121 *carder*: card player.
122 *gleeker*: a player of gleek, a card game.
124 *tour*: a crescent of false hair.
129 *matadore*: the name given to the principal cards (the black aces and a variable third card) in ombre.
134 *Soliciting his affairs*: (1) pursuing his amours (2) but playing on another meaning, 'conducting law business' (see following note).
135 *depending*: pending, like a lawyer's cases ('causes').

LADY TOWNLEY. How strangely love and jealousy rage in that poor woman!

MEDLEY. She could not have picked out a devil upon earth so proper to torment her, has made her break a dozen or two of fans already, tear half a score points in pieces, and destroy hoods and knots without number.

LADY TOWNLEY. We heard of a pleasant serenade he gave her t'other night.

MEDLEY. A Danish serenade with kettledrums, and trumpets.

EMILIA. Oh barbarous!

MEDLEY. What, you are of the number of the ladies whose ears are grown so delicate since our operas, you can be charmed with nothing but flûtes douces, and French hautboys.

EMILIA. Leave your raillery, and tell us, is there any new wit come forth, songs or novels?

MEDLEY. A very pretty piece of gallantry, by an eminent author, called, *The Diversions of Bruxelles*, very necessary to be read by all old ladies who are desirous to improve themselves at questions and commands, blindman's buff, and the like fashionable recreations.

---

143 *points*: see note to *She Would*, I ii 116.

143 *knots*: see note to *She Would*, III i 176.

148 *Danish serenade*: Carnochan compares *Hamlet*, I iv 8–12: 'The King doth wake tonight and takes his rouse, / Keeps wassail, and the swaggering upspring reels; / And as he drains his draughts of Rhenish down, / The kettledrum and trumpet thus bray out / The triumph of his pledge.'

152 *operas*: see Additional Note.

153 *flûtes douces*: 'Flute doux' (*1676*); the *flûte douce* (the recorder), a recent arrival in England, was in the process of succeeding the flageolet in popularity.

154 *hautboys*: oboes.

155 *raillery*: this word is another recent arrival from France (*OED*'s first example dates from 1653).

158 *The Diversions of Bruxelles*: '*Bruxells*' (*1676*), 'Brussels' (Carnochan, Barnard). The work referred to under this parodic title was identified by R.S. Cox, Jr (*Modern Language Quarterly*, 29 (1968), 183–9) as Richard Flecknoe's *A Treatise of the Sports of Wit* (1675).

160–1 *questions and commands*: an unfashionable game in which one person addressed ludicrous questions and commands to each member of the company.

EMILIA. Oh ridiculous!

MEDLEY. Then there is *The Art of Affectation*, written by a late beauty of quality, teaching you how to draw up your breasts, stretch up your neck, to thrust out your breech, to play with your head, to toss up your nose, to bite your lips, to turn up your eyes, to speak in a silly soft tone of a voice, and use all the foolish French words that will infallibly make your person and conversation charming, with a short apology at the latter end, in the behalf of young ladies, who notoriously wash, and paint, though they have naturally good complexions.

EMILIA. What a deal of stuff you tell us!

MEDLEY. Such as the town affords madam. The Russians hearing the great respect we have for foreign dancing, have lately sent over some of their best baladines, who are now practising a famous ballet which will be suddenly danced at the Bear Garden.

LADY TOWNLEY. Pray forbear your idle stories, and give us an account of the state of love, as it now stands.

MEDLEY. Truly there has been some revolutions in those affairs, great chopping and changing among the old, and some new lovers, whom malice, indiscretion, and misfortune, have luckily brought into play.

LADY TOWNLEY. What think you of walking into the next room, and sitting down before you engage in this business?

---

164 *The Art of Affectation*: 'Medley is poking fun at *The Gentlewoman's Companion*, printed in 1675 as by Hannah Woolley' (Conaghan). It recommends some of the behaviour here mocked.

173 *wash, and paint*: use cosmetic washes and make-up.

179 *baladines*: theatrical dancers; mountebanks, buffoóns.

179 *ballet*: another recent importation from French; originally used to illustrate dramatically the costumes and manners of other nations.

180 *suddenly*: soon.

180 *Bear Garden*: 'a hit both at the contemporary craze for music and dancing by foreign troupes, and at the proverbial barbarity of the Russians' (Barnard), since the Bear Garden was, as its name suggests, a venue for beat-baiting.

185 *chopping and changing*: 'the phrase meant, originally, "bartering with, trading"; here, it keeps something of that meaning' (Carnochan).

MEDLEY. I wait upon you, and I hope (though women are commonly unreasonable) by the plenty of scandal I shall discover, to give you very good content ladies.

Exeunt.

SCENE II

Enter MRS LOVEIT *and* PERT.
MRS LOVEIT *putting up a letter, then pulling out her pocket glass, and looking in it.*

MRS LOVEIT. Pert.

PERT. Madam.

MRS LOVEIT. I hate myself, I look so ill today.

PERT. Hate the wicked cause on't, that base man Mr Dorimant, who makes you torment and vex yourself continually.

MRS LOVEIT. He is to blame indeed.

PERT. To blame to be two days without sending, writing, or coming near you, contrary to his oath and covenant; 'twas to much purpose to make him swear; I'll lay my life there's not an article but he has broken, talked to the vizards i' the pit, waited upon the ladies from the boxes to their coaches; gone behind the scenes, and fawned upon those little insignificant creatures, the players; 'tis impossible for a man of his inconstant temper to forbear I'm sure.

MRS LOVEIT. I know he is a devil, but he has something of the angel yet undefaced in him, which makes him so charming and agreeable, that I must love him be he never so wicked.

PERT. I little thought madam to see your spirit tamed to this degree, who banished poor Mr Lackwit but for taking up another lady's fan in your presence.

MRS LOVEIT. My knowing of such odious fools, contributes to the making of me love Dorimant the better.

PERT. Your knowing of Mr Dorimant, in my mind, should rather make you hate all mankind.

MRS LOVEIT. So it does, besides himself.

---

s.d. *putting up*: putting away.

PERT. Pray, what excuse does he make in his letter?

MRS LOVEIT. He has had business.

PERT. Business in general terms would not have been a current excuse for another; a modish man is always very busy when he is in pursuit of a new mistress.

MRS LOVEIT. Some fop has bribed you to rail at him; he had business, I will believe it, and will forgive him.

PERT. You may forgive him anything, but I shall never forgive him his turning me into ridicule, as I hear he does.

MRS LOVEIT. I perceive you are of the number of those fools his wit had made his enemies.

PERT. I am of the number of those he's pleased to rally, madam; and if we may believe Mr Wagfan, and Mr Caperwell, he sometimes makes merry with yourself too, among his laughing companions.

MRS LOVEIT. Blockheads are as malicious to witty men, as ugly women are to the handsome; 'tis their interest, and they make it their business to defame 'em.

PERT. I wish Mr Dorimant would not make it his business to defame you.

MRS LOVEIT. Should he, I had rather be made infamous by him, than owe my reputation to the dull discretion of those fops you talk of. Bellinda! (*Running to her*)

Enter BELLINDA.

BELLINDA. My dear.

MRS LOVEIT. You have been unkind of late.

BELLINDA. Do not say unkind, say unhappy!

MRS LOVEIT. I could chide you, where have you been these two days?

BELLINDA. Pity me rather my dear, where I have been so tired with two or three country gentlewomen, whose conversation has been more unsufferable than a country fiddle.

---

33 *current*: acceptable, valid.
33 *modish*: see note to *Comical Revenge*, IV ii 12.
42 *rally*: make fun of.
43–4 *Mr Caperwell*: see note to *Comical Revenge*, III v 47.
45 *companions*: see note to *Comical Revenge*, I ii 88.

MRS LOVEIT. Are they relations?

BELLINDA. No. Welsh acquaintance I made when I was last year at St Winifrid's, they have asked me a thousand questions of the modes and intrigues of the town, and I have told 'em almost as many things for news that hardly were so, when their gowns were in fashion.

MRS LOVEIT. Provoking creatures, how could you endure 'em?

BELLINDA. (*aside*) Now to carry on my plot, nothing but love could make me capable of so much falsehood; 'tis time to begin, lest Dorimant should come before her jealousy has stung her; (*Laughs and then speaks on*) I was yesterday at a play with 'em, where I was fain to show 'em the living, as the man at Westminster does the dead; that is Mrs Such-a-one admired for her beauty, this is Mr Such-a-one cried up for a wit; that is sparkish Mr Such-a-one who keeps reverend Mrs Such-a-one, and there sits fine Mrs Such-a-one who was lately cast off by my Lord Such-a-one.

MRS LOVEIT. Did you see Dorimant there?

BELLINDA. I did, and imagine you were there with him, and have no mind to own it.

MRS LOVEIT. What should make you think so?

BELLINDA. A lady masked in a pretty *déshabillé* whom Dorimant entertained with more respect, than the gallants do a common vizard.

MRS LOVEIT. (*aside*) Dorimant at the play entertaining a mask, oh heavens!

BELLINDA. (*aside*) Good.

MRS LOVEIT. Did he stay all the while?

BELLINDA. Till the play was done, and then led her out, which confirms me it was you!

MRS LOVEIT. Traitor!

PERT. Now you may believe he had business, and you may forgive him too.

MRS LOVEIT. Ingrateful perjured man!

BELLINDA. You seem so much concerned my dear, I

---

78 *fain*: obliged.

78–9 *the man at Westminster*: the guide at Westminster Abbey.

88 *déshabillé*: a dress of a negligent style.

fear I have told you unawares what I had better have concealed for your quiet.

MRS LOVEIT. What manner of shape had she?

BELLINDA. Tall and slender, her motions were very genteel, certainly she must be some person of condition.

MRS LOVEIT. Shame and confusion be ever in her face when she shows it.

BELLINDA. I should blame your discretion for loving that wild man my dear, but they say he has a way so bewitching, that few can defend their hearts who know him.

MRS LOVEIT. I will tear him from mine, or die i' the attempt.

BELLINDA. Be more moderate.

MRS LOVEIT. Would I had daggers, darts, or poisoned arrows in my breast, so I could but remove the thoughts of him from thence.

BELLINDA. Fie, fie, your transports are too violent, my dear. This may be but an accidental gallantry, and 'tis likely ended at her coach.

PERT. Should it proceed farther, let your comfort be, the conduct Mr Dorimant affects, will quickly make you know your rival, ten to one let you see her ruined, her reputation exposed to the town, a happiness none will envy her but yourself madam.

MRS LOVEIT. Whoe'er she be, all the harm I wish her, is, may she love him as well as I do, and may he give her as much cause to hate him.

PERT. Never doubt the latter end of your curse madam!

MRS LOVEIT. May all the passions that are raised by neglected love, jealousy, indignation, spite, and thirst of revenge, eternally rage in her soul, as they do now in mine. (*Walks up and down with a distracted air*)

Enter a PAGE.

PAGE. Madam, Mr Dorimant –

MRS LOVEIT. I will not see him.

---

106 *genteel*: graceful, stylish.
107 *condition*: social position, rank.
111 *wild man*: see note to *She Would*, I ii 47.
124 *affects*: (1) has an affection for (2) assumes artificially.

PAGE. I told him you were within, madam.

MRS LOVEIT. Say you lied, say I'm busy, shut the door; say anything.

PAGE. He's here madam.

Enter DORIMANT.

DORIMANT. 'They taste of death who do at heav'n arrive,
But we this paradise approach alive.'
(*To* MRS LOVEIT) What dancing the galloping nag without a fiddle? (*Offers to catch her by the hand, she flings away and walks on*) (*Pursuing her*) I fear this restlessness of the body, madam, proceeds from an unquietness of the mind. What unlucky accident puts you out of humour; a point ill-washed, knots spoiled i' the making up, hair shaded awry, or some other little mistake in setting you in order?

PERT. A trifle in my opinion, sir, more inconsiderable than any you mention.

DORIMANT. Oh Mrs Pert, I never knew you sullen enough to be silent, come let me know the business.

PERT. The business, sir, is the business that has taken you up these two days; how have I seen you laugh at men of business, and now to become a man of business yourself!

DORIMANT. We are not masters of our own affections, our inclinations daily alter; now we love pleasure, and anon we shall dote on business; human frailty will have it so, and who can help it?

MRS LOVEIT. Faithless, inhuman, barbarous man –

DORIMANT. Good, now the alarm strikes –

MRS LOVEIT. Without sense of love, of honour, or of gratitude, tell me, for I will know, what devil masked she was, you were with at the play yesterday?

DORIMANT. Faith I resolved as much as you, but the devil was obstinate, and would not tell me.

142–3 *They taste . . . alive*: the first two lines of Waller's 'Of her Chamber' (*Works*, ed. Thorn Drury, vol. 1, p. 26); Dorimant substitutes 'who' for 'that' in the original.

144 *dancing the galloping nag*: Carnochan glosses this as a 'country dance', and this seems a reasonable surmise, but no evidence has been produced to substantiate it.

165 *alarm*: call to arms.

MRS LOVEIT. False in this as in your vows to me, you do know!

DORIMANT. The truth is I did all I could to know.

MRS LOVEIT. And dare you own it to my face; hell and furies! (*Tears her fan in pieces*)

DORIMANT. Spare your fan, madam, you are growing hot, and will want it to cool you.

MRS LOVEIT. Horror and distraction seize you, sorrow and remorse gnaw your soul, and punish all your perjuries to me – (*Weeps*)

DORIMANT. 'So thunder breaks the cloud in twain,
And makes a passage for the rain.'

Turning to BELLINDA.

(*To* BELLINDA) Bellinda, you are the devil that have raised this storm; you were at the play yesterday, and have been making discoveries to your dear.

BELLINDA. Y'are the most mistaken man i' the world.

DORIMANT. It must be so, and here I vow revenge; resolve to pursue, and persecute you more impertinently than ever any loving fop did his mistress, hunt you i' the Park, trace you i' the Mail, dog you in every visit you make, haunt you at the plays, and i' the drawing room, hang my nose in your neck, and talk to you whether you will or no, and ever look upon you with such dying eyes, till your friends grow jealous of me, send you out of town, and the world suspect your reputation. (*In a lower voice*) At my Lady Townley's when we go from hence. (*He looks kindly on* BELLINDA)

BELLINDA. I'll meet you there.

DORIMANT. Enough.

MRS LOVEIT. Stand off, you sha' not stare upon her so. (*Pushing* DORIMANT *away*)

181–2 *So thunder . . . rain*: identified by R.G. Howarth (*Notes and Queries*, 188 (1945), 281) as coming from Matthew Roydon's 'An Elegie, or Friend's Passion, for his Astrophill' (published in *The Phoenix Nest* (1593)). Where the original reads 'rends' Dorimant substitutes 'breaks'.

190 *the Park*: see note to *Comical Revenge*, II i 103.

190 *the Mail*: the Mall, a walk bordering St James's Park.

192 *drawing room*: formal reception held by the king.

DORIMANT. Good! There's one made jealous already.

MRS LOVEIT. Is this the constancy you vowed?

DORIMANT. Constancy at my years! 'tis not a virtue in season, you might as well expect the fruit the autumn ripens i' the spring.

MRS LOVEIT. Monstrous principle!

DORIMANT. Youth has a long journey to go, madam, should I have set up my rest at the first inn I lodged at, I should never have arrived at the happiness I now enjoy.

MRS LOVEIT. Dissembler, damned dissembler!

DORIMANT. I am so I confess, good nature, and good manners corrupt me. I am honest in my inclinations, and would not, wer't not to avoid offence, make a lady a little in years believe I think her young, wilfully mistake art for nature; and seem as fond of a thing I am weary of, as when I doted on't in earnest.

MRS LOVEIT. False man.

DORIMANT. True woman.

MRS LOVEIT. Now you begin to show yourself!

DORIMANT. Love gilds us over, and makes us show fine things to one another for a time, but soon the gold wears off, and then again the native brass appears.

MRS LOVEIT. Think on your oaths, your vows and protestations, perjured man.

DORIMANT. I made 'em when I was in love.

MRS LOVEIT. And therefore ought they not to bind? Oh impious!

DORIMANT. What we swear at such a time may be a certain proof of a present passion, but to say truth, in love there is no security to be given for the future.

MRS LOVEIT. Horrid and ingrateful, begone, and never see me more.

DORIMANT. I am not one of those troublesome coxcombs, who because they were once well received, take the privilege to plague a woman with their love

---

201 *Good! There's one made . . .* : most modern editions mark this as an aside; but *1676* does not do so. Treating it as an aside might be marginally preferable in performance; but Dorimant could also intend to sting Mrs Loveit further by letting her hear this evidence of his dispassionateness.

208 *set up my rest*: take up permanent residence.

223 *native*: natural.

ever after; I shall obey you, madam, though I do myself some violence. (*He offers to go, and* MRS LOVEIT *pulls him back*)

MRS LOVEIT. Come back, you sha' not go. Could you have the ill nature to offer it?

DORIMANT. When love grows diseased the best thing we can do is to put it to a violent death; I cannot endure the torture of a lingering and consumptive passion.

MRS LOVEIT. Can you think mine sickly?

DORIMANT. Oh, 'tis desperately ill! what worse symptoms are there than your being always uneasy when I visit you, your picking quarrels with me on slight occasions, and in my absence kindly listening to the impertinences of every fashionable fool that talks to you?

MRS LOVEIT. What fashionable fool can you lay to my charge?

DORIMANT. Why the very cock-fool of all those fools, Sir Fopling Flutter.

MRS LOVEIT. I never saw him in my life but once.

DORIMANT. The worse woman you at first sight to put on all your charms, to entertain him with that softness in your voice, and all that wanton kindness in your eyes, you so notoriously affect, when you design a conquest.

MRS LOVEIT. So damned a lie did never malice yet invent; who told you this?

DORIMANT. No matter; that ever I should love a woman that can dote on a senseless caper, a tawdry French riband, and a formal cravat.

MRS LOVEIT. You make me mad.

DORIMANT. A guilty conscience may do much, go on, be the game-mistress o' the town, and enter all our young fops, as fast as they come from travel.

MRS LOVEIT. Base and scurrilous!

---

254 *cock-fool*: 'a nonce-formation' (Barnard).
269 *game-mistress*: for 'game' in this sense, see note to *She Would*, I i 12–13.
269 *enter*: initiate.

DORIMANT. A fine mortifying reputation 'twill be for a woman of your pride, wit, and quality!

MRS LOVEIT. This jealousy's a mere pretence, a cursed trick of your own devising; I know you.

DORIMANT. Believe it and all the ill of me you can, I would not have a woman have the least good thought of me, that can think well of Fopling; farewell, fall to, and much good may do you with your coxcomb.

MRS LOVEIT. Stay, oh stay, and I will tell you all.

DORIMANT. I have been told too much already.

Exit DORIMANT.

MRS LOVEIT. Call him again.

PERT. E'en let him go, a fair riddance.

MRS LOVEIT. Run I say, call him again, I will have him called.

PERT. The devil should carry him away first, were it my concern. *Exit* PERT.

BELLINDA. H'as frighted me from the very thoughts of loving men; for heaven's sake, my dear, do not discover what I told you; I dread his tongue as much as you ought to have done his friendship.

Enter PERT.

PERT. He's gone, madam.

MRS LOVEIT. Lightning blast him.

PERT. When I told him you desired him to come back, he smiled, made a mouth at me, flung into his coach, and said –

MRS LOVEIT. What did he say?

PERT. 'Drive away', and then repeated verses.

MRS LOVEIT. Would I had made a contract to be a witch when first I entertained this greater devil, monster, barbarian; I could tear myself in pieces.

---

272 *mortifying*: *OED*'s earliest example of the word in the sense of 'humiliating' comes from 1726; but that must surely be the meaning here.

278–9 *fall to*: (1) set to work (2) 'good appetite!' ('to fall to (food)' meant 'to begin eating').

279 *much good may do you*: Verity emended this to 'much good may it do you'; but this is unnecessary, since the phrase as it stands in *1676* is a conventional seventeenth-century ironic formula.

300 *entertained*: gave a kind reception, received as lover.

Revenge, nothing but revenge can ease me; plague, war, famine, fire, all that can bring universal ruin and misery on mankind, with joy I'd perish to have you in my power but this moment. *Exit* MRS LOVEIT.

PERT. Follow madam, leave her not in this outrageous passion. (PERT *gathers up the things*)

BELLINDA. H'as given me the proof which I desired of his love, but 'tis a proof of his ill nature too; I wish I had not seen him use her so.

I sigh to think that Dorimant may be,
One day as faithless, and unkind to me.

Exeunt.

ACT III

SCENE [I]

Lady Woodvill's lodgings.

Enter HARRIET, *and* BUSY *her woman.*

BUSY. Dear madam! Let me set that curl in order.

HARRIET. Let me alone, I will shake 'em all out of order.

BUSY. Will you never leave this wildness?

HARRIET. Torment me not.

BUSY. Look! there's a knot falling off.

HARRIET. Let it drop.

BUSY. But one pin, dear madam.

HARRIET. How do I daily suffer under thy officious fingers!

BUSY. Ah the difference that is between you and my Lady Dapper! how uneasy she is if the least thing be amiss about her!

HARRIET. She is indeed most exact! nothing is ever wanting to make her ugliness remarkable!

BUSY. Jeering people say so!

---

4 *wildness*: 'restiveness' (Barnard).

HARRIET. Her powdering, painting, and her patching never fail in public to draw the tongues and eyes of all the men upon her.

BUSY. She is indeed a little too pretending.

HARRIET. That women should set up for beauty as much in spite of nature, as some men have done for wit.

BUSY. I hope without offence one may endeavour to make one's self agreeable.

HARRIET. Not, when 'tis impossible. Women then ought to be no more fond of dressing than fools should be of talking; hoods and modesty, masks and silence, things that shadow and conceal; they should think of nothing else.

BUSY. Jesu! Madam, what will your mother think is become of you? for heaven's sake go in again.

HARRIET. I won't!

BUSY. This is the extravagant'st thing that ever you did in your life, to leave her and a gentleman who is to be your husband.

HARRIET. My husband! Hast thou so little wit to think I spoke what I meant when I overjoyed her in the country, with a low curtsy, and 'What you please, madam, I shall ever be obedient'.

BUSY. Nay, I know not, you have so many fetches.

HARRIET. And this was one, to get her up to London! Nothing else I assure thee.

BUSY. Well, the man, in my mind, is a fine man!

HARRIET. The man indeed wears his clothes fashionably, and has a pretty negligent way with him, very courtly, and much affected; he bows, and talks, and smiles so agreeably as he thinks.

BUSY. I never saw anything so genteel!

HARRIET. Varnished over with good breeding, many a blockhead makes a tolerable show.

BUSY. I wonder you do not like him.

HARRIET. I think I might be brought to endure him, and that is all a reasonable woman should expect in a

---

17 *patching*: wearing a small patch, usually of black silk, on the face as an ornament.

41 *fetches*: tricks, dodges.

husband, but there is duty i' the case – and like the haughty Merab, I
'Find much aversion in my stubborn mind,'
which
'Is bred by being promised and designed.'

BUSY. I wish you do not design your own ruin! I partly guess your inclinations madam – that Mr Dorimant –

HARRIET. Leave your prating, and sing some foolish song or other.

BUSY. I will, the song you love so well ever since you saw Mr Dorimant. [*Sings.*]

SONG.

'When first Amintas charmed my heart,
My heedless sheep began to stray;
The wolves soon stole the greatest part,
And all will now be made a prey.

Ah, let not love your thoughts possess,
'Tis fatal to a shepherdess;
The dang'rous passion you must shun,
Or else like me be quite undone.'

HARRIET. Shall I be paid down by a covetous parent for a purchase? I need no land; no, I'll lay myself out all in love. It is decreed –

Enter YOUNG BELLAIR.

YOUNG BELLAIR. What generous resolution are you making madam?

HARRIET. Only to be disobedient, sir.

YOUNG BELLAIR. Let me join hands with you in that –

56–9 *Merab . . . designed*: Merab, elder daughter of Saul, who was promised to David but then married to Adriel (1 Samuel 18, verse 19). Harriet is invoking Abraham Cowley's description of her in his *Davideis* (1656): 'And much aversion in her stubborn mind / Was bred by being *promis'd* and *design'd*' (*Poems*, ed. A.R. Waller (Cambridge University Press, 1905), p. 341).

58 *which*: printed in *1676* as a catchword at the bottom of p. 32, but accidentally omitted from its appropriate place at the head of p. 33.

75 *purchase*: prize, booty.

75 *lay myself out*: spend myself.

HARRIET. With all my heart, I never thought I should have given you mine so willingly. Here I Harriet –

YOUNG BELLAIR. And I Harry –

HARRIET. Do solemnly protest –

YOUNG BELLAIR. And vow –

HARRIET. That I with you –

YOUNG BELLAIR. And I with you –

BOTH. Will never marry –

HARRIET. A match!

YOUNG BELLAIR. And no match! How do you like this indifference now?

HARRIET. You expect I should take it ill I see!

YOUNG BELLAIR. 'Tis not unnatural for you women to be a little angry, you miss a conquest, though you would slight the poor man were he in your power.

HARRIET. There are some it may be have an eye like Bart'lomew, big enough for the whole fair, but I am not of the number, and you may keep your gingerbread. 'Twill be more acceptable to the lady, whose dear image it wears sir.

YOUNG BELLAIR. I must confess madam, you came a day after the fair.

HARRIET. You own then you are in love –

YOUNG BELLAIR. I do.

HARRIET. The confidence is generous, and in return I could almost find in my heart to let you know my inclinations.

YOUNG BELLAIR. Are you in love?

---

95 *a little angry, you miss a conquest*: thus *1676*; but most modern editions remove the comma, thus making 'you miss a conquest' a subordinate clause depending on the preceding main clause. This is a plausible reading; but, since taking 'you miss a conquest' as a main clause in its own right makes completely adequate sense, the comma has been retained in the present text.

98 *Bart'lomew*: i.e. Bartholomew Cokes in Ben Jonson's *Bartholomew Fair* (1614). He gullibly buys all the knick-knacks which the fair (held annually in Smithfield on 24 August) sets before him and is then robbed of them and much that he brought into the fair with him, including the heiress he was to marry. Itemizing his losses, however, it is (he says) the theft of the gingerbread 'which grieves me worst of all' (IV ii 86).

99–100 *gingerbread*: sold at fairs in the shape of human figures.

102–3 *a day after the fair*: i.e. too late (proverbial).

HARRIET. Yes, with this dear town, to that degree, I can scarce endure the country in landscapes and in hangings.

YOUNG BELLAIR. What a dreadful thing 'twould be to be hurried back to Hampshire!

HARRIET. Ah – name it not! –

YOUNG BELLAIR. As for us, I find we shall agree well enough! would we could do something to deceive the grave people!

HARRIET. Could we delay their quick proceeding, 'twere well, a reprieve is a good step towards the getting of a pardon.

YOUNG BELLAIR. If we give over the game, we are undone! What think you of playing it on booty?

HARRIET. What do you mean?

YOUNG BELLAIR. Pretend to be in love with one another! 'twill make some dilatory excuses we may feign, pass the better.

HARRIET. Let us do't, if it be but for the dear pleasure of dissembling.

YOUNG BELLAIR. Can you play your part?

HARRIET. I know not what it is to love, but I have made pretty remarks by being now and then where lovers meet. Where did you leave their gravities?

YOUNG BELLAIR. I' th' next room! your mother was censuring our modern gallant.

Enter OLD BELLAIR, *and* LADY WOODVILL.

HARRIET. Peace! Here they come, I will lean against this wall, and look bashfully down upon my fan, while you like an amorous spark modishly entertain me.

LADY WOODVILL. Never go about to excuse 'em, come, come, it was not so when I was a young woman.

OLD BELLAIR. A dod, they're something disrespectful –

---

111 *landscapes*: landscape-paintings.
112 *hangings*: wall-tapestries.
123 *playing it on booty*: joining with a confederate in order to victimize another player.
132 *remarks*: observations.

LADY WOODVILL. Quality was then considered, and not rallied by every fleering fellow.

OLD BELLAIR. Youth will have its jest, a dod it will.

LADY WOODVILL. 'Tis good breeding now to be civil to none but players and Exchange women, they are treated by 'em as much above their condition, as others are below theirs.

OLD BELLAIR. Out a pize on 'em, talk no more, the rogues ha' got an ill habit of preferring beauty, no matter where they find it.

LADY WOODVILL. See your son, and my daughter, they have improved their acquaintance since they were within.

OLD BELLAIR. A dod methinks they have! Let's keep back and observe.

YOUNG BELLAIR. Now for a look and gestures that may persuade 'em I am saying all the passionate things imaginable –

HARRIET. Your head a little more on one side, ease yourself on your left leg, and play with your right hand.

YOUNG BELLAIR. Thus, is it not?

HARRIET. Now set your right leg firm on the ground, adjust your belt, then look about you.

YOUNG BELLAIR. A little exercising will make me perfect.

HARRIET. Smile and turn to me again very sparkish!

YOUNG BELLAIR. Will you take your turn and be instructed?

HARRIET. With all my heart.

YOUNG BELLAIR. At one motion play your fan, roll your eyes, and then settle a kind look upon me.

HARRIET. So.

YOUNG BELLAIR. Now spread your fan, look down upon it, and tell the sticks with a finger.

HARRIET. Very modish.

YOUNG BELLAIR. Clap your hand up to your bosom, hold down your gown. Shrug a little, draw up your

---

146 *fleering*: jeering, mocking.

149 *Exchange women*: women serving in the shops of the New Exchange.

179 *tell*: run the finger across them as if counting them.

breasts, and let 'em fall again, gently, with a sigh or two, etc.

HARRIET. By the good instructions you give, I suspect you for one of those malicious observers who watch people's eyes, and from innocent looks, make scandalous conclusions.

YOUNG BELLAIR. I know some indeed who out of mere love to mischief are as vigilant as jealousy itself, and will give you an account of every glance that passes at a play, and i' th' Circle!

HARRIET. 'Twill not be amiss now to seem a little pleasant.

YOUNG BELLAIR. Clap your fan then in both your hands, snatch it to your mouth, smile, and with a lively motion fling your body a little forwards. So – now spread it; fall back on the sudden, cover your face with it, and break out into a loud laughter – take up! look grave, and fall a-fanning of yourself – admirably well acted.

HARRIET. I think I am pretty apt at these matters!

OLD BELLAIR. A dod I like this well.

LADY WOODVILL. This promises something.

OLD BELLAIR. Come! there is love i' th' case, a dod there is, or will be; what say you young lady?

HARRIET. All in good time sir, you expect we should fall to, and love as game-cocks fight, as soon as we are set together, a dod y'are unreasonable!

OLD BELLAIR. A dod sirrah, I like thy wit well.

---

184 *etc.*: Carnochan regards this as a stage direction, adding the comment that 'the actors were, evidently, to improvise'. But it seems to me equally, or more, plausible to read it as Young Bellair's jovially kind permission to Harriet to improvise along the lines he has now prescribed and, hence, most certainly a part of the spoken dialogue.

192 *i' the Circle*: the most likely meaning, as Brett-Smith pointed out, is 'the "tour" or Ring in Hyde Park, where the fashionable world paraded' (cf. III ii 000). But Carnochan also suggested that the reference might possibly be to the assembly at Court (cf. IV i 100).

200 *take up!*: stop.

210 *sirrah*: 'applied to a woman seriously or in jest up to 1711, but almost certainly used here to indicate Old Bellair's old-fashioned vulgarity' (Barnard).

Enter a SERVANT.

SERVANT. The coach is at the door madam.

OLD BELLAIR. Go, get you and take the air together.

LADY WOODVILL. Will not you go with us?

OLD BELLAIR. Out a pize: a dod I ha' business and cannot. We shall meet at night at my sister Townley's.

YOUNG BELLAIR. (*aside*) He's going to Emilia. I overheard him talk of a collation.

Exeunt.

SCENE II

Enter LADY TOWNLEY, EMILIA, *and* MR MEDLEY.

LADY TOWNLEY. I pity the young lovers we last talked of, though to say truth their conduct has been so indiscreet, they deserve to be unfortunate.

MEDLEY. Y'have had an exact account, from the great lady i' the box down to the little orange wench.

EMILIA. Y'are a living libel, a breathing lampoon; I wonder you are not torn in pieces.

MEDLEY. What think you of setting up an office of intelligence for these matters? the project may get money.

LADY TOWNLEY. You would have great dealings with country ladies.

MEDLEY. More than Muddiman has with their husbands.

Enter BELLINDA.

LADY TOWNLEY. Bellinda, what has been become of you! we have not seen you here of late with your friend Mrs Loveit.

BELLINDA. Dear creature, I left her but now so sadly afflicted.

---

6 *libel*: a satirical attack on others' characters, in manuscript or printed form; hence, like the 'lampoon', capable of being 'torn'.

13 *Muddiman*: Henry Muddiman (1629–92), author of a newsletter with a wide circulation among readers outside the capital.

LADY TOWNLEY. With her old distemper jealousy!

MEDLEY. Dorimant has played her some new prank.

BELLINDA. Well, that Dorimant is certainly the worst man breathing.

EMILIA. I once thought so.

BELLINDA. And do you not think so still?

EMILIA. No indeed!

BELLINDA. Oh Jesu!

EMILIA. The town does him a great deal of injury, and I will never believe what it says of a man I do not know again for his sake!

BELLINDA. You make me wonder!

LADY TOWNLEY. He's a very well-bred man.

BELLINDA. But strangely ill-natured.

EMILIA. Then he's a very witty man!

BELLINDA. But a man of no principles.

MEDLEY. Your man of principles is a very fine thing indeed.

BELLINDA. To be preferred to men of parts by women who have regard to their reputation and quiet. Well were I minded to play the fool, he should be the last man I'd think of.

MEDLEY. He has been the first in many ladies' favours, though you are so severe, madam.

LADY TOWNLEY. What he may be for a lover I know not, but he's a very pleasant acquaintance I am sure.

BELLINDA. Had you seen him use Mrs Loveit as I have done, you would never endure him more –

EMILIA. What he has quarrelled with her again!

BELLINDA. Upon the slightest occasion, he's jealous of Sir Fopling.

LADY TOWNLEY. She never saw him in her life but yesterday, and that was here.

EMILIA. On my conscience! he's the only man in town that's her aversion, how horribly out of humour she was all the while he talked to her!

BELLINDA. And somebody has wickedly told him –

EMILIA. Here he comes.

---

19 *distemper*: (1) illness, disease but also (2) ill-temper, ill-humour.

Enter DORIMANT.

MEDLEY. Dorimant! you are luckily come to justify yourself – here's a lady –

BELLINDA. Has a word or two to say to you from a disconsolate person.

DORIMANT. You tender your reputation too much I know madam, to whisper with me before this good company.

BELLINDA. To serve Mrs Loveit, I'll make a bold venture.

DORIMANT. Here's Medley the very spirit of scandal.

BELLINDA. No matter!

EMILIA. 'Tis something you are unwilling to hear, Mr Dorimant.

LADY TOWNLEY. Tell him Bellinda whether he will or no!

BELLINDA. (*aloud*) Mrs Loveit –

DORIMANT. Softly, these are laughers, you do not know 'em.

BELLINDA. (*to* DORIMANT *apart*) In a word y'ave made me hate you, which I thought you never could have done.

DORIMANT. In obeying your commands.

BELLINDA. 'Twas a cruel part you played! how could you act it?

DORIMANT. Nothing is cruel to a man who could kill himself to please you; remember five a clock tomorrow morning.

BELLINDA. I tremble when you name it.

DORIMANT. Be sure you come.

BELLINDA. I sha'not.

DORIMANT. Swear you will!

BELLINDA. I dare not.

DORIMANT. Swear I say.

BELLINDA. By my life! by all the happiness I hope for –

DORIMANT. You will.

BELLINDA. I will.

DORIMANT. Kind.

BELLINDA. I am glad I've sworn, I vow I think I should ha' failed you else!

DORIMANT. Surprisingly kind! in what temper did you leave Loveit?

BELLINDA. Her raving was prettily over, and she began to be in a brave way of defying you, and all your works. Where have you been since you went from thence?

DORIMANT. I looked in at the play.

BELLINDA. I have promised and must return to her again.

DORIMANT. Persuade her to walk in the Mail this evening.

BELLINDA. She hates the place and will not come.

DORIMANT. Do all you can to prevail with her.

BELLINDA. For what purpose?

DORIMANT. Sir Fopling will be here anon, I'll prepare him to set upon her there before me.

BELLINDA. You persecute her too much, but I'll do all you'll ha' me.

DORIMANT. (*aloud*) Tell her plainly, 'tis grown so dull a business I can drudge on no longer.

EMILIA. There are afflictions in love Mr Dorimant.

DORIMANT. You women make 'em, who are commonly as unreasonable in that as you are at play; without the advantage be on your side, a man can never quietly give over when he's weary!

MEDLEY. If you would play without being obliged to complaisance Dorimant, you should play in public places.

DORIMANT. Ordinaries were a very good thing for that, but gentlemen do not of late frequent 'em; the deep play is now in private houses.

BELLINDA *offering to steal away.*

LADY TOWNLEY. Bellinda, are you leaving us so soon?

BELLINDA. I am to go to the Park with Mrs Loveit, madam – *Exit* BELLINDA.

---

99 *prettily over*: almost ended.

100 *brave*: excellent, 'capital'.

100–1 *defying you, and all your works*: an ironic reference to the promise made by the godparents on behalf of the infant in the Anglican baptismal service to 'renounce the devil and all his works'.

119 *play*: gambling.

123 *complaisance*: see note to I i 464.

125 *Ordinaries*: see note to *Comical Revenge*, I iii 2.

LADY TOWNLEY. This confidence will go nigh to spoil this young creature.

MEDLEY. 'Twill do her good madam. Young men who are brought up under practising lawyers prove the abler counsel when they come to be called to the bar themselves –

DORIMANT. The town has been very favourable to you this afternoon, my Lady Townley, you use to have an *embarras* of chairs and coaches at your door, an uproar of footmen in your hall, and a noise of fools above here.

LADY TOWNLEY. Indeed my house is the general rendezvous, and next to the playhouse is the common refuge of all the young idle people.

EMILIA. Company is a very good thing, madam, but I wonder you do not love it a little more chosen.

LADY TOWNLEY. 'Tis good to have an universal taste, we should love wit, but for variety, be able to divert ourselves with the extravagancies of those who want it.

MEDLEY. Fools will make you laugh.

EMILIA. For once or twice! but the repetition of their folly after a visit or two grows tedious and unsufferable.

LADY TOWNLEY. You are a little too delicate Emilia.

Enter a PAGE.

PAGE. Sir Fopling Flutter, madam, desires to know if you are to be seen.

LADY TOWNLEY. Here's the freshest fool in town, and one who has not cloyed you yet. Page!

PAGE. Madam!

LADY TOWNLEY. Desire him to walk up.

[*Exit* PAGE.]

DORIMANT. Do not you fall on him, Medley, and snub

---

131 *confidence*: i.e. Loveit's and Dorimant's confiding in Bellinda.
137 *favourable*: well-disposed.
139 *embarras of chairs and coaches*: cf. *embarras de voitures* (Fr.), a congestion of carriages.
140 *uproar*: loud outcry; but it also perhaps retains some element of an older meaning, 'an insurrection or popular rising'.
154 *delicate*: fastidious.

him. Soothe him up in his extravagance! he will show the better.

MEDLEY. You know I have a natural indulgence for fools, and need not this caution, sir!

Enter SIR FOPLING FLUTTER, *with his* PAGE *after him.*

SIR FOPLING. Page! Wait without. [*Exit* PAGE.] (*To* LADY TOWNLEY) Madam, I kiss your hands, I see yesterday was nothing of chance, the *belles assemblées* form themselves here every day. (*To* EMILIA) Lady your servant; Dorimant, let me embrace thee, without lying I have not met with any of my acquaintance, who retain so much of Paris as thou dost, the very air thou hadst when the marquise mistook thee i' th' Tuileries, and cried 'Hey chevalier', and then begged thy pardon.

DORIMANT. I would fain wear in fashion as long as I can, sir, 'tis a thing to be valued in men as well as baubles.

SIR FOPLING. Thou art a man of wit, and understands the town: prithee let thee and I be intimate, there is no living without making some good man the confident of our pleasures.

DORIMANT. 'Tis true! but there is no man so improper for such a business as I am.

SIR FOPLING. Prithee! why hast thou so modest an opinion of thyself?

DORIMANT. Why first, I could never keep a secret in my life, and then there is no charm so infallibly makes me fall in love with a woman as my knowing a friend loves her. I deal honestly with you.

SIR FOPLING. Thy humour's very gallant or let me perish, I knew a French count so like thee.

LADY TOWNLEY. Wit I perceive has more power over

---

162 *Soothe him up*: encourage him by expressing approval.
168–9 *belles assemblées*: fashionable gatherings.
174 *th' Tuileries*: the garden of the Palais de Tuileries in Paris.
174 *Hey chevalier*: Carnochan and Barnard emend to 'Hé' here – a plausible step, if it were not for the possibility that Etherege does not intend Sir Fopling to be gifted with great accuracy in such matters (cf. his '*à revoir*', line 287).

you than beauty, Sir Fopling, else you would not have let this lady stand so long neglected.

SIR FOPLING. (*to* EMILIA) A thousand pardons madam, some civilities due of course upon the meeting a long absent friend. The *éclat* of so much beauty I confess ought to have charmed me sooner.

EMILIA. The *brillant* of so much good language sir has much more power than the little beauty I can boast.

SIR FOPLING. I never saw anything prettier than this high work on your *point d'Espagne* –

EMILIA. 'Tis not so rich as *point de Venise* –

SIR FOPLING. Not altogether, but looks cooler, and is more proper for the season. Dorimant, is not that Medley?

DORIMANT. The same, sir.

SIR FOPLING. Forgive me sir in this *embarras* of civilities, I could not come to have you in my arms sooner. You understand an equipage the best of any man in town I hear.

MEDLEY. By my own you would not guess it.

SIR FOPLING. There are critics who do not write sir.

MEDLEY. Our peevish poets will scarce allow it.

SIR FOPLING. Damn 'em, they'll allow no man wit, who does not play the fool like themselves and show it! Have you taken notice of the gallesh I brought over?

MEDLEY. Oh yes! 't has quite another air, than th'English makes.

SIR FOPLING. 'Tis as easily known from an English tumbril, as an Inns of Court man is from one of us.

---

197 *due of course*: i.e. customary.
198 *éclat*: brilliance.
200 *brillant*: glitter.
203 *high work*: raised needlework.
203 *point d'Espagne*: Spanish lace.
204 *point de Venise*: Venetian lace.
209 *embarras*: see note to line 139.
211 *equipage*: either (1) retinue or (2) apparel, accoutrements.
218 *gallesh*: *calèche* (Fr.): a light carriage with low wheels and a removable folded hood or top (a new fashion from France).
223 *tumbril*: two-wheeled cart which tips to empty its load, especially a dung-cart.
223 *Inns of Court man*: lawyer.

DORIMANT. Truly there is a *bel air* in galleshes as well as men.

MEDLEY. But there are few so delicate to observe it.

SIR FOPLING. The world is generally very *grossier* here indeed.

LADY TOWNLEY. He's very fine.

EMILIA. Extreme proper.

SIR FOPLING. A slight suit I made to appear in at my first arrival, not worthy your consideration ladies.

DORIMANT. The pantaloon is very well mounted.

SIR FOPLING. The tassels are new and pretty.

MEDLEY. I never saw a coat better cut.

SIR FOPLING. It makes me show long-waisted, and I think slender.

DORIMANT. That's the shape our ladies dote on.

MEDLEY. Your breech though is a handful too high in my eye Sir Fopling.

SIR FOPLING. Peace Medley, I have wished it lower a thousand times, but a pox on't 'twill not be.

LADY TOWNLEY. His gloves are well-fringed, large and graceful.

SIR FOPLING. I was always eminent for being *bien ganté.*

EMILIA. He wears nothing but what are originals of the most famous hands in Paris.

SIR FOPLING. You are in the right madam.

LADY TOWNLEY. The suit.

SIR FOPLING. Barroy.

EMILIA. The garniture.

---

224 *bel air*: elegant style.
227 *grossier*: coarse, crude.
230 *proper*: admirable, of good appearance, handsome.
233 *pantaloon*: a kind of skirt-like breeches in fashion for some time after the Restoration; they had very wide legs pleated into a waist band above and reaching to the knees below.
233 *mounted*: i.e. puffed out.
245–6 *bien ganté*: well-gloved.
251 *Barroy*: presumably the list of fashionable Parisian merchants which follows is authentic, but the only one who has been confidently identified is Chedreux, who gave his name to a type of wig.
252 *garniture*: ornamental trimmings (e.g. of jewellery and ribbons) added to clothing (the word was a recent importation from French).

SIR FOPLING. Le Gras –

MEDLEY. The shoes!

SIR FOPLING. Piccar!

DORIMANT. The periwig!

SIR FOPLING. Chedreux.

LADY TOWNLEY.
EMILIA. } The gloves!

SIR FOPLING. Orangerie! You know the smell ladies! Dorimant, I could find in my heart for an amusement to have a gallantry with some of our English ladies.

DORIMANT. 'Tis a thing no less necessary to confirm the reputation of your wit, than a duel will be to satisfy the town of your courage.

SIR FOPLING. Here was a woman yesterday –

DORIMANT. Mrs Loveit.

SIR FOPLING. You have named her!

DORIMANT. You cannot pitch on a better for your purpose.

SIR FOPLING. Prithee! what is she?

DORIMANT. A person of quality, and one who has a rest of reputation enough to make the conquest considerable: besides I hear she likes you too!

SIR FOPLING. Methoughts she seemed though very reserved, and uneasy all the time I entertained her.

DORIMANT. Grimace and affectation: you will see her i' th' Mall tonight.

SIR FOPLING. Prithee, let thee and I take the air together.

DORIMANT. I am engaged to Medley, but I'll meet you at St James's, and give you some information, upon the which you may regulate your proceedings.

SIR FOPLING. All the world will be in the Park tonight: ladies, 'twere pity to keep so much beauty longer within doors, and rob the Ring of all those charms that should adorn it – hey page.

Enter PAGE, *and goes out again.*

---

259 *Orangerie*: perfume extracted from the orange-flower.
271–2 *a rest of reputation enough*: sufficient reputation left.
276 *Grimace*: pretence.
285 *the Ring*: see note to III i 192.

See that all my people be ready. Dorimant *à revoir.*

[*Exit* SIR FOPLING.]

MEDLEY. A fine mettled coxcomb.

DORIMANT. Brisk and insipid –

MEDLEY. Pert and dull.

EMILIA. However you despise him gentlemen, I'll lay my life he passes for a wit with many.

DORIMANT. That may very well be, nature has her cheats, stums a brain, and puts sophisticate dullness often on the tasteless multitude for true wit and good humour. Medley, come.

MEDLEY. I must go a little way, I will meet you i' the Mail.

DORIMANT. (*to the* WOMEN) I'll walk through the garden thither, we shall meet anon and bow.

LADY TOWNLEY. Not tonight! we are engaged about a business, the knowledge of which may make you laugh hereafter.

MEDLEY. Your servant ladies.

DORIMANT. *À revoir*, as Sir Fopling says –

Exeunt MEDLEY *and* DORIMANT.

LADY TOWNLEY. The old man will be here immediately.

EMILIA. Let's expect him i' th' garden –

LADY TOWNLEY. Go, you are a rogue.

EMILIA. I can't abide you.

Exeunt.

---

287 *à revoir*: repeated mockingly by Dorimant later (line 305), so presumably this spelling deliberately reflects either a blunder by Sir Fopling or his affected pronunciation.

288 *fine mettled*: thus *1676*; most modern editions print this as 'fine-mettled', but they may, in fact, be two independent adjectives rather than a compound.

294 *stums*: to stum wine is to renew it by mixing it with stum or must and raising a new fermentation.

294 *sophisticate*: adulterated, mixed with some foreign substance, impure.

308 *expect*: wait for.

SCENE III

The Mail.

Enter HARRIET, YOUNG BELLAIR, *she pulling him.*

HARRIET. Come along.

YOUNG BELLAIR. And leave your mother.

HARRIET. Busy will be sent with a hue and cry after us; but that's no matter.

YOUNG BELLAIR. 'Twill look strangely in me.

HARRIET. She'll believe it a freak of mine, and never blame your manners.

YOUNG BELLAIR. What reverend acquaintance is that she has met?

HARRIET. A fellow beauty of the last king's time, though by the ruins you would hardly guess it.

Exeunt.

Enter DORIMANT *and crosses the stage.*
Enter YOUNG BELLAIR, *and* HARRIET.

YOUNG BELLAIR. By this time your mother is in a fine taking.

HARRIET. If your friend Mr Dorimant were but here now, that she might find me talking with him.

YOUNG BELLAIR. She does not know him but dreads him I hear of all mankind.

HARRIET. She concludes if he does but speak to a woman she's undone, is on her knees every day to pray heaven defend me from him.

YOUNG BELLAIR. You do not apprehend him so much as she does.

HARRIET. I never saw anything in him that was frightful.

YOUNG BELLAIR. On the contrary, have you not observed something extreme delightful in his wit and person?

---

6 *freak*: whim.

10 *the last king's time*: Charles I's, more than a quarter of a century earlier.

13 *taking*: disturbed or agitated state of mind.

HARRIET. He's agreeable and pleasant I must own, but he does so much affect being so, he displeases me.

YOUNG BELLAIR. Lord madam, all he does and says, is so easy, and so natural.

HARRIET. Some men's verses seem so to the unskilful, but labour i' the one, and affectation in the other to the judicious plainly appear.

YOUNG BELLAIR. I never heard him accused of affectation before.

Enter DORIMANT *and stares upon her.*

HARRIET. It passes on the easy town, who are favourably pleased in him to call it humour.

Exeunt YOUNG BELLAIR *and* HARRIET.

DORIMANT. 'Tis she! it must be she, that lovely hair, that easy shape, those wanton eyes, and all those melting charms about her mouth, which Medley spoke of; I'll follow the lottery, and put in for a prize with my friend Bellair. *Exit* DORIMANT *repeating* –
'In love the victors from the vanquished fly;
They fly that wound, and they pursue that die.'

Enter YOUNG BELLAIR, *and* HARRIET, *and after them* DORIMANT *standing at a distance.*

YOUNG BELLAIR. Most people prefer High Park to this place.

HARRIET. It has the better reputation I confess: but I abominate the dull diversions there, the formal bows, the affected smiles, the silly by-words, and amorous tweers, in passing; here one meets with a little conversation now and then.

YOUNG BELLAIR. These conversations have been fatal to some of your sex, madam.

---

37 *It passes on*: it is accepted by.
37–8 *favourably*: indulgently, with undue favour or partiality.
38 *humour*: i.e. part of his natural temperament.
44–5 *'In love . . . that die'*: the last lines of Waller's 'To a Friend, of the Different Success of their Loves' (*Poems*, ed. Thorn Drury, vol. 1, p. 103).
46 *High Park*: Hyde Park.
50 *by-words*: tricks of speech, pet phrases.
51 *tweers*: glances, leers.

HARRIET. It may be so; because some who want temper have been undone by gaming, must others who have it wholly deny themselves the pleasure of play?

DORIMANT. (*coming up gently, and bowing to her*) Trust me, it were unreasonable madam.

HARRIET. Lord! who's this? (*She starts and looks grave*)

YOUNG BELLAIR. Dorimant.

DORIMANT. Is this the woman your father would have you marry?

YOUNG BELLAIR. It is.

DORIMANT. Her name?

YOUNG BELLAIR. Harriet.

DORIMANT. I am not mistaken, she's handsome.

YOUNG BELLAIR. Talk to her, her wit is better than her face; we were wishing for you but now.

DORIMANT. (*to* HARRIET) Overcast with seriousness o' the sudden! A thousand smiles were shining in that face but now; I never saw so quick a change of weather.

HARRIET. (*aside*) I feel as great a change within; but he shall never know it.

DORIMANT. You were talking of play, madam, pray what may be your stint?

HARRIET. A little harmless discourse in public walks, or at most an appointment in a box barefaced at the playhouse; you are for masks, and private meetings; where women engage for all they are worth I hear.

DORIMANT. I have been used to deep play, but I can make one at small game, when I like my gamester well.

HARRIET. And be so unconcerned you'll ha' no pleasure in't.

DORIMANT. Where there is a considerable sum to be won, the hope of drawing people in, makes every trifle considerable.

---

55 *temper*: self-control.

66 *I am not mistaken*: Carnochan and Barnard print this as an aside; but the *1676* arrangement (adhered to here) is perfectly playable.

76 *stint*: upper limit.

82 *make one at*: participate in.

HARRIET. The sordidness of men's natures I know makes 'em willing to flatter and comply with the rich, though they are sure never to be the better for 'em.

DORIMANT. 'Tis in their power to do us good, and we despair not but at some time or other they may be willing.

HARRIET. To men who have fared in this town like you, 'twould be a great mortification to live on hope; could you keep a Lent for a mistress?

DORIMANT. In expectation of a happy Easter, and though time be very precious, think forty days well lost, to gain your favour.

HARRIET. Mr Bellair! let us walk, 'tis time to leave him, men grow dull when they begin to be particular.

DORIMANT. Y'are mistaken, flattery will not ensue, though I know y'are greedy of the praises of the whole Mail.

HARRIET. You do me wrong.

DORIMANT. I do not, as I followed you, I observed how you were pleased when the fops cried 'She's handsome, very handsome, by God she is', and whispered aloud your name – the thousand several forms you put your face into; then, to make yourself more agreeable, how wantonly you played with your head, flung back your locks, and looked smilingly over your shoulder at 'em.

HARRIET. I do not go begging the men's as you do the ladies' good liking with a sly softness in your looks, and a gentle slowness in your bows, as you pass by 'em – as thus sir – (*Acts him*) is not this like you?

Enter LADY WOODVILL *and* BUSY.

YOUNG BELLAIR. Your mother madam. (*Pulls* HARRIET. *She composes herself*)

LADY WOODVILL. Ah my dear child Harriet.

BUSY. Now is she so pleased with finding her again she cannot chide her.

LADY WOODVILL. Come away!

DORIMANT. 'Tis now but high Mail madam, the most entertaining time of all the evening.

---

124 *high Mail*: the busiest, most fashionable time of day for visiting the Mall.

HARRIET. I would fain see that Dorimant mother, you so cry out of for a monster, he's in the Mail I hear.

LADY WOODVILL. Come away then! the plague is here and you should dread the infection.

YOUNG BELLAIR. You may be misinformed of the gentleman?

LADY WOODVILL. Oh no! I hope you do not know him. He is the prince of all the devils in the town, delights in nothing but in rapes and riots.

DORIMANT. If you did but hear him speak madam!

LADY WOODVILL. Oh! he has a tongue they say would tempt the angels to a second fall.

Enter SIR FOPLING *with his equipage, six* FOOTMEN, *and a* PAGE.

SIR FOPLING. Hey, Champagne, Norman, La Rose, La Fleur, La Tour, La Verdure. Dorimant –

LADY WOODVILL. Here, here he is among this rout, he names him; come away Harriet, come away.

Exeunt LADY WOODVILL, HARRIET, BUSY *and* YOUNG BELLAIR.

DORIMANT. This fool's coming has spoiled all, she's gone, but she has left a pleasing image of herself behind that wanders in my soul – it must not settle there.

SIR FOPLING. What reverie is this! speak man.

DORIMANT. 'Snatched from myself how far behind
Already I behold the shore!'

Enter MEDLEY.

MEDLEY. Dorimant, a discovery! I met with Bellair.

DORIMANT. You can tell me no news sir, I know all.

126–7 *you so cry out of*: i.e. whom you so denounce.

137 s.d. *equipage*: retinue.

138–9 *Champagne . . . La Verdure*: Arthur Sherbo (*Modern Language Notes*, 64 (1949), 343–4) pointed out that Sir Fopling's entry derives from scene 11 of Molière's *Les Précieuses Ridicules* (1659), where Mascarille calls to his servants: 'Hola, Champagne, Picard, Bourguignon, Casquaret, Basque, la Verdure, Lorrain, Provençal, la Violette.'

140 *rout*: disorderly crowd.

147–8 *'Snatched from myself . . . the shore'*: lines 3–4 from Waller's 'Of Loving at First Sight' (*Works*, ed. Thorn Drury, vol. 1, p. 100).

MEDLEY. How do you like the daughter?

DORIMANT. You never came so near truth in your life, as you did in her description.

MEDLEY. What think you of the mother?

DORIMANT. Whatever I think of her, she thinks very well of me I find.

MEDLEY. Did she know you?

DORIMANT. She did not, whether she does now or no I know not. Here was a pleasant scene towards, when in came Sir Fopling, mustering up his equipage, and at the latter end named me, and frighted her away.

MEDLEY. Loveit and Bellinda are not far off, I saw 'em alight at St James's.

DORIMANT. Sir Fopling hark you, a word or two – (*Whispers*) – look you do not want assurance.

SIR FOPLING. I never do on these occasions.

DORIMANT. Walk on, we must not be seen together, make your advantage of what I have told you, the next turn you will meet the lady.

SIR FOPLING. Hey – follow me all.

Exeunt SIR FOPLING *and his equipage.*

DORIMANT. Medley, you shall see good sport anon between Loveit and this Fopling.

MEDLEY. I thought there was something toward by that whisper.

DORIMANT. You know a worthy principle of hers?

MEDLEY. Not to be so much as civil to a man who speaks to her in the presence of him she professes to love.

DORIMANT. I have encouraged Fopling to talk to her tonight.

MEDLEY. Now you are here she will go nigh to beat him.

DORIMANT. In the humour she's in, her love will make her do some very extravagant thing doubtless.

MEDLEY. What was Bellinda's business with you at my Lady Townley's?

DORIMANT. To get me to meet Loveit here in order to

---

159 *towards*: imminent, in preparation.

163 *St James's*: 'probably St James's Palace, opposite the park to the west end of the Mall' (Carnochan).

168–9 *the next turn*: i.e. the next circuit of the Mall.

an *éclairicissement*; I made some difficulty of it, and have prepared this rancounter to make good my jealousy.

MEDLEY. Here they come!

Enter MRS LOVEIT, BELLINDA *and* PERT.

DORIMANT. I'll meet her and provoke her with a deal of dumb civility in passing by, then turn short and be behind her, when Sir Fopling sets upon her –
'See how unregarded now
That piece of beauty passes' –

Exeunt DORIMANT *and* MEDLEY.

BELLINDA. How wonderful respectfully he bowed!

PERT. He's always over-mannerly when he has done a mischief.

BELLINDA. Methoughts indeed at the same time he had a strange despising countenance.

PERT. The unlucky look he thinks becomes him.

BELLINDA. I was afraid you would have spoke to him my dear.

LOVEIT. I would have died first; he shall no more find me the loving fool he has done.

BELLINDA. You love him still!

MRS LOVEIT. No.

PERT. I wish you did not.

MRS LOVEIT. I do not, and I will have you think so: what made you hale me to this odious place Bellinda?

BELLINDA. I hate to be hulched up in a coach; walking is much better.

MRS LOVEIT. Would we could meet Sir Fopling now.

BELLINDA. Lord! would you not avoid him?

MRS LOVEIT. I would make him all the advances that may be.

---

188 *éclaircissement*: clearing up (of a misunderstanding).
189 *rancounter*: encounter, skirmish.
195–6 *See how . . . passes*: the opening of Sir John Suckling's 'Sonnet I' (*Non-Dramatic Works*, ed. Thomas Clayton (Oxford, Clarendon Press, 1971), p. 47); the original first line is 'Do'st see how . . . '
199 *mischief*: injury.
202 *unlucky*: malicious.
212 *hulched up*: hunched up, doubled up.

BELLINDA. That would confirm Dorimant's suspicion, my dear.

MRS LOVEIT. He is not jealous; but I will make him so, and be revenged a way he little thinks on.

BELLINDA. (*aside*) If she should make him jealous, that may make him fond of her again: I must dissuade her from it. – Lord! my dear, this will certainly make him hate you.

MRS LOVEIT. 'Twill make him uneasy though he does not care for me; I know the effects of jealousy on men of his proud temper.

BELLINDA. 'Tis a fantastic remedy, its operations are dangerous and uncertain.

MRS LOVEIT. 'Tis the strongest cordial we can give to dying love, it often brings it back when there's no sign of life remaining: but I design not so much the reviving his, as my revenge.

Enter SIR FOPLING *and his equipage.*

SIR FOPLING. Hey! bid the coachman send home four of his horses, and bring the coach to Whitehall, I'll walk over the Park – madam, the honour of kissing your fair hands is a happiness I missed this afternoon at my Lady Townley's!

MRS LOVEIT. You were very obliging, Sir Fopling, the last time I saw you there.

SIR FOPLING. The preference was due to your wit and beauty. Madam, your servant, there never was so sweet an evening.

BELLINDA. 'T has drawn all the rabble of the town hither.

SIR FOPLING. 'Tis pity there's not an order made, that none but the *beau monde* should walk here.

MRS LOVEIT. 'Twould add much to the beauty of the place: see what a sort of nasty fellows are coming.

---

228 *temper*: temperament, character.
231 *cordial*: medicine to invigorate the heart.
236 *Whitehall*: a royal palace, across the park from the Mall; it was destroyed by fire in 1698.
248 *beau monde*: fashionable society.
250 *a sort*: crowd, company.

Enter four ill-fashioned FELLOWS *singing, ' 'Tis not for kisses alone', &c.*

MRS LOVEIT. Foh! Their periwigs are scented with tobacco so strong –

SIR FOPLING. It overcomes our pulvilio – methinks I smell the coffee-house they come from.

FIRST MAN. Dorimant's convenient, Madam Loveit.

SECOND MAN. I like the oily buttock with her.

THIRD MAN. What spruce prig is that?

FIRST MAN. A caravan, lately come from Paris.

SECOND MAN. Peace, they smoke.

All of them coughing; exeunt singing, 'There's something else to be done', etc.

Enter DORIMANT *and* MEDLEY.

DORIMANT. They're engaged –

MEDLEY. She entertains him as if she liked him.

DORIMANT. Let us go forward – seem earnest in discourse and show ourselves. Then you shall see how she'll use him.

BELLINDA. Yonder's Dorimant my dear.

MRS LOVEIT. (*aside*) I see him, he comes insulting; but I will disappoint him in his expectation. (*To* SIR FOPLING) I like this pretty nice humour of yours Sir

---

250 s.d. *four*: only '*Three Slovenly Bullies*' are listed in the *Dramatis Personae*, and only three speak. But Conaghan suggests that Etherege 'may have considered the theatrical effectiveness of having the "nasty Fellows" outnumber the people of fashion on stage'. Barnard surmises, however, that the *Dramatis Personae* might reflect 'an economy made for production'.

250 s.d. *'Tis not for kisses alone'*: Carnochan identified this as line 15 of an anonymous song, 'Tell me no more you love', published in *A New Collection of the Choicest Songs* (1676); lines 5–8 run, ' 'Tis not for kisses alone / So long I have made my address. / There's something else to be done, / Which you cannot choose but guess.'

253 *pulvilio*: scented powder.

255 *convenient*: mistress.

256 *oily buttock*: smooth whore.

257 *spruce prig*: fop, coxcomb.

258 *caravan*: object of plunder (thieves' slang).

259 *smoke*: take notice (of us).

259 s.d. *'There's something else to be done'*: see note to line 250 s.d.

266 *insulting*: see note to *She Would*, II i 8.

268 *nice*: fastidious.

Fopling: with what a loathing eye he looked upon those fellows!

SIR FOPLING. I sat near one of 'em at a play today, and was almost poisoned with a pair of cordivant gloves he wears –

MRS LOVEIT. Oh! filthy cordivant, how I hate the smell! (*Laughs in a loud affected way*)

SIR FOPLING. Did you observe, madam, how their cravats hung loose an inch from their neck, and what a frightful air it gave 'em.

MRS LOVEIT. Oh I took particular notice of one that is always spruced up with a deal of dirty sky-coloured riband.

BELLINDA. That's one of the walking flageolets who haunt the Mail o'nights –

MRS LOVEIT. Oh! I remember him! H'has a hollow tooth enough to spoil the sweetness of an evening.

SIR FOPLING. I have seen the tallest walk the streets with a dainty pair of boxes, neatly buckled on.

MRS LOVEIT. And a little footboy at his heels pocket-high, with a flat-cap – a dirty face –

SIR FOPLING. And a snotty nose –

MRS LOVEIT. Oh – odious, there's many of my own sex with that Holborn equipage trig to Gray's Inn Walks; and now and then travel hither on a Sunday.

MEDLEY. She takes no notice of you.

DORIMANT. Damn her! I am jealous of a counter-plot!

MRS LOVEIT. Your liveries are the finest, Sir Fopling – oh that page! that page is the prettily'st dressed – they are all Frenchmen.

SIR FOPLING. There's one damned English blockhead among 'em, you may know him by his mien.

---

272 *cordivant*: cordovan, Spanish leather.

282 *flageolets*: see note to *She Would*, III iii 178.

287 *boxes*: some form of ungainly footwear; 'wooden overshoes(?)' (Carnochan).

289 *flat-cap*: round cap with a low, flat crown, worn by London citizens, especially apprentices.

292 *Holborn equipage*: retinue characteristic of the mercantile community, Holborn being a centre for business and trading activity.

292 *trig*: walk quickly.

292–3 *Gray's Inn Walks*: see note to *She Would*, IV i 36–7.

295 *jealous*: suspicious.

MRS LOVEIT. Oh! that's he, that's he, what do you call him?

SIR FOPLING. Hey – I know not what to call him –

MRS LOVEIT. What's your name?

FOOTMAN. John Trott, madam!

SIR FOPLING. Oh unsufferable! Trott, Trott, Trott! there's nothing so barbarous as the names of our English servants. What countryman are you sirrah?

FOOTMAN. Hampshire, sir?

SIR FOPLING. Then Hampshire be your name. Hey, Hampshire!

MRS LOVEIT. Oh that sound, that sound becomes the mouth of a man of quality!

MEDLEY. Dorimant you look a little bashful on the matter!

DORIMANT. She dissembles better than I thought she could have done.

MEDLEY. You have tempted her with too luscious a bait. She bites at the coxcomb.

DORIMANT. She cannot fall from loving me to that?

MEDLEY. You begin to be jealous in earnest.

DORIMANT. Of one I do not love –

MEDLEY. You did love her.

DORIMANT. The fit has long been over –

MEDLEY. But I have known men fall into dangerous relapses when they have found a woman inclining to another.

DORIMANT. (*to himself*) He guesses the secret of my heart! I am concerned, but dare not show it, lest Bellinda should mistrust all I have done to gain her.

BELLINDA. (*aside*) I have watched his look, and find no alteration there. Did he love her some signs of jealousy would have appeared?

---

308 *What countryman are you*: i.e. from what part of the country do you come?

310 *Then Hampshire be your name*: Brett-Smith cites a comment of Congreve's on this passage: 'The Ancients us'd to call their Servants by the names of the Countries from whence they came . . . The French to this Day do the same, and call their Footmen *Champagne le Picard, le Gascon, le Bourgignon*, &c. And Sir *George Etheridge* in his *Fopling Flutter*, the *Hampshire*, &c. speaking to his Valet, imitates this Custom.' See also the note to lines 138–9.

DORIMANT. I hope this happy evening, madam, has reconciled you to the scandalous Mail, we shall have you now hankering here again –

MRS LOVEIT. Sir Fopling will you walk –

SIR FOPLING. I am all obedience madam –

MRS LOVEIT. Come along then – and let's agree to be malicious on all the ill-fashioned things we meet.

SIR FOPLING. We'll make a critick on the whole Mail madam.

MRS LOVEIT. Bellinda you shall engage –

BELLINDA. To the reserve of our friends my dear.

MRS LOVEIT. No! No! Exceptions –

SIR FOPLING. We'll sacrifice all to our diversion –

MRS LOVEIT. All – all –

SIR FOPLING. All.

BELLINDA. All? Then let it be.

Exeunt SIR FOPLING, MRS LOVEIT, BELLINDA, *and* PERT *laughing.*

MEDLEY. Would you had brought some more of your friends, Dorimant, to have been witnesses of Sir Fopling's disgrace and your triumph –

DORIMANT. 'Twere unreasonable to desire you not to laugh at me; but pray do not expose me to the town this day or two.

MEDLEY. By that time you hope to have regained your credit.

DORIMANT. I know she hates Fopling, and only makes use of him in hope to work me on again; had it not been for some powerful considerations which will be removed tomorrow morning, I had made her pluck off this mask, and show the passion that lies panting under.

Enter a FOOTMAN.

---

336 *hankering*: 'hanging about', lingering (expectantly).

341 *critick*: critique (the latter spelling, and the pronunciation it represents, displaced the previously normal form, 'critick', in the course of the eighteenth century).

343 *engage*: take part.

345 *No! No! Exceptions –* : thus *1676*; most modern texts follow the precedent of *1693* and emend to some version of 'No! No exceptions', but the *1676* version is easily actable and therefore retained here.

MEDLEY. Here comes a man from Bellair, with news of your last adventure.

DORIMANT. I am glad he sent him. I long to know the consequence of our parting.

FOOTMAN. Sir, my master desires you to come to my Lady Townley's presently, and bring Mr Medley with you. My Lady Woodvill and her daughter are there.

MEDLEY. Then all's well Dorimant –

FOOTMAN. They have sent for the fiddles and mean to dance! He bid me tell you, sir, the old lady does not know you, and would have you own yourself to be Mr Courtage. They are all prepared to receive you by that name.

DORIMANT. That foppish admirer of quality, who flatters the very meat at honourable tables, and never offers love to a woman below a lady-grandmother.

MEDLEY. You know the character you are to act I see!

DORIMANT. This is Harriet's contrivance – wild, witty, lovesome, beautiful and young – come along Medley –

MEDLEY. This new woman would well supply the loss of Loveit.

DORIMANT. That business must not end so, before tomorrow sun is set, I will revenge and clear it.
And you and Loveit to her cost shall find,
I fathom all the depths of womankind.

Exeunt.

---

365 *last*: latest.

381–2 *wild . . . young*: Brett-Smith hears an echo here of Waller's 'Of the Danger his Majesty (being Prince) Escaped in the Road at Saint Andrews', lines 13–14: 'Of the Fourth Edward was his noble song, / Fierce, goodly, valiant, beautiful, and young' (*Works*, ed. Thorn Drury, vol. 1, p. 1).

ACT IV

[SCENE I]

The scene opens with the fiddles playing a country dance.

Enter DORIMANT, LADY WOODVILL, YOUNG BELLAIR, *and* MRS HARRIET, OLD BELLAIR, *and* EMILIA, MR MEDLEY *and* LADY TOWNLEY*; as having just ended the dance.*

OLD BELLAIR. So, so, so! a smart bout, a very smart bout a dod!

LADY TOWNLEY. How do you like Emilia's dancing, brother?

OLD BELLAIR. Not at all! not at all.

LADY TOWNLEY. You speak not what you think I am sure.

OLD BELLAIR. No matter for that, go, bid her dance no more, it don't become her, it don't become her, tell her I say so; (*Aside*) a dod I love her.

DORIMANT. (*to* LADY WOODVILL) All people mingle nowadays madam. And in public places women of quality have the least respect showed 'em.

LADY WOODVILL. I protest you say the truth, Mr Courtage.

DORIMANT. Forms and ceremonies, the only things that uphold quality and greatness, are now shamefully laid aside and neglected.

LADY WOODVILL. Well! this is not the women's age, let 'em think what they will, lewdness is the business now, love was the business in my time.

DORIMANT. The women indeed are little beholding to the young men of this age, they're generally only dull admirers of themselves, and make their court to nothing but their periwigs and their cravats, and would be more concerned for the disordering of 'em, though on a good occasion, than a young maid would be for the tumbling of her head or handkercher.

LADY WOODVILL. I protest you hit 'em.

DORIMANT. They are very assiduous to show themselves at court well dressed to the women of quality, but their business is with the stale mistresses of the town, who are prepared to receive their lazy addresses by industrious old lovers, who have cast 'em off, and made 'em easy.

HARRIET. He fits my mother's humour so well, a little more and she'll dance a kissing dance with him anon.

MEDLEY. Dutifully observed madam.

DORIMANT. They pretend to be great critics in beauty, by their talk you would think they liked no face, and yet can dote on an ill one, if it belong to a laundress or a tailor's daughter: they cry a woman's past her prime at twenty, decayed at four-and-twenty, old and unsufferable at thirty.

LADY WOODVILL. Unsufferable at thirty! That they are in the wrong, Mr Courtage, at five-and-thirty, there are living proofs enough to convince 'em.

DORIMANT. Ay madam! there's Mrs Setlooks, Mrs Droplip, and my Lady Loud! show me among all our opening buds, a face that promises so much beauty as the remains of theirs.

LADY WOODVILL. The depraved appetite of this vicious age tastes nothing but green fruit, and loaths it when 'tis kindly ripened.

DORIMANT. Else so many deserving women, madam, would not be so untimely neglected.

LADY WOODVILL. I protest Mr Courtage, a dozen such good men as you, would be enough to atone for that wicked Dorimant, and all the under-debauchees of the town.

HARRIET, EMILIA, YOUNG BELLAIR, MEDLEY, LADY TOWNLEY *break out into a laughter.*

What's the matter there?

---

28 *tumbling*: disordering.

28 *handkercher*: a kerchief for the neck or head.

37 *kissing dance*: a cushion-dance, a round-dance, formerly danced at weddings, in which the women and men alternately knelt on a cushion to be kissed.

53 *tastes*: has a taste for.

54 *kindly*: naturally, seasonably.

MEDLEY. A pleasant mistake, madam, that a lady has made, occasions a little laughter.

OLD BELLAIR. Come, come, you keep 'em idle! they are impatient till the fiddles play again.

DORIMANT. You are not weary, madam?

LADY WOODVILL. One dance more! I cannot refuse you Mr Courtage.

They dance.

After the dance, OLD BELLAIR, *singing and dancing up to* EMILIA.

EMILIA. You are very active, sir.

OLD BELLAIR. A dod sirrah; when I was a young fellow I could ha' capered up to my woman's gorget.

DORIMANT. You are willing to rest yourself madam –

LADY WOODVILL. We'll walk into my chamber and sit down.

MEDLEY. Leave us Mr Courtage, he's a dancer, and the young ladies are not weary yet.

LADY WOODVILL. We'll send him out again.

HARRIET. If you do not quickly, I know where to send for Mr Dorimant.

LADY WOODVILL. This girl's head, Mr Courtage, is ever running on that wild fellow.

DORIMANT. 'Tis well you have got her a good husband madam, that will settle it.

Exeunt LADY TOWNLEY, LADY WOODVILL *and* DORIMANT.

OLD BELLAIR. (*to* EMILIA) A dod sweetheart be advised, and do not throw thyself away on a young idle fellow.

EMILIA. I have no such intention sir.

OLD BELLAIR. Have a little patience! Thou shalt have the man I spake of. A dod he loves thee, and will make a good husband, but no words –

EMILIA. But sir –

OLD BELLAIR. No answer – out a pize! peace! and think on't.

Enter DORIMANT.

---

71 *capered up to my woman's gorget*: a gorget was a garment worn by women to cover the neck and shoulders. Thus Old Bellair is boasting of having once been able, in dancing, to kick as high as his partner's neck.

DORIMANT. Your company is desired within sir.

OLD BELLAIR. I go! I go! good Mr Courtage – (*To* EMILIA) fare you well! go! I'll see you no more.

EMILIA. What have I done sir?

OLD BELLAIR. You are ugly, you are ugly! Is she not Mr Courtage?

EMILIA. Better words or I sha'nt abide you.

OLD BELLAIR. Out a pize – a dod, what does she say! Hit her a pat for me there. *Exit* OLD BELLAIR.

MEDLEY. You have charms for the whole family.

DORIMANT. You'll spoil all with some unseasonable jest, Medley.

MEDLEY. You see I confine my tongue, and am content to be a bare spectator, much contrary to my nature.

EMILIA. Methinks, Mr Dorimant, my Lady Woodvill is a little fond of you.

DORIMANT. Would her daughter were.

MEDLEY. It may be you may find her so! try her, you have an opportunity.

DORIMANT. And I will not lose it! Bellair, here's a lady has something to say to you.

YOUNG BELLAIR. I wait upon her. Mr Medley we have both business with you.

DORIMANT. Get you all together then. (*To* HARRIET) That demure curtsy is not amiss in jest, but do not think in earnest it becomes you.

HARRIET. Affectation is catching I find; from your grave bow I got it.

DORIMANT. Where had you all that scorn, and coldness in your look?

HARRIET. From nature sir, pardon my want of art: I have not learnt those softnesses and languishings which now in faces are so much in fashion.

DORIMANT. You need 'em not, you have a sweetness of your own, if you would but calm your frowns and let it settle.

HARRIET. My eyes are wild and wandering like my passions, and cannot yet be tied to rules of charming.

DORIMANT. Women indeed have commonly a method of managing those messengers of love! now they will look as if they would kill, and anon they will look as

---

107 *bare*: mere.

if they were dying. They point and rebate their glances, the better to invite us.

HARRIET. I like this variety well enough; but hate the set face that always looks as it would say 'Come love me'. A woman, who at plays makes the *doux yeux* to a whole audience, and at home cannot forbear 'em to her monkey.

DORIMANT. Put on a gentle smile and let me see, how well it will become you.

HARRIET. I am sorry my face does not please you as it is, but I shall not be complaisant and change it.

DORIMANT. Though you are obstinate, I know 'tis capable of improvement, and shall do you justice madam, if I chance to be at court, when the critics of the circle pass their judgment; for thither you must come.

HARRIET. And expect to be taken in pieces, have all my features examined, every motion censured, and on the whole be condemned to be but pretty, or a beauty of the lowest rate. What think you?

DORIMANT. The women, nay the very lovers who belong to the drawing-room will maliciously allow you more than that; they always grant what is apparent, that they may the better be believed when they name concealed faults they cannot easily be disproved in.

HARRIET. Beauty runs as great a risque exposed at court as wit does on the stage, where the ugly and the foolish, all are free to censure.

DORIMANT. (*aside*) I love her, and dare not let her know it, I fear sh'as an ascendant o'er me and may

---

135 *point and rebate*: sharpen and blunt.

139 *makes the doux yeux*: makes eyes at; 'Deux yeux' (*1676*).

140–1 *cannot forbear 'em to her monkey*: cf. John Wilmot Earl of Rochester's 'A Letter from Artemisia in the Town to Chloe in the Country', lines 135ff. (*Complete Poems*, ed. David M. Vieth (New Haven and London, Yale University Press, 1968), p. 106).

145 *complaisant*: see note to I i 464.

149 *circle*: either (1) assembly at Court or (2) fashionable set.

156 *drawing-room*: see note to II ii 192.

161 *risque*: as the spelling suggests, a recent importation from French.

165 *ascendant*: dominance (originally an astrological term).

revenge the wrongs I have done her sex. (*To her*) Think of making a party madam, love will engage.

HARRIET. You make me start! I did not think to have heard of love from you.

DORIMANT. I never knew what 'twas to have a settled ague yet, but now and then have had irregular fits.

HARRIET. Take heed, sickness after long health is commonly more violent and dangerous.

DORIMANT. (*aside*) I have took the infection from her, and feel the disease now spreading in me. (*To her*) Is the name of love so frightful that you dare not stand it?

HARRIET. 'Twill do little execution out of your mouth on me I am sure.

DORIMANT. It has been fatal –

HARRIET. To some easy women, but we are not all born to one destiny, I was informed you use to laugh at love, and not make it.

DORIMANT. The time has been, but now I must speak –

HARRIET. If it be on that idle subject, I will put on my serious look, turn my head carelessly from you, drop my lip, let my eyelids fall, and hang half o'er my eyes – thus while you buzz a speech of an hour long in my ear, and I answer never a word! why do you not begin?

DORIMANT. That the company may take notice how passionately I make advances of love! and how disdainfully you receive 'em.

HARRIET. When your love's grown strong enough to make you bear being laughed at, I'll give you leave to trouble me with it. Till when pray forbear, sir.

Enter SIR FOPLING *and others in masks.*

DORIMANT. What's here masquerades?

HARRIET. I thought that foppery had been left off, and people might have been in private with a fiddle.

---

167 *making a party*: i.e. entering the lists.
167 *engage*: offer support.
170–1 *settled ague*: lasting fever.
182 *use to*: are accustomed to.
189 *buzz*: murmur, whisper.
198 *masquerades*: see Additional Note to *She Would*, III iii 255.

DORIMANT. 'Tis endeavoured to be kept on foot still by some who find themselves the more acceptable, the less they are known.

YOUNG BELLAIR. This must be Sir Fopling.

MEDLEY. That extraordinary habit shows it.

YOUNG BELLAIR. What are the rest?

MEDLEY. A company of French rascals whom he picked up in Paris and has brought over to be his dancing equipage on these occasions! make him own himself; a fool is very troublesome when he presumes he is incognito.

SIR FOPLING. (*to* HARRIET) Do you know me?

HARRIET. Ten to one but I guess at you!

SIR FOPLING. Are you women as fond of a vizard as we men are?

HARRIET. I am very fond of a vizard that covers a face I do not like, sir.

YOUNG BELLAIR. Here are no masks you see, sir, but those which came with you, this was intended a private meeting, but because you look like a gentleman, if you will discover yourself and we know you to be such, you shall be welcome.

SIR FOPLING. (*pulling off his mask*) Dear Bellair.

MEDLEY. Sir Fopling! how came you hither?

SIR FOPLING. Faith as I was coming late from Whitehall, after the king's *couchée*, one of my people told me he had heard fiddles at my Lady Townley's, and –

DORIMANT. You need not say any more, sir.

SIR FOPLING. Dorimant, let me kiss thee.

DORIMANT. Hark you Sir Fopling! (*Whispers*)

SIR FOPLING. Enough, enough, Courtage. A pretty kind of young woman that, Medley, I observed her in

---

205 *habit*: dress.

207 *rascals*: see note to *Comical Revenge*, I ii 103.

226 *king's couchée*: reception preceding the king's going to bed (*OED* cites this as the first English instance).

the Mail more *éveillée* than our English women commonly are, prithee what is she?

MEDLEY. The most noted coquette in town; beware of her.

SIR FOPLING. Let her be what she will, I know how to take my measures, in Paris the mode is to flatter the *prude*, laugh at the *faux-prude*, make serious love to the *demi-prude*, and only rally with the coquette. Medley, what think you?

MEDLEY. That for all this smattering of the mathematics, you may be out in your judgment at tennis.

SIR FOPLING. What a *coq-à-l'âne* is this? I talk of women and thou answer'st tennis.

MEDLEY. Mistakes will be for want of apprehension.

SIR FOPLING. I am very glad of the acquaintance I have with this family.

MEDLEY. My lady truly is a good woman.

SIR FOPLING. Ah! Dorimant, Courtage I would say, would thou hadst spent the last winter in Paris with me. When thou wert there La Corneus and Sallyes

---

234 *éveillée*: wide-awake, vivacious. Verity quotes Addison in *Spectator*, no. 45, who, advising women to keep their 'Sprightliness from degenerating into Levity', comments that 'the whole Discourse and Behaviour of the *French* is to make the Sex more Fantastical, or (as they are pleased to term it) *more awakened*, than is consistent either with Virtue or Discretion'.

239 *take my measures*: make my plans (from the Fr. *prendre des mesures*). *OED* does not list the English use before 1698, so Sir Fopling may be actually translating a French idiom as he speaks.

239 *in Paris*: Brett-Smith cites a contemporary French parallel to such advice from a poem by Roger de Rabutin, Comte de Bussy, bound in a volume (*c.* 1670) with the *Histoire Amoureuse* (see note to line 266).

240 *faux-prude*: false prude.

241 *demi-prude*: half prude.

243–4 *mathematics*: see note to *She Would*, I ii 176.

245 *coq-à-l'âne*: string of nonsense.

253 *La Corneus and Sallyes*: Verity suggests Mesdames Cornuel and Selles, minor literary figures of the day, both mentioned in works by Bussy.

were the only *habitudes* we had, a comedian would have been a *bonne fortune*. No stranger ever passed his time so well as I did some months before I came over. I was well received in a dozen families, where all the women of quality used to visit, I have intrigues to tell thee, more pleasant, than ever thou read'st in a novel.

HARRIET. Write 'em, sir, and oblige us women! our language wants such little stories.

SIR FOPLING. Writing madam's a mechanic part of wit! A gentleman should never go beyond a song or a *billet*.

HARRIET. Bussy was a gentleman.

SIR FOPLING. Who D'Ambois?

MEDLEY. Was there ever such a brisk blockhead?

HARRIET. Not D'Ambois, sir, but Rabutin. He who writ the *Loves of France*.

SIR FOPLING. That may be, madam! many gentlemen do things that are below 'em. Damn your authors, Courtage, women are the prettiest things we can fool away our time with.

HARRIET. I hope ye have wearied yourself tonight at court, sir, and will not think of fooling with anybody here.

SIR FOPLING. I cannot complain of my fortune there, madam – Dorimant –

DORIMANT. Again!

SIR FOPLING. Courtage, a pox on't, I have something

---

254 *habitudes*: acquaintance (derived from the French idiom, *avoir des habitudes dans une maison*, 'to be at home in some-one's house').

254–5 *a comedian would have been a bonne fortune*: 'The impli-cation is that *even* a comic actor would have been a "piece of good luck." Probably Sir Fopling shows his ignorance; Madame Cornuel was known for her wit' (Carnochan).

263 *mechanic*: mean, lowly.

266 *Bussy*: Roger de Rabutin, Comte de Bussy (1618–93), author of the *Histoire Amoureuse des Gaules* (cf. line 270).

267 *D'Ambois*: Louis de Clermont d'Amboise, Sieur de Bussy, a sixteenth-century French adventurer (the central character of George Chapman's still performed *Bussy D'Ambois* (1607)). Sir Fopling's 'French veneer fails him, and he knows only the Bussy of a former age, who had long been familiar to English theatre-goers' (Brett-Smith).

to tell thee. When I had made my court within, I came out and flung myself upon the mat under the state i' th' outward room, i' th' midst of half a dozen beauties who were withdrawn to jeèr among themselves, as they called it.

DORIMANT. Did you know 'em?

SIR FOPLING. Not one of 'em by heavens! not I. But they were all your friends.

DORIMANT. How are you sure of that?

SIR FOPLING. Why we laughed at all the town; spared nobody but yourself, they found me a man for their purpose.

DORIMANT. I know you are malicious to your power.

SIR FOPLING. And faith! I had occasion to show it, for I never saw more gaping fools at a ball or on a birthday.

DORIMANT. You learned who the women were.

SIR FOPLING. No matter! they frequent the drawing-room.

DORIMANT. And entertain themselves pleasantly at the expense of all the fops who come there.

SIR FOPLING. That's their business, faith I sifted 'em and find they have a sort of wit among them – (*Pinches a tallow candle*) ah filthy.

DORIMANT. Look he has been pinching the tallow candle.

SIR FOPLING. How can you breathe in a room where there's grease frying! Dorimant thou art intimate with my lady, advise her for her own sake and the good company that comes hither to burn wax lights.

HARRIET. What are these masquerades who stand so obsequiously at a distance?

SIR FOPLING. A set of baladines, whom I picked out of the best in France and brought over, with a *flûte douce* or two, my servants; they shall entertain you.

---

282 *my court within*: i.e. to the king.
283–4 *the state*: canopy.
285 *jeèr*: presumably indicating a piece of affected pronunciation.
294 *to your power*: to the extent of your power.
296–7 *birthday*: celebration of the king's birthday.
303 *sifted*: examined closely.
315–16 *flûte douce*: see note to II i 153; 'Flutes deux' (*1676*).

HARRIET. I had rather see you dance yourself Sir Fopling.

SIR FOPLING. And I had rather do it – all the company knows it – but madam –

MEDLEY. Come, come! no excuses Sir Fopling.

SIR FOPLING. By heavens Medley –

MEDLEY. Like a woman I find you must be struggled with before one brings you to what you desire.

HARRIET. (*aside*) Can he dance?

EMILIA. And fence and sing too, if you'll believe him.

DORIMANT. He has no more excellence in his heels than in his head. He went to Paris a plain bashful English blockhead, and is returned a fine undertaking French fop.

MEDLEY. I cannot prevail.

SIR FOPLING. Do not think it want of complaisance, madam.

HARRIET. You are too well-bred to want that, Sir Fopling. I believe it want of power.

SIR FOPLING. By heavens and so it is. I have sat up so damned late and drunk so cursed hard since I came to this lewd town, that I am fit for nothing but low dancing now, a *courante*, a *bourrée*, or a *menuet*: but St André tells me, if I will but be regular in one month I shall rise again. Pox on this debauchery. (*Endeavours at a caper*)

EMILIA. I have heard your dancing much commended.

SIR FOPLING. It had the good fortune to please in Paris. I was judged to rise within an inch as high as

---

324 *you to what you desire*: 'you what you desire' (*1676*); 'you to what' (*1704*).

329 *undertaking*: bold, forward.

338–9 *low dancing*: the three dances he names are low because they do not involve high leaping or capers of the kind at which Old Bellair boasts he once excelled (see lines 70–1).

340 *St André*: a French choreographer brought over with a troop to stage the dances in the opera *Psyche* which (after long preparation) had been finally produced on 27 February 1675.

the Basque in an entry I danced there.

HARRIET. I am mightily taken with this fool, let us sit: here's a seat Sir Fopling.

SIR FOPLING. At your feet, madam; I can be nowhere so much at ease: by your leave gown.

HARRIET.
EMILIA. } Ah! you'll spoil it.

SIR FOPLING. No matter, my clothes are my creatures. I make 'em to make my court to you ladies, hey – *qu'on commence.*

Dance.

To an English dancer English motions. I was forced to entertain this fellow, one of my set miscarrying – oh horrid! leave your damned manner of dancing, and put on the French air: have you not a pattern before you. – Pretty well! imitation in time may bring him to something.

---

345 *the Basque*: most probably a reference to 'le Basque sauteur', a French dancer, a liaison of whose with Madame de Berthillac is (as Barnard points out) recounted in a work attributed to Bussy. Brett-Smith's suggestion ('the skirt of a coat') is, however, not impossible.

345 *entry*: a dance performed as an interlude during an entertainment.

352–3 *hey – qu'on commence*: Conaghan identified that *1676* existed in uncorrected and corrected forms. At this point the uncorrected reads, 'Quon Comencè, English motions', while the corrected provides, 'Quon Comencè to an English Dancer English motions'. Conaghan comments that lack of punctuation in the corrected version 'suggests that the compositor made the insertion without attending to its purpose: *to an English Dancer* is almost certainly a stage direction'. I find this confidence difficult to share and have therefore stayed loyal here to the version followed by Verity, Brett-Smith and Carnochan.

353 *qu'on commence*: begin!

355 *entertain*: hire, employ.

355 *miscarrying*: coming to harm, or going astray, leaving my service.

357 *not a*: thus *1676* corrected; the uncorrected version reads 'not had a'. Conaghan comments that the 'change allows for a demonstration of dancing by Sir Fopling', and Barnard, going one step further, adds a stage direction ('*Dances*') before 'Pretty well!' Again these deductions seem unsure to me. Sir Fopling's remark surely can equally well (or better) apply to the French dancers surrounding the unfortunate English one.

After the dance enter OLD BELLAIR, LADY WOODVILL *and* LADY TOWNLEY.

OLD BELLAIR. Hey a dod! what have we here, a mumming?

LADY WOODVILL. Where's my daughter? – Harriet.

DORIMANT. Here, here, madam! I know not but under these disguises there may be dangerous sparks, I gave the young lady warning!

LADY WOODVILL. Lord! I am so obliged to you, Mr Courtage.

HARRIET. Lord! how you admire this man!

LADY WOODVILL. What have you to except against him?

HARRIET. He's a fop.

LADY WOODVILL. He's not a Dorimant, a wild extravagant fellow of the times.

HARRIET. He's a man made up of forms and common-places, sucked out of the remaining lees of the last age.

LADY WOODVILL. He's so good a man that were you not engaged –

LADY TOWNLEY. You'll have but little night to sleep in.

LADY WOODVILL. Lord! 'tis perfect day –

DORIMANT. (*aside*) The hour is almost come I appointed Bellinda, and I am not so foppishly in love here to forget; I am flesh and blood yet.

LADY TOWNLEY. I am very sensible, madam.

LADY WOODVILL. Lord, madam!

HARRIET. Look in what a struggle is my poor mother yonder!

YOUNG BELLAIR. She has much ado to bring out the compliment!

DORIMANT. She strains hard for it.

HARRIET. See, see! her head tottering, her eyes staring, and her under-lip trembling –

DORIMANT. Now, now, she's in the very convulsions of her civility. (*Aside*) 'Sdeath I shall lose Bellinda: I

---

369 *except*: object.
381 *perfect day*: i.e. broad daylight.
385 *sensible*: aware, appreciative (of your courtesy).

must fright her hence! she'll be an hour in this fit of good manners else. (*To* LADY WOODVILL) Do you not know, Sir Fopling, madam?

LADY WOODVILL. I have seen that face – oh heaven, 'tis the same we met in the Mail, how came he here?

DORIMANT. A fiddle in this town is a kind of fop-call; no sooner it strikes up, but the house is besieged with an army of masquerades straight.

LADY WOODVILL. Lord! I tremble Mr Courtage! for certain Dorimant is in the company.

DORIMANT. I cannot confidently say he is not, you had best begone. I will wait upon you; your daughter is in the hands of Mr Bellair.

LADY WOODVILL. I'll see her before me. Harriet, come away.

[*Exeunt* LADY WOODVILL *and* HARRIET.]

YOUNG BELLAIR. Lights! Lights!

LADY TOWNLEY. Light down there.

OLD BELLAIR. A dod it needs not –

DORIMANT. Call my Lady Woodvill's coach to the door quickly.

[*Exeunt* LADY TOWNLEY, DORIMANT, EMILIA, *and* YOUNG BELLAIR.]

OLD BELLAIR. Stay Mr Medley, let the young fellows do that duty; we will drink a glass of wine together. 'Tis good after dancing! what mumming spark is that?

MEDLEY. He is not to be comprehended in few words.

SIR FOPLING. Hey! La Tour.

MEDLEY. Whither away Sir Fopling?

SIR FOPLING. I have business with Courtage –

MEDLEY. He'll but put the ladies into their coach and come up again.

OLD BELLAIR. In the meantime I'll call for a bottle.

Exit OLD BELLAIR.

Enter YOUNG BELLAIR.

MEDLEY. Where's Dorimant?

YOUNG BELLAIR. Stolen home! he has had business waiting for him there all this night, I believe, by an impatience I observed in him.

MEDLEY. Very likely, 'tis but dissembling drunkenness, railing at his friends, and the kind soul will embrace the blessing, and forget the tedious expectation.

SIR FOPLING. I must speak with him before I sleep!

YOUNG BELLAIR. Emilia and I are resolved on that business.

MEDLEY. Peace here's your father.

Enter OLD BELLAIR, *and* BUTLER *with a bottle of wine.*

OLD BELLAIR. The women are all gone to bed. Fill boy! Mr Medley begin a health.

MEDLEY. To Emilia. (*Whispers*)

OLD BELLAIR. Out a pize! she's a rogue and I'll not pledge you.

MEDLEY. I know you well.

OLD BELLAIR. A dod drink it then.

SIR FOPLING. Let us have the new bachique.

OLD BELLAIR. A dod that is a hard word! What does it mean sir?

MEDLEY. A catch or drinking song.

OLD BELLAIR. Let us have it then.

SIR FOPLING. Fill the glasses round, and draw up in a body. Hey! Music!

They sing.

'The pleasures of love and the joys of good wine,
To perfect our happiness wisely we join.
We to beauty all day
Give the sovereign sway,
And her favourite nymphs devoutly obey.
At the plays we are constantly making our court
And when they are ended we follow the sport,
To the Mall and the Park
Where we love till 'tis dark;
Then sparkling champagne

---

441 *pledge*: see note to *Comical Revenge*, II iii 53.

442 *I know you well*: thus *1676* and editions to *1711*; most modern editors (Conaghan being one exception) emend to 'I know you will', but this is unnecessary.

444 *bachique*: drinking song (cf. line 447); *OED* gives this as its single example, so Sir Fopling is perhaps importing a word from French.

445 *hard*: (1) difficult but also (2) cant (cf. Samuel Butler, *Hudibras*, Part I, Canto 1, 3 and note, in John Wilders' edition (Oxford, Clarendon Press, 1967)).

460 *champagne*: a recent importation (both as a commodity and a word from the French).

Puts an end to their reign;
It quickly recovers
Poor languishing lovers,
Makes us frolic and gay, and drowns all our sorrow.
But alas! we relapse again on the morrow.
  Let every man stand
  With his glass in his hand,
And briskly discharge at the word of command.
  Here's a health to all those
  Whom tonight we depose.
Wine and beauty by turns great souls should inspire.
Present all together; and now boys give fire – '

OLD BELLAIR. A dod a pretty business and very merry.

SIR FOPLING. Hark you Medley, let you and I take the fiddles and go waken Dorimant.

MEDLEY. We shall do him a courtesy, if it be as I guess. For after the fatigue of this night, he'll quickly have his belly full: and be glad of an occasion to cry, 'Take away, Handy'.

YOUNG BELLAIR. I'll go with you, and there we'll consult about affairs Medley.

OLD BELLAIR. (*looks on his watch*) A dod, 'tis six a clock.

SIR FOPLING. Let's away then.

OLD BELLAIR. Mr Medley, my sister tells me you are an honest man. And a dod I love you. Few words and hearty, that's the way with old Harry, old Harry.

SIR FOPLING. Light your flambeaux. Hey.

OLD BELLAIR. What does the man mean?

MEDLEY. 'Tis day Sir Fopling.

SIR FOPLING. No matter. Our serenade will look the greater.

Exeunt Omnes.

---

464 *frolic*: mirthful, sportive.
472 *Present all together*: raise your weapons (i.e. your drinks) and take aim (the conclusion of a series of military metaphors).
488 *flambeaux*: torches.
491 *serenade*: see note to *Comical Revenge*, V ii 10.

SCENE II

Dorimant's lodging, a table, a candle, a toilet, &c. HANDY *tying up linen.*

Enter DORIMANT *in his gown and* BELLINDA.

DORIMANT. Why will you be gone so soon?

BELLINDA. Why did you stay out so late?

DORIMANT. Call a chair, Handy! what makes you tremble so?

[*Exit* HANDY.]

BELLINDA. I have a thousand fears about me: have I not been seen think you?

DORIMANT. By nobody but myself and trusty Handy.

BELLINDA. Where are all your people?

DORIMANT. I have dispersed 'em on sleeveless errands. What does that sigh mean?

BELLINDA. Can you be so unkind to ask me? – well – (*Sighs*) were it to do again –

DORIMANT. We should do it, should we not?

BELLINDA. I think we should: the wickeder man you to make me love so well – will you be discreet now?

DORIMANT. I will –

BELLINDA. You cannot.

DORIMANT. Never doubt it.

BELLINDA. I will not expect it.

DORIMANT. You do me wrong.

BELLINDA. You have no more power to keep the secret, than I had not to trust you with it.

DORIMANT. By all the joys I have had, and those you keep in store –

BELLINDA. You'll do for my sake what you never did before –

DORIMANT. By that truth thou hast spoken, a wife shall sooner betray herself to her husband –

---

9 *sleeveless*: purposeless, trifling.

23–6 *By all . . . before* – : 'Dorimant may or may not have intended his asseveration to take the form of an Alexandrine, but she is quick to interrupt his heroics with her rhyming reply' (Brett-Smith).

BELLINDA. Yet I had rather you should be false in this than in another thing you promised me.

DORIMANT. What's that?

BELLINDA. That you would never see Loveit more but in public places, in the Park, at court and plays.

DORIMANT. 'Tis not likely a man should be fond of seeing a damned old play when there is a new one acted.

BELLINDA. I dare not trust your promise.

DORIMANT. You may –

BELLINDA. This does not satisfy me. You shall swear you never will see her more.

DORIMANT. I will! a thousand oaths – by all –

BELLINDA. Hold – you shall not, now I think on't better.

DORIMANT. I will swear –

BELLINDA. I shall grow jealous of the oath, and think I owe your truth to that, not to your love.

DORIMANT. Then, by my love! no other oath I'll swear.

Enter HANDY.

HANDY. Here's a chair.

BELLINDA. Let me go.

DORIMANT. I cannot.

BELLINDA. Too willingly I fear.

DORIMANT. Too unkindly feared. When will you promise me again?

BELLINDA. Not this fortnight.

DORIMANT. You will be better than your word.

BELLINDA. I think I shall. Will it not make you love me less?

Fiddles without.

(*Starting*) Hark! what fiddles are these?

DORIMANT. Look out, Handy!

Exit HANDY *and returns.*

HANDY. Mr Medley, Mr Bellair, and Sir Fopling, they are coming up.

DORIMANT. How got they in?

HANDY. The door was open for the chair.

BELLINDA. Lord! let me fly –

DORIMANT. Here, here, down the back stairs. I'll see you into your chair.

BELLINDA. No, no! stay and receive 'em. And be sure

you keep your word and never see Loveit more. Let it be a proof of your kindness.

DORIMANT. It shall – Handy direct her. Everlasting love go along with thee. (*Kissing her hand*)

Exeunt BELLINDA *and* HANDY.

Enter YOUNG BELLAIR, MEDLEY, *and* SIR FOPLING.

YOUNG BELLAIR. Not abed yet!

MEDLEY. You have had an irregular fit Dorimant.

DORIMANT. I have.

YOUNG BELLAIR. And is it off already?

DORIMANT. Nature has done her part gentlemen, when she falls kindly to work, great cures are effected in little time, you know.

SIR FOPLING. We thought there was a wench in the case by the chair that waited. Prithee make us a *confidence.*

DORIMANT. Excuse me.

SIR FOPLING. *Le sage* Dorimant – was she pretty?

DORIMANT. So pretty she may come to keep her coach and pay parish duties if the good humour of the age continue.

MEDLEY. And be of the number of the ladies kept by public-spirited men for the good of the whole town.

SIR FOPLING. Well said Medley. (SIR FOPLING *dancing by himself*)

YOUNG BELLAIR. See Sir Fopling dancing.

DORIMANT. You are practising and have a mind to recover I see.

SIR FOPLING. Prithee Dorimant! why hast not thou a glass hung up here? a room is the dullest thing without one!

YOUNG BELLAIR. Here is company to entertain you.

SIR FOPLING. But I mean in case of being alone. In a glass a man may entertain himself –

---

73 *irregular fit*: Medley is recalling Dorimant's earlier remark (IV i 171).

80–1 *make us a confidence*: i.e. confide in us.

83 *Le sage*: prudent, discreet.

84 *keep her coach*: 'An instance of Dorimant's discretion. The description could hardly apply to Bellinda, who is not mercenary' (Conaghan).

DORIMANT. The shadow of himself indeed.

SIR FOPLING. Correct the errors of his motions and his dress.

MEDLEY. I find Sir Fopling in your solitude, you remember the saying of the wise man, and study yourself.

SIR FOPLING. 'Tis the best diversion in our retirements. Dorimant thou art a pretty fellow and wear'st thy clothes well, but I never saw thee have a handsome cravat. Were they made up like mine, they'd give another air to thy face. Prithee let me send my man to dress thee but one day. By heavens an Englishman cannot tie a ribbon.

DORIMANT. They are something clumsy-fisted –

SIR FOPLING. I have brought over the prettiest fellow that ever spred a toilet, he served some time under Mérille the greatest *génie* in the world for a *valet de chambre.*

DORIMANT. What he who formerly belonged to the Duke of Candale?

SIR FOPLING. The same, and got him his immortal reputation.

DORIMANT. Y'have a very fine brandenburgh on Sir Fopling.

SIR FOPLING. It serves to wrap me up, after the fatigue of a ball.

MEDLEY. I see you often in it, with your periwig tied up.

SIR FOPLING. We should not always be in a set dress,

103–4 *study yourself*: the injunction 'Know thyself' was inscribed on the temple of Apollo; Plato (*Protagoras*, 343b) ascribes the saying to the Seven Wise Men.

115 *Mérille*: at the time of the play in the service of the Duc d'Orléans. According to Conaghan, 'Bussy speaks of him in 1677 as "*premier valet de chambre de Monsieur*" '.

115 *génie*: man of genius.

115–16 *valet de chambre*: see note to *Comical Revenge*, II i 77–8.

118 *Duke of Candale*: Louis-Charles-Gaston de Nogaret de Foix (1627–58), a French general; mentioned as a leader of fashion by Bussy in the *Histoire Amoureuse* (he ascribes, however, the credit for this to his mistress, not his valet).

121 *brandenburgh*: morning gown.

125–6 *periwig tied up*: 'i.e. to save combing' (Conaghan).

'tis more *en cavalier* to appear now and then in a *déshabillé*.

MEDLEY. Pray how goes your business with Loveit?

SIR FOPLING. You might have answered yourself in the Mail last night. Dorimant! did you not see the advances she made me? I have been endeavouring at a song!

DORIMANT. Already!

SIR FOPLING. 'Tis my *coup d'essai* in English, I would fain have thy opinion of it.

DORIMANT. Let's see it.

SIR FOPLING. Hey page give me my song – Bellair, here thou hast a pretty voice sing it.

YOUNG BELLAIR. Sing it yourself Sir Fopling.

SIR FOPLING. Excuse me.

YOUNG BELLAIR. You learnt to sing in Paris.

SIR FOPLING. I did, of Lambert the greatest master in the world: but I have his own fault, a weak voice, and care not to sing out of a *ruelle*.

DORIMANT. A *ruelle* is a pretty cage for a singing fop indeed.

YOUNG BELLAIR *reads the song.*

'How charming Phillis is, how fair!
  Ah that she were as willing,
To ease my wounded heart of care
  And make her eyes less killing.
I sigh! I sigh! I languish now,
  And love will not let me rest,
I drive about the Park, and bow
  Still as I meet my dearest.'

SIR FOPLING. Sing it, sing it man, it goes to a pretty

---

128 *en cavalier*: dashing.

129 *in a déshabillé*: informally dressed.

136 *coup d'essai*: first attempt.

144 *Lambert*: Michel Lambert (1610–96), master of chamber music to Louis XIV and a teacher much sought after by the fashionable.

146 *ruelle*: 'a bedroom, where ladies of fashion in the seventeenth and eighteenth centuries, especially in France, held a morning reception of persons of distinction; hence, a reception of this kind' (*OED*).

156 *Still as*: whenever.

new tune which I am confident was made by Baptiste.

MEDLEY. Sing it yourself Sir Fopling, he does not know the tune.

SIR FOPLING. I'll venture. (SIR FOPLING *sings*)

DORIMANT. Ay marry! now 'tis something. I shall not flatter you, Sir Fopling, there is not much thought in't. But 'tis passionate and well-turned.

MEDLEY. After the French way.

SIR FOPLING. That I aimed at – does it not give you a lively image of the thing? Slap down goes the glass, and thus we are at it.

DORIMANT. It does indeed, I perceive, Sir Fopling, you'll be the very head of the sparks, who are lucky in compositions of this nature.

Enter Sir Fopling's FOOTMAN.

SIR FOPLING. La Tour, is the bath ready?

FOOTMAN. Yes sir.

SIR FOPLING. *Adieu donc mes chers.*

Exeunt SIR FOPLING [*and* FOOTMAN.]

MEDLEY. When have you your revenge on Loveit, Dorimant?

DORIMANT. I will but change my linen and about it.

MEDLEY. The powerful considerations which hindered have been removed then.

DORIMANT. Most luckily this morning, you must along with me, my reputation lies at stake there.

MEDLEY. I am engaged to Bellair.

DORIMANT. What's your business?

---

158 *Baptiste*: 'Baptist' (*1676*). This is the usual abbreviation at this time of the name of Giovanni Battista Draghi, an Italian musician well-known in London, having settled there after the Restoration. But, given Sir Fopling's French devotions, the more likely candidate here is Jean-Baptiste Lully (1638–87), the famous composer and master of Court music to Louis XIV.

167 *glass*: of the coach-window. For a description of the rituals associated with courtship between the occupants of passing coaches in the Park, see the opening conversation in Shadwell's *A True Widow* (1678).

172 *La Tour*: '*La Tower*' (*1676*), as also at IV i 420.

174 *Adieu donc mes chers*: farewell then, my friends.

MEDLEY. Ma-tri-mony an't like you.

DORIMANT. It does not, sir.

YOUNG BELLAIR. It may in time Dorimant, what think you of Mrs Harriet?

DORIMANT. What does she think of me?

YOUNG BELLAIR. I am confident she loves you.

DORIMANT. How does it appear?

YOUNG BELLAIR. Why she's never well but when she's talking of you, but then she finds all the faults in you she can. She laughs at all who commend you, but then she speaks ill of all who do not.

DORIMANT. Women of her temper betray themselves by their over-cunning. I had once a growing love with a lady, who would always quarrel with me when I came to see her, and yet was never quiet if I stayed a day from her.

YOUNG BELLAIR. My father is in love with Emilia.

DORIMANT. That is a good warrant for your proceedings, go on and prosper, I must to Loveit. Medley I am sorry you cannot be a witness.

MEDLEY. Make her meet Sir Fopling again in the same place, and use him ill before me.

DORIMANT. That may be brought about I think. I'll be at your aunt's anon and give you joy Mr Bellair.

YOUNG BELLAIR. You had not best think of Mrs Harriet too much, without church security there's no taking up there.

DORIMANT. I may fall into the snare too. But –
The wise will find a difference in our fate,
You wed a woman, I a good estate.

Exeunt.

SCENE III

Enter the chair with BELLINDA, *the* MEN *set it down and open it.* BELLINDA *starting.*

---

184 *Ma-tri-mony an't like you*: 'Medley mimics tradesmen's speech, in response to Dorimant's "business" ' (Conaghan).

184 *an't*: if it.

207 *give you joy*: congratulate you.

210 *taking up*: (1) possessing yourself of her (2) borrowing at interest, purchasing (playing on 'church security').

BELLINDA. (*surprised*) Lord! where am I? in the Mail! Whither have you brought me?

FIRST CHAIRMAN. You gave us no directions, madam?

BELLINDA. (*aside*) The fright I was in made me forget it.

FIRST CHAIRMAN. We use to carry a lady from the squire's hither.

BELLINDA. (*aside*) This is Loveit, I am undone if she sees me. – Quickly carry me away.

FIRST CHAIRMAN. Whither an't like your honour?

BELLINDA. Ask no questions –

Enter Loveit's FOOTMAN.

FOOTMAN. Have you seen my lady, madam?

BELLINDA. I am just come to wait upon her –

FOOTMAN. She will be glad to see you, madam. She sent me to you this morning to desire your company, and I was told you went out by five a clock.

BELLINDA. (*aside*) More and more unlucky!

FOOTMAN. Will you walk in madam?

BELLINDA. I'll discharge my chair and follow, tell your mistress I am here.

Exit FOOTMAN.

(*Gives the* CHAIRMEN *money*) Take this! and if ever you should be examined, be sure you say, you took me up in the Strand over against the Exchange, as you will answer it to Mr Dorimant.

CHAIRMEN. We will an't like your honour.

Exit CHAIRMEN.

BELLINDA. Now to come off, I must on –
In confidence and lies some hope is left;
'Twere hard to be found out in the first theft. *Exit.*

---

27 *confidence*: hardihood, impudence.

ACT V

[SCENE I]

Enter MRS LOVEIT *and* PERT *her woman.*

PERT. Well! in my eyes Sir Fopling is no such despicable person.

MRS LOVEIT. You are an excellent judge.

PERT. He's as handsome a man as Mr Dorimant, and as great a gallant.

MRS LOVEIT. Intolerable! is't not enough I submit to his impertinences, but must I be plagued with yours too?

PERT. Indeed madam –

MRS LOVEIT. 'Tis false, mercenary malice –

Enter her FOOTMAN.

FOOTMAN. Mrs Bellinda madam –

MRS LOVEIT. What of her?

FOOTMAN. She's below.

MRS LOVEIT. How came she?

FOOTMAN. In a chair, ambling Harry brought her.

MRS LOVEIT. He bring her! His chair stands near Dorimant's door and always brings me from thence – run and ask him where he took her up; go, there is no truth in friendship neither. Women, as well as men, all are false, or all are so to me at least.

PERT. You are jealous of her too?

MRS LOVEIT. You had best tell her I am. 'Twill become the liberty you take of late. This fellow's bringing of her, her going out by five a clock – I know not what to think.

Enter BELLINDA.

Bellinda, you are grown an early riser I hear!

BELLINDA. Do you not wonder my dear, what made me abroad so soon?

MRS LOVEIT. You do not use to be so.

BELLINDA. The country gentlewomen I told you of (lord! they have the oddest diversions!) would never let me rest till I promised to go with them to the markets this morning to eat fruit and buy nosegays.

MRS LOVEIT. Are they so fond of a filthy nosegay?

BELLINDA. They complain of the stinks of the town, and are never well but when they have their noses in one.

MRS LOVEIT. There are essences and sweet waters.

BELLINDA. Oh they cry out upon perfumes they are unwholesome, one of 'em was falling into a fit with the smell of these narolii.

MRS LOVEIT. Methinks in complaisance you should have had a nosegay too.

BELLINDA. Do you think, my dear, I could be so loathsome to trick myself up with carnations and stock-gillyflowers? I begged their pardon and told them I never wore anything but orange-flowers and tuberose. That which made me willing to go was, a strange desire I had to eat some fresh nectarines.

MRS LOVEIT. And had you any?

BELLINDA. The best I ever tasted.

MRS LOVEIT. Whence came you now?

BELLINDA. From their lodgings, where I crowded out of a coach and took a chair to come and see you my dear.

MRS LOVEIT. Whither did you send for that chair?

BELLINDA. 'Twas going by empty.

MRS LOVEIT. Where do these country gentlewomen lodge I pray?

BELLINDA. In the Strand over against the Exchange.

PERT. That place is never without a nest of 'em, they

---

33 *nosegays*: bunches of sweet-smelling flowers.
38 *sweet waters*: liquid perfumes or scents.
41 *narolii*: (usually in the singular form and spelt 'neroli' or 'neroly') oil distilled from the flowers of the bitter orange and used as a perfume.
45 *trick myself up*: see note to *She Would*, III iii 104.
46 *stock-gillyflowers*: white stock.
47 *orange-flowers*: i.e. in the form of perfume.
48 *tuberose*: perfume extracted from very fragrant flowers of the tuberose, a lilaceous plant; Barnard noted that 'Like the orange-flower this was an exotic having only recently reached England.'
53 *crowded*: hurriedly pressed.

are always as one goes by fleering in balconies or staring out of windows.

Enter FOOTMAN.

MRS LOVEIT. (*to the* FOOTMAN) Come hither. (*Whispers*)

BELLINDA. (*aside*) This fellow by her order has been questioning the chairmen! I threatened 'em with the name of Dorimant, if they should have told truth I am lost for ever.

MRS LOVEIT. 'In the Strand' said you?

FOOTMAN. Yes madam over against the Exchange.

Exit FOOTMAN.

MRS LOVEIT. She's innocent and I am much to blame.

BELLINDA. (*aside*) I am so frighted, my countenance will betray me.

MRS LOVEIT. Bellinda! what makes you look so pale?

BELLINDA. Want of my usual rest, and jolting up and down so long in an odious hackney.

FOOTMAN *returns.*

FOOTMAN. Madam! Mr Dorimant!

MRS LOVEIT. What makes him here?

BELLINDA. (*aside*) Then I am betrayed indeed, h'has broke his word, and I love a man that does not care for me.

MRS LOVEIT. Lord! you faint Bellinda!

BELLINDA. I think I shall! such an oppression here on the sudden.

PERT. She has eaten too much fruit I warrant you.

MRS LOVEIT. Not unlikely!

PERT. 'Tis that lies heavy on her stomach.

MRS LOVEIT. Have her into my chamber, give her some surfeit-water, and let her lie down a little.

PERT. Come, madam! I was a strange devourer of fruit when I was young, so ravenous –

Exeunt BELLINDA *and* PERT *leading her off.*

MRS LOVEIT. Oh that my love would be but calm

---

78 *What makes him here?*: 'What is he doing here?', or 'what brings him here?'

83 *oppression*: pain.

89 *surfeit-water*: medicinal drink.

90 *strange*: unusual, exceptional.

awhile! that I might receive this man with all the scorn and indignation he deserves.

Enter DORIMANT.

DORIMANT. Now for a touch of Sir Fopling to begin with. Hey – page – give positive order that none of my people stir – let the *canaille* wait as they should do – since noise and nonsense have such powerful charms,

'I that I may successful prove,
Transform myself to what you love.'

MRS LOVEIT. If that would do, you need not change from what you are, you can be vain and loud enough.

DORIMANT. But not with so good a grace as Sir Fopling. Hey, Hampshire – oh – that sound, that sound becomes the mouth of a man of quality.

MRS LOVEIT. Is there a thing so hateful as a senseless mimic?

DORIMANT. He's a great grievance indeed to all who like yourself, madam, love to play the fool in quiet.

MRS LOVEIT. A ridiculous animal, who has more of the ape, than the ape has of the man in him.

DORIMANT. I have as mean an opinion of a sheer mimic as yourself, yet were he all ape I should prefer him to the gay, the giddy, brisk-insipid noisy fool you dote on.

MRS LOVEIT. Those noisy fools, however you despise 'em, have good qualities, which weigh more (or ought at least) with us women, than all the pernicious wit you have to boast of.

DORIMANT. That I may hereafter have a just value for their merit, pray do me the favour to name 'em.

---

97 *canaille*: rabble.

100–1 *I that I may . . . love*: lines 5–6 from Waller's 'To the Mutable Fair' (*Works*, ed. Thorn Drury, vol. 1, p. 106), with the first word changed from 'And' to 'I'.

113 *sheer*: *OED* lists 'sheer wit' as a Restoration and eighteenth-century term for a particular form of fashionable humour, and the adjective perhaps carries some element of that meaning here.

115 *brisk-insipid*: thus *1676*. Dorimant is presumably recalling his own earlier description of Sir Fopling (III ii 289), and the hyphen underlines the paradox involved in naming the two qualities side by side.

MRS LOVEIT. You'll despise 'em as the dull effects of ignorance and vanity! yet I care not if I mention some. First, they really admire us, while you at best but flatter us well.

DORIMANT. Take heed! Fools can dissemble too –

MRS LOVEIT. They may! but not so artificially as you – there is no fear they should deceive us! Then they are assiduous, sir, they are ever offering us their service, and always waiting on our will.

DORIMANT. You owe that to their excessive idleness! They know not how to entertain themselves at home, and find so little welcome abroad, they are fain to fly to you who countenance 'em as a refuge against the solitude they would be otherwise condemned to.

MRS LOVEIT. Their conversation too diverts us better.

DORIMANT. Playing with your fan, smelling to your gloves, commending your hair, and taking notice how 'tis cut and shaded after the new way –

MRS LOVEIT. Were it sillier than you can make it, you must allow 'tis pleasanter to laugh at others than to be laughed at ourselves though never so wittily. Then though they want skill to flatter us, they flatter themselves so well, they save us the labour! we need not take that care and pains to satisfy 'em of our love which we so often lose on you.

DORIMANT. They commonly indeed believe too well of themselves, and always better of you than you deserve.

MRS LOVEIT. You are in the right, they have an implicit faith in us which keeps 'em from prying narrowly into our secrets, and saves us the vexatious trouble of clearing doubts which your subtle and causeless jealousies every moment raise.

DORIMANT. There is an inbred falsehood in women, which inclines 'em still to them, whom they may most easily deceive.

MRS LOVEIT. The man who loves above his quality, does not suffer more from the insolent impertinence of his mistress, than the woman who loves above her understanding does from the arrogant presumptions of her friend.

---

128 *artificially*: see note to I i 254.

150–1 *an implicit faith*: see note to *She Would*, III iii 300–1.

DORIMANT. You mistake the use of fools, they are designed for properties and not for friends, you have an indifferent stock of reputation left yet. Lose it all like a frank gamester on the square, 'twill then be time enough to turn rook, and cheat it up again on a good substantial bubble.

MRS LOVEIT. The old and the ill-favoured are only fit for properties indeed, but young and handsome fools have met with kinder fortunes.

DORIMANT. They have, to the shame of your sex be it spoken; 'twas this, the thought of this made me by a timely jealousy endeavour to prevent the good fortune you are providing for Sir Fopling – but against a woman's frailty all our care is vain.

MRS LOVEIT. Had I not with a dear experience bought the knowledge of your falsehood, you might have fooled me yet. This is not the first jealousy you have feigned to make a quarrel with me, and get a week to throw away on some such unknown inconsiderable slut, as you have been lately lurking with at plays.

DORIMANT. Women, when they would break off with a man, never want th'address to turn the fault on him.

MRS LOVEIT. You take a pride of late in using of me ill, that the town may know the power you have over me. Which now (as unreasonably as yourself) expects that I (do me all the injuries you can) must love you still.

DORIMANT. I am so far from expecting that you should, I begin to think you never did love me.

MRS LOVEIT. Would the memory of it were so wholly worn out in me that I did doubt it too! what made you come to disturb my growing quiet?

DORIMANT. To give you joy of your growing infamy.

MRS LOVEIT. Insupportable! insulting devil! this from

---

164 *properties*: tools, mere instruments.
165 *indifferent*: reasonable, moderate.
166 *frank*: lavish, generous, bounteous.
166 *on the square*: (1) face to face, openly, directly (2) (from the 1660s, especially in reference to gambling) without artifice or trickery.
167 *rook*: see note to *She Would*, II i 27.
168 *substantial*: see note to *She Would*, III i 41.
168 *bubble*: see note to *She Would*, II i 28.

you, the only author of my shame! this from another had been but justice, but from you, 'tis a hellish and inhuman outrage. What have I done?

DORIMANT. A thing that puts you below my scorn, and makes my anger as ridiculous as you have made my love.

MRS LOVEIT. I walked last night with Sir Fopling.

DORIMANT. You did madam, and you talked and laughed aloud 'Ha, ha, ha' – oh that laugh, that laugh becomes the confidence of a woman of quality.

MRS LOVEIT. You who have more pleasure in the ruin of a woman's reputation than in the endearments of her love, reproach me not with yourself, and I defy you to name the man can lay a blemish on my fame.

DORIMANT. To be seen publicly so transported with the vain follies of that notorious fop, to me is an infamy below the sin of prostitution with another man.

MRS LOVEIT. Rail on, I am satisfied in the justice of what I did, you had provoked me to't.

DORIMANT. What I did was the effect of a passion, whose extravagancies you have been willing to forgive.

MRS LOVEIT. And what I did was the effect of a passion you may forgive if you think fit.

DORIMANT. Are you so indifferent grown?

MRS LOVEIT. I am.

DORIMANT. Nay! then 'tis time to part. I'll send you back your letters you have so often asked for: I have two or three of 'em about me.

MRS LOVEIT. Give 'em me.

DORIMANT. You snatch as if you thought I would not – there – and may the perjuries in 'em be mine if e'er I see you more. (*Offers to go, she catches him*)

MRS LOVEIT. Stay!

DORIMANT. I will not.

MRS LOVEIT. You shall.

DORIMANT. What have you to say?

MRS LOVEIT. I cannot speak it yet.

DORIMANT. Something more in commendation of the fool. Death! I want patience, let me go.

MRS LOVEIT. I cannot. (*Aside*) I can sooner part with the limbs that hold him. – I hate that nauseous fool, you know I do.

DORIMANT. Was it the scandal you were fond of then?

MRS LOVEIT. Y'had raised my anger equal to my love, a thing you ne'er could do before, and in revenge I did – I know not what I did: – would you would not think on't any more.

DORIMANT. Should I be willing to forget it, I shall be daily minded of it, 'twill be a commonplace for all the town to laugh at me, and Medley, when he is rhetorically drunk, will ever be declaiming on it in my ears.

MRS LOVEIT. 'Twill be believed a jealous spite! Come forget it.

DORIMANT. Let me consult my reputation, you are too careless of it. (*Pauses*) You shall meet Sir Fopling in the Mail again tonight.

MRS LOVEIT. What mean you?

DORIMANT. I have thought on it, and you must. 'Tis necessary to justify my love to the world: you can handle a coxcomb as he deserves, when you are not out of humour madam!

MRS LOVEIT. Public satisfaction for the wrong I have done you! This is some new device to make me more ridiculous!

DORIMANT. Hear me!

MRS LOVEIT. I will not!

DORIMANT. You will be persuaded.

MRS LOVEIT. Never.

DORIMANT. Are you so obstinate?

MRS LOVEIT. Are you so base?

DORIMANT. You will not satisfy my love?

MRS LOVEIT. I would die to satisfy that, but I will not, to save you from a thousand racks, do a shameless thing to please your vanity.

DORIMANT. Farewell false woman.

MRS LOVEIT. Do! go!

DORIMANT. You will call me back again.

MRS LOVEIT. Exquisite fiend! I knew you came but to torment me.

Enter BELLINDA *and* PERT.

DORIMANT. (*surprised*) Bellinda here!

---

246 *commonplace*: stock theme.

BELLINDA. (*aside*) He starts! and looks pale, the sight of me has touched his guilty soul.

PERT. 'Twas but a qualm as I said, a little indigestion; the surfeit-water did it madam, mixed with a little mirabilis.

DORIMANT. [*aside*] I am confounded! and cannot guess how she came hither!

MRS LOVEIT. 'Tis your fortune Bellinda ever to be here, when I am abused by this prodigy of ill nature.

BELLINDA. I am amazed to find him here! How has he the face to come near you?

DORIMANT. (*aside*) Here is fine work towards! I never was at such a loss before.

BELLINDA. One who makes a public profession of breach of faith and ingratitude! I loath the sight of him.

DORIMANT. [*aside*] There is no remedy, I must submit to their tongues now, and some other time bring myself off as well as I can.

BELLINDA. Other men are wicked, but then they have some sense of shame! he is never well but when he triumphs, nay! glories to a woman's face in his villainies.

MRS LOVEIT. You are in the right Bellinda, but methinks your kindness for me makes you concern yourself too much with him.

BELLINDA. It does indeed my dear! His barbarous carriage to you yesterday, made me hope you ne'er would see him more, and the very next day to find him here again, provokes me strangely: but because I know you love him I have done.

DORIMANT. You have reproached me handsomely, and I deserve it for coming hither, but –

PERT. You must expect it, sir! all women will hate you for my lady's sake!

DORIMANT. [*aside*] Nay, if she begins too, 'tis time to fly! I shall be scolded to death else. (*Aside to* BELLINDA) I am to blame in some circumstances I confess; but as to the main, I am not so guilty as you

---

281 *qualm*: see note to *Comical Revenge*, I ii 28.

283 *mirabilis*: *aqua mirabilis*, a medicinal drink of wine and spices.

306 *carriage*: behaviour.

imagine. – I shall seek a more convenient time to clear myself.

MRS LOVEIT. Do it now! what impediments are here?

DORIMANT. I want time, and you want temper.

MRS LOVEIT. These are weak pretences!

DORIMANT. You were never more mistaken in your life, and so farewell. DORIMANT *flings off.*

MRS LOVEIT. Call a footman! Pert! quickly, I will have him dogged.

PERT. I wish you would not for my quiet and your own. [*Exit* PERT.]

MRS LOVEIT. I'll find out the infamous cause of all our quarrels, pluck her mask off, and expose her bare-faced to the world.

BELLINDA. (*aside*) Let me but escape this time, I'll never venture more.

MRS LOVEIT. Bellinda! you shall go with me.

BELLINDA. I have such a heaviness hangs on me with what I did this morning, I would fain go home and sleep, my dear.

MRS LOVEIT. Death! and eternal darkness. I shall never sleep again. Raging fevers seize the world and make mankind as restless all as I am. *Exit* MRS LOVEIT.

BELLINDA. I knew him false and helped to make him so! Was not her ruin enough to fright me from the danger? It should have been, but love can take no warning. *Exit* BELLINDA.

SCENE II

Lady Townley's house.

Enter MEDLEY, YOUNG BELLAIR, LADY TOWNLEY, EMILIA *and* CHAPLAIN.

MEDLEY. Bear up Bellair, and do not let us see that repentance in thine we daily do in married faces.

LADY TOWNLEY. This wedding will strangely surprise my brother when he knows it.

MEDLEY. Your nephew ought to conceal it for a time,

---

334 *heaviness*: torpor, want of animation.

madam, since marriage has lost its good name, prudent men seldom expose their own reputations till 'tis convenient to justify their wives'.

OLD BELLAIR. (*without*) Where are you all there? Out, a dod will nobody hear?

LADY TOWNLEY. My brother, quickly Mr Smirk into this closet, you must not be seen yet.

[CHAPLAIN] *goes into the closet.*

Enter OLD BELLAIR *and Lady Townley's* PAGE.

OLD BELLAIR. Desire Mr Fourbe to walk into the lower parlour, I will be with him presently. [*Exit* PAGE] (*To* YOUNG BELLAIR) Where have you been, sir, you could not wait on me today?

YOUNG BELLAIR. About a business.

OLD BELLAIR. Are you so good at business? a dod I have a business too, you shall dispatch out of hand, sir. Send for a parson, sister; my Lady Woodvill and her daughter are coming.

LADY TOWNLEY. What need you huddle up things thus?

OLD BELLAIR. Out a pize, youth is apt to play the fool, and 'tis not good it should be in their power.

LADY TOWNLEY. You need not fear your son.

OLD BELLAIR. H'has been idling this morning, and a dod I do not like him. (*To* EMILIA) How dost thou do sweetheart?

EMILIA. You are very severe, sir, married in such haste!

OLD BELLAIR. Go to, thou'rt a rogue, and I will talk with thee anon. Here's my Lady Woodvill come.

Enter LADY WOODVILL, HARRIET *and* BUSY.

Welcome, madam; Mr Fourbe's below with the writings.

LADY WOODVILL. Let us down and make an end then.

OLD BELLAIR. Sister, show the way. (*To* YOUNG

---

12 *closet*: see note to *Comical Revenge*, V ii 172.
22 *huddle up*: hasten along unceremoniously.
31 *Go to*: used to express disapproval.
34 *writings*: legal documents concerning the marriage settlement.

BELLAIR *who is talking to* HARRIET) Harry your business lies not there yet! Excuse him till we have done lady, and then a dod he shall be for thee. Mr Medley we must trouble you to be a witness.

MEDLEY. I luckily came for that purpose, sir.

Exeunt OLD BELLAIR, MEDLEY, YOUNG BELLAIR, LADY TOWNLEY *and* LADY WOODVILL.

BUSY. What will you do madam?

HARRIET. Be carried back and mewed up in the country again, run away here, anything, rather than be married to a man I do not care for – dear Emilia, do thou advise me!

EMILIA. Mr Bellair is engaged you know.

HARRIET. I do; but know not what the fear of losing an estate may fright him to.

EMILIA. In the desperate condition you are in, you should consult with some judicious man; what think you of Mr Dorimant?

HARRIET. I do not think of him at all.

BUSY. She thinks of nothing else I am sure –

EMILIA. How fond your mother was of Mr Courtage!

HARRIET. Because I contrived the mistake to make a little mirth, you believe I like the man.

EMILIA. Mr Bellair believes you love him.

HARRIET. Men are seldom in the right when they guess at a woman's mind, would she whom he loves loved him no better.

BUSY. (*aside*) That's e'en well enough on all conscience.

EMILIA. Mr Dorimant has a great deal of wit.

HARRIET. And takes a great deal of pains to show it.

EMILIA. He's extremely well-fashioned.

HARRIET. Affectedly grave, or ridiculously wild and apish.

BUSY. You defend him still against your mother.

HARRIET. I would not were he justly rallied, but I cannot hear anyone undeservedly railed at.

EMILIA. Has your woman learnt the song you were so taken with?

---

43 *mewed up*: see note to *She Would*, I ii 149.
65 *well-fashioned*: i.e. in the fashion.
67 *apish*: (1) silly, trifling (2) ridiculously imitative.

HARRIET. I was fond of a new thing, 'tis dull at second hearing.

EMILIA. Mr Dorimant made it.

BUSY. She knows it madam, and has made me sing it at least a dozen times this morning.

HARRIET. Thy tongue is as impertinent as thy fingers.

EMILIA. You have provoked her.

BUSY. 'Tis but singing the song and I shall appease her.

EMILIA. Prithee do.

HARRIET. She has a voice will grate your ears worse than a catcall, and dresses so ill she's scarce fit to trick up a yeoman's daughter on a holyday.

BUSY *sings.* *Song by Sir C.S.*

'As Amoret with Phillis sat
One evening on the plain,
And saw the charming Strephon wait
To tell the nymph his pain,

The threat'ning danger to remove
She whispered in her ear,
"Ah Phillis, if you would not love,
This shepherd do not hear.

None ever had so strange an art
His passion to convey
Into a list'ning virgin's heart
And steal her soul away.

Fly, fly betimes, for fear you give
Occasion for your fate."
"In vain" said she, "in vain I strive,
Alas! 'tis now too late." '

Enter DORIMANT.

---

83 *catcall*: a kind of whistle, used to express disapproval or impatience (later in the century, if not already, in the playhouses).

83 *dresses*: i.e. her mistress.

84 s.d. *Sir C.S.*: attributed by a 1722 collection of his *Works* to Sir Charles Sedley; but, on balance, more likely to have been written by Sir Car Scroope (see first note to Prologue).

97 *betimes*: speedily.

DORIMANT. 'Music so softens and disarms the mind – '

HARRIET. 'That not one arrow does resistance find.'

DORIMANT. Let us make use of the lucky minute then.

HARRIET. (*aside, turning from* DORIMANT) My love springs with my blood into my face, I dare not look upon him yet.

DORIMANT. What have we here, the picture of celebrated Beauty, giving audience in public to a declared lover?

HARRIET. Play the dying fop, and make the piece complete sir.

DORIMANT. What think you if the hint were well improved? The whole mystery of making love pleasantly designed and wrought in a suit of hangings?

HARRIET. 'Twere needless to execute fools in effigy who suffer daily in their own persons.

DORIMANT. (*to* EMILIA *aside*) Mistress Bride, for such I know this happy day has made you –

EMILIA. Defer the formal joy you are to give me, and mind your business with her – (*aloud*) here are dreadful preparations Mr Dorimant, writings sealing, and a parson sent for –

DORIMANT. To marry this lady –

BUSY. Condemned she is, and what will become of her I know not, without you generously engage in a rescue.

DORIMANT. In this sad condition, madam, I can do no less than offer you my service.

HARRIET. The obligation is not great, you are the

101–2 *Music . . . find*: the sixth couplet of Waller's 'Of my Lady Isabella, Playing on the Lute' (*Works*, ed. Thorn Drury, vol. 1, p. 90), with 'one' substituted for the original 'an'.

108 *celebrated Beauty*: thus *1676*, and thus reprinted down to *1735*. Verity also printed this, but Brett-Smith emended to 'a celebrated beauty', comparing 'a declared lover', and has been followed in this by most subsequent editors. Etherege, however, may have intended 'the personification of beauty' rather than 'one particular beautiful lady', thus making the *1676* reading apt.

113 *improved*: i.e. put to good use.

114 *suit of hangings*: set of tapestry wall-hangings.

115 *execute*: (1) do execution upon (2) paint.

119 *the formal joy you are to give me*: see note to IV ii 207.

common sanctuary for all young women who run from their relations.

DORIMANT. I have always my arms open to receive the distressed. But I will open my heart and receive you, where none yet did ever enter – you have filled it with a secret, might I but let you know it –

HARRIET. Do not speak it, if you would have me believe it; your tongue is so famed for falsehood 'twill do the truth an injury. (*Turns away her head*)

DORIMANT. Turn not away then; but look on me and guess it.

HARRIET. Did you not tell me there was no credit to be given to faces? that women nowadays have their passions as much at will as they have their complexions, and put on joy and sadness, scorn and kindness, with the same ease they do their paint and patches – are they the only counterfeits?

DORIMANT. You wrong your own, while you suspect my eyes, by all the hope I have in you, the inimitable colour in your cheeks is not more free from art than are the sighs I offer.

HARRIET. In men who have been long hardened in sin, we have reason to mistrust the first signs of repentance.

DORIMANT. The prospect of such a heaven will make me persevere, and give you marks that are infallible.

HARRIET. What are those?

DORIMANT. I will renounce all the joys I have in friendship and in wine, sacrifice to you all the interest I have in other women –

HARRIET. Hold – though I wish you devout, I would not have you turn fanatic – could you neglect these a while and make a journey into the country?

DORIMANT. To be with you I could live there: and never send one thought to London.

HARRIET. Whate'er you say, I know all beyond High Park's a desert to you, and that no gallantry can draw you farther.

DORIMANT. That has been the utmost limit of my love – but now my passion knows no bounds, and there's no measure to be taken of what I'll do for you from anything I ever did before.

HARRIET. When I hear you talk thus in Hampshire, I

shall begin to think there may be some little truth enlarged upon.

DORIMANT. Is this all? – will you not promise me –

HARRIET. I hate to promise! what we do then is expected from us, and wants much of the welcome it finds, when it surprises.

DORIMANT. May I not hope?

HARRIET. That depends on you, and not on me, and 'tis to no purpose to forbid it. (*Turns to* BUSY)

BUSY. Faith madam, now I perceive the gentleman loves you too, e'en let him know your mind and torment yourselves no longer.

HARRIET. Dost think I have no sense of modesty?

BUSY. Think, if you lose this you may never have another opportunity.

HARRIET. May he hate me, (a curse that frights me when I speak it!) if ever I do a thing against the rules of decency and honour.

DORIMANT. (*to* EMILIA) I am beholding to you for your good intentions, madam.

EMILIA. I thought the concealing of our marriage from her might have done you better service.

DORIMANT. Try her again –

EMILIA. What have you resolved, madam? The time draws near.

HARRIET. To be obstinate and protest against this marriage.

Enter LADY TOWNLEY *in haste.*

LADY TOWNLEY. (*to* EMILIA) Quickly, quickly, let Mr Smirk out of the closet.

SMIRK *comes out of the closet.*

HARRIET. A parson! had you laid him in here?

DORIMANT. I knew nothing of him.

HARRIET. Should it appear you did, your opinion of my easiness may cost you dear.

---

172 *little*: *1676* uncorrected omits this adjective.

172–3 *some little truth enlarged upon*: some element of truth in what you say.

Enter OLD BELLAIR, YOUNG BELLAIR, MEDLEY, *and* LADY WOODVILL.

OLD BELLAIR. Out a pize! the canonical hour is almost past; sister, is the man of God come?

LADY TOWNLEY. He waits your leisure –

OLD BELLAIR. By your favour sir. A dod a pretty spruce fellow! What may we call him?

LADY TOWNLEY. Mr Smirk! my Lady Bigot's chaplain.

OLD BELLAIR. A wise woman! a dod she is. The man will serve for the flesh as well as the spirit. Please you sir to commission a young couple to go to bed together a God's name? – Harry.

YOUNG BELLAIR. Here sir –

OLD BELLAIR. Out a pize without your mistress in your hand!

SMIRK. Is this the gentleman?

OLD BELLAIR. Yes sir!

SMIRK. Are you not mistaken sir?

OLD BELLAIR. A dod, I think not sir.

SMIRK. Sure you are sir?

OLD BELLAIR. You look as if you would forbid the banns Mr Smirk, I hope you have no pretension to the lady!

SMIRK. Wish him joy sir! I have done him the good office today already.

OLD BELLAIR. Out a pize what do I hear?

LADY TOWNLEY. Never storm brother, the truth is out.

OLD BELLAIR. How say you sir! is this your wedding day?

YOUNG BELLAIR. It is sir.

OLD BELLAIR. And a dod it shall be mine too, (*To* EMILIA) give me thy hand sweetheart, what dost thou mean? give me thy hand I say.

EMILIA *kneels and* YOUNG BELLAIR.

LADY TOWNLEY. Come, come, give her your blessing, this is the woman your son loved and is married to.

OLD BELLAIR. Ha! cheated! cozened! and by your contrivance sister!

---

205 *canonical hour*: hours during which marriage could be legally performed (8 a.m.–noon).

238 *cozened*: defrauded.

LADY TOWNLEY. What would you do with her, she's a rogue and you can't abide her.

MEDLEY. Shall I hit her a pat for you sir?

OLD BELLAIR. A dod you are all rogues, and I never will forgive you.

LADY TOWNLEY. Whither! whither away?

MEDLEY. Let him go and cool awhile!

LADY WOODVILL. (*to* DORIMANT) Here's a business broke out now Mr Courtage, I am made a fine fool of.

DORIMANT. You see the old gentleman knew nothing of it.

LADY WOODVILL. I find he did not. I shall have some trick put upon me if I stay in this wicked town any longer. Harriet! dear child! where art thou? I'll into the country straight.

OLD BELLAIR. A dod madam, you shall hear me first –

Enter MRS LOVEIT, *and* BELLINDA.

MRS LOVEIT. Hither my man dogged him! –

BELLINDA. Yonder he stands my dear.

MRS LOVEIT. I see him. – (*Aside*) And with him the face that has undone me! oh that I were but where I might throw out the anguish of my heart, here it must rage within and break it.

LADY TOWNLEY. Mrs Loveit! are you afraid to come forward?

MRS LOVEIT. I was amazed to see so much company here in a morning, the occasion sure is extraordinary –

DORIMANT. (*aside*) Loveit and Bellinda! the devil owes me a shame today, and I think never will have done paying it.

MRS LOVEIT. Married! dear Emilia! how am I transported with the news!

HARRIET. (*to* DORIMANT) I little thought Emilia was the woman Mr Bellair was in love with – I'll chide her for not trusting me with the secret.

DORIMANT. How do you like Mrs Loveit?

HARRIET. She's a famed mistress of yours I hear –

DORIMANT. She has been on occasion!

267–8 *the devil owes me a shame*: see note to *Comical Revenge*, II ii 108.

OLD BELLAIR. (*to* LADY WOODVILL) A dod madam I cannot help it.

LADY WOODVILL. You need make no more apologies sir!

EMILIA. (*to* MRS LOVEIT) The old gentleman's excusing himself to my Lady Woodvill.

MRS LOVEIT. Ha, ha, ha! I never heard of anything so pleasant.

HARRIET. (*to* DORIMANT) She's extremely overjoyed at something.

DORIMANT. At nothing, she is one of those hoiting ladies, who gaily fling themselves about, and force a laugh, when their aching hearts are full of discontent and malice.

MRS LOVEIT. Oh heaven! I was never so near killing myself with laughing – Mr Dorimant! are you a brideman?

LADY WOODVILL. Mr Dorimant! is this Mr Dorimant, madam?

MRS LOVEIT. If you doubt it, your daughter can resolve you I suppose.

LADY WOODVILL. I am cheated too, basely cheated.

OLD BELLAIR. Out a pize, what's here more knavery yet!

LADY WOODVILL. Harriet! on my blessing come away I charge you.

HARRIET. Dear mother! do but stay and hear me.

LADY WOODVILL. I am betrayed and thou art undone I fear.

HARRIET. Do not fear it – I have not, nor never will do anything against my duty – believe me! dear mother do.

DORIMANT. (*to* MRS LOVEIT) I had trusted you with this secret but that I knew the violence of your nature would ruin my fortune as now unluckily it has: I thank you madam.

MRS LOVEIT. She's an heiress I know, and very rich.

DORIMANT. To satisfy you I must give up my interest wholly to my love, had you been a reasonable woman, I might have secured 'em both, and been happy –

MRS LOVEIT. You might have trusted me with any-

---

288 *hoiting*: noisy, giddy.

thing of this kind, you know you might. Why did you go under a wrong name?

DORIMANT. The story is too long to tell you now, be satisfied, this is the business; this is the mask has kept me from you.

BELLINDA. (*aside*) He's tender of my honour, though he's cruel to my love.

MRS LOVEIT. Was it no idle mistress then?

DORIMANT. Believe me a wife, to repair the ruins of my estate that needs it.

MRS LOVEIT. The knowledge of this makes my grief hang lighter on my soul; but I shall never more be happy.

DORIMANT. Bellinda!

BELLINDA. Do not think of clearing yourself with me, it is impossible – do all men break their words thus?

DORIMANT. Th'extravagant words they speak in love; 'tis as unreasonable to expect we should perform all we promise then, as do all we threaten when we are angry – when I see you next –

BELLINDA. Take no notice of me and I shall not hate you.

DORIMANT. How came you to Mrs Loveit?

BELLINDA. By a mistake the chairmen made for want of my giving them directions.

DORIMANT. 'Twas a pleasant one. We must meet again.

BELLINDA. Never.

DORIMANT. Never!

BELLINDA. When we do, may I be as infamous as you are false.

LADY TOWNLEY. Men of Mr Dorimant's character, always suffer in the general opinion of the world.

MEDLEY. You can make no judgment of a witty man from common fame, considering the prevailing faction, madam –

---

344 *pleasant*: humorous, amusing.

352–3 *prevailing faction*: Conaghan aptly cites Dryden who, in dedicating *The Assignation* (1673) to Sir Charles Sedley, speaks of 'the ignorant and ridiculous Descriptions which some Pedants have given of the Wits . . . those wretches Paint leudness, Atheism, Folly, Ill-Reasoning, and all manner of Extravagances amongst us, for want of understanding what we are' (*Dramatic Works*, ed. Montague Summers (London, Nonesuch Press, 1932), vol. 3, p. 276).

OLD BELLAIR. A dod he's in the right.

MEDLEY. Besides 'tis a common error among women, to believe too well of them they know, and too ill of them they don't.

OLD BELLAIR. A dod he observes well.

LADY TOWNLEY. Believe me, madam, you will find Mr Dorimant as civil a gentleman as you thought Mr Courtage.

HARRIET. If you would but know him better –

LADY WOODVILL. You have a mind to know him better! Come away – you shall never see him more –

HARRIET. Dear mother stay –

LADY WOODVILL. I wo'not be consenting to your ruin –

HARRIET. Were my fortune in your power –

LADY WOODVILL. Your person is.

HARRIET. Could I be disobedient I might take it out of yours and put it into his.

LADY WOODVILL. 'Tis that you would be at, you would marry this Dorimant.

HARRIET. I cannot deny it! I would, and never will marry any other man.

LADY WOODVILL. Is this the duty that you promised?

HARRIET. But I will never marry him against your will –

LADY WOODVILL. (*aside*) She knows the way to melt my heart. – (*To* HARRIET) Upon yourself light your undoing.

MEDLEY. (*to* OLD BELLAIR) Come, sir, you have not the heart any longer to refuse your blessing.

OLD BELLAIR. A dod I ha'not – rise and God bless you both – make much of her Harry, she deserves thy kindness – (*To* EMILIA) a dod sirrah I did not think it had been in thee.

Enter SIR FOPLING *and's* PAGE.

SIR FOPLING. 'Tis a damned windy day! hey page! is my periwig right?

PAGE. A little out of order, sir!

SIR FOPLING. Pox o' this apartment, it wants an ante-chamber to adjust one's self in. (*To* MRS LOVEIT) Madam! I came from your house and your servants directed me hither.

MRS LOVEIT. I will give order hereafter they shall direct you better.

SIR FOPLING. The great satisfaction I had in the Mail last night has given me much disquiet since.

MRS LOVEIT. 'Tis likely to give me more than I desire.

SIR FOPLING. What the devil makes her so reserved? Am I guilty of an indiscretion, madam?

MRS LOVEIT. You will be of a great one, if you continue your mistake, sir.

SIR FOPLING. Something puts you out of humour.

MRS LOVEIT. The most foolish inconsiderable thing that ever did.

SIR FOPLING. Is it in my power?

MRS LOVEIT. To hang or drown it, do one of 'em, and trouble me no more.

SIR FOPLING. So *fière*! *serviteur*, madam – Medley! where's Dorimant?

MEDLEY. Methinks the lady has not made you those advances today she did last night, Sir Fopling –

SIR FOPLING. Prithee do not talk of her.

MEDLEY. She would be a *bonne fortune.*

SIR FOPLING. Not to me at present.

MEDLEY. How so?

SIR FOPLING. An intrigue now would be but a temptation to me to throw away that vigour on one which I mean shall shortly make my court to the whole sex in a ballet.

MEDLEY. Wisely considered, Sir Fopling.

SIR FOPLING. No one woman is worth the loss of a cut in a caper.

MEDLEY. Not when 'tis so universally designed.

LADY WOODVILL. Mr Dorimant, everyone has spoke so much in your behalf, that I can no longer doubt but I was in the wrong.

MRS LOVEIT. There's nothing but falsehood and impertinence in this world! all men are villains or

---

410 *fière*: haughty.
410 *serviteur*: your servant.
415 *bonne fortune*: echoing Sir Fopling's earlier remark, IV i 254–5.
423 *a cut*: a step in dancing, defined by *OED* as to 'spring from the ground, and, while in the air, to twiddle the feet one in front of the other alternately with great rapidity'.

fools; take example from my misfortunes. Bellinda, if thou wouldst be happy, give thyself wholly up to goodness.

HARRIET. (*to* MRS LOVEIT) Mr Dorimant has been your God Almighty long enough, 'tis time to think of another –

MRS LOVEIT. Jeered by her! I will lock myself up in my house, and never see the world again.

HARRIET. A nunnery is the more fashionable place for such a retreat, and has been the fatal consequence of many a *belle passion.*

MRS LOVEIT. [*aside*] Hold heart! till I get home! should I answer 'twould make her triumph greater. (*Is going out*)

DORIMANT. Your hand Sir Fopling –

SIR FOPLING. Shall I wait upon you madam?

MRS LOVEIT. Legion of fools, as many devils take thee.

Exit MRS LOVEIT.

MEDLEY. Dorimant! I pronounce thy reputation clear – and henceforward when I would know anything of woman, I will consult no other oracle.

SIR FOPLING. Stark mad, by all that's handsome! Dorimant thou hast engaged me in a pretty business.

DORIMANT. I have not leisure now to talk about it.

OLD BELLAIR. Out a pize, what does this man of mode do here again?

LADY TOWNLEY. He'll be an excellent entertainment within brother, and is luckily come to raise the mirth of the company.

LADY WOODVILL. Madam, I take my leave of you.

LADY TOWNLEY. What do you mean madam?

LADY WOODVILL. To go this afternoon part of my way to Hartley –

OLD BELLAIR. A dod you shall stay and dine first! come we will all be good friends, and you shall give

---

441 *belle passion*: violent passion.

446 *Legion of fools*: a multitude, with an echo of Mark 5, verse 9 (the story of the casting out of the devils from the 'man with an unclean spirit'): 'My name *is* Legion; for we are many' (cf. Epilogue, line 18).

461 *Hartley*: Barnard identifies three possible candidates in Hampshire, Hartley Wespall, Hartley Mauditt and Hartley Wintney.

Mr Dorimant leave to wait upon you and your daughter in the country.

LADY WOODVILL. If his occasions bring him that way, I have now so good an opinion of him, he shall be welcome.

HARRIET. To a great rambling lone house, that looks as it were not inhabited, the family's so small; there you'll find my mother, an old lame aunt, and myself sir, perched up on chairs at a distance in a large parlour; sitting moping like three or four melancholy birds in a spacious volary – does not this stagger your resolution?

DORIMANT. Not at all, madam! The first time I saw you, you left me with the pangs of love upon me, and this day my soul has quite given up her liberty.

HARRIET. This is more dismal than the country! Emilia! pity me, who am going to that sad place. Methinks I hear the hateful noise of rooks already – kaw, kaw, kaw – there's music in the worst cry in London! 'My dill and cowcumbers to pickle.'

OLD BELLAIR. Sister! knowing of this matter, I hope you have provided us some good cheer.

LADY TOWNLEY. I have brother, and the fiddles too –

OLD BELLAIR. Let 'em strike up then, the young lady shall have a dance before she departs.

Dance.

(*After the dance*) So now we'll in, and make this an arrant wedding day –
(*To the pit*) And if these honest gentlemen rejoice,
A dod the boy has made a happy choice.

Exeunt omnes.

---

466 *occasions*: business, affairs.

469–70 *as it were*: i.e. as if it were.

474 *volary*: aviary.

482 *cry*: street-vendor's cry.

483 *dill and cowcumbers to pickle*: Brett-Smith quoted Addison in *Spectator*, no. 251 on the cries of the London street-traders: 'I am always pleased with that particular Time of the Year which is proper for the pickling of Dill and Cucumbers; but alas this Cry, like the Song of the Nightingales, is not heard above two Months.'

THE EPILOGUE
by MR DRYDEN

Most modern wits, such monstrous fools have shown,
They seemed not of heav'n's making but their own.
Those nauseous harlequins in farce may pass,
But there goes more to a substantial ass!
Something of man must be exposed to view,
That, gallants, they may more resemble you:
Sir Fopling is a fool so nicely writ,
The ladies would mistake him for a wit,
And (when he sings, talks loud, and cocks) would cry,
'I vow methinks he's pretty company,
So brisk, so gay, so travelled, so refined!
As he took pains to graff upon his kind.'
True fops help nature's work, and go to school,
To file and finish God A'mighty's fool.
Yet none Sir Fopling him, or him can call;
He's knight o' th' shire, and represents ye all.
From each he meets, he culls whate'er he can,
Legion's his name, a people in a man.
His bulky folly gathers as it goes,
And, rolling o'er you, like a snowball grows.
His various modes from various fathers follow,
One taught the toss, and one the new French wallow.

Epilogue: see Additional Note.
Dryden: Dryden was a friend of Etherege's, paying a tribute to him as 'gentle George' in *MacFlecknoe*, lines 151–4, and sending him an amiable verse *Letter to Etherege* while the latter was in Ratisbon.
3 *harlequins in farce*: Harlequin was a traditional figure in Italian and French comedy; there were many complaints from (among others) Dryden in the 1670s about a prevailing taste for farce and the importation of stylistic features and personnel from abroad.
9 *cocks*: (1) swaggers, struts, brags (2) cocks his hat; cf. note to *She Would*, I ii 173.
12 *graff*: graft.
12 *upon his kind*: upon properties naturally his own.
16 *knight o' th' shire*: Member of Parliament for a county.
18 *Legion*: see note to V ii 446.
22 *toss*: i.e. of the head.
22 *wallow*: rolling walk or gait.

His sword-knot, this; his cravat, this designed,
And this, the yard-long snake he twirls behind.
From one the sacred periwig he gained,
Which wind ne'er blew, nor touch of hat profaned.
Another's diving bow he did adore,
Which with a shog casts all the hair before:
Till he with full decorum brings it back,
And rises with a water spaniel shake.
As for his songs (the ladies' dear delight)
Those sure he took from most of you who write.
Yet ev'ry man is safe from what he feared,
For no one fool is hunted from the herd.

---

23 *sword-knot*: a ribbon or tassel tied to the hilt of a sword.

24 *snake*: a long curl or tail attached to a wig.

26 *touch of hat*: some gallants carried their hats in their hands so that their periwigs would not be put out of order.

28 *shog*: shake, jerk.

ADDITIONAL NOTES

ADDITIONAL NOTES

The Comical Revenge

Dedication. Charles Sackville, Lord Buckhurst (1643–1706), later fourth Earl of Middlesex (1675) and sixth Earl of Dorset (1677). One of the young wits of Charles II's court, and himself both a poet of modest distinction and the patron of numerous writers from Dryden to Prior. He was also the companion and accomplice of Sir Charles Sedley in two notorious incidents recorded by Pepys (1 July 1663 and 23 October 1668). He was to be present at the first performance of *She Would* in the company of Etherege, Buckingham and Sedley (Pepys, 6 February 1668).

Prologue, 11. After the Restoration Norwich quickly established itself as a busy centre for touring, and in Dublin John Ogilby's company played at the Theatre Royal in Smock Alley. At least one actor played in both Norwich and Dublin; see William Smith Clark, *The Early Irish Stage: The Beginnings to 1720* (Oxford, Clarendon Press, 1955), pp. 57–8.

Prologue, 20. For post-1660 writers John Fletcher (1579–1625) and Ben Jonson (1573–1637) were (with Shakespeare) the most remarkable of the early seventeenth-century dramatists, and their plays figured prominently in the repertoires of the reopened theatres. Their distinctive merits were frequently contrasted in the terms used here; for 'the art of Ben', see, for example, Gunnar Sorelius, *'The Giant Race before the Flood': Pre-Restoration Drama on the Stage and in the Criticism of the Restoration* (Uppsala, Almqvist and Wiksell, 1966), pp. 91–2.

I i 22. 'Ian Villian' (*1664*). Early eighteenth-century editions emend the second word to 'Villain'; Verity printed 'Ian villain' with a hesitant footnote, 'Meant for "damn villains"?' Brett-Smith, returning to 'Villian', added the exclamation marks also included in the present edition and, in justification of this procedure, offered the most plausible interpretation of the passage yet: 'Dufoy is merely calling the footmen, John and William, in his broken English.'

I ii 33–4. *squib*: in addition to meaning 'an explosive firework', the word was also used for 'an explosive device used as a missile or means of attack'.
wild-fire: (1) an inflammable compound, readily ignited and very difficult to extinguish (used in warfare, etc.); (2) various inflammatory diseases, especially those in which the eruption spreads from one part to another. Both these senses were used figuratively to mean 'violent, excited states of feeling'. Given Sir Frederick's later jokes about the likely evanescence of Beaufort's passion, however, yet another meaning is worth bearing in mind – i.e. 'an *ignis fatuus*, a will-o'-the-wisp'.
huzzay: 'Huzzéé' (*1664*, Verity, Brett-Smith). Presumably intended (like 'crack') as an onomatopoeic representation of the sound of the 'squib'. I have ventured to emend the spelling to 'huzzay' which *OED* lists as a variant form of 'huzza', meaning 'to make an exultant noise'. As a noun, 'huzza' was also in this period a term for 'one given to noisy or riotous conduct; a rake, a gallant'.

I iv 21–2. Brett-Smith suggested that there is a reminiscence here of Christopher Marlowe's *Hero and Leander* (*Works*, ed. C.F. Tucker

Brooke (Oxford, Clarendon Press, 1910), p. 496):

> It lies not in our power to love, or hate,
> For will in us is over-rul'd by fate
>
> (i 167–8)

II ii 55. From *1723* onwards editions have tended to emend here to 'excess', and Verity and Brett-Smith followed suit. The original, however, is perfectly plausible, 'access' being used by contemporaries in the sense of 'increase, enlargement, addition'. One might perhaps paraphrase its meaning here as 'the extreme delicacy of discrimination (in matters concerning virtue) which Lovis has now attained'.

II ii 70. Surely an echo of Richard Lovelace's 'To Lucasta, *Going to the Warres*' (*Poems*, ed. C.H. Wilkinson (Oxford, Clarendon Press, 1930), p. 18):

> True; a new Mistresse now I chase,
> The first Foe in the Field;
> And with a stronger Faith imbrace
> A Sword, a Horse, a Shield.
>
> Yet this Inconstancy is such,
> As you too shall adore;
> I could not love thee (Deare) so much,
> Lov'd I not Honour more.
>
> (lines 5–12)

II ii 154. 'Considering the early date of this play, the arbor probably concealed two professional singers (or at least one – to sing Aurelia's part), since main characters rarely sing in early plays. But even if these two actresses did sing the song, the arbor helped to solve another practical problem of performance: it brings singer and accompanist(s) into close proximity', since the latter could be concealed behind or within it (Curtis A. Price, *Music in the Restoration Theatre* (Ann Arbor, UMI Research Press, 1979), pp. 45–6).

II iii 137. For an account of the scale of this kind of activity in the 1650s, see David Underdown, *Royalist Conspiracy in England 1649–1660* (New Haven, Yale University Press, 1960). Taverns were among the securest places where men engaged in such plots could meet without attracting undue attention to themselves (see Edward Hyde Earl of Clarendon, *Life* (3rd edition: Oxford, 1761), vol. 2, p. 35).

II iii 161. For the game's addictive qualities and, therefore, its aptness to the plot Wheadle has proposed, see [Charles Cotton], *The Compleat Gamester* (London, 1674), p. 127: 'Certainly *Hazzard* is the most bewitching Game that is plaid on the Dice; for when a man begins to play he knows not when to leave off; and having once accustom'd himself to play at *Hazzard* he hardly ever after minds any thing else.'

III iv 39. The activities available at such an academy are described by Frederick Bracher, 'Etherege at Clement's Inn', *Huntington Library Quarterly*, 43 (1979–80), 130–1.

III v 8. One of the judges at the trial of Charles I in 1649 and a signatory of the king's death warrant. On one notorious occasion, in December 1659, he ordered 'a file of musketeers' to fire (with fatal results) on a crowd of apprentices petitioning for a free parliament. He was frequently mocked in satires of the 1650s and 1660s as a man of base origin promoted by the upheavals of war and revolution to an eminence of which he was comically unworthy – see, for instance, the jokes about 'single-eyed *Hewson* the Cobler' and 'Lord *Hughson* the Cobler' in *Rump* (London, 1662), Part 1, p. 342 and Part 2, p. 102. He fled the country on the restoration of Charles II and died in exile in 1662.

IV i 39–40. A gloss is perhaps suggested by a sentence of George Eliot's *Daniel Deronda* (Book 4, chapter 32): 'he seemed to himself like the Sabine warriors in the memorable story – with nothing to meet his spear but flesh of his flesh, and objects that he loved' – i.e. when the Sabine women, now grown attached to their ravishers, threw themselves between the latter and the Sabine warriors who sought revenge.

IV v 41. G. Cross (*Notes and Queries*, 203 (1960), 532–3) suggested that this line echoes the opening line of John Donne's *Twickenham Garden*, 'Blasted with sighs, and surrounded with tears' (*Songs and Sonets*, ed. Theodore Redpath (London, Methuen & Co., 1959), p. 42).

V v 143. A kind of breeches or trousers in fashion for some time after the Restoration (cf. *Man of Mode*, III ii 233 and note). Evelyn (cited in *OED*) said that they were taken by the French from the costume of the stage-character of the period 'when the freak takes our Monsieurs to appear like so many Farces or Jack Puddings on the stage'. For Dufoy's association with Jack Pudding, see III iv 16 and note.

She Would if She Could

I i 158. This theological doctrine refers to the freeing of men by Christ from the burden of the Mosaic law and human ordinances (see Arthur Barker, *Milton and the Puritan Dilemma, 1641–1660* (University of Toronto Press, 1942), pp. 37–42). Libertine variations on it claimed to find in it a justification for a freedom from all restraints, and it is clearly such an interpretation that Courtall has in mind.

I i 265. In addition to the more obvious senses of the word, Samuel Butler (*Characters*, ed. Charles W. Daves (Cleveland, Case Western Reserve University Press, 1970), p. 282) offers a definition apt to Lady Cockwood's character: an impertinent, he writes, 'Is one that straggles always from the purpose, and goes about every thing he undertakes, and fetches a compass, as if he meant to attack it in the rear, but never comes near enough to engage.'

I ii 47. Used in this period for a man brought up far from, and unshaped by, the restraints of civil society; see Edward Dudley and Maximillian E. Novak (eds.), *The Wild Man Within: An Image in Western Thought from the Renaissance to Romanticism* (University of Pittsburgh Press, 1972), which quotes Dryden (p. 188) aptly describing contemporary libertines as not so much wild in the woods, as 'wild within Doors, in Chambers, And in Closets'.

I ii 171–2. There are frequent references in the period to this habit – for instance, in the Prologue to Part 2 of John Dryden's *The Conquest of Granada* (*Dramatic Works*, ed. Montague Summers (London, Nonesuch Press, 1932), vol. 3, p. 91):

when Vizard Masque appears in Pit,
Straight, every man who thinks himself a Wit,

Perks up; and, managing his Comb, with grace,
With his white Wigg sets off his Nut-brown Face.

III iii 173. 'Champagne' (*1668*). The drink was just becoming known in England (*OED*'s first example is from 1664) and so might possibly be what is intended here. Taylor and Davison emend to 'champaign', Davison providing as gloss 'open country', which is certainly a current Restoration meaning for the word. With neither 'champagne' nor 'champaign', however, does the preceding 'this' make much sense. Verity (without comment) emends to '*campagne*', a word Etherege uses frequently in his letters from Ratisbon in the sense of 'military campaign', and 'this *campagne*' does make sense – i.e. Rakehell's brother has set off to be a gentlemanly spectator at 'this year's, the current' campaign. I have, therefore, adopted that emendation in the present text.

III iii 255. Cf. Gilbert Burnet, *History of my Own Time*, ed. O. Airy (Oxford, Clarendon Press, 1897), Part I, i, 473: 'At this time [i.e. 1669] the court fell into much extravagance in masquerading; both king and queen, and all the court, went about masked, and came into houses unknown, and danced. People were so disguised, that without being on the secret none could distinguish them.'

The Man of Mode

I i 281–2. Not, in fact, a penalty suffered by any atheist during Charles II's reign, although there were rumours soon after the Restoration that some aggrieved bishops were planning to revive it in an attempt to put an end to the career of their prime bogeyman, Thomas Hobbes. The prosecution never materialized, but Hobbes was sufficiently disturbed by the possibility to produce a manuscript attempting to demonstrate that '*de haeretico comburendo* was a writ that no longer ran' – see the articles by Samuel I. Mintz and Robert Willman, *Journal of the History of Ideas*, 29 (1968), 409–14, and 31 (1970), 606–15.

I i 333. The adverbial use of 'bloody' as an intensifier in colloquial language was in 1676 of very recent origin. *OED* describes its derivation as uncertain, but speculates that 'it was at first a reference to the habits of the "bloods" or aristocratic rowdies of the end of the 17th and beginning of the 18th C.' This, if true, would give an extra edge to its use in a conversation about the nature of genteel and plebeian sinfulness.

I i 335–6. Brett-Smith commented: 'i.e. tope is the word for gentleman to use; the Shoomaker is humorously rebuking Medley for his "bloody drunk". Or, with a pause after "World", the last five words might go with a piece of by-play, the Shoomaker winking at the footman, and performing, in anticipation, the motions of drinking Dorimant's health.' Both Carnochan and Barnard suggest a pause by adding a full-stop or comma after 'world'. But the whole speech could be read as being addressed to Handy and meaning: 'Well then, let's drink together very publicly for the honour of my master, Robin.' (For 'Tope', see note to *Comical Revenge*, II iii 52).

II i 73. This is the reading of the seventeenth-century quartos. Carnochan (followed by Barnard) changed the punctuation to an exclamation mark after 'mum' and added a stage direction '*Aloud*' before 'I can't abide you.' His only authority for this is slightly heavier pointing (i.e. a semi-colon) in two eighteenth-century reprintings. But the *1676* reading makes perfectly good sense and is therefore reproduced here.

II i 152. A number of musical dramas variously described as 'dramatick operas', 'semi-operas' and 'ambigue entertainments' achieved popularity with the theatrical public in the early 1670s – see Richard Luckett, 'Exotick but rational entertainments: the English dramatick operas', in Marie Axton and Raymond Williams (eds.), *English Drama: Forms and Development* (Cambridge University Press, 1977), pp. 123ff.

Epilogue. Three manuscript versions of the epilogue have been discovered and are collated in John Dryden, *Works*, ed. E.N. Hooker and H.T. Swedenberg, Jr (Berkeley, University of California Press, 1956–), vol. 1, pp. 397–8, where the editors argue that it is unlikely that the *1676* text derives from any of the MSS. No variant readings from them have therefore been admitted here; but British Museum MS Sloane 203, folio 95r, adds an extra couplet after line 12: 'Labouring to put in more as Mr. Bayes / Thrums in Additions to his ten yeares playes' (Bodleian MS Don. b. 8, pp. 558–9, also includes this couplet, but after line 14, and with minor variations). The reference is to a play which was long in the writing, Buckingham's *The Rehearsal* (1671), in which the character of Bayes is designed as a mocking portrait of Dryden. The couplet does not, however, figure in later editions of *The Man of Mode* and has therefore been omitted from the present text.